# POLITICAL SCIENCE:
# AN OVERVIEW OF THE FIELDS

Second Edition

James W. Peterson
Lee M. Allen
Nolan J. Argyle

Cover background image courtesy of Corel.

Copyright © 1994, 1997 by Kendall/Hunt Publishing Company

ISBN 0-7872-4179-2

All rights reserved. No part of this publication may be reproduced, stored in a retrieval system, or transmitted, in any form or by any means, electronic, mechanical, photocopying, recording, or otherwise, without the prior written permission of the copyright owner.

Printed in the United States of America
10   9   8   7   6   5   4   3   2   1

*Jim Peterson dedicates his portion of this project to his parents,
Walter and Ellen Peterson*

*Lee Allen dedicates his portion of this project to
Stephen J. Allen and Joyce D. Allen*

*Nolan Argyle dedicates his portion of this project to the memory
of his father, Rell F. Argyle, and to his mother, Lilly Argyle*

# Contents

*Introduction*  vii

## Part One
## THE FOUNDATIONS OF POLITICAL SCIENCE

### POLITICAL THEORY
1. The Political Association — *Aristotle* — 4
2. The Reputation of the Prince — *Niccolò Machiavelli* — 9
3. The State of Nature, Property, and the Development of Civil Society — *John Locke* — 13
4. Why Study Plato? The Link Between Political Theory and Practical Politics — *Nolan J. Argyle* — 19

### METHODOLOGY AND POLITICAL SCIENCE
5. Methods, "Science," and Politics: Modes of Analysis in Political Science — *Nolan J. Argyle* — 30
6. On Learning or Remembering — *Plato* — 39
7. Survey Research: The Role of the Family in Political Socialization — *James LaPlant* — 47
8. Legal Research — *Jane Elza and Lee M. Allen* — 55

## Part Two
## FIELDS WITH A DOMESTIC EMPHASIS

### AMERICAN POLITICS
9. Selected excerpts from the *Federalist Papers* — *James Madison* — 66
10. The Constitutional Setting — *Louis Fisher* — 75
11. American Voting Behavior: Partisanship, Turnout, and Types of Elections — *David W. Winder* — 87
12. Partners in Power: Federalism in the U.S — *Richard T. Saeger* — 97

### PUBLIC LAW
13. Federalist Paper Number 78 — *Alexander Hamilton* — 106
14. Constitutional Interpretation: Distinctions Without Differences — *Clyde Willis* — 113
15. The History of Mainstream Legal Thought — *Elizabeth Mensch* — 123
16. Judicial Review — *Sarah Ellerbee* — 137

### PUBLIC ADMINISTRATION
17. Concerning the Secretaries of the Prince — *Niccolò Machiavelli* — 146
18. What Is Public Administration? — *Herbert A. Simon, Donald W. Smithburg, and Victor A. Thompson* — 151
19. Legal, Political, and Managerial Approaches to Public Administration — *David Rosenbloom* — 159
20. Performance in Public Administration: Measuring Government Efficiency and Effectiveness — *Robert T. Aldinger* — 167

## Part Three
## FIELDS WITH A GLOBAL EMPHASIS

### COMPARATIVE POLITICS
21. The Varieties of the Main Types of Constitutions — *Aristotle* — 178
22. The European Union in Transition: From Independent Nation-States to a United States of Europe? — *Carol Glen* — 183
23. Democratization and Structural Adjustment Programs in Africa: Failures and Successes of Two Development Strategies — *Napoleon Bamfo* — 193
24. Elections and Electoral Reform in Comparative Perspective — *Malcolm Punnett* — 201

### INTERNATIONAL RELATIONS

25. Inquiry into the Lawfulness of War 210
    —*Hugo Grotius*
26. Obligation and Post World War II Order and State Action 215
    —*Marc G. Pufong*
27. Technology, Power, and Competiveness Among Developed States 223
    —*Robert S. Walters & David H. Blake*
28. American Foreign Policy in the Post Cold War World 229
    —*James W. Peterson*

## Part Four
## THE INTEGRATIVE FIELD

### PUBLIC POLICY

29. Analyzing the Causes of Revolution 240
    —*Aristotle*
30. Factors in Policy Making: Human Population and Technology 247
    —*Lee M. Allen*
31. Policy Here, Policy There, Policy Everywhere 255
    —*Gary Misch*
32. Comparative Public Policy: Environmental Policy in the United States and Germany 263
    —*Michael J. Baun*

*Conclusion*  272
*Bibliography*  273
*Index*  281

# Introduction

Political science is a fascinating discipline, indeed, as argued by Plato and Aristotle, it is the "master science." It is the master science for the simple reason that politics control and determine so much of what we do—and that includes what we do in other sciences. The question of when a fetus becomes a living person is not being decided by biologists, but by the political system. The discipline is complex and many-faceted. In order to examine it, one must break it down into its component parts, and look at them one at a time. This text breaks the field down into fields specified by the American Political Science Association: political theory, methodology, American government, public law, public administration, comparative politics, international relations, and public policy. The editors of this text see these fields organized into one structure, much as shown on the cover. Political theory and methodology are the two foundation fields of the discipline. The pillars of the discipline include those fields with a domestic focus—American government, public law, and public administration—and those fields with a more global focus—comparative government and international relations. Public policy integrates the fields back into a whole, and thus serves as the capstone of the discipline.

## Political Theory

Political theory, or normative political thought, is the primary foundation of the discipline of political science. Indeed, for much of our history, it was political science. Classical Greek writings, including Plato's *Republic* and Aristotle's *Politics* helped shape the development of Western civilization. Not only did these works influence later thinkers like Cicero, Hobbes, and Rousseau, they helped mold the governing structure of most of Europe and later that of the United States. It is impossible to truly understand the modern political world without having some appreciation of the thinking that helped shape it over the centuries.

The first three readings in this chapter provide a cross-section of some of the classic works that underpin Western political development. Aristotle discusses the nature of the political association and, within that context, what it means to be a "citizen." Niccolò Machiavelli discusses the traits necessary to be an effective ruler. John Locke presents a theory of government based upon a compact among the people; a theory that underpins the American view of the state. The final reading discusses the relevance of ancient political thought for understanding modern political actions.

Aristotle uses the analogy of a ship's crew to indicate that a "good citizen," like a "good sailor," can be judged not so much on the basis of whether he is a good person, but on his contribution to the whole. A political association, like a ship's crew, needs people with different capacities and abilities working together for a common purpose.

Aristotle sees that political association, the polis, as natural. Individuals, not being self-sufficient, require the contributions of others in order to achieve their own potential humanity. Aristotle tells us that one "who is unable to share in the benefits of political associations, or has no need to share . . . must therefore be either a beast or a god." It is the polis that makes one human. Man, for Aristotle, is "the best of animals" when perfected through the polis; the "the worst of all" when isolated from it.

Aristotle gives us a view of politics based upon the concept that political associations are natural. The next theorist presented counters this view. Niccolò Machiavelli, in "The Reputation of the Prince," argues that any order in the state must be imposed by the prince; that the prince "understand how to avail himself of the beast and the man." The prince must "be a fox to discover the snares and a lion to terrify the wolves." And it is through his ability to use both the beast and the man—through what modern theorists would call impression management—that the prince becomes an effective ruler. Above all, Machiavelli tells us, "the most efficacious remedies that a prince can have against conspiracies is not to be hated and despised by the people."

Machiavelli's assertion that the political association, rather than being a natural order serving to define humanity, was instead an artificial creation whose order was imposed by the prince raised some troubling questions. If the state was not natural, either in the Aristotelian sense or in the modifications made by the Christian Fathers, how could one justify the state? How could one state be classified as "better" than another? Machiavelli's response seemed to be that the state was justified through the princely imposition of order, and that a more orderly state was "better" than a less orderly one. He seemed to cut politics loose from any moral foundation. Rather than the polis defining humanity, or serving as part of God's plan, it became an instrument of order.

The next author is one of a group of theorists who provided government with an alternate foundation; a foundation that returned a definition of morality to governments, and thereby provided a means for evaluating whether one government was "better" than another. Government, in the view of these theorists, results in a compact among individuals. And the definition of the compact that captured the American mind was that put forth by John Locke.

Like other compact theorists, Locke begins with a state-of-nature argument. Unlike many other compact theorists, however, Locke does not present that state of nature as either an intolerable state nor as a utopian society. Man, being reasonable, can coexist with his fellow men in a state of nature. Reason, however, is not equally shared, leading to disputes among men in such a state; disputes that create "inconveniences" for those who reside there. And it is to remedy these inconveniences that man forms first a civil society and then a government. Government, then, is based upon the consent of those who create it; it draws its legitimate power from the citizenry, who retain sovereignty in their hands.

Locke's arguments are part of the foundation of the American state. His views were paraphrased by Jefferson in the *Declaration of Independence*, and have become part of American political culture. Yet that culture draws upon each of the individuals mentioned in this chapter, and upon innumerable others. Other political cultures also draw upon this heritage; often with results that differ from the American experience. The final section of this chapter discusses how an understanding of political thought can help us understand contemporary events.

Argyle takes two themes from political theory and traces their development, showing how they underpin current debate. He first looks at compact theory, tracing it from Seneca through Locke to its influence on the Founding Fathers of the American state. He shows how much of the current rhetoric of politics in the United States is influenced by divided opinion concerning the nature of the compact that forms our government. He then analyzes nationalist thought, starting with Machiavelli. He emphasizes that thread of nationalist thought developed by de Gobineau, linked with Nietzsche's distinction between the lower man and "superman," placed in context by Chamberlain, and operationalized by Adolph Hitler. Argyle then examines how this nationalist thinking is affecting the current conflicts in Eastern Europe, including the recent war in the former Yugoslavia.

Studying political theory can give the student of political science a greater appreciation for the possibilities and the limits of political action. It gives one a sense of perspective in which current events take on clearer meaning. Political theory remains the primary foundation of political science.

# Methodology

Methodology is the other foundation field of political science. It provides the tools one needs to analyze the complexity of several billion individuals interacting in a political setting. Yet it is not the most popular field in the discipline; indeed, the very word is enough to make many political science students suffer an anxiety attack. Yet one cannot study politics—or anything else, for that matter—without using a methodology to direct that study. Many students simply prefer an implicit, rather than an explicit methodology. One is better off, however, if one explicitly recognizes what methodological approach one is using, and understands the strengths and weaknesses of that approach.

Political science is often regarded as lagging behind other social sciences in developing explicit methodological approaches; indeed, many of the methodological tools used in the discipline were developed in other social science disciplines, including sociology and economics. Yet politics, and therefore political methodology, was at the heart of the earliest writings in all societies. Part of the confusion concerning the status of methodology in political science stems from the tendency for many social scientists, including many political scientists, to equate "methods" with those techniques used in data analysis. Yet this is only **one** methodological approach, and it is not necessarily the **best** approach under all circumstances.

The first reading in this chapter addresses the question of what methodology in political science is, and what it ought to be. Argyle presents a brief history of the discipline of political science, and discusses the role methodology has played in defining that history. He argues that Aristotle may be considered the first "true political scientist," and that Machiavelli is the "first modern political scientist." Argyle then traces the evolution of the modern discipline within the United States, starting with Columbia University's establishment of the first Department of History and Political Science in 1856. He points out that the contemporary debate concerning what does and does not constitute methodology stems from a split occurring within the discipline during the decades of the 1920s through the 1960s. He concludes with an analysis of the current status of methodology in political science.

The next reading is taken from one of the most famous pieces in political science literature, Plato's *Meno*. Using Socrates as his foil, Plato demonstrates the power of **deductive reasoning**. Socrates leads a boy through a series of logical steps to enable him to "remember" geometry. In doing so, he presents an argument that we are born with full knowledge within us; we merely must "discover" those things we already know. The method of discovery outlined in *Meno*, the Socratic method, dominated political science methodology for centuries, and it remains a powerful form of political inquiry. As Meno tells Socrates: "You seem to me to argue well. . . . I don't know how you do it."

The reading by James LaPlant is representative of the behavioral, quantitative approach to political science methodology. LaPlant examines the role of the family in political socialization and, in so doing, illustrates the scientific method as it is applied to research in political science. He points out that a political scientist's research "is only as good as the theory and hypotheses that provide the foundation" for the research project.

Jane Elza and Lee Allen's article on legal research illustrates the continuing utility of qualitative research in political science. The article illustrates the role that historical analysis and logic play in research. The authors point out that this type of research can be very time consuming, and requires excellent preparation by the researcher.

Methodology. The very word should not make any political science student suffer an anxiety attack. It is a process we are engaged in at all times; understanding that process can help us understand ourselves and the world about us.

# American Politics

The study of American politics is the first pillar forming the structure of the discipline, resting upon the twin foundations of theory and methodology. American politics occurs within a framework of constitutional democracy. A constitutional democracy is a limited government originating with the people, consented to by the people, and elected and monitored by the people. And all the people are considered equally important and sovereign in a constitutional democracy. Accordingly, the United States has universal adult suffrage: all persons over the age of eighteen who are not convicted felons have the right to vote. Thus, the U.S., like all true constitutional democracies, is committed to political equality.

The framers of the Constitution of the United States were learned men. They were also practical men, and one of their first practical challenges following the Convention of 1787 was to persuade the delegates to the various state ratifying conventions to give their approval to the framer's work. Particularly crucial was the approval of New York. Without the large state's ratification, the legitimacy of this new constitution might very well have been questioned. The task of persuading the ratifying convention delegates was undertaken primarily by two of the delegates to the Philadelphia Convention, James Madison of Virginia and Alexander Hamilton of New York. John Jay, also of New York, played a lesser role. *The Federalist Papers*, penned by these three Founding Fathers, is arguably America's single greatest contribution to political theory. The pseudonym under which the three wrote these papers, which were published in the New York newspapers, was *Publius*.

Included here are two of the best known *Federalist* papers: Nos. 51 and 10, both authored by Madison. No. 51 addresses the importance of checking and balancing power with power. In order to prevent any one branch of the national government—executive, legislative, judicial—from riding roughshod over the others, the Constitution, Madison argues, "partitions" power.

*Federalist No. 10* discusses "factions," or what today we would call political parties and interest groups. In any nation characterized by a plurality of different interests—political, religious, and economic—there will be different opinions vying to be heard and groups desiring to dominate. The task of the Constitution will be to prevent that domination from happening by checking faction with faction by allowing all to compete. Thus, another kind of limiting of power—this one with private organizations—is facilitated by the Constitution.

Louis Fisher discusses the Constitution, and how it has developed as the underpinning of American government in "The Constitutional Setting." Fisher discusses the nature of constitutions and constitutional government, and points out how these ideas have developed throughout our history. He indicates that presidents have seen the Constitution of the United States differently, particularly when it comes to the powers it confers upon the national versus the state governments.

David Winder discusses what is happening to American electoral behavior. Starting with the seminal work on American voting behavior, *The American Voter*, Winder analyzes the changes that have taken place in the electorate in the past four decades and speculates on the overall significance of the 1996 election. Electoral behavior is vitally important in terms of the three branches operating under a constitutional system. American voters elect our Congress and choose the president, who in turn appoints members of the Supreme Court and other federal courts as vacancies occur. The voting public has continued to pick winners for the presidency and virtually all seats in Congress from only two major parties.

This chapter finishes with a look at state governments in the American political system. As Richard T. Saeger points out, states form a critical element in the pillar of American politics. Seager starts with the question, "Does anybody really care about state government?" He does an excellent job of pointing out that we all should care. Saeger discusses various views of federalism, and how those views affect the role state governments play. He then examines the role of states in the current federal system, concluding that "states are as vibrant and as vital as they've ever been."

## Public Law

The second pillar in the discipline of political science is public law. The courts have played a key role in developing and defining the American nation. That role has been controversial from the start, as indicated in the first reading, *Federalist 78*, by Alexander Hamilton.

Hamilton argued for the courts to serve as an independent check on the other branches of government. In order to do this, he pointed out the need for judicial independence; independence he felt could only be obtained by appointing judges for life, allowing them to hold office *"during good behavior."*

Clyde Willis focuses upon judicial decision making—upon how judges come to understand and apply the meaning of law. Instead of a focus on **what** the judge decided, the focus is on **how** the judge decided in the first place. The inquiry goes to the philosophical essence of interpretation rather than its practical implication, although the inquiry has profound practical implications.

Elizabeth Mensch examines the history of legal thought in America. She points out that in the period immediately following the Revolutionary War, law, as the embodiment of reason, "seemed to offer the only source of stability in a nation that otherwise threatened to dissolve into the chaotic, leveling passions of a people now so dangerously declared to be sovereign." Yet the legal profession has never come to a final resolution on how it is to provide that stability—if it is to be a "value-neutral" or a "participation-oriented" profession.

Sarah Ellerbee adds to this discussion by focusing upon judicial review. Pointing out that "the roots of judicial review are found in British legal theory," she goes on to show how those British roots took on a decidedly American twist. She shows how the concept of judicial review fits within a democratic society. A strong, independent judiciary may pose a risk to democratic society, she tells us, but it may also serve to protect that society from public passions that become to strong to be resisted by elected officials.

## Public Administration

Public administration is the final pillar in the structure of political science with a primarily domestic focus. As the first reading in this chapter indicates, however, public administration, and the other pillars with domestic foci, cannot be studied in isolation from the rest of the political world. The first modern political scientist, Niccolò Machiavelli was very much a public administrator. Machiavelli was concerned with how the medieval Italian Prince could evict foreign invaders and create a strong stable government based on civic and administrative principles. In his "Concerning the Secretaries of the Prince," he advises the Medicis concerning how to choose good public servants and on why and how one should avoid appointing mere flatterers to public office.

Machiavelli helps to usher in our contemporary era, and the remaining three sections in this chapter focus on public administration concepts and practices in a modern context.

First, Herbert Simon and others describe reasons for the growth of public administration, and problems that have emerged with its evolution. They also introduce us to comparisons and contrasts between public and private administrative systems, and show why government cannot always simply be run like a business.

While acknowledging the need to understand the human elements at work in public organizations, these authors tend to view organizations as rational, more science than art, in structure and processes. However, focusing on issues amenable to rationality, such as efficiency, may be insufficient to guide organizations in other areas, such as ethical considerations, and in decision making, in leadership, etc. This polemic sets the stage for the next article, which focuses on some of the competing and often contradictory values faced by public administrators.

In this next article David Rosenbloom continues our review and examination of individuals interacting in an organizational setting, and the different values which affect managing public organizations. David Rosenbloom looks to the U.S. Constitution and its amendments for the principles that circumscribe the field of public administration. According to Rosenbloom, the checks and balances of the three branches of government provided for in the Constitution create tensions among managerial, political, and legal forces—these tensions dominate and restrict management in the public sector. He neatly defines this approach, and describes several implications each of these values holds in terms of organization structure, view of the individual, decision making, and other organizational considerations. When you think about it, balancing the demands of managerial efficiency (getting the most output for the input), political responsiveness and representativeness, and legal compliance and due process, all at the same time, is a real juggling act, where it is all too easy to drop the ball.

The fourth and last section in this chapter, by Robert Aldinger, examines a major issue in public administration: finding a reliable and valid method to measure performance in public organizations. This topic fits in well with all of the articles, but especially with both the Rosenbloom and Simon pieces, because many of the difficulties public administrators have in measuring performance are based on the nature of public administration itself: the type of services the agencies provide and the diverse array of customers they serve.

Aldinger begins by looking at the traditional quantitative approach for measuring performance: counting and measuring outputs of an organization. One of the most widely used methods that exemplifies this approach is Management by Objectives, (MBO). He briefly presents the history, features, and application of MBO. Next he introduces an approach for performance evaluation that focuses on continuous quality improvement for the production of goods and services. This approach, Total Quality Management (TQM), has been used in private business for decades, but recently public agencies have adopted its principles in an effort to make long-lasting changes in the process, and even culture, of organizations. After presenting some of the major problems and benefits of TQM, the article offers some conclusions about the prospects for its future success in the realm of public administration.

# Comparative Politics

Comparative politics is the first pillar in the structure of political science with a predominantly global focus. Just as one cannot study those pillars with a domestic focus without placing them in the larger global political system, one cannot examine comparative politics without using the American political system as part of that comparison. This is brought out particularly well in the reading by Malcolm Punnett.

The first reading in this section is by the first true political scientist, Aristotle. In *The Varieties of the Main Types of Constitutions*, he laid the groundwork of modern comparative study of political systems by arguing that governments as well as the constitutions by which they operate are a reflection of the essential elements of society. He identified two main forms of government; democracy, where the free are rulers, and oligarchy, where the few rule. However, classifying political systems solely on these two broad categories, he argued, completely misses the essential elements peculiar to each form of government. He identified five forms of democracy and four forms of oligarchy to show how broad categorizations of political systems could lead to inaccurate and misleading conclusions.

The next two readings provide comparative studies of key regions of the world. Carol Glen provides a contemporary comparative study focusing upon Western Europe, while Napoleon Bamfo looks at Africa.

Carol Glen examines a region that has always held special significance for American policy, and it is a region that has experienced "dramatic and sudden change" in the past few years. Governments in Europe are being forced to rethink traditional relations with the continued development of the European Union. Pointing out that the European Union has "come a long way" from its early days, she nevertheless indicates that it has many obstacles to overcome before it can come close to being a "United States of Europe."

Napoleon Bamfo examines democratic and structural programs in Africa, an area of the world that has occupied an increasing amount of American policymakers attention. Bamfo discusses the continent's checkered political and economic past, pointing out the many problems African states have faced in trying to develop into nations that are both politically and economically viable. He finds reason for hope in recent developments on the continent, arguing that Africans have gained "invaluable experience" from the events of the past few years. To consolidate these gains, however, Bamfo believes that "governments must adopt a common sense approach" in their efforts to develop while at the same time strengthening civic culture.

Finally, Malcolm Punnett's article is an example of a comparative study of one topic, elections and electoral reform, which draws upon examples from a variety of countries drawn primarily from two regions: America and Europe. Malcolm Punnett provides an excellent overview of various electoral systems that have been developed. He argues that constitution makers and electoral reformers need to move beyond the question of what is the best electoral system to a determination of what outcomes are desired, and which system is most conducive to obtaining those outcomes.

## International Relations

International relations is the other pillar in the structure of political science with a primarily global focus. There are a wide variety of methodologies used in the study of international relations. In earlier decades of this century there was an historical concern with the evolution of the modern international state system. However, in recent decades there has been a strong effort to apply quantitative methods to the study of international affairs. In part, this latter focus reflects changed approaches within political science as well as in all of the social sciences during the last thirty years. Scholars have applied quantitative techniques to the study of international politics in hopes of providing systematic advice and verifiable conclusions to those who seek to overcome international disorder and its accompanying violence and bloodshed.

Issues of war and peace have affected the lives of many of us in recent years whether we have family members in the uniformed services or whether we have a concern about the present and future role of the United States in the world. In this light, the article by Hugo Grotius provides a seventeenth-century perspective on such issues. He wrestles with the question of what the grounds are that justify the decision of a people to go to war.

The questions raised by Grotius continue today. As shown in the reading by Marc Pufong, such questions have preoccupied American foreign policymakers in situations such as the Persian Gulf War of 1991 and the war in Bosnia in 1992–95.

In recent decades emergent technology has reshaped the global order in so many ways. Walters & Blake focus on the extent to which technology can change the power dimension of a nation and its competitive position in the world. There are countless additional ways in which technology has revamped the outlines of world politics. Modern post-war technology made possible the development of weapons of destruction unimaginable early in this century. During the Cold War the United States and the Soviet Union stockpiled far more nuclear weapons than would have been needed to destroy the other in a real military conflict. On a more positive note, modern communications and computer technology offer global linkages that were unanticipated even thirty years ago. Coverage of the Gulf War by CNN offered the possibility to follow a war minute by minute without missing much of the action. Internet makes possible nearly personal communications between individuals in different corners of the world. Political leaders understand that technological power is a key ingredient of national strength that may affect decisions leading to war or strategies designed to protect the national interest.

James W. Peterson describes the changing nature of American foreign policy in a post Cold War world. Arguing that American foreign policy has been at a crossroad during the 1990s, Peterson poses three related questions we must address in trying to come to terms with post Cold War dilemmas. First, what attempts have American leaders made to codify objectives and uncover a replacement for Cold War-style containment? Second, how much have domestic forces and variables affected the process of developing a new foreign policy for the next century: And third, what kinds of policy themes have recently emerged in the areas with which American leaders must deal on a daily basis?

# Public Policy

Public policy is shown as the capstone, or roof, of the edifice that makes up the structure of political science. While it has not lived up to Harold Lasswell's hope for a fully integrative field that would unify the social sciences, it is the most integrative subfield within political science.

The chapter begins with an excerpt from Aristotle's *Politics*. In this piece, Aristotle focuses on the single most fundamental question of public policy, that of national survival. He does so by looking at the extreme method of public policy change: political revolution. His article demonstrates the deep roots that a policy focus has in political science. He explains that revolutions, based on varying interpretations of justice and equality, lead to conflict, political struggles, and constitutional changes. The objective political scientist is interested in the various methods by which revolutionary threats may be created and/or averted.

Lee Allen looks at modern factors in emerging policy issues, but, in so doing, once again illustrates the long history of the field. His argument that population growth and technology drive policy issues echoes a famous argument made by Malthus in the eighteenth century. Allen presents us with a number of policy problems we must address if we are to ensure our future. He also points out a number of policy "myths" that prevent us from dealing with these problems as rationally as we might.

In the next reading, Gary Misch examines the use of symbolic words and phrases in the development of public policy. Arguing that the "development of public policy is far more art than science," he analyzes policy making practices in the United States. Utilizing mini case studies drawn from both domestic and foreign policy making, Misch demonstrates how political actors use symbolic terms to build support for their policies. He concludes with the observation that "public policies must ultimately be evaluated in terms of their real outcomes, not rhetoric."

In the final reading in this chapter, Michael J. Baun shows how a policy approach assists one in studying comparative politics. He examines environmental policy in the United States and Germany, a public policy area that has emerged as a major focus within the past few decades. He finds many similarities in the two countries approaches to this policy area, but he also finds a number of differences. Both countries demonstrate the important role of political leadership in environmental policy, as well as the effect of external forces such as the oil crisis of the 1970s. Differences in the two countries policies are attributed to a number of factors, including the difference in their political party structure and Germany's role within the European Union. His article helps us understand the unique features of different national political systems and contributes to our knowledge of politics.

## Part One

# THE FOUNDATIONS OF POLITICAL SCIENCE

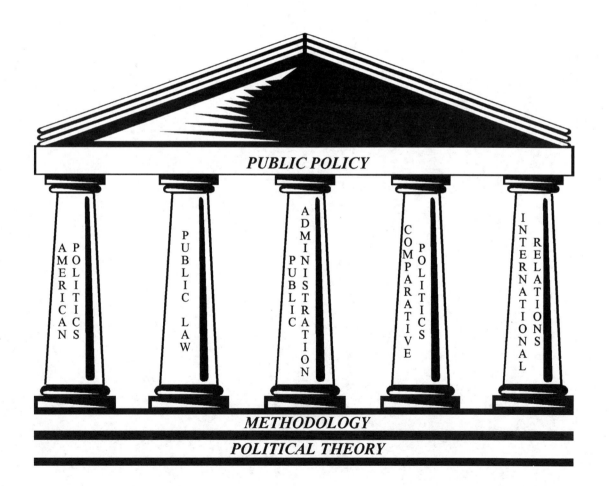

*Chapter One*

# POLITICAL THEORY

**POLITICAL THEORY**

# THE POLITICAL ASSOCIATION

## Aristotle*

*[Editor's note: Aristotle's definition of the political association takes the form of the polis; the all-encompassing political community. In the following passage he makes it clear that the state—the polis—is essential for human development.]*

## THE STATE AS NATURAL

Every state is a community of some kind, and every community is established with a view to some good; for mankind always act in order to obtain that which they think good. But, if all communities aim at some good, the state or political community, which is the highest of all, and which embraces all the rest, aims at good in a greater degree than any other, and at the highest good.

Some people think that the qualifications of a statesman, king, householder, and master are all the same, and that they differ, not in kind, but only in the number of their subjects. For example, the ruler over a few is called a master; over more, the manager of a household; over a still larger number, a statesman or king, as if there were no difference between a great household and a small state. The distinction which is made between the king and the statesman is as follows: When the government is personal, the ruler is a king; when, according to the rules of the political science, the citizens rule and are ruled in turn, then he is called a statesman. . . .

*Aristole*

When several villages are united in a single complete community, large enough to be nearly or quite nearly self-sufficing, the state comes into existence, originating in the bare needs of life, and continuing in existence for the sake of a good life. And therefore, if the earlier forms of society are natural, so is the state, for it is the end of them and the nature of a thing is its end. For what each thing is when fully developed, we call its nature, whether we are speaking of a man, a horse, or a family. Besides, the final cause and end of a thing is the best, and to be self-sufficing is the end and the best.

Hence it is evident that the state is a creation of nature, and that man is by nature a political animal. And he who by nature and not by mere accident is without a state, is either a bad man or above humanity. . . .

Now, that man is more of a political animal than bees or any other gregarious animals is evident. Nature, as we often say, makes nothing in vain, and man is the only animal whom she has endowed with the gift of speech. And whereas mere voice is but an indication of pleasure or pain, and is therefore found in other animals, the power of speech is intended to set forth the expedient and inexpedient, and therefore likewise the just and the unjust. And it is a characteristic of man that he alone has any sense of good and evil, of just and unjust, and the like, and the association of living beings who have this sense makes a family and a state.

Further, the state is by nature clearly prior to the family and to the individual, since the whole is of necessity prior to the part; for example, if the whole body be destroyed, there will be no foot or hand, except in an equivocal sense, as we might speak of a stone hand; for when destroyed the hand will be no better than that. But things are defined by their working and power; and we

---

* Aristotle. (1905). *Politics* (Trans. Benjamin Jowett). Oxford: Clarendon Press. Book III.

ought not to say that they are the same when they no longer have their proper quality, but only that they have the same name. The proof that the state is a creation of nature and prior to the individual is that the individual, when isolated, is not self-sufficing; and therefore he is like a part in relation to the whole. But he who is unable to live in society, or who has no need because he is sufficient for himself, must be either a beast or a god: he is no part of a state. A social instinct is implanted in all men by nature, and yet he who first founded the state was the greatest of benefactors. For man, when perfected, is the best of animals, but, when separated from law and justice, he is the worst of all; since armed injustice is the more dangerous, and he is equipped at birth with arms, meant to be used by intelligence and virtue, which he may use for the worst ends. Wherefore, if he have not virtue, he is the most unholy and the most savage of animals, and the most full of lust and gluttony. But justice is the bond of men in states, for the administration of justice, which is the determination of what is just, is the principle of order in political society.

## THE NATURE OF THE GOOD CITIZEN

He who would inquire into the essence and attributes of various kinds of governments must first of all determine "What is a state?" . . . [A] state is a composite, like any other whole made up of many parts;—these are the citizens, who compose it. It is evident, therefore, that we must begin by asking, Who is the citizen, and what is the meaning of the term?

There is a point nearly allied to the preceding: Whether the virtue of a good man and a good citizen is the same or not. But, before entering on this discussion, we must certainly first obtain some general notion of the virtue of the citizen. Like the sailor, the citizen is a member of a community. Now, sailors have different functions, for one of them is a rower, another a pilot, and a third a look-out man, a fourth is described by some similar term; and while the precise definition of each individual's virtue applies exclusively to him, there is, at the same time, a common definition applicable to them all. For they have all of them a common object, which is safety in navigation. Similarly, one citizen differs from another, but the salvation of the community is the common business of them all. This community is the constitution; the virtue of the citizen must therefore be relative to the constitution of which he is a member. If, then, there are many forms of government, it is evident that there is not one single virtue of the good citizen which is perfect virtue. But we say that the good man is he who has one single virtue which is perfect virtue. Hence it is evident that the good citizen need of necessity possess the virtue which makes a good man.

The same question may also be approached by another road, from a consideration of the best constitution. If the state cannot be entirely composed of good men, and yet each citizen is expected to do his own business as well, and must therefore have virtue, still, inasmuch as all the citizens cannot be alike, the virtue of the good citizen and of the good man cannot coincide. All must have the virtue of the good citizen—thus, and thus only, can the state be perfect; but they will not have the virtue of a good man, unless we assume that in the good state all the citizens must be good.

Again, the state, as composed of unlikes, may be compared to the living being: as the first elements into which a living being is resolved are soul and body, as soul is made up of rational principle and appetite, the family of husband and wife, property of master and slave, so of all these, as well as other dissimilar elements, the state is composed; and, therefore, the virtue of all the citizens cannot possibly be the same, any more than the excellence of the leader of a chorus is the same as that of the performer who stands by his side. I have said enough to show why the two kinds of virtue cannot be absolutely and always the same.

But will there then be no case in which the virtue of the good citizen and the virtue of the good man coincide? To this we answer that the good ruler is a good and wise man, and that he who would be a statesman must be a wise man. And some persons say that even the education of the ruler should be of a special kind: for are not the children of kings instructed in riding and military exercises? As Euripides says:

*"No subtle arts for me, but what the state requires."*

As though there were a special education needed by a ruler. If then the virtue of a good ruler is the same as that of a good man, and we assume further that the subject is a good citizen and the virtue of the good man cannot be absolutely the same, although in some cases they may; for the virtue of a ruler differs from that of a citizen. It was the sense of this difference which made Jason say that "he felt hungry when he was not a tyrant," meaning that he could not endure to live in the private station. But, on the other hand, it may be argued that men are praised for knowing both how to rule and how to obey, and he is said to be a citizen of approved virtue who is able to do both. Now if we suppose the virtue of a good man to be that which rules, and the virtue of the citizen to include ruling and obeying, it cannot be said that they are equally worthy of praise. Since, then, it is sometimes thought that the ruler and the ruled must learn different things and not the same, but that the citizen must know and share in them both, the inference is obvious. There is, indeed, the rule of a master, which is concerned with menial offices—the master need not know how to perform these, but may employ others in the execution of them: the other would be degrading; and by the other I mean the power actually to do menial duties, which vary much in character and are executed by various classes of slaves, such, for example, as handicraftsmen, who, as their name signifies, live by the labor of their hands: under these the mechanic is included. Hence in ancient times, and among some nations, the working classes had no share in the government—a privilege which they only acquired under the extreme democracy. Certainly the good man and the statesman and the good citizen ought not to learn the crafts of inferiors except for their occasional use; if they habitually practice them, there will cease to be a distinction between master and slave.

# ARISTOTLE

NAME: _____

SECTION: _____

DATE: _____

1. What arguments does Aristotle use to assert that man is by nature a political animal?

   _____
   _____
   _____
   _____
   _____
   _____
   _____

2. What argument does Aristotle use to assert that the virtue of a citizen is different from the virtue of a good person?

   _____
   _____
   _____
   _____
   _____
   _____
   _____

3. Why, according to Aristotle, is the Polis necessary for human development?

   _____
   _____
   _____
   _____
   _____
   _____
   _____

4. What does Aristotle mean when he talks about the Constitution of the Polis?

_____
_____
_____
_____
_____
_____

5. Why should people be praised because they know both how to obey and how to rule?

_____
_____
_____
_____
_____
_____

**Group Exercise:** Study your local community and report on which necessary commodities must be imported from other places.

**Individual Project:** Examine any government textbook and show that at least six parts cover the same subject matter as Aristotle's work.

# The Reputation of the Prince

## Niccolò Machiavelli*

### CONCERNING THE WAY IN WHICH PRINCES SHOULD KEEP FAITH

Every one admits how praiseworthy it is in a prince to keep faith, and to live with integrity and not with craft. Nevertheless our experience has been that those princes who have done great things have held good faith of little account, and have known how to circumvent the intellect of men by craft, and in the end have overcome those who have relied on their word. You must know there are two ways of contesting, the one by the law, the other by force; the first method is proper to men, the second to beasts; but because the first is frequently not sufficient, it is necessary to have recourse to the second. Therefore it is necessary for a prince to understand how to avail himself of the beast and the man. . . . A prince, therefore, being compelled knowingly to adopt the beast, ought to choose the fox and lion; because the lion cannot defend himself against snares and the fox cannot defend himself against wolves. Therefore, it is necessary to be a fox to discover the snares and a lion to terrify the wolves. Those who rely simply on the lion do not understand what they are about. Therefore a wise lord cannot, nor ought he to, keep faith when such observance may be turned against him, and when the reasons that caused him to pledge it exist no longer. If men were entirely good this precept would not hold, but because they are bad, and will not keep faith with you, you too are not bound to observe it with them. . . .

But it is necessary to know well how to disguise this characteristic and to be a great pretender and dissembler; and men are so simple, and so subject to present necessities, that he who seeks to deceive will always find some one who will allow himself to be deceived. . . .

Therefore it is unnecessary for a prince to have all the good qualities I have enumerated, but it is very necessary to appear to have them. And I shall dare to say this also, that to have them and always to observe them is injurious, and that to appear to have them is useful; to appear merciful, faithful, humane, religious, upright, and to be so, but with a mind so framed that should you require not to be so, you may be able to know how to change to the opposite.

And you have to understand this, that a prince, especially a new one, cannot observe all those things for which men are esteemed, being often forced, in order to maintain the state, to act contrary to fidelity, friendship, humanity, and religion. Therefore it is necessary for him to have a mind ready to turn itself accordingly as the winds and variations of fortune force it, yet, as I have said above, not to diverge from the good if he can avoid doing so, but if compelled, then to know how to set about it.

### THAT ONE SHOULD AVOID BEING DESPISED AND HATED

. . . The prince must consider, as has been in part said before, how to avoid those things which will make him hated or contemptible; and as often as he shall have succeeded he will have fulfilled his part, and he need not fear any danger in other reproaches.

It makes him hated above all things, as I have said, to be rapacious, and to be a violator of the property and women of his subjects, from both of which he must abstain. And when neither their property nor honor is touched, the majority of men live content, and he has only to contend with the ambition of a few, whom he can curb with ease in many ways.

---

* Excerpted from: Machiavelli, N. (1908) *The Prince*. (Trans. W. K. Marriott). New York: E. P. Dutton & Co. Chpts. 18 & 19.

It makes him contemptible to be considered fickle, frivolous, effeminate, mean-spirited, irresolute, from all of which a prince should guard himself as from a rock; and he should endeavor to show in his actions greatness, courage, gravity, and fortitude; and in his private dealings with his subjects let him show that his judgements are irrevocable, and maintain himself in such reputation that no one can hope either to deceive him or to get round him.

... For this reason a prince ought to have two fears, one from within on account of his subjects, the other from without, on account of external powers. From the latter he is defended by being well armed and having good allies, and if he is well armed he will have good friends, and affairs will always remain quiet within when they are quiet without, unless they should have been already disturbed by conspiracy; and even should affairs outside be disturbed, if he has carried out his preparations and has lived as I have said, as long as he does not despair, he will resist every attack, as I said Nabis the Spartan did.

But concerning his subjects, when affairs outside are disturbed he has only to fear that they will conspire secretly, from which a prince can easily secure himself by avoiding being hated and despised, and by keeping the people satisfied with him, which it is most necessary for him to accomplish, as I have said above at length. And one of the most efficacious remedies that a prince can have against conspiracies is not to be hated and despised by the people, for he who conspires against a prince always expects to please them by his removal; but when the conspirator can only look forward to offending them, he will not have the courage to take such a course, for the difficulties that confront a conspirator are infinite. And as experience shows, many have been the conspiracies, but few have been successful; because he who conspires cannot act alone, nor can he take a companion except from those whom he believes to be malcontents, and as soon as you have opened your mind to a malcontent you have given him the material with which to content himself, for by denouncing you he can look for every advantage; so that, seeing the gain from this course to be assured, and seeing the other to be doubtful and full of dangers, he must be a very rare friend, or a thoroughly obstinate enemy of the prince, to keep faith with you.

And, to reduce the matter into a small compass, I say that, on the side of the conspirator, there is nothing but fear, jealousy, prospect of punishment to terrify him; but on the side of the prince there is the majesty of the principality, the laws, the protection of friends and the state to defend him; so that, adding to all these things the popular goodwill, it is impossible that any one should be so rash as to conspire. For whereas in general the conspirator has to fear before the execution of his plot, in this case he has also to fear the sequel to his crime; because on account of it he has the people for an enemy, and thus cannot hope for any escape. . . .

For this reason I consider that a prince ought to reckon conspiracies of little account when his people hold him in esteem; but when it is hostile to him, and bears hatred towards him, he ought to fear everything and everybody. And well-ordered states and wise princes have taken every care not to drive the nobles to desperation, and to keep the people satisfied and contented, for this is one of the most important objects a prince can have.

# MACHIAVELLI

NAME: _____

SECTION: _____

DATE: _____

1. Why should a ruler know how to be both a lion and a fox?

   _____
   _____
   _____
   _____
   _____
   _____
   _____
   _____

2. What is the purpose, according to Machiavelli, that justifies a prince in acting contrary to fidelity, friendship, humanity, and religion?

   _____
   _____
   _____
   _____
   _____
   _____
   _____
   _____

3. What kinds of actions, according to Machiavelli, are likely to make a prince despised and hated?

   _____
   _____
   _____
   _____
   _____
   _____
   _____

4. What are the four virtues that Machiavelli said a prince must show in his actions?

___

5. What is the main difficulty confronting a potential conspirator when attempting to find companions?

___

**Group Exercise:** Identify a possible problem facing the President in which the solution can be either acting like a lion or like a fox.

**Individual Project:** Explain the similarities between a little white lie between friends and a public speech misrepresenting the truth.

# The State of Nature, Property, and the Development of Civil Society

## John Locke*

### Of the State of Nature

To understand political power right, and derive it from its original, we must consider what state all men are naturally in, and that is, a state of perfect freedom to order their actions and dispose of their possessions and persons, as they think fit, within the bounds of the law of nature; without asking leave, or depending upon the will of any other man.

A state of equality, wherein all the power and jurisdiction is reciprocal, no one having more than another; there being nothing more evident than that creatures of the same species and rank, promiscuously born to all the same advantages of nature, and the use of the same faculties, should also be equal one amongst another without subordination or subjection; unless the Lord and Master of them all should, by manifest declaration of his will, set one above another, and confer on him, by an evident and clear appointment, an undoubted right to dominion and sovereignty. . . .

But though this be a state of liberty, yet it is not a state of license; though man in that state have an uncontrollable liberty to dispose of his person or possessions, yet he has not liberty to destroy himself, or so much as any creature in his possession, but where some nobler use than its bare preservation calls for it. The state of nature has a law to govern it, which obliges every one: and reason, which is that law, teaches all mankind, who will but consult it, that being all equal and independent, no one ought to harm another in his life, health, liberty, or possessions: for men being all the workmanship of one omnipotent and infinitely wise Maker; all the servants of one sovereign Master, sent into the world by his order, and about his business; they are his property, whose workmanship they are, made to last during his, not another's pleasure: and being furnished with like faculties, sharing all in one community of nature, there cannot be supposed any such subordination among us that may authorize us to destroy another, as if we were made for one another's uses, as the inferior ranks of creatures are for ours. Every one, as he is bound to preserve himself, and not to quit his station wilfully, so by the like reason, when his own preservation comes not in competition, ought he, as much as he can, to preserve the rest of mankind, and may not, unless it be to do justice to an offender, take away or impair the life, . . . liberty, health, limb, or goods of another.

And that all men nay be restrained from invading others' rights, and from doing hurt to one another, the law of nature be observed, which willeth the peace and preservation of all mankind, the execution of the law of nature is, in that state, put into every man's hands, whereby every one has a right to punish the transgressors of that law to such a degree as may hinder its violation: for the law of nature would, as all other laws that concern men in this world, be in vain, if there were nobody that in the state of nature had a power to execute that law, and thereby preserve the innocent, and restrain offenders. And if any one in the state of nature may punish another for any evil he has done, every one may do so: for in that state of perfect equality, where naturally there is no superiority or jurisdiction of one over another, what any may do in prosecution of that law every one must needs have a right to do.

. . . In transgressing the law of nature, the offender declares himself to live by another rule than that of reason and common equity, which is that measure God has set to the actions of men for their mutual security; and so he becomes dangerous to mankind, the tie, which is to secure them

---

* Excerpted from: Locke, J. (1823). *The works of John Locke*, Vol. 5. London: Thomas Tegg.

from injury and violence, being slighted and broken by him: which being a trespass against the whole species, and the peace and safety of it, provided for by the law of nature; every man upon this score, by the right he hath to preserve mankind in general, may restrain, or where it is necessary, destroy things noxious to them, as so may bring such evil on any one, who hath transgressed that law, as may make him repent the doing of it, and thereby deter him, and by his example others, from doing the like mischief. . . .

To this strange doctrine, viz. That "in the state of nature every one has the executive power" of the law of nature, I doubt not but it will be objected, that it is unreasonable for men to be judges in their own cases, that self-love will make men partial to themselves and their friends: and, on the other side, that ill-nature, passion, and revenge will carry them too far in punishing others; and hence nothing but confusion and disorder will follow: and that therefore God hath certainly appointed government to restrain the partiality and violence of men. I easily grant, that civil government is the proper remedy for the inconveniences of the state of nature, which must certainly be great, where men may be judges in their own case; . . . but I shall desire those who make this objection to remember, that absolute monarchs are but men; and if government is to be the remedy of those evils, which necessarily follow from men's being judges in their own cases, and the state of nature is therefore not to be endured; I desire to know what kind of government that is, and how much better it is than the state of nature, where one man, commanding a multitude, has the liberty to be judge in his own case, and may do to all his subjects whatever he pleases, without the least liberty to any one to question of control those who execute his pleasure? and in whatsoever he doth, whether led by reason, mistake or passion, must be submitted to? Much better it is in the state of nature, wherein men are not bound to submit to the unjust will of another: and if he that judges, judges amiss in his own, or any other case, he is answerable for it to the rest of mankind.

## OF POLITICAL OR CIVIL SOCIETY

God having made man such a creature, that in his own judgement it was not good for him to be alone, put him under strong obligations of necessity, convenience, and inclination, to drive him into society, as well as fitted him with understanding and language to continue and enjoy it. The first society was between man and wife, which gave beginnings to that between parents and children; to which, in time, that between master and servant came to be added: and though all these might, and commonly did meet together, and make up but one family, wherein the master or mistress of it had some sort of rule proper to a family; each of these, or all together, came short of political society. . . .

Man being born . . . with a title to perfect freedom, and uncontrolled enjoyment of all the rights and privileges of the law of nature, equally with any other man, or number of men in the world, hath by nature a power, not only to preserve his property, that is, his life, liberty and estate, against the injuries and attempts of other men; but to judge of and punish the breaches of that law in others, as he is persuaded that offence deserves, even with death itself, in crimes where the heinousness of the fact, in his opinion, requires it. But because no political society can be, nor subsist, without having in itself the power to preserve the property, and in order thereunto, punish the offenses of those of that society; there, and there only is political society, where every one of the members hath quitted this natural power, resigned it up into the hands of the community in all cases that exclude him not from appealing for to the law established by it. And thus all private judgements of every particular member being excluded, the community comes to be umpire, by settled standing rules, indifferent, and the same to all parties; and by men having authority from the community, for the execution of those rules, decides all the differences that may happen between any members of that society concerning any matter of right; and punishes those offenses which any member hath committed against the society, with such penalties as the law has established: whereby it is easy to discern who are, and who are not, in political society together. Those who are united in one body, and have a common established law and judicature to appeal to, with authority to decide controversies between them, and punish offenders, are in civil society one with another: but those who have no such common appeal, I mean on earth, are still in the state of nature, each being, where there is no other, judge for himself and executions: which is, as I have before showed it, the perfect state of nature.

# OF THE ENDS OF POLITICAL SOCIETY AND GOVERNMENT

If man in the state of nature be so free as has been said; if he be absolute lord of his own person and possessions, equal to the greatest, and subject to nobody, why will he part with his freedom, why will he give up this empire, and subject himself to the dominion and control of any other power? To which it is obvious to answer, that though in the state of nature he hath such a right, yet the enjoyment of it is very uncertain, and constantly exposed to the invasion of others; for all being kings as much as he, every man his equal, and the greater part no strict observers of equity and justice, the enjoyment of the property he has in this state is very unsafe, very insecure. This makes him willing to quit a condition, which, however free, is full of fears and continual dangers; and it is not without reason that he seeks out, and is willing to join in society with others, who are already united, or have a mind to unite, for the mutual preservation of their lives, liberties, and estates, which I call by the general name property.

The great and chief end, therefore, of men's uniting into commonwealths, and putting themselves under government, is the preservation of their property. To which in the state of nature there are many things wanting.

First, There wants an established, settled, known law, received and allowed by common consent to be the standard of right and wrong, and the common measure to decide all controversies between them: for though the law of nature be plain and intelligible to all rational creatures; yet men being biased by their interest, as well as ignorant for want of studying it, are not apt to allow of it as a law binding to them in the application of it to their particular cases.

Secondly, In the state of nature there wants a known and indifferent judge, with authority to determine all differences according to the established law: for every one in that state being both judge and executioner of the law of nature, men being partial to themselves, passion and revenge is very apt to carry them too far, and with too much heat, in their own cases; as well as negligence and unconcernedness, to make them too remiss in other men's.

Thirdly, In the state of nature there often wants power to back and support the sentence when right, and to give it due execution. They who by any injustice offend, will seldom fail, where they are able, by force to make good their injustice; such resistance many times makes the punishment dangerous, and frequently destructive to those who attempt it.

Thus mankind, notwithstanding all the privileges of the state of nature, being but in an ill condition, while they remain in it, are quickly driven into society. Hence it comes to pass, that we seldom find any number of men live any time together in this state. The inconveniences that they are therein exposed to, by the irregular and uncertain exercise of the power every man has of punishing the transgressions of others, make them take sanctuary under the established laws of government, and therein seek the preservation of their property. It is this makes them so willingly give up every one his single power of punishing, to be exercised by such alone as shall be appointed to it amongst them; and by such rules as the community, or those authorized by them to that purpose, shall agree on. And in this we have the original right of both the legislative and executive power, as well as of the governments and societies themselves.

# LOCKE

NAME: _____

SECTION: _____

DATE: _____

1. What is Locke's basic argument that people ought not to harm others in their life, health, liberty, or possessions?

   _____
   _____
   _____
   _____
   _____
   _____
   _____
   _____

2. When Locke says the community should be an umpire, what standard should it use concerning matters of rights and offenses?

   _____
   _____
   _____
   _____
   _____
   _____
   _____
   _____

3. According to Locke, why do people part with their freedom and subject themselves to governmental power?

   _____
   _____
   _____
   _____
   _____
   _____

4. Does Locke agree that under some conditions private judgements and punishment ought to be allowed?

_____
_____
_____
_____
_____
_____
_____

5. Do you agree that, according to Locke, in the state of nature each person is the judge in his/her own case?

_____
_____
_____
_____
_____
_____
_____

**Group Exercise:** Obtain some small article, such as a water glass or pencil, and write a law explaining who can use it and when.

**Individual Project:** Give an example of when it would be good to have an umpire when there is a dispute between two people.

# Why Study Plato? The Link between Political Theory and Practical Politics

## Nolan J. Argyle

*The classics of political thought are an indispensable component of a liberal arts education simply because their authors addressed themselves primarily to politically engaged intellectuals and intellectually sophisticated citizens. By understanding in historical context the reflections of each age's greatest sage, the serious student of political thought can gain a heightened appreciation of the possibilities and limits of political action.*

*Edward Bryan Portis*

Until approximately a century ago, the study of politics meant the study of political philosophy. One examined the ideas of the great philosophers in order to determine what a good state ought to be. Then, responding to growing complexity and resultant specialization, those scholars whose primary venue was political institutions formed the American Political Science Association, and began to work to "professionalize" the discipline. In doing so they began to adopt tools and techniques from other emerging social science professions, particularly sociology and economics. And, as the new tools and techniques occupied an increasingly central position in political science, study of the great philosophers began to decline.

As the discipline became more adept at using "scientific" tools of analysis Plato's cave gave way to dummy variables. Many of today's political scientists can discuss beta weights for hours, but have no conception of St. Thomas Aquinas' hierarchy of laws. This is not to argue that beta weights aren't important—the author has spent a fair amount of time discussing them—but it is to argue that an over-emphasis upon newly-developed tools and techniques robs the discipline of a needed foundation. Plato's cave can help us put the findings of a regression analysis of social frustration and political stability in perspective.

Political theory—the "reflections of each age's greatest sage," as Portis puts it, can help us understand the results of our analysis; these works did not become "classics because academicians considered them fine examples of scholarship and taught them to students. Instead, political actors and critics found in them useful or challenging arguments to justify or criticize existing political decisions or arrangements."

This study examines two concepts developed in political theory and relates those concepts to current political events in an attempt to illustrate the answer to the question of "why study Plato"; an answer that hinges upon the utility of such study for enhancing our understanding of the practical world of politics. The study looks at compact theory, which underpins the American political system; and at nationalism, which is heavily influencing events in Eastern Europe and elsewhere in the world at this time.

## Compact Theory and the Nature of the State

Compact theory argues that the legitimacy of a state, and therefore the legitimacy of the actions a state may take, are dependent upon an agreement—or compact—between those who rule and those who are ruled. In the United States, that agreement is spelled out in the *Constitution*; a document who's preamble, memorized by every school child of the author's generation, is written in pure compact terminology:

> We, the people of the United States, in order to form a more perfect Union, establish justice, insure domestic tranquility, provide for the common defense, promote the general welfare, and secure the blessings of liberty to ourselves and our posterity do ordain and establish this Constitution for the United States of America.

It is the *people* who establish the government; not the thirteen *states* existing at that time. Indeed, each of these states was established on a similar compact. This fact, and arguments over its real meaning, have defined what we are as a nation.

Virtually all compact theorists build their arguments upon a "state-of-nature" theory. In its most simple form, such a theory asks: "if there is no government, no society, what condition does humanity find itself in?" The answer to that question is different for different theorists, and those differences lead to different states and to different state powers.

While state-of-nature arguments go back as far as written history—and probably farther—the first major political theorist to base his arguments on a state-of-nature, and thus to begin to develop the theory of the compact, was Seneca. We will start by examining his arguments.

## Seneca and the Origins of Government

Seneca (4? B.C.–65 A.D.) lived in Rome at a time when the state was moving from republic to empire; at a time of great stress and political upheaval. There is an old Chinese curse: may you live in interesting times. Seneca, like most great philosophers, lived in interesting times, and his arguments reflected an attempt to understand the events occurring around him. Rome appeared to be moving from a "good" form of government—republic, to a "bad" form—dictatorship and empire. Seneca, believing in the equality of man, turned to Stoic philosophy to place the events of his time in context.

For Seneca, the virtuous man is one who devotes himself to the contemplation of and the understanding of natural law, which predates and is superior to government. "Good comes with reason," he states. A good man, then, is one with "a free and upstanding mind which subjects other things to itself and itself to nothing."

Seneca argues that man once lived contentedly in a primitive state, a "golden age." All goods were held in common, there were rulers (although "leaders" may be a more appropriate term); however, there were no laws, and no agencies of enforcement. As nature's dictates were always just, man did not have to be coerced into obedience. Man was virtuous because he had no knowledge of evil. This virtue was disrupted by the introduction of private property. Man became jealous of his own property and covetous of his neighbor's. Avarice replaced virtue as a dominant force. Government, with its trappings of laws and enforcement agencies, was created as a result of man's fall from his virtuous primitive condition.

Seneca's arguments meshed well with Christian thought when Rome adopted Christianity as a state religion. His golden age became the Garden of Eden, Adam's Fall introduced a knowledge of good and evil, and government therefore became a necessary outcome of the Fall. Under this view, government became part of God's plan to lead people back to virtue.

This view of man in a fallen state, with government therefore necessary to control us and require us to live a more virtuous life was developed most prominently in the work of John Calvin. His arguments, mixed with a Hobbesian view of the state of nature, play a major role in developing an American political ideology.

## Calvin and Theocracy

Central to Calvin's arguments was the sovereignty of God in all matters. The state, then, had significance only to the extent that it furthered God's plan. The church was a necessary intermediary to man's salvation, and thus princes, as agents of God, were subordinate to it. God was the origin of all good. Man, since Adam's Fall, was evil and corrupt, born in sin, and afflicted with the curse of Adam's transgression. If man were to overcome this fallen state, both temporal and ecclesiastical discipline were required. The state provided the sword, but it was to be wielded under the guidance of the church: "civil government is designed, as long as we live in this world, to cherish and support the external worship of God...."

Both church and state were to be controlled by those few in society with the capability of understanding God's purpose. Society was to be a directed commonwealth.

Calvin provides a purpose for government—to establish general peace and tranquility—but he didn't provide a rationale for people subjugating themselves to it. After all, if people were disposed to evil as a result of the Fall, why would they tolerate a government that sought to limit their evil actions? Sir Thomas Hobbes provided the theoretical justification for the Calvinist directed commonwealth.

## *Thomas Hobbes*

Thomas Hobbes was born prematurely at Malmesbury, England, on April 5, 1588. His early birth has been attributed to his mother's fright upon hearing or the approach of the Spanish Armada; a story that Hobbes himself promoted. Whether true of not, it seems a fitting portent for his life, for Hobbes lived through some bloody and dangerous times. England underwent a civil war that dominated political developments during Hobbes' lifetime, giving him a pessimistic view of human nature. And this pessimism affected his political theory; a theory that began with a state of nature argument.

For Hobbes, the two fundamental drives within each of us are to attain whatever we see as desirable, and to avoid anything we see as undesirable. We desire self-preservation above all else, and what we seek most is to avoid the loss of life. Thus security becomes the greatest good, and security is obtainable only through the acquisition of power. The desire for power is unlimited, the supply of power is limited, and thus conflict develops as each of us seeks more and more power.

This struggle for power is never ending, as no one is capable of obtaining enough power to be secure. No one dare refrain from the struggle, as others will seek to exercise power over him or her. Thus, we are all equally aggressive. For Hobbes, then, our true nature is individualistic, self-seeking, fearful, and competitive to the point of combativeness. If each of us follows our natural inclinations, we would be in a constant state of warfare.

Yet we are not without reason, and reason does provide a way out of this intolerable situation. We are capable of realizing that, unless we are willing to accept the discipline imposed upon us by superior authority, our possessions and our lives may be forfeit. We therefore come together to enter a compact in which we surrender our sovereignty to a state that will be strong enough to ensure peace. And, once established, the sovereign—the state—is not to be resisted, as such resistance returns people to the intolerable conditions found in a state of nature.

Hobbes' arguments fit well with the Calvinist vision of fallen man, and became part of the political arguments of the Puritans, first in England, and then in New England. His arguments were too harsh to have wider appeal in England, however, and it was left to another compact theorist, Sir John Locke, to define the nature of the compact that triumphed there.

## *John Locke*

John Locke (1632–1704) lived in an England that was moving away from civil war and developing a stable political system. Reason and sanity seemed to be returning to the political arena, and his writings reflect a more optimistic view of humanity.

Locke sets forth his basic philosophy in the second of his *Two Treatises of Government*. For Locke, the state of nature has two defining characteristics. First, it is a state of perfect freedom, in which people may do as they choose within the limits imposed by natural law. Second, it is a state of equality for its inhabitants; they are not equal in their capacities, as Hobbes argued, but in the rights they possess. This equality does not create the abysmal conditions Hobbes sees in a state of nature; instead, people, being reasonable, do get along with one another fairly well.

For Locke, we are governed in a natural state by natural law; a law we each can understand and apply. However, while each of us is reasonable, we are not each equally endowed with reason. While rational, we are not perfect. We do suffer from some of the problems of selfishness that Hobbes focused on. Thus we have disagreements concerning what natural law really is. Specifically, Locke argues that there are three defects in the state of nature: 1) there is no known and established law, 2) there is no known and indifferent judge to resolve disagreements over the law, and 3) there is no executive power to enforce judgements. "Thus Mankind, notwithstanding all the privileges of the State of Nature, being but an ill condition, while they remain in it, are quickly driven into society."

Like Hobbes, Locke sees people coming together to form a compact establishing government. Unlike Hobbes, however, he does not see people driven into this compact out of fear for their very lives and property, but rather entering the compact for convenience. Thus the compact is a voluntary one based upon the reasoned consent of the governed.

Both the Hobbesian and Lockean compacts form part of American political culture. We need to examine how these views enter into our political psyche, and how they continue to influence debate on the nature of the American state.

## American Adaptations

American adaptations of compact theory draw upon both the Hobbesian compact, as brought to America by the Puritans, and the Lockean compacts. They are best illustrated in their views concerning church-state relations; relations that have long been characterized by Jesus' statement: (Luke 22:38) "But they said, 'Lord, behold, here are two swords.' And he said to them, 'It is enough.'" The two swords are the state and the church. The relationship between them, including which sword is superior, differs in the Hobbesian and Lockean compacts.

*The Puritan Compact.* Puritan leaders saw man in a fallen state, whose carnal nature must be controlled for the good of the commonwealth by strong magistrates operating under God's laws. The England of the Puritans certainly lent credence to the view of man dominated by desire. The civil strife within England of this period illustrated man at his worst. The Puritan view, however, did not become dominant in England.

This Calvinist model dominated the early political life of Puritan New England. Church and state were to be separate but complementary institutions, tied together to preserve peace in the commonwealth, and to promote the virtue of the citizenry. As Cotton stated, "if the church and people of God fall away from God, God will visit the city and country with public calamity, if not captivity, for the church's sake."

Cotton's arguments are echoed in those of Richard Viguerie, a contemporary spokesman for the Christian right, who argues that "America was founded upon a belief in God. . . . And as long as America held fast to that belief, God blessed us." Ronald Reagan, while serving as governor of California, wrote that "what we need is a spiritual awakening and return to the morals of a Christian society."

This belief in a nation founded upon a Puritan view of Christian morality provides absolute standards of behavior. Echoing Cotton's view that "church governors and civil governors do herein stand parallel one to another," the Christian right rejects a clear separation between religion and politics, between church and state. Thus Jerry Falwell argues that "it is unpopular in some circles to equate the two. But I say that they must be viewed as cousins of the same family. . . ." Ronald Reagan, addressing the abortion issue, rejected public opinion polls as a guide for state action, calling instead for an adherence to "Judeo-Christian traditions . . . to return to standards we know are based on solid moral principles." James Watt argues that conflict in America is the result of governmental policies that are at odds with "absolute moral values as given to us in the Judeo-Christian teachings."

Reagan paraphrased Winthrop's "Citty vpon a Hill" speech in many of his major addresses, from his early debates with then President Carter to his final State of the Union message. And it was, he argued, a city under attack. As Jerry Falwell put it, "there can be no questioning the retrogression of America's stability as a free and healthy nation. In the last several years, Americans have literally stood by and watched as godless, spineless leaders have brought our nation floundering to the brink of death." And Reagan's first Secretary of the Interior, James Watt, makes it clear that "fuzzy-headed liberals" who control "every institution in this nation except the Oval Office" [and who now control that] are responsible for this retrogression.

The response needed to bring government back, to place it firmly at the helm of a nation moving forward, is to tie government back to the views of the Puritans, to reunify the two swords under the watchful eye of the Church; to ensure that the ecclesiastical sword is primary. Yet those who make these arguments, whether it is in the form of re-introducing prayer in public schools, overturning *Roe v. Wade,* or any of the myriad of items on their agenda, overlook the fact that the "Church" is not so clear-cut in today's world.

Current efforts of Fundamentalist "Christian right" movements have focused on grass-roots politics, including supporting candidates for state and local office, with a special emphasis upon capturing control of local school boards. Much of the opposition to this movement comes from those who have a more Lockean view of the compact.

*The Lockean Compact.* Those supporting the Lockean compact would agree with Jefferson "that our civil rights have no dependence on our religious opinions," and "that to suffer the civil magistrate to intrude his powers into the field of opinion . . . is a dangerous fallacy, which at once destroys all religious liberty."

Jefferson's views reflect a tradition that comes down from St. Thomas Aquinas through a diverse group of theorists, including Martin Luther and John Locke. While Luther was authoritarian, he based that position upon the need to control man in a fallen state—indeed, this was why God had ordained secular power. He did not, however, see the Church controlling that power; indeed, for Luther, the prince controlled the Church in secular matters. Nor, for Luther, could the state control the religious beliefs of its citizens.

Locke further developed the argument for separation of church and state in his *A Letter Concerning Toleration*. Government, he argued, exists to protect life, liberty, and property. These are *civil*, not *religious*, functions. Churches are voluntary organizations devoted to saving mens' souls. As such, they are not entitled to use secular power to enforce belief. Pointing out that any religious conformity that would be obtained through the use of secular power would be an outer conformity only, he concludes that the use of such power for ecclesiastical purposes is both impractical and contrary to Christian morality.

This position, stated as a "wall of separation" between church and state, dominated American political development during the decade of the 1960s and into the 1970s. The Supreme Court, through decisions such as *Engle v. Vitale* (1962) and *Roe v. Wade* (1973) served both to confirm this position and at the same time to energize those opposing it.

The debate concerning the nature of the compact will continue. And the role of the political scientist, both in joining the debate and in analyzing that debate will continue. Those on both sides would find it informative to examine the origins of the debate, however, for insights such an examination can give them in framing that debate.

## NATIONALISM, "RACE," AND CONFLICT AMONG STATES

Seneca's statement that the truly wise man would serve the commonwealth, that greater society of all mankind, was reflected in the writings of the early Christian Fathers, who saw the universal Christian commonwealth as an integral part of God's plan. The Church was to bring reality to Cicero's vision of a Roman Empire built upon the concept of universal brotherhood.

With the fall of Rome in 476, central authority collapsed and Europe moved to a feudal system, but the dream of a universal Christian brotherhood remained. Any unifying framework that did exist was due largely to the influence of the Church, which, in a very real sense, emerged as the only centralized governing body in Europe. As Curtis points out, "[i]n this unified but localized social structure, the Church pressed the idea of a universal Christian Commonwealth. In a period of barbarian kingdoms, the argument was put forward of a single society with two governments, each with separate powers."

As Europe began to emerge from the localized chaos of the middle ages, and started to develop the modern nation-state system, this vision of a universal brotherhood began to be replaced by a growing nationalism. One of the first to give voice to this nationalist movement was Niccolò Machiavelli.

### Niccolò Machiavelli

Machiavelli (1469–1527) was a citizen of the city-state of Florence during a period when Italy was a collection of small, disorganized states dominated by foreign powers. While Florentine by citizenship, however, Machiavelli saw himself as Italian. And, as an ardent patriot, his primary goal was Italian unity.

England, France, and Spain were emerging as modern nation states. Strong monarchs were unifying these states under central control, but no similar monarch had emerged in Italy. Dominated by four small states—Florence, Naples, Milan, and Venice—the Italian peninsula was open to invasion and exploitation by the stronger powers of France and Spain. This was an intolerable situation for Machiavelli, and he devoted his time to finding a remedy.

Machiavelli clearly understood the forces that barred Italian unity. Primary among those forces was the existence of the Papal States, a collection of small states sprawled across the center of the peninsula and ruled directly by the Pope. A series of popes had turned this into the strongest and best administered state in Italy. None of these popes had been strong enough to extend his rule over the whole of Italy, but each had been strong enough to prevent anyone else from extending his control. Therefore, Machiavelli was convinced that the Church must relinquish temporal control to a prince who could unify Italy. The universal Christian brotherhood had to be replaced by Italian nationalism. Machiavelli's greatest work, *The Prince*, was written as both a plea and a guide for the Medicis to assume that role.

*This opportunity must not . . . be allowed to pass, so that Italy may at length find her liberator. I cannot express the love with which he would be received in all those provinces which have suffered under these foreign invasions, with what thirst for vengeance. . . . What Italian would withhold allegiance? This barbarous domination stinks in the nostrils of every one. May your illustrious house therefore assume this task with that courage and those hopes which are inspired by a just cause, so that under its banner our fatherland may be raised up, and under its auspices be verified that saying of Petrarch:*

> *Valour against fell wrath*
> *Will take up arms; and be the combat quickly sped!*
> *For, sure, the ancient worth,*
> *That in Italians stirs the heart, is not yet dead.*

Calling for a "liberator," a great prince who exemplified the nation, Machiavelli helped set the tone for nationalist movements. The Church must be subordinate to the prince if the nation were to prosper. He did not, however, argue that Italians were naturally superior to others; he simply called for them to achieve an equal status.

## Nationalism, Religion, and Luther

Martin Luther contributed to the growth of nationalism with his defection from the Catholic Church and his allegiance with German princes. While his arguments contained elements of democratic ideology, Luther himself was more totalitarian. He strongly supported the efforts of German princes to suppress a series of peasant revolts, and he called upon the state to suppress any outward display of religious deviationism. The state could not control individual belief, but that did not mean that it couldn't control the expression of that belief. Luther was ardently anti-Semitic, and his attacks on Jews helped set the stage for an ethnic, if not racial, element in nationalism.

Three key German philosophers of the nineteenth century—Schopenhouer, Treitschke, and Nietzsche—contributed to the growth of nationalist thought. Schopenhouer's arguments that it is the will to power, rather than reason, that rules the world contributed to the "great man" thesis that is often an integral part of nationalist movements. Treitschke's anti-Semitism, militarism, and his calls for a greater Germany helped fuel the rise of nationalism. Nietzsche had nothing but contempt for Christianity, democracy, or conventional morality, and his distinction between the lower man and "superman" became part of German nationalism; an interesting fact when one considers that Nietzsche himself was neither a nationalist nor an anti-Semite, and indeed he held a low opinion of Germans in general.

It was not a German, but a Frenchman who, along with a Germanized Englishman, were to develop the racial aspect of nationalism, an aspect that found its strongest voice in German National Socialism.

## The "Volk" and the Theory of Race

The theory of the "folkish" state adds a particularly interesting twist to nationalist thought, as it does not exalt the state, but the people—the *Volk*. Rather than the state being of supreme importance, it is the "racial existence" of the people that counts; a people who are defined by blood and soil. The state merely serves as an entity to protect the *Volk*; the state must protect the "fatherland."

The principle bond holding the folkish state together is race, and maintaining "racial purity," then, becomes essential for the maintenance of the *Volk*. German National Socialists—Nazis—built their theory of race upon the works of Count Arthur de Gobineau, a Frenchman; and Houston Stewart Chamberlain, an English expatriate and German imperialist. And, while the arguments of these individuals are bizarre, to say the least, they influenced millions of Germans, and, more tragically, continue to influence many people—including people in the United States—today.

De Gobineau (1816–1882) argued that the capacity of the races is determined mainly by their color. The white race is superior, the black race inferior, and the yellow race fits somewhere in between. Further, among those of the white race, Aryans were superior, with those select Aryans of Teutonic descent the best of all. Coincidentally, de Gobineau argued that the French aristocracy, including himself, were all Teutonic.

These views seemed eminently reasonable to Richard Wagner's son-in-law: Houston Stewart Chamberlain. All, that is, except the part about the French nobility. Chamberlain elaborated—and changed—de Gobineau's arguments to support the concept of German superiority. Rome became great by eliminating Jewish influence, and the invading Germanic tribes then took from Rome everything suitable to Nordic culture and Germanized it. Germans constituted the highest race in the world, of that day and it followed that they were not only entitled to rule the world, it was their destiny. But it was a destiny that could only be fulfilled by wiping out all traces of Jewry.

De Gobineau and Chamberlain's ideas found fertile soil in a Germany that was undergoing great stress following World War I. The result was the rise of the National Socialist German Workers' Party, World War II, and the extermination of millions of Jews and others of the "lesser races" by Nazi supermen.

## National Socialist German Workers' Party

In 1928 the National Socialist German Workers' Party—the Nazis—ran candidates for seats in the German legislature. The party polled less than three percent of the popular vote, but did manage to elect 12 delegates. Then came the Great Depression, and with it, the conditions that gave rise to Hitler. Promising all things to all Germans, and above all, to "correct" the wrongs done to Germany after World War I, the party gained widespread support. In 1932, the Nazis had increased their seats in the legislature from the initial 12 to 230, and in January 1933, the aging president Hindenburg named Adolf Hitler chancellor of the German Reich. When Hindenburg died in 1934, Hitler combined the offices of president and chancellor and became *Fuhrer* and *Reichskanzler*. He immediately outlawed competing parties, and assumed dictatorial power.

Hitler argued a twisted form of Darwinism as the basis of Nazi philosophy. Germans, he stated, were the product of a continuing struggle for survival among the races; a struggle that occurred within the race as well as between the races. This led to the creation of a natural elite. There are, according to Hitler, three races in the world. The Aryan includes the Scandinavian, Dutch, and English peoples, as well as the superior Germans; it is the "culture creating" race, and is superior to the others. Then come the "culture carrying" race, of which the Japanese are the best example; such people are not capable of creating culture, but they can maintain it. Finally come the "culture destroyers": Jews and Negroes. These races, Hitler states, are devoted to, and responsible for, the degradation of culture. They pursue their own end of world destruction through intermingling with superior races.

The arguments of Hitler and other Nazis are beyond contempt from any rational, scientific basis. Yet they had great appeal for many Germans—and for many non-Germans. They were given a legitimacy they did not deserve when they were at least partially endorsed by leading intellectuals. Among the most prominent political philosophers to climb aboard the Nazi bandwagon was Martin Heidegger, an intense nationalist.

Heidegger was a passionate supporter of the *Volk*, the folkish state based upon blood tied to a specific homeland. In a Europe struggling with the reality of the Great Depression the call for a "return" to the purity of the fatherland and a recommitment to nationalist ideals seemed the only goal worth pursuing for Heidegger. In the spring of 1933, he joined the Nazi party and became rector of Freiburg University, an institution which he planned to develop into the "intellectual flagship of a spiritually revived German nation." Later in the year, he called upon all Germans to support their *führer* in an upcoming national election. Until his death in 1976, Heidegger never recanted his support for the Nazi cause.

Support by recognized intellectuals such as Heidegger helped legitimate arguments that defy any rational examination. Those arguments continue to persist, and continue to influence contemporary political development, particularly in Eastern Europe.

## Nationalism, "Race," and Eastern Europe

Eastern Europe is undergoing a period as stressful as the Great Depression; it is going through "interesting times." And many in the region are turning to some of the same nationalist fervor found in Nazi Germany to find answers to the problems and dilemmas they face. The collapse of communism in this region has left an intellectual vacuum, the economic infrastructure cannot compete with the capitalist West, and long-suppressed ethnic tensions are re-emerging. Given these conditions, it is not surprising that many intellectuals in the area have turned to a passionate nationalism as the only idea worth cherishing. Like Heidegger in the 1930s, the attraction of the fatherland, and a passionate commitment to a state of blood and soil provides an answer to the problems of the world.

Resurgent nationalism is found in every country of Eastern Europe, including the former East Germany. Nietzsche's works are becoming increasingly popular among former Marxist professors, replacing Marx and Engels. And the image of a "pure" people linked to the land is again growing in appeal.

In Hungary, open to the West long before most of East Europe, nationalist fervor has been growing. Responding to what they see as the "Americanization" of Hungary a number of Hungarian intellectuals are calling for a return to their Magyar roots. This includes a call for a Greater Hungary, which can be achieved only by seizing "Hungarian" land from Romania and Croatia. This has been accompanied by growing antisemitism. The old, discredited arguments of Hitler are gaining new adherents.

Nowhere has the rebirth of nationalist movements had more impact than in the former Yugoslavia. Nationalist movements emerged among Croatians, Bosnians, Slovenians, and most of all Serbians. Serbs are seeking to reclaim their "folkish state"—a state whose heart is found in Kosovo Polje. On this site in 1389 forces of the Ottoman Empire defeated a Serbian army, sending the nation into six centuries of obscurity. Kosovo, now populated mostly by Albanians, is seen as the spiritual heartland of Serbia, a mystical cradle of true Serbhood where faith and history become one on the walls of ancient Orthodox monasteries.

In 1986 two hundred Serbian intellectuals signed a document demanding "the right to spiritual identity, to the defense of the foundations of Serb national culture and to the physical survival" of the Serb nation. "More than any other single document," states Marks, "this memorandum . . . laid the ideological groundwork for Milosevic's rise to power, the military occupation of Kosovo and the annihilation of Bosnia." With the breakup of Yugoslavia, Serb nationalism demanded that all of Greater Serbia be included in a new Serb homeland, including areas where Serbs were a distinct minority. The result has been the ongoing conflict in the Balkans. Many of the atrocities of the recent war—atrocities that were perpetrated by all sides, but with Serbs in the forefront—were designed to ensure a "purity" of "race."

Serbian attempts to seize what they saw—and still see—as their soil, soil that belongs to them because of the Serbian blood that has been mixed with it over the centuries, is supported by most Serbian intellectuals. In Belgrade a group of 40 young women, including musicians and playwrights, formed a group whose English translation is "Only a Serbian Woman Can Save a Serbian Man." The women made trips to the Bosnian and Croatian fronts, singing folk songs to boost the morale of their soldiers.

Major fighting in the Balkans stopped in 1995 when NATO forces, including a strong American contingent, moved in to enforce a cease fire. There is some reason to hope that the fragile peace created by the presence of NATO troops may remain after those troops are gone, but there is no guarantee. Certainly there has been no decline in nationalist rhetoric. Yugoslavia (dominated by Serbians), Croatia, and Slovenia are attempting to "purify" their languages, with Serbs eliminating Croatian terms, Croatians eliminating Serb terms, and so on. One problem people are finding in attempting to do this is that the languages—or dialects— are more regional than national. Recently Croatia's president used the Serbian term for bread in a broadcast. News accounts of the broadcast were carefully edited, with the proper Croatian term substituted.

The final outcome of the Balkan conflict remains uncertain, as does the final outcome for East European nationalist movements in general. At a minimum, however, one can conclude that the area will continue to be reflective of the old Chinese curse: it will continue to have some interesting times.

## Summary and Conclusions

Political theory provides political actors and critics useful or challenging arguments to justify or criticize existing political decisions or arrangements. Arguments advanced by political theorists become part of our political consciousness. Whether one has ever heard of Thomas Hobbes or John Locke, one has ideas shaped by those theorists. Americans continue to argue the nature of the compact upon which our government rests based upon ideas developed by these two and others. And those ideas are incredibly powerful, as is seen in nationalist thought.

As indicated earlier, the arguments of Hitler and other Nazis are beyond contempt from any rational, scientific basis. When examined using all of the powerful tools and techniques of modern, quantitative political science, they can be "rejected." Yet they have influenced and continue to influence political development. Beta weights and correlations will not make them go away. As Diamond points out: "Our survival depends on whether we progress with understanding how people behave, why some societies become frustrated, whether their governments tend to become unstable, and how political leaders make decisions like whether to press a red button." Political scientists need to be familiar with the arguments developed by political theorists over the centuries in order to evaluate their impact upon contemporary political development.

# ARGYLE

NAME: _____

SECTION: _____

DATE: _____

1. What is Seneca's explanation for the downfall of the "Golden Age"?

2. What did John Calvin believe was the purpose of Government?

3. Thomas Hobbes said that human beings had two major drives. What were they?

4. Thomas Hobbes and John Locke had conflicting views of the "State of Nature." What are their opposing views?

_____

_____

_____

_____

_____

_____

_____

5. Describe how Nazi type ideology has been used to foster war in the Balkans.

_____

_____

_____

_____

_____

_____

_____

**Group Project:** Identify the basic elements of Nazi ideology and show how they can be used by any radical ethnic group in an attempt to oppress other groups.

**Individual Project:** Find a recently reported speech by some ethnic leader and identify in it examples of "Volk" ideology.

*Chapter Two*

# METHODOLOGY AND POLITICAL SCIENCE

*METHODOLOGY*
*POLITICAL THEORY*

# METHODS, "SCIENCE," AND POLITICS: MODES OF ANALYSIS IN POLITICAL SCIENCE

### Nolan J. Argyle

> ... When Albert Somit and Joseph Tanenhaus wrote their semi-official history, *The Development of Political Science*, they said, "We deliberately limited our attention to those aspects of the past which bear directly on the present 'state of the discipline.'" That took them back not to Plato's cave but to New York in 1880.
>
> Michael Nelson

The first Department of History and Political Science was established at Columbia University in 1856; in 1880 Columbia established the first independent Department of Political Science. In 1903 the American Political Science Association was formed. These are the events that many in political science use to date the origins of the discipline. Yet political commentary occupied much of the earliest writing in every civilization, and "political science" is as old as civilization itself. Gladden points out that "the official ranked early among the first professionals," and that "[t]he widening of our knowledge of human activity by the discovery of cave and rock paintings going back into pre-cultivation ages, and thus providing evidence of very early concerted or communal activity, suggests that the public official must have emerged long before the dawn of history."

This study examines the discipline of political science by examining how we study politics. It agrees with Nelson, quoted at the beginning of this study, that any such examination of the study of politics must go back beyond the 1880s. And, while the author agrees with Gladden that politics "emerged long before the dawn of history," one cannot really study politics much before the dawn of written records. Thus, in the development of Western politics, starting with Plato's cave is not a bad idea.

## FOUNDATIONS OF POLITICAL SCIENCE

The foundations of Western political institutions are found in the polis—the Greek city-states established during the first millennium B.C. throughout the Mediterranean basin. These city-states developed a variety of governing structures, as well as developing Western concepts about politics in general. In this regard, Athens, as the intellectual center of the Greek world, provides the fullest expression of the concepts and ideas that underpin Western development.

### Reason and Observation: Development of a "Science" of Politics

A triumvirate of Greek philosophers, Socrates, Plato, and Aristotle, provided a framework through which political events were to be examined for the next two thousand years. The first member of this great triumvirate, Socrates (470–399 BC), is the least known of the three. He left no written works to evaluate him by; what we know of him comes from the commentaries of his contemporaries and of his students. Most of our knowledge of Socrates comes from his student, Plato. As Curtis points out: "For Plato, Socrates was the great example of intellectual integrity, the man always prepared to discuss, the professor who sought not to profess, the teacher who refused to indoctrinate, who aimed to make men think."

For Socrates, justice can come only through the nurturing of one's soul; the virtuous state is one that not only allows for but provides that nurturing. Law is natural; it pre-exists the state, and indeed, is present even without the state. This law, if properly understood and applied, can insure justice. From this, Socrates develops the principle that was to guide his study and which he imparted to his students: that **virtue is knowledge, that it is discoverable, and that it can be taught and learned**. His pupil, Plato, sought to show how that knowledge could be discovered and, once discovered, put to use by the statesman.

Plato (427?–347 B.C.) was, in many ways, a typical Athenian. Born of aristocratic parents, he prepared himself for a career in public service. The disastrous outcome of the Pelopennesian War and the rise of the Thirty Tyrants ended those plans. Plato became disenchanted with Athens after the city condemned and executed his mentor, Socrates. Plato traveled widely, viewing various forms of political organization, and developing his own concepts concerning them. These concepts did not always sit well with those he critiqued. In Syracuse Plato lectured Dionysus I on the proper role of a ruler—lectures that resulted in Plato's enslavement. Ransomed by friends, Plato returned to Athens and founded his Academy, the first of the great schools of philosophy. In his Academy, Plato developed the theories of organization and politics that were to secure his place in history; "in them," states Harmon, "we find the origin of European political thought." We also find the earliest method of studying politics.

Plato's greatest work is unquestionably *The Republic*. In it he uses Socrates to lead the reader through a dialectic argument in which "truth" is eventually discovered. In this and in other works, he develops the **Socratic method**, based upon deductive logic. This method is the first true methodology of politics, but it is not political science. It emphasizes reason alone as a guide; as such, it becomes an incomplete model for science. The oft-cited example of the bumblebee illustrates this. Deductive reasoning clearly shows that the wing span of the insect in question is too small to support the size of the body in flight; yet the bumblebee, ignorant of this conclusion, buzzes right along on its business. Reason needs to be tempered with observation. And one of Plato's students, Aristotle, provides this model.

*Aristole*

Aristotle (384–322 B.C.) enrolled in Plato's Academy at the age of seventeen. This young colonial, newly arrived in Athens, was to develop into one of the greatest thinkers in history. While he openly disagreed with his mentor on many subjects, there is no question that he was profoundly affected by Plato's arguments.

He established his own school, the Lyceum, in 335 B.C., a period during which Athens was a Macedonian protectorate. The school prospered, with Aristotle emerging as the best-known and most popular teacher in Athens. Aristotle divided knowledge into specific disciplines—biology, ethics, politics, psychology, physics, and metaphysics. The approach to the study of each discipline was based upon **science**, which he then divided into the theoretical, the practical, and the productive. The aim of the first was disinterested knowledge, of the second the guidance of conduct, and the third the guidance of the arts. The science of logic constituted a discipline preliminary to the others, as its purpose was to set forth the conditions that must be observed by all thinking which has truth as its aim. He argued that science, in a strict sense, was *demonstrated knowledge of the causes of things*. His method of teaching became imprinted upon the Greek system, and influenced instructional methodology from that point onward, earning him the title of the first **true** political scientist.

The center of Aristotelian logic is *syllogism*; the form of reasoning whereby, given two propositions, a third follows necessarily from them. Descartes' famous observation may be used to illustrate this. First, Descartes developed two propositions: 1) thinking proves existence, and 2) I think. From these, it necessarily followed: 3) I think, therefore I am.

In both the natural and social sciences Aristotle favored the evolutionary view of scientific investigation. The student must examine the process involved in creating the condition being studied; in studying states he must consider the historic process. For Aristotle the state was constantly evolving from a lesser form toward perfection, and the ultimate state would be crafted by drawing upon the past.

The writings of Plato and Aristotle dominated political development for centuries. While there were key disagreements in their thinking, they both agreed that the state was natural, that it served to define what humanity was, and that the state was a necessary vehicle for moving humanity toward perfection. The first challenge to this Greek foundation of politics came during the Renaissance.

### Empiricism as a Challenge to Normativism:

Niccolò Machiavelli (1469–1527) was a child of the Renaissance, an era during which the communal view of man was being challenged by an insurgent individualism, coupled with new views of economics. Self-interest became not only a legitimate, but a noble motive. It was an era begging for a new approach to studying and analyzing politics, and Machiavelli provided a new paradigm.

Machiavelli rejected the natural, communal state, arguing instead that the state had no reality apart from the individuals it comprised. He also rejected the idea that these individuals were themselves governed by natural law determined through reason. Instead, he argued that there is no inherent purpose in the state. Any direction it may receive must be imposed upon it by the ruler. This being the case, the ruler must carefully apply proper principles of organization, based upon an understanding of human nature. And human nature, for Machiavelli, was a mixture of reason (man) and desire (beast). The wise prince must "know well how to use both the beast and the man," he "must know how to use both natures, and that one without the other is not durable."

Machiavelli's focus was empirical and individualistic. He rejected natural law, determined through reason, as a guide for political analysis. Natural law may or may not exist; that was beside the point. We can understand only those things we are capable of determining through our own senses. His emphasis on empirical data and upon the individual as the unit to be studied earns him the title of the first **modern** political scientist.

The concepts and ideas concerning the appropriate way to study and analyze political systems, and the appropriate purpose behind such analysis, continues to this day. We now need to examine more recent arguments, and evaluate their relevance for methodology.

## Modern Political Science and Methodology: Aristotle and Machiavelli Revisited

As indicated earlier, many political scientists date the discipline from the sequence of events between the establishment of a department of political science in 1880 and the establishment of a professional society in 1903. This period, then, may be used to date the beginning of "modern" political science; thus "modern" political science has been a development largely of this century. It occurred at a time when social scientists began to see themselves as "professionals," and as professionals operating within narrowly defined spheres. Historians, sociologists, and economists led the way in developing professional associations with all of the attendant trappings; political science followed in 1903.

In establishing the American Political Science Association, those who studied and taught about government hoped to move the discipline to the status of a profession that would hold its own with other newly-established professions. The problem with this, as Nelson points out, was that:

> *because political scientists abandoned their own philosophical heritage for the sake of aping their colleagues, it was now hard to find two of them who agreed on what their newly professionalized discipline was. Was it contemporary history, as some argued, or political economy, or political sociology, or law, or what?*

This confusion remains to this day, but the discipline has made some progress in sorting itself out. One can now talk about periods of development during which clear themes dominated. And, one hopes, we can now speak of a growing consensus about the nature of the discipline. These periods are included in Table 1, along with other key events in the development of the discipline.

## TABLE 1 SELECTED KEY EVENTS IN THE DEVELOPMENT OF POLITICAL METHODOLOGY

| Date | Event |
| --- | --- |
| 470–350 B.C. | Development of the Socratic Method |
| 384–322 B.C. | Life of Aristotle. He becomes the first "true" political scientist, defining a science of inquiry that shaped future study. |
| 5 B.C.–65 A.D. | Life of Seneca. The Roman stoic begins the development of compact theory. |
| 492–496 | Pope Gelasius begins the development of the "two swords" theory of Church-State relations. Political arguments become dominated by theological interpretation. |
| 1100 | Irnerius begins lectures on Roman Law at Bologna, establishing a distinguished school of law which starts tradition of legalism in political methodology. |
| 1469–1532 | Life of Niccolò Machiavelli. His emphasis on empiricism earns him the title of the first "modern" political scientist. |
| 1856 | Columbia University establishes the first Department of History and Political Science in the United States. |
| 1880 | John W. Burgess convinces Columbia University to establish the first separate Department of Political Science. |
| 1880–1903 | Formative period. The emphasis is on legal status of political institutions, with constitutional law the dominant theme. |
| 1903 | American Political Science Association founded. |
| 1903–1921 | Emergent period. Legalist approach begins to see challenges from those who emphasize a "science" of politics and from those who argue for a prescriptive approach. |
| 1920–1945 | Transition period, characterized by the Reed–Merriam split. |
| 1929–1932 | Studies conducted at the Hawthorne Works of the Western Electric Company in Cicero, Illinois. The studies set the stage for the "behavioral revolution" in political science. |
| 1939 | American Society for Public Administration founded. The Society represents the first formal split within the discipline of political science. |
| 1945–present | "Behavioral revolution" in the social sciences, which creates great friction between "traditionalists" and "behavioralists" in political science. |
| 1951 | Harold D. Lasswell calls for a policy orientation which he argues would cut across fragmented specializations and create a unified social science. |
| 1967–present | Postbehavioralism. Movement arguing that political scientists must become more "relevant" and value-oriented. |
| 1970s–present | Contingency period. Attempts are made to integrate various approaches into a coherent whole, arguing each approach is valid under given conditions. |

## THE FORMATIVE AND EMERGENT PERIODS

When the American Political Science Association was founded in 1903, those few individuals who saw themselves as political scientists had reached a loose consensus that the study of politics meant the study of government. And, if one was to study government, the appropriate focus of that study was upon the rules and legal structures that formed its foundation. In short, political scientists studied constitutions and the legal relationships that flowed from them. If one studied Congress, for example, the starting point—indeed, often the ending point—of that study was the Constitution of the United States. Woodrow Wilson wrote the definitive text on Congress while he was in residence at Johns Hopkins University, forty miles from the Capitol Building. He didn't make a single trip down to look at Congress or to talk to a congressman; everything he needed was in the 'Hopkins library.

Research in this period relied largely on historical methodology, and concentrated on the analysis of written documents. As Richard Jensen put it, the motto of this generation of political scientists was "[h]istory is past politics and politics present history." In addition to constitutions, scholars analyzed court decisions and newspapers—anything to make a good footnote. There was a tendency to take the written word at face value. The result was the compilation of great masses of descriptive data, with little attempt to relate that data to developments in other disciplines or to even critically analyze it. The result, as Nelson points out, was that "the typical scholarly *oeuvre* consisted of sleep-inducing, legalistic descriptions of the formal institutions of government."

There were political scientists in this period who went against the trend, calling for a more rigorous empiricism or for prescriptive rather than descriptive political science. And these people helped set the stage for what became a struggle for the heart and soul of the discipline; a struggle that was to eventually see political scientists divided into two camps, each convinced that theirs was the truth, each mistrusting the other.

## THE TRANSITION YEARS

In the quarter-century between 1920 and 1945, two separate attempts were made to re-define American political science. Charles Merriam launched his campaign for a "scientific" approach in 1921, and strengthened that bid through three national conferences held from 1923 through 1925. The second attempt was led by Thomas Reed under the aegis of the American Political Science Association's Committee on Policy. Beginning in the late 1920s, Reed and his followers pressed for a focus on the immediate questions of public policy, with training for the public service to be a priority. Neither movement succeeded in remaking political science in its image, but both movements left lasting impressions.

Merriam's emphasis on a "science" of politics meshed well with studies being conducted in the business world by people like Elton Mayo, studies that were trying to determine a "one best way" of organizing and ended up concluding that more attention had to be paid to the social nature of man in organizations. Mayo's famous studies conducted at the Hawthorne Works of the Western Electric Company, along with similar studies, put the focus on social interaction as an explanatory variable; the techniques developed by Merriam's followers sought to examine those interactions in terms of their relevance for *political behavior*.

Reed's followers lost influence within the discipline in the post-World War II era. Dismissed by the new "behavioralists" as mere "traditionalists," they found few resources available to them. The Reed tradition, however, was to re-emerge in the late 1960s as part of postbehavioralism.

## BEHAVIORALISM AND POLITICAL METHODS

Following World War II, *behavioralism* emerged as a dominant theme in the social sciences, including political science. Advocates of this approach argued for a scientific investigation of political behavior. In a book that helped define the field, Hienz Eulau stated:

*The root is man. I don't think it is possible to say anything meaningful about the governance of man without talking about the political behavior of man—his acts, goals, drives, feelings, beliefs, commitments, and values. . . . Politics is the study of why man finds it necessary or desirable to build government, of how he adapts government to his changing needs or demands, of how and why he decides on public policies. Politics is concerned with the conditions and consequences of human action.*

*A study of politics which leaves man out of its equation is a rather barren politics. Yet such is the propensity of man that he can consider his own creations without measuring them by himself.*

In order to "measure ourselves," behavioralists developed an impressive array of rigorous and systematic methodologies. They sought to discover uniformities or regularities in human behavior through formulation and testing of empirical hypotheses. This could only be done, it was argued, by first developing sound *theories* concerning human behavior. Only then, it was argued, could political science be other than an oxymoron.

Another key figure in the field, David Easton, also argued that the emphasis should not be placed on institutions, but on "a kind of activity that may express itself through a variety of institutions." Politics is the "authoritative allocation of values," and that is the type of activity we should focus upon. Easton helped popularize *systems theory* as a method for analyzing that activity. Systems theory and its offshoot, functional analysis, became dominant models during the 1960s and 1970s. Morton Kaplan, a prominent political scientist who applied systems theory to the study of international politics, argued that "a scientific politics can develop only if the materials of politics are treated in terms of systems of action." While this statement was a little strong for most political scientists, they nevertheless adopted many of the concepts of systems theory and incorporated them into their own methodological approaches. Key to these approaches was the facts-values dichotomy. Political scientists were to deal with "facts," unclouded by value systems that interfered with a "scientific" interpretation of those facts. Empiricism, not normativism, was the operative approach.

The center of the behavioral movement in political science is found at the University of Michigan's Center for Political Studies. The Center has the most impressive data base in the discipline, with an emphasis upon election studies. For a discipline eager to convince itself and the outside world that it was a "true science," the Center became Mecca. As Michael Nelson put it: "As wealthy Midwesterners once sent their daughters East for finishing, so graduate departments now pack off their progeny to Michigan each summer to learn the latest in statistics and modeling."

By the late 1960s a reaction to the dominance of behavioralism was setting in within the discipline, resulting in *postbehavioralism*.

## POSTBEHAVIORALISM

In 1967 a number of young political scientists got together at the APSA meeting and organized the Caucus for a New Political Science. In calling for a "new" political science, they argued for political activism. Methods were useful, in their view, only if they obtained knowledge needed for the resolution of policy problems. They sought to rethink the linkage of political power and the dominant methods of political inquiry. They rejected the facts-values dichotomies of behavioralism, arguing instead that facts took on meaning only through the application of values.

One of the more interesting aspects of postbehavioralism was the apparent conversion of many of the mainline behavioralists to this point of view, among them David Easton. In an address to the American Political Science Association in 1969, he blasted behavioralism, charging that it had served to "conceal the brute realities of politics," and that "political science as usual" had failed to predict the social and political upheavals of the 1960s. Scientific information had to be made more consumable for the purposes of informing political action by non-intellectuals—it had to become "relevant." Following Easton's lead, a number of behavioralists issued their own *mea culpas*. In 1974 APSA President Avery Leiserson stated that the "new revolution" in political science was better conceived of as a counter-reformation.

Leiserson's analogy may be appropriate; rather than replace behavioralism—which itself never replaced earlier approaches—postbehavioralism emerged as yet another model for political scientists to follow. Behavioralism remains alive and well. Methods and modeling for their own sake still dominate the pages of the discipline's leading journal. Little has changed since Nelson wrote that "one could pick up the current issue of the *American Political Science Review* and come away blissfully ignorant of all the burning political questions of the day."

## THE CONTINGENCY VIEW

The past two decades have seen the emergence of a *contingency approach* to the study of political phenomena. Those advocating this approach accept the legitimacy of legalism, behavioralism, postbehavioralism, and all other "isms." Each approach is valid under certain conditions. The motto of contingency theorists is "it all depends." The approach should be determined by what one is studying, and what the purpose of the study is. Contingency theorists believe that there is room for Aristotle's syllogistic approach to co-exist with Machiavelli's emphasis upon empiricism and observation.

## BACK TO THE FUTURE: WHERE WE GO FROM HERE

Political methodology continues to evolve, and arguments over what methodology is appropriate continue. The discipline of political science has and will continue to have its factions, its behavioralists and postbehavioralists; its legal scholars and its systems analysts. Each faction finds a particular class of methods to be advantageous to the questions it is interested in; the problem comes when one faction rejects the legitimacy of other factions because they are "methodological primitives" or because they are so enamored of sophisticated methodologies that "they can't see the forest for the trees."

The future political scientist would do well to keep Michael Nelson's advice in mind: "We ought to begin by recognizing that wisdom is the result of equal parts of philosophy and experience, of thinking and doing." Methods can help us order our thinking and allow us to better understand our experiences.

# ARGYLE

NAME: _____

SECTION: _____

DATE: _____

1. Explain why Aristotle's emphasis on "causality" may well make him the first "true" political scientist.

2. Describe the techniques used in data analysis, one of the most common methodological approaches used in political science.

3. List the major types of methodology used in political science, and explain why there is no single "best" approach.

4. Explain why an emerging emphasis on political behaviorism created a split in the discipline of political science.

___

5. What is the idea of a contingency approach to the study of political science, and why does it seem particularly appropriate in the 20th Century and 21st Century?

___

**Group Exercise:** Review and discuss the causal and syllogistic approaches of Aristotle and the empiricism of Machiavelli. Should either be disregarded in the modern world?

**Individual Project:** Choose a recent edition of a scholarly journal and see how many examples you can find of ideas that were discussed by one of the great political theorists.

# ON LEARNING OR REMEMBERING

## Plato*

*[Editor's note: In the following excerpt from* Meno, *Plato presents a dialogue between Socrates and Meno (Menon), a wealthy young nobleman from Thessaly. Meno asks if virtue can be taught. Socrates responds that what we call teaching is instead remembering. In illustrating this point, Socrates presents a powerful argument for deductive reasoning as a means of understanding our environment.]*

*Socrates & Meno: Is it learning or remembering?*

**SOCRATES:** As the soul is immortal and often born, having seen what is on earth and what is in the house of Hades, and everything, there is nothing it has not learnt; so there is no wonder it can remember about virtue and other things, because it knew about these before. For as all nature is akin, and the soul has learnt everything, there is nothing to hinder a man, remembering one thing only—which men call learning—from himself finding out all else, if he is brave and does not weary in seeking; for seeking and learning is all remembrance.... I have faith that this is true, and I wish with your help to try to find out what virtue is.

**MENO:** Yes, Socrates. But what do you mean by saying that we do not learn, but what we call learning is remembering? Can you teach me how this is?

---

\* Excerpted from: Plato. (1914). Meno. In *Plato: With an English Translation* (Trans. Harold North Fowler). New York: G. P. Putnam's Sons.

**SOCRATES:** You are a young rogue, as I said a moment ago, Meno, and now you ask me if I can teach you, when I tell you there is no such thing as teaching, only remembering. I see you want to show me up at once as contradicting myself.

**MENO:** I swear that isn't my purpose, my dear Socrates; I never thought of that, it was just habit. But if you know any way to show me how this can be as you say, show away!

**SOCRATES:** That is not easy, but still I want to do my best for your sake. Here, just call up one of your own men from among this crowd of servants, any one you like, and I'll prove my case in him.

**MENO:** All right. *(To a lad)* Come here.

**SOCRATES:** Is he Greek, can he speak our language?

**MENO:** Rather! Born in my house.

**SOCRATES:** Now, kindly attend and see whether he seems to be learning from me, or remembering.

**MENO:** All right, I will attend.

**SOCRATES:** Now my lad, tell me: Do you know that a four-cornered space is like this?

**LAD:** I do.

**SOCRATES:** Is this a four-cornered space having all these lines equal, all four?

**LAD:** Surely

**SOCRATES:** And these across the middle, are they not equal too?

**LAD:** Yes.

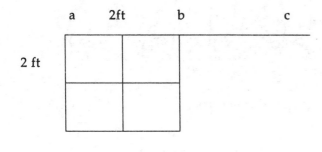

*Diagram 1*

**SOCRATES:** Such a space might be larger or smaller?

**LAD:** Oh yes.

**SOCRATES:** Then if this side is two feet long and this two, how many feet would the whole be? Or look at it this way: if it were two feet this way, and only one the other, would not the space be once two feet?

**LAD:** Yes.

**SOCRATES:** But as it is two feet this way also, isn't it twice two feet?

**LAD:** Yes, so it is.

**SOCRATES:** So the space is twice two feet?

**LAD:** Yes.

**SOCRATES:** Then how many are twice two feet? Count and tell me.

**LAD:** Four, Socrates.

**SOCRATES:** Well, could there be another such space, twice as big, but of the same shape, with all the lines equal like this one?

**LAD:** Yes.

**SOCRATES:** How many feet will there be in that, then?

**LAD:** Eight.

**SOCRATES:** Very well, now try to tell me how long will be each line of that one. The line of this one is two feet; how long would the line of the double one be?

**LAD:** The line would be double, Socrates, that is clear.

**SOCRATES:** (aside to Meno): You see, Meno, that I am not teaching this lad anything: I ask him everything; and now he thinks he knows what the line is from which the eight-square-foot space is to be made. Don't you agree?

**MENO:** Yes, I agree.

**SOCRATES:** Does he know then?

**MENO:** Not at all.

**SOCRATES:** He *thinks* he knows, from the double size which is wanted?

**MENO:** Yes.

**SOCRATES:** Well, observe him while he remembers bit by bit, as he ought to remember.

Now, lad, answer me. You say the double space is made from the double line. You know what I mean; not long this way and short this way, it must be equal every way like this, but double this—eight square feet. Just look and see if you think it will be made from the double line.

**LAD:** Yes, I do.

**SOCRATES:** Then this line is double this, if we add as much to it on this side.

**LAD:** Of course!

**SOCRATES:** Then if we put four like this, you say we shall get the eight-foot space.

**LAD:** Yes.

**SOCRATES:** Then let us draw these four equal lines. Is that the space which you say will be eight feet?

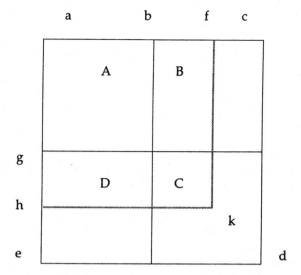

*Diagram 2*

**LAD:** Of course.

**SOCRATES:** Can't you see in it these four spaces here each of them equal to the one we began with, the four-foot space?

**LAD:** Yes.

**SOCRATES:** Well, how big is the new one? Is it not four times the old one?

**LAD:** Surely it is!

**SOCRATES:** Is four times the old one, double?

**LAD:** Why no, upon my word!

**SOCRATES:** How big, then?

**LAD:** Four times as big!

**SOCRATES:** Then, my lad, from a double line we get a space four times as big, not double.

**LAD:** That's true.

**SOCRATES:** Four times four is sixteen, isn't it?

**LAD:** Yes.

**SOCRATES:** But what line will make an eight-foot space? This line makes one four times as big, sixteen, doesn't it?

**LAD:** That's what I say.

**SOCRATES:** And this four-foot space comes from this line, half the length of the long one?

**LAD:** Yes.

**SOCRATES:** Good. The eight-foot space will be double this and half this.

**LAD:** Yes.

**SOCRATES:** Then its line must be longer than this, and shorter than this. What do you think?

**LAD:** That's what I think.

**SOCRATES:** That's right, just answer what you think. Tell me also: Was not this line two feet, and this four?

**LAD:** Yes.

**SOCRATES:** Then the line of the eight-foot space must be longer than this line of two feet, and shorter than the line of four feet.

**LAD:** Yes. It must.

**SOCRATES:** Try to tell me, then, how long you say it must be.

**LAD:** Three feet.

**SOCRATES:** Three feet, very well: If we take half this bit and add it on, that makes three feet, doesn't it? For here we have two, and here one, the added bit; and, on the other side, in the same way, here are two, here one; and that makes the space you say.

**LAD:** Yes.

**SOCRATES:** Then if the space is three feet this way and three feet that way, the whole space will be three times three feet?

**LAD:** It looks like it.

**SOCRATES:** How much is three times three feet?

**LAD:** Nine.

**SOCRATES:** How many feet was the double to be?

**LAD:** Eight.

**SOCRATES:** So we have not got the eight-foot space from the three-foot line after all.

**LAD:** No, we haven't.

**SOCRATES:** Then how long ought the line to be? Try to tell us exactly, or if you don't want to give it in numbers, show it if you can.

**LAD:** Indeed, Socrates, on my word I don't know.

**SOCRATES:** Now, Meno, do you notice how this lad is getting on in his remembering? At first he did not know what line made the eight-foot space, and he does not know yet; but he thought he knew then, and boldly answered as if he did know, and did not think there was any doubt; now he thinks there is a doubt, and as he does not know, so he does not think he does know.

**MENO:** Quite true.

**SOCRATES:** Then he is better off as regards the matter he did not know?

**MENO:** Yes, I think so too.

**SOCRATES:** So now we have put him into a difficulty, and like the stingray we have made him numb, have we done him any harm?

**MENO:** I don't think so.

**SOCRATES:** At least we have brought him a step onwards, as it seems, to find out how he stands. For now he would go on contentedly seeking, since he does not know; but then he could easily have thought he would be talking well about the double space, even before any number of people again and again, saying how it must have a line of double length.

*On Learning or Remembering* 41

MENO: It seems so.

SOCRATES: Then do you think he would have tried to find out or to learn what he thought he knew, not knowing, until he tumbled into a difficulty by thinking he did not know, and longed to know?

MENO: I do not think he would, Socrates.

SOCRATES: So he gained by being numbed?

MENO: I think so.

SOCRATES: Just notice now that after this difficulty he will find out by seeking along with me, while I do nothing but ask questions and give no instruction. Look out if you find me teaching and explaining to him, instead of asking for his opinions.

Now, lad, answer me. Is not this our four-foot space? Do you understand?

LAD: I do.

SOCRATES: Shall we add another equal to it, thus?

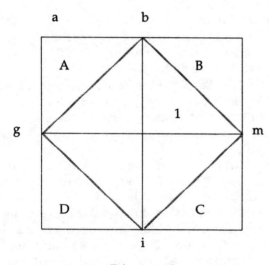

Diagram 3

LAD: Yes.

SOCRATES: And a third equal to either of them, thus?

LAD: Yes.

SOCRATES: Now shall we not also fill in this space in the corner?

LAD: Certainly.

SOCRATES: Won't these be four equal spaces?

LAD: Yes.

SOCRATES: Very well. How many times the small one is this whole space?

LAD: Four times.

SOCRATES: But we wanted a double space; don't you remember?

LAD: Oh yes, I remember.

SOCRATES: Then here is a line running from corner to corner, cutting each of these spaces in two parts.

LAD: Yes.

SOCRATES: Are not these four lines equal, and don't they contain this space within them?

LAD: Yes, that is right.

SOCRATES: Just consider: How big is the space?

LAD: I don't understand.

SOCRATES: Does not each of these lines cut each of the spaces, four spaces, in half? Is that right?

LAD: Yes.

SOCRATES: How many spaces as big as that are in this middle space?

LAD: Four.

SOCRATES: How many in this one?

LAD: Two.

SOCRATES: How many times two is four?

LAD: Twice.

SOCRATES: Then how many square feet is this middle space?

LAD: Eight square feet.

SOCRATES: Made from what line?

LAD: This one.

SOCRATES: From the line drawn from corner to corner of the four-foot space?

LAD: Yes.

SOCRATES: The professors call this a diagonal: so if this is a diagonal, the double space would be made from the diagonal, as you say, Meno's lad!

LAD: Certainly, Socrates.

SOCRATES: Now then, Meno, what do you think? Was there one single opinion which the lad did not give as his own?

MENO: No, they were all his own opinions.

SOCRATES: Yet he did not know, as we agreed shortly before.

MENO: Quite true, indeed.

SOCRATES: Were these opinions in him, or not?

MENO: They were.

SOCRATES: Then in one who does not know, about things he does not know, there are true opinions about the things which he does not know?

MENO: So it appears.

SOCRATES: And now these opinions have been stirred up in him as in a dream; and if someone will keep asking him these same questions often and in various forms, you can be sure that in the end he will know about them as accurately as anybody.

MENO: It seems so.

SOCRATES: And no one having taught him, only asked questions, yet he will know, having got the knowledge out of himself?

MENO: Yes.

SOCRATES: But to get knowledge out of yourself is to remember, isn't it?

MENO: Certainly it is.

SOCRATES: Well then: This knowledge which he now has—he either got it sometime, or he had it always?

MENO: Yes.

SOCRATES: Then if he had it always, he was also always one who knew; but if he got it sometime, he could not have got it in this present life. Or has someone taught him geometry? For he will do just these same things in all matters of geometry, and so with all other sciences. Then is there anyone who has taught him everything? You are sure to know that, I suppose, especially since he was born and brought up in your house.

MENO: Well, I indeed know that no one has ever taught him.

SOCRATES: Has he all these opinions, or not?

MENO: He has, Socrates, it must be so.

SOCRATES: Then if he did not get them in this life, is it not clear now that he had them and had learnt at some other time?

MENO: So it seems.

SOCRATES: Is not that the time when he was not a man?

MENO: Yes.

SOCRATES: Then if both in the time when he is a man and when he isn't there are to be true opinions in him, which are awakened by questioning and become knowledge, will not his soul have understood them for all time? For it is clear that through all time he either is or is not a man.

MENO: That's clear.

SOCRATES: Then if the truth of things is always in our soul, the soul must be immortal; so that what you do not know now by any chance—that is, what you do not remember—you must boldly try and find out and remember?

MENO: You seem to me to argue well, Socrates. I don't know how you do it.

# PLATO

NAME: _____

SECTION: _____

DATE: _____

1. If Deductive Reasoning must begin from at least one accepted assumption, is it similar to syllogistic reasoning?

2. Why does Socrates seem to believe that intellectual difficulty can be a product of both "numbness" and learning?

3. Explain why a true political scientist is never content to "believe" anything, but must keep an open mind.

4. Why is it said that Plato used Socrates "like a foil"?

_____
_____
_____
_____
_____
_____
_____

5. Were you convinced by Plato's Meno that people "remember" rather than learn? Why, or why not?

_____
_____
_____
_____
_____
_____
_____

**Group Exercise:** Convene, and try to re-enact the Meno dialogues with some young person not in college. Report the results.

**Individual Project:** In Meno, Socrates says that he is not teaching the lad anything, he says that he is not a teacher. Could he be something else, like a guide?

# Survey Research: The Role of the Family in Political Socialization

## James LaPlant

Clarence Darrow once declared that "I shall not follow my friend into the labyrinth of statistics. Statistics are a pleasant indoor sport, not so good as crossword puzzles, and they prove nothing to any sensible person who is familiar with statistics." Quantitative political science research, which involves numerical analysis and often utilizes statistics, can find itself open to this criticism. Many political scientists take the "science" in political science very seriously. To guard against Darrow's popular criticism, quantitative political science research follows a rigorous scientific method. This essay will outline the scientific method and provide an example of survey research that follows the method.

The three main elements of the scientific method are *theory*, *operationalization*, and *observation*. The order of these elements is extremely important. The political scientist begins with theory, moves to operationalization of the research concepts, and then the observations are made of the political world. As we examine each of the elements of the scientific method, an example of research on adolescent political socialization will help to highlight the process of conducting political science research.

## THEORY

Our motivation for conducting political science research usually begins with an interest in studying some aspect of the political world. Many political scientists are interested in studying the factors that influence the decision of a citizen whether or not to vote. Students of the United States Congress often investigate the determinants of the voting behavior of members of Congress. Scholars of comparative politics have explored the forces that lead to the outbreak of a revolution. Research in the subfield of international relations has examined the social, political, and economic forces that can drive a nation into warfare. The expectation of a good theory is that it is not only interesting but also addresses an important question about politics. If you think of a research project as similar to building a house, the role of theory in the research project is equivalent to pouring the foundation of a new home. Theory is the first and arguably the most important element of our project. Good theory is the bedrock of the research project and it provides support for the rest of our work.

The theory that guides the research in this essay involves an investigation of how adolescents come to think about politics. Erikson et al. argue that "just as one learns how to read and write and what is fashionable in clothing, one learns about politics. A considerable portion of this learning occurs before the individual is old enough to enter the voting booth." The study of political socialization focuses on how an individual acquires a political identity, political knowledge, and a sense of what it means to be a good citizen. Political socialization research investigates the development of our attitudes and feelings about government and politics.

Scholars of political socialization pay particular attention to the role of the family. The family is often cited as the most powerful agent in pre-adult political socialization. Quite simply, children spend a tremendous amount of time with their parents and there are numerous opportunities for parents to influence the political learning of their children. The most widely discussed evidence for parental influence on adolescents is the transmission of partisan identification. Adolescents often identify with the same political party as their parents, although this relationship has weakened in recent years.

The role of the family in political socialization may well be determined by the level of "family politicization." Family politicization refers to how often the family discusses politics and whether or not the parents encourage an interest in politics. We would expect the influence of the family on political socialization to be greatest in those families that are politicized. Jennings and Niemi report that the level of family politicization affects the party identification and political cynicism of high school seniors. Langton and Karns discover that "children reared in families where parents are interested in politics, discuss politics among themselves, and also participate in political activities, are more likely to have developed a sense of political efficacy than those students from less politicized families." These studies are more than twenty-five years old. Families now follow hectic schedules between school, homework, soccer games, and other recreational activities. Does family politicization continue to play a role in political learning?

The influence of the family on political socialization may also be conditioned by changes in family structure. David Popenoe somberly notes that "only about 50 percent of the children born during the 1970–1984 'baby-bust' period will still live with their natural parents by age 17—a staggering drop from nearly 80 percent." Also, the percentage of out-of-wedlock births has skyrocketed in the last few decades. We know that a divorce can be highly disruptive for children and adolescents. Does divorce also disrupt the political learning of adolescents?

## OPERATIONALIZATION

Babbie notes that "operationalization refers simply to a specification of steps, procedures, or operations that you will go through in actually measuring and identifying the variables you want to observe." Quantitative political science research is discussed in the language of variables. There are two main types of variables: dependent and independent. A **dependent variable** is the political phenomenon that we are attempting to explain. An **independent variable** is presumed to cause or produce changes in the dependent variable. A research **hypothesis** is a statement of the expected relationship between an independent variable and a dependent variable. A researcher might hypothesize that individuals who read a daily newspaper have higher levels of political knowledge than individuals who do not read a newspaper. The independent variable is reading a newspaper and the dependent variable is political knowledge.

Hypotheses must be carefully formulated since they determine how we operationalize our research project. Champney explains that there are five components of a good hypothesis in political science research:

- politically interesting
- plausible
- positive and nontautological
- addressed to the same set of cases
- addressed to more than one case

A good hypothesis should be relevant to our study of politics and it must be plausible. A researcher might hypothesize that people with brown hair are more likely to vote for Democratic candidates than people with blonde hair. Champney notes that such a hypothesis makes no sense. The hypothesis is plausible if it can be supported by reasonable theories of human behavior. A positive hypothesis posits a relationship between the independent and dependent variables that can be tested.

Furthermore, a hypothesis should not be a tautology (a statement that is true by definition). "Rich people have more money than poor people" and "belligerent nations are more likely to go to war than peaceful nations" are examples of tautologies. The independent and dependent variables should be addressed to the same set of cases. A political scientist might hypothesize that the number of high school dropouts in a city is positively associated with the juvenile crime rate. If the researcher selects fifty cities for the study, data must be collected on the number of high school dropouts and the juvenile crime rates in each of the cities. If the researcher collects data on high school dropout rates in fifty cities and then juvenile crime rates in fifty *different cities*, the hypothesis simply cannot be tested since the research does not address the same set of cases. Finally, the hypothesis must address more than one case. Champney notes "the hypothesis that the rise of Hitler in Germany altered the course of world history cannot be tested comparatively and scientifically because it encompasses only one case. Obviously, we cannot compare several worlds where Hitler rose to several worlds where he did not rise to determine which worlds possessed altered courses of history!"

Champney reminds us that "some variables may be treated both as dependent and independent within the discipline of political science." If we are interested in studying the development of political cynicism (dependent variable), we might consider the influence of independent variables such as race, income, or age. Political cynicism could be utilized as an independent variable in the study of political participation (dependent variable). Individuals that are highly cynical about politics might be less likely to participate in politics.

From the discussion of the role of the family in political socialization, several research hypotheses can be formulated:

*Adolescents in politicized families will have higher levels of political identification than adolescents in less politicized families.*

*Adolescents in politicized families will have higher levels of political efficacy than adolescents in less politicized families.*

The independent variable is the level of politicization in the family. The dependent variable is political identification in the first hypothesis and political efficacy in the second hypothesis. The concept of **political efficacy** refers to the belief that you can influence the actions of government. Adolescents growing up in families that regularly discuss politics may learn about the political parties and they may come to appreciate a citizen's ability to influence government.

## OBSERVATION

Babbie notes that the final step in the scientific method involves looking at the world and making measurements of what is observed. Babbie emphasizes that observation can include conducting experiments, interviewing people, or visiting what you are interested in and watching it. Survey research, the administration of a questionnaire to a group of respondents, is one of the most popular forms of observation in quantitative political science research. The major studies of voting behavior, most public opinion surveys, and government censuses utilize this mode of observation. Political socialization studies have relied heavily on survey research, particularly in the administration of questionnaires to students while they are in school. Surveying students in the schools enables the researcher to observe large and diverse groups of adolescents.

Quantitative political science research will often make reference to the terms population and sample. A **population** is the total set of items that a researcher is concerned about and a **sample** is a subset of a population. If a sample is selected randomly (every member of the population has an equal chance of being selected), the researcher can make inferences about the population based upon a sample. Consider the example of research on public opinion. The Gallup organization will conduct public opinion surveys of roughly 1,000 Americans and then make inferences about the entire American electorate. These surveys often utilize random-digit dialing techniques in which computer programs randomly select telephone numbers for interviewing. Although such techniques are often heralded as giving everyone in the population an equal chance of being selected, the poorest of citizens may not have a phone and rich families might have multiple phone numbers listed to their home. The fact that many Americans utilize their answering machines to screen calls also creates a problem. It is important to keep in mind that the statement "everyone in the population has an equal chance of being selected" is often easier said than done.

To test the hypotheses on the role of the family in adolescent political socialization, we will examine the results of a recent survey of middle school students. In the spring of 1996, a written questionnaire was administered to 942 middle school students in the Oklahoma City Public Schools. Four hundred and seventy-six seventh graders and 466 eighth graders were surveyed in randomly selected social studies courses in five middle schools. The five middle schools were selected in different geographic quadrants of Oklahoma City to capture a diverse mix of students. The sample for the study is the 942 students and the population is all the seventh and eighth grade students in the Oklahoma City school district. It is important to note that the population for the study is not all the seventh and eighth grade students in the United States. From a sample of middle school students in Oklahoma City, a researcher could not reasonably make inferences about all the middle school students across the country.

The first research hypothesis on political socialization argues that adolescents in politicized families will have higher levels of political identification than adolescents in less politicized families. In the Oklahoma City survey, the students were asked "do you hear anyone in your family talk about politics, voting, and things like that?" Students could select "very often," "occasionally" or "not at all" as possible responses. This question serves as the measure of family politicization. Students were also asked "if you could register to vote, would you be a Democrat, a Republican, or an Independent?" Students were

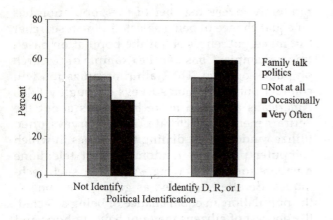

*Figure 1 Political Identification and Family Discussion of Politics*

classified as having a sense of political identification if they selected Democrat, Republican, or Independent. Students that answered "don't know" or "don't know what Republican and Democrat means" were classified as not having a sense of political identification.

Figure 1 reveals the relationship between family politicization and political identification. Of the adolescents that report discussing politics very often in their family, 60% identify with the Democrats, Republicans, or Independents. For students that live in families that occasionally discuss politics, approximately 50% are classified as political identifiers and 50% do not identify with the Democrats, Republicans, or Independents. For adolescents living in families that do not discuss politics, almost 70% do not have a sense of political identification. Only 30% of the students living in families that do not discuss politics would register to vote as a Democrat, Republican, or Independent. Family discussions about politics may well contribute to an adolescent's identification with politics. For those adolescents growing up in families that do not discuss politics, the political parties and the act of voting may not appear to be relevant or important.

Figure 2 helps to further clarify the role of family politicization in adolescent political socialization. The students were asked to name an important difference between the Democrats and the Republicans. Two hundred and twelve students in the sample were able to identify a difference between the parties. Students gave responses such as "Democrats help the working people," "Republicans help the rich," "Democrats give too much welfare," and "Democrats spend more money." As Figure 2 reveals, students in politicized families are more likely to identify an important difference between the parties than students from families that never discuss politics. For those adolescents growing up in families that do not discuss politics, almost 93% did not identify a major difference between the two parties. Only 7% of the students living in families that do not discuss politics identified a difference between the parties. For students that report their families discuss politics very often, roughly one-third identified a difference between the Democrats and Republicans. Family discussions of politics may impart to adolescents an understanding of the key differences between the political parties.

The second research hypothesis contends that adolescents in politicized families will have higher levels of political efficacy than adolescents in less politicized families. It is difficult to measure political efficacy with a single question in a survey. A series of questions is often utilized to measure the extent to which citizens believe they can influence the political process. The middle school students were asked five questions relating to political efficacy. Student responses to these questions provided the basis for categorizing students as low, medium, and high on political efficacy. A student scoring low on political efficacy would strongly agree with statements such as "citizens don't have a chance to say what they think about running the government" and "there are some big, powerful people in the government who are running the whole thing, and they do not care about us ordinary people." A student scoring high on political efficacy would

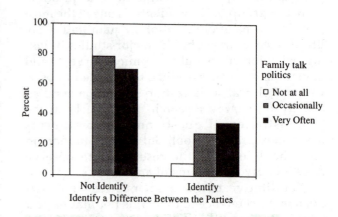

*Figure 2 Party Difference and Family Discussion of Politics*

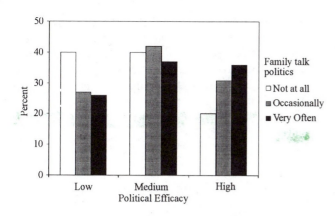

*Figure 3 Political Efficacy and Family Discussion of Politics*

strongly disagree with such statements. Figure 3 illustrates the relationship between family politicization and political efficacy. For students living in families that do not discuss politics, approximately 40% have a low sense of political efficacy and only 20% have a high sense of political efficacy. The category of a high sense of political efficacy is largely composed of adolescents living in families that very often and occasionally discuss politics. Family discussions of politics may inculcate into adolescents the belief that citizens can make a difference in the political process.

When investigating the relationship between two variables, the researcher must also consider the potential influence of a third variable. The relationship between two variables might be explained away by the introduction of a third variable. Meier and Brudney provide the whimsical example of a research analyst who is investigating the recent upsurge of juvenile crime in a large city. The analyst "discovers" a relationship between ice-cream consumption and juvenile crime. In the precincts of the city where ice-cream consumption is high, the juvenile crime rate is very low. In the precincts of the city where ice-cream consumption is low, juvenile crime rates are high. Does it make sense to argue that ice-cream consumption lowers juvenile crime rates? Should the city purchase ice-cream trucks to deliver delicious treats to all the teenagers in the city to help eradicate juvenile crime? The research analyst might want to consider the influence of a third variable such as the income level of a precinct. The higher income areas of the city have lower rates of juvenile crime. They also happen to have adolescents that eat a lot of ice-cream. The poorer precincts in the city have high levels of juvenile crime and there is little ice-cream consumption.

The income level in the precinct is the key predictor of juvenile crime. Income level also explains the different rates of ice-cream consumption. Once we consider the role of income, the original relationship between ice-cream consumption and juvenile crime is clearly spurious. A **spurious relationship** means that the "apparent" relationship between two variables is explained away by the introduction of a third variable.

In the case of adolescent political socialization, it might be argued that the key variable is family composition. There appears to be a relationship between family politicization and political efficacy. The level of politicization in a family may be determined by the composition of the family. Families in which both natural parents are in the home might have more opportunities and more of an incentive to discuss politics with their children. We might hypothesize that single parents lead hectic lives and they simply are not able to frequently discuss politics with their children. Figure 4 explores the connection between family composition and discussing politics. Adolescents living with both natural parents are no more likely to discuss politics in the family than adolescents that live with one parent. Close inspection of Figure 4 reveals that family politicization is roughly equivalent across all major categories of family composition.

Although family composition does not appear to influence the level of family politicization, there might be a connection between family composition and political efficacy. Sociologists have explored the negative impact that divorce can have on school achievement, law-abiding behavior, and learning societal norms of cooperation.

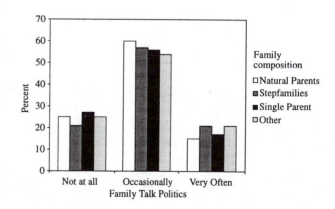

*Figure 4 Family Composition and Discussing Politics*

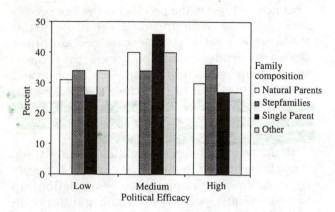

*Figure 5 Political Efficacy and Family Composition*

Can growing up in a single-parent family also impair the development of a sense of political efficacy? Figure 5 helps to answer that question. There appears to be no major difference in the levels of political efficacy based on family composition. Of the adolescents living with single parents, 27% have a high sense of political efficacy compared to 30% of the adolescents living with both natural parents. This does not mean that family politicization is *the* driving force behind political efficacy. Other variables such as race and income are likely to have an influence on political efficacy. Minorities often have a lower sense of political efficacy than whites. Rich citizens are more likely to believe that they can influence the political process than poor citizens. Champney reminds us that because of the myriad of independent variables in the study of human behavior "no hypothesis is completely and unconditionally true. At best, hypotheses *tend toward confirmation*."

## Conclusion

Numerical analysis is often derided with the criticism that "figures lie, and liars figure!" This type of criticism can be healthy for quantitative political science research if it helps to keep us focused on the scientific method. In some social science research, it appears that the primary focus is on sophisticated statistical techniques and theory is more of an afterthought. It is no accident that theory comes first and foremost in the scientific method. Computers, statistical techniques, and survey instruments are only *tools* for our research. Our research is only as good as the theory and hypotheses that provide the foundation for our research project. Political science may not be able to articulate the equivalent of a "law of gravity" or the "laws of thermodynamics," but carefully crafted research can provide valuable scientific insights into the world of politics.

# LAPLANT

NAME: _____

SECTION: _____

DATE: _____

1. What are the three main elements of the scientific method in political science?

2. Do families influence the developing political ideas of children and adolescents? Why or why not?

3. Apparently, some people argued that eating ice cream reduces criminal activity. Do you think this is true? Why or why not?

4. What are the five major components of a good political research hypothesis?

5. Some people argue that children who are reared in single-parent households are handicapped in political socialization. What does the research say about this theory?

**Group Exercise:** Obtain a recent newspaper story about some political event. What theory does it suggest to the group? Then construct a research project to test the plausibility of that theory.

**Individual Project:** Review Figure 4 in the LaPlant article. Briefly summarize in words what that figure shows.

# LEGAL RESEARCH

## Jane Elza and Lee M. Allen

### INTRODUCTION

Courts resolve disputes by applying and interpreting the law. State courts apply and interpret state law and federal courts apply preexisting norms or principles enacted by legislatures into statutory law or articulated by administrators in administrative law. Judges, of course, are not supposed to make law. Instead, they are supposed to apply the norms objectively to particular fact situations. Legal research, to a large extent, consists of matching individual fact situations or of finding statutory language compatible with the client's problem or applying previous court decisions to unique situations.

Of the three branches of government, students usually know the least about the courts. The Founding Fathers wrote a constitution that makes the courts active players in every political dispute. Therefore, some understanding of the perspectives and rationales of the courts is critical to any aspiring political scientist. The history, power, and functions of the courts need to be understood. Similarly, every political researcher knows that some familiarity with the materials, vocabulary, and techniques of legal research are necessary in any mastery of political science research methodology.

There are two basic approaches to researching Law. The first approach uses statutory materials and case law and also focuses on procedural issues. This is the type of research used by attorneys and paralegals in researching cases for clients. The second approach is much broader, emphasizing the more routine scholarly research and writing skills, and this type is used in academic settings or in writing background papers for proposed legislative changes in the law.

Both approaches require some familiarity with the courts, the judicial process, and cases. How much familiarity depends, frequently, on the topic or topics being investigated and on the amount of resources and time available to the researcher. Still, researching the law is basically similar to ordinary research. This should give novices confidence in their abilities to find legal information. It must be emphasized that legal indexes work the same way as other reference materials. Realizing this helps alleviate the shock that result from a researcher's first exposure to the vast amount of legal information that is available.

### PROBLEMS

The first major problem in legal research is searching through tons of chaff for the few tiny kernels of useful and relevant information and precedent. And the legal records are vast indeed. In the United States alone, law has been cranked out, supplemented and amended and changed for over two hundred years. It has been generated by Congress, state legislatures, and even city councils. It has also been created by legal court decisions at the federal, state, and local levels. In addition, legally binding decrees may be declared by presidents, governors, and mayors; and bureaucracies make regulations which are also an important area of law and case decisions. There are literally millions and millions of laws and court opinions available in the legal record.

As if this were not enough, American courts often recognize the laws of Great Britain as relevant to contemporary litigation. The laws of merry old England can be useful, providing both information and legal precedent for varying interpretations of the great historical body of law which the American colonies inherited from the British Empire. And to a certain extent, the laws of Spain and France have on occasion been found relevant as well, particularly in the southwestern United States and in Louisiana. Anything may be useful in legal research.

For example, in the well known and highly controversial case of *Roe v. Wade*, in which the Supreme Court of the United States found that women have rights to an abortion procedure under certain circumstances, the research net was cast very widely indeed. If one reads the official court opinion in that case, one sees that the legal record that was found relevant to American law included reference to ancient Babylonian laws, the laws of classical Greece including the Hippocratic Oath, the laws of the Roman Empire and the Medieval Christian Church, and of course the laws of England and colonial America. What the court found in its review of this extensive legal record of actual cases and controversies covering over two thousand years of lawmaking was that abortion law and policy is peculiarly subject to current public opinion. It is never resolved, just re-cycled.

When abortion is illegal, general public opinion becomes horrified over what is seen as a "bloodbath" of young women dying because of suicide, or due to self-inflicted wounds incurred in attempts to abort, or because of bad treatment by incompetent quacks in back alleys. Thus, over a time frame of about twenty years, a generation, public pressure always mounts to make abortion legal. But as soon as it becomes legal, the general public opinion then tends to become horrified over what is now seen as a "bloodbath" of foetuses dying because of abortions by physicians or by self-administered abortions. Then pressure mounts to make it illegal, succeeds in another twenty years or so, and the cycle continues without end.

In short, historical legal records show that there has been no simple legal solution to this biological problem for thousands of years, just an endless cycle during which adult women and developing foetuses take turns in being the temporary winners or losers of contemporary legal policy. But because the cycle requires generations to complete, the average layperson is incapable of seeing the big picture.

In 1973 the Supreme Court of the United States took notice of this intractable area of law and made a historically remarkable attempt to deal with it. In its almost Solomonic "trimester" decision, the court keyed the law to two factors: the viability of the foetus, and the rights of the adult female. It was hoped that this approach would be seen as the fairest possible solution and would be accepted by public opinion. However it seems obvious that today the pendulum is swinging slowly in the other direction, due to increasing political pressure and radical activism by anti-abortionists.

Figure 6 shows how this cycle changes over a time-frame of about three hundred years, with a legal policy change at intervals of a generation, or about twenty years, on average. The result is a sine wave, a fluctuation of policy, and historical failure to come up with a definitive answer to this perennial legal problem.

Legal research is usually a problem solving activity, although it is rarely necessary to probe as deep into the historical legal record as in the example above. But always, if a person wants to convince a jury, courts, or legislature to do something, or to decide on issues in a certain way, then he/she must find the correct rule to apply in their legal reasoning and argument. As a result, legal research is often a lot like a treasure hunt. But legal treasure hunting requires both a large vocabulary and a lot of persistence. It also is most rewarding to researchers who have developed

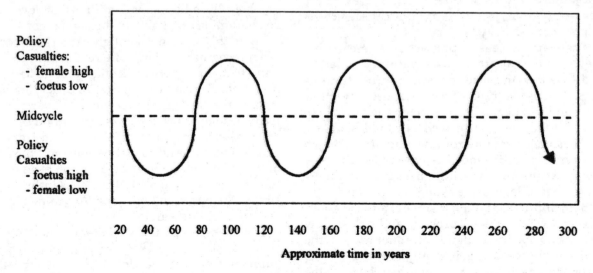

*Figure 6*

good strategies and efficient techniques for their information searches.

In this effort, a major goal of any legal researcher must be to acquaint himself or herself with the basic kinds of resources that are available in their local community or area, including not only basic materials but also any indexes to legal materials. And the researcher may have another problem: what to do when local indexes have not been updated! If finding and using the official materials like the *United States Reports* or the *Supreme Court Reporter* is impossible, there are any number of lawbooks, summaries, hornbooks and casebooks that can be used to get started. The basic research goal is to find the legal reasoning and the rule that can be applied to the client's situation. Another of the advantages in using these materials is that they may provide order and consistency to an overwhelming volume of legal material.

The second problem that most legal researchers encounter is vocabulary. Students and other novices rarely know even the most basic terms used in judicial proceedings, such as "plaintiff" and "defendant." One way to deal with this problem is to acquire a legal dictionary. Irving Shapiro's *Dictionary of Legal Terms*, Gould Publications, is but one example of an inexpensive, easy to use, and understandable legal dictionary; there are many such useful reference works listed in the bibliography.

And if monetary expense is a consideration, as it often is, the researcher could try to prepare a list of relevant terms and definitions. Many lawbooks have glossaries that can be helpful. Once the researcher has access to a glossary, a dictionary, or a list of terms, it is advisable to immediately learn how to use these terms in the search into the court system and the larger legal system.

The third problem most of the novice legal researchers face is deciding just how extensively they want to pursue the complexities of their case, both in the preliminary search for information and later in pursuing their cases in the legal system, where any case can often be appealed again and again and again. Once again, resources and time are key factors in these decisions. In any event, the information has to be organized and clearly written for notes, arguments, and for casebriefs. There are books that emphasize writing skills; however, they may assume a far broader knowledge than the average introductory student possesses.

For example, Block's *Effective Legal Writing*, Flesch's *How to Write Plain English*, and Shapo's *Writing and Analysis in the Law*, and Statsky,'s *Legal Research and Writing* may be useful. Other books, like the well known Dwyer's *Law Writer's Guide*, concentrate almost exclusively on proper citations. For the beginner, another very good book is Melone's *Researching Constitutional Law*. The book has a glossary, sample questions for students to research, advice on style and proper citation for a research paper, and summaries of the basic books used for such research.

Books designed specifically for legal research are especially useful. Teply's *Legal Research and Citation* has sample problems which allow the student to answer questions using the illustrated examples. If students have access to a fully stocked law library, standard texts like Jacobstein's *Fundamentals of Legal Research* or Cohen's *Finding the Law* are particularly easy to use and to read. Elias' *Legal Research* gives helpful hints for dealing with common problems students may have.

Standard practice research problems for students usually involve the interesting areas of the law, like the Freedom of Information Act or the Privacy Act, but can focus on any well known law which affects many people. Always, legal case research should be geared to the interests of the client or to professional development of the researcher. It is usually necessary to pose questions geared towards the client's individual interests and any unique circumstances of the case.

Finally, there are also problems with using the case research method itself. This method tends to overemphasize procedure and the role of courts. In fact, it often is aggravating because its focus tends to be too narrow. An advantage of the case method is its immediate applicability to the clients case. Whereas popular writings and even legal authorities may require a lot of arguing to be accepted, prior decisions usually receive a more sympathetic hearing from judges.

Newspapers, magazines, and television presentations can all supplement case citations and are frequently a part of legislative research projects, but these are generally only accepted in court cases when they help to establish facts, not in the wording or reasoning of the law or the courts.

Many of the problems of legal research are inherent in the subject itself. Unless one is dealing with a narrow subdivision of law, there is little coherence from jurisdiction to jurisdiction. Even the vocabulary may be inconsistent. Indeed, one of the continuing controversies of every case is the location of boundaries of relevancy, what material or evidence may be allowed and what may not be allowed. Given these difficulties, how well the researchers integrate their findings into their arguments will often determine how successful they will be in getting their information recognized and entered into the official case record. However, experience with small projects over time will build confidence in any researcher.

It is important to realize that there is no such thing as THE LAW. Law evolves through application and interpretation, mainly by courts, which then explain their reasons for making incremental adjustments to resolve the specific issue before them. Courts make these incremental adjustments by applying the explanations, legal norms, and wording of prior cases. A prior case similar to the case being decided is a precedent. This formalistic process makes no concession to changes in the values of the community or even to the idea that new situations do not always conform comfortably with the past. The past is always the authority for the present and the present is rarely the authority for the future.

If a lawyer has a client with a problem, he/she will turn first to the law written by those authorized to make law—legislatures. If the client's problem falls within the state's authority, the lawyer looks in the state's statutes. In Georgia, the laws passed by the Georgia Legislature are published in *Georgia Laws*, a book that contains laws that apply to local governments as well. These laws are published yearly and each book contains an index for that volume. However, the lawyer would have to know which laws were passed when to effectively use the *Georgia Laws*. It is easier to use the *Official Code of Georgia Annotated*, usually abbreviated as O.C.Ga.A.

Codes organize statutes by topic and they include all the laws passed by the legislature on that topic. An index allows the lawyer to find the statute by topic and, if the code is annotated, he/she can find what decisions of courts or the state's Attorney General have affected that particular statute.

This is more difficult than it sounds because the indexes may use archaic legal terms, *e.g.*, Master and Servant rules in the area of employment law. It is much like using a phonebook. One looks up "drug stores" and gets referred to "pharmacies." The lawyer, then, wants to have as many words to look up as he/she can in order to pinpoint the relevant parts for the client's particular problem. One word leads to another; one law leads to another. And there are millions and millions of laws which have been recorded for thousands of years. Thus the legal researcher faces a very daunting task in trying to find just the "right" law.

However, in the modern world this process can be made easier by using the new Westlaw or Lexis electronic data bases which match the words to the cases, codes, or statutes. Each word is linked by "connectors" which tell the computer where to look and how to limit the search. If one typed in the words, "prisoner" and "due process," one would be flooded by cases. To a large extent, a client pays a lawyer for knowing what to look for and how to present what is found to a court in an acceptable format.

Since there is no such thing as THE LAW, computerized research merely makes it easier to find information which can be used as arguments, as well as highly detailed information like how many cases a particular judge decided on a given day on this particular topic. Most people outside of academia have little use for the last type of information.

What the lawyer really wants to find is a decision by the highest court in the state that supports his/her interpretation of the law and/or facts. That is because the highest court is the highest authority on what the law means. State supreme court decisions are usually published, if not by the state, then by private publishing companies like West. These private companies may not include all the court's opinions or even all of a single opinion. If a private publisher publishes the state supreme court decisions, the legislature will have to decide whether these publications are to be classified as "official" or not. This information is routinely printed inside each book. In the State of Georgia, the *Supreme Court Reporter*, (usually abbreviated *Ga.*), is an official publication.

It is quite possible that the lawyer will not know enough about the legal principles or specific law that applies in a new client's case. (Law schools do not teach THE LAW. They teach how to find the law and use it to achieve a specific goal.) To gather background for the case, the lawyer may look in legal encyclopedias, the *American Law Reports* (a research tool in legal authorities), legal periodicals, or looseleaf services (special reporters of specialized law.) Again, the information the lawyer finds is condensed into key words through which he hopes to find THE case that settles his client's problem as the client wants it settled.

Each of the research tools mentioned above contain references to cases the lawyer should find helpful. If he or she is certain of the general boundaries of the law or knowledgeable about specific divisions of the law, the lawyer might want to start the search for THE case with a digest. Digests are not authoritative and cannot be cited in support of an argument, but they are collections of condensed cases by topic and so are good tools to find a relevant case, which the lawyer would then read, just as he/she would have read the appropriate statute or code section at the beginning of the search.

Someone who does not like to read, who dislikes making subtle distinctions, and who cannot make minor differences into arguments for broader principles would probably not like being a lawyer.

It is, of course, unusual to find a case "on point," one which exactly matches the client's problem and settles the issue the way the client wants. The lawyer must then use the research tools above to find the reasons why a court should interpret the statute, administrative order, or previous court case in a way favorable to the client. This can be done by invoking the authority of a higher court or law (the highest is of course the U.S. Supreme Court's interpretation of the U.S. Constitution). Or the lawyer may rely on leading experts in the field or Model Laws proposed by the American Bar Association or even the usual tactics of debate. (It should be noted, however, that most lawyers are not trial lawyers and the arguments they make are primarily written according to forms designated by legislatures and/or courts. The ability to express oneself clearly in writing is essential to being a lawyer.)

Once the lawyer has found the case or statute he/she wants to use to lend the argument authority, the next step is to Shepardize it. Shepardizing tells the attorney whether the case or law is still current or whether it has been changed by some court or legislature at a later date. What the lawyer does is look up the case or statute in a series of special books commonly called *Shepard's Citations*.

There is one set of books for each type of court on the state and federal level, and several specialty editions focusing on topics in the law. This type of research is called "shepardizing" and it is essential because the lawyer can't win if he/she's relying on information that is out of date or on a case that has been overturned, especially if it has been overturned by the U.S. Supreme Court. Sometimes, the good researcher will try to predict what the law will be, not what it was.

For example, it is often advisable for researchers to consult the *Federal Register* if possible. It is especially important if the researcher is interested in finding out about new or proposed federal laws or regulations. Unfortunately, it, like all too many other legal resources, is rarely available in every library. There are so many legal materials and data bases that no library can carry them all, not even the Congressional Library in Washington, D.C.! But the text is carried by both the *Westlaw* and *Lexis* data bases, so a researcher with a modem and access to the electronic world wide web has a very real advantage over researchers who lack computer training.

Legal research is not really difficult, but it is usually very time consuming, even with computerized help. It can be tedious, as one goes from legal authority to legal authority without finding exactly what is needed to convince the judge of one's position. To be morally right is not enough to win a case, neither is citing the necessities of the moment or the degree of injury to the client. For a client to win, the advocate must have the client's argument accepted, and one must be able to argue that the result is dictated by this legal principle or that legal authority. One must be able to fit the argument into the wording and/or the tradition of the existing laws.

# Elza and Allen

NAME: _____

SECTION: _____

DATE: _____

1. Describe why word and topic search strategies for electronic databases should be used in legal research.

   _____
   _____
   _____
   _____
   _____
   _____
   _____
   _____

2. What are some of the types of data bases that can be accessed when trying to do research for a legal client?

   _____
   _____
   _____
   _____
   _____
   _____
   _____
   _____

3. What is a legal code, and how does it differ from legislative laws?

   _____
   _____
   _____
   _____
   _____
   _____

4. What do courts of law do when cases are brought to them?

___

5. What does a lawyer look for when searching for precedent for his client?

___

**Group Exercise:** Go to *Shepard's Citations* and randomly choose two cases for research. Photocopy the two citations. Find the original case and photocopy the first page of the court's opinion.

**Individual Project:** Choose a published court case and report on its significance.

*Part Two*

# Fields with a Domestic Emphasis

*Chapter Three*

# **AMERICAN POLITICS**

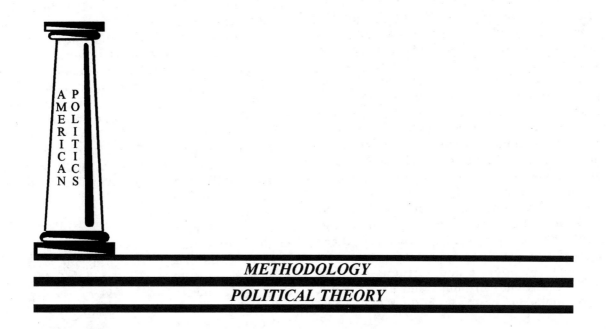

# Selected Excerpts from the Federalist Papers

## *James Madison**

### Federalist No. 10

Among the numerous advantages promised by a well-constructed Union, none deserves to be more accurately developed than its tendency to break and control the violence of faction. The friend of popular governments never finds himself so much alarmed for their character and fate, as when he contemplates their propensity to this dangerous vice. He will not fail, therefore, to set a due value on any plan which, without violating the principles to which he is attached, provides a proper cure for it. The instability, injustice, and confusion introduced into the public councils, have, in truth, been the mortal diseases under which popular governments have everywhere perished; as they continue to be the favorite and fruitful topics from which the adversaries to liberty derive their most specious declamations. The valuable improvements made by the American constitutions on the popular models, both ancient and modern, cannot certainly be too much admired; but it would be an unwarrantable partiality, to contend that they have as effectually obviated the danger on this side, as was wished and expected. Complaints are everywhere heard from our most considerate and virtuous citizens, equally the friends of public and private faith, and of public and personal liberty, that our governments are too unstable, that the public good is disregarded in the conflicts of rival parties, and that measures are too often decided, not according to the rules of justice and the rights of the minor party, but by the superior force of an interested and overbearing majority. However anxiously we may wish that these complaints had no foundation, the evidence, of known facts will not permit us to deny that they are in some degree true. It will be found, indeed, on a candid review of our situation, that some of the distresses under which we labor have been erroneously charged on the operation of our governments; but it will be found, at the same time, that other causes will not alone account for many of our heaviest misfortunes; and, particularly, for that prevailing and increasing distrust of public engagements, and alarm for private rights, which are echoed from one end of the continent to the other. These must be chiefly, if not wholly, effects of the unsteadiness and injustice with which a factious spirit has tainted our public administrations.

By a faction, I understand a number of citizens, whether amounting to a majority or a minority of the whole, who are united and actuated by some common impulse of passion, or of interest, adverse to the rights of other citizens, or to the permanent and aggregate interests of the community.

There are two methods of curing the mischiefs of faction: the one, by removing its causes; the other, by controlling its effects. There are again two methods of removing the causes of faction: the one, by destroying the liberty which is essential to its existence; the other, by giving to every citizen the same opinions, the same passions, and the same interests.

It could never be more truly said

*James Madison*

---

\* Madison, James. (1901). Federalist 10 and Federalist 51. In *The Federalist: A commentary on the Constitution of the United States: Being a collection of essays written by Alexander Hamilton, James Madison, and John Jay.* (Intro. E. Gaylord). Washington, D.C.: M. W. Dunne.

than of the first remedy, that it was worse than the disease. Liberty is to faction what air is to fire, an aliment without which it instantly expires. But it could not be less folly to abolish liberty, which is essential to political life, because it nourishes faction, than it would be to wish the annihilation of air, which is essential to animal life, because it imparts to fire its destructive agency.

The second expedient is as impracticable as the first would be unwise. As long as the reason of man continues fallible, and he is at liberty to exercise it, different opinions will be formed. As long as the connection subsists between his reason and his self-love, his opinions and his passions will have a reciprocal influence on each other; and the former will be objects to which the latter will attach themselves. The diversity in the faculties of men, from which the rights of property originate, is not less an insuperable obstacle to a uniformity of interests. The protection of these faculties is the first object of government. From the protection of different and unequal faculties of acquiring property, the possession of different degrees and kinds of property immediately results; and from the influence of these on the sentiments and views of the respective proprietors, ensues a division of the society into different interests and parties.

The latent causes of faction are thus sown in the nature of man; and we see them everywhere brought into different degrees of activity, according to the different circumstances of civil society. A zeal for different opinions concerning religion, concerning government, and many other points, as well of speculation as of practice; an attachment to different leaders ambitiously contending for pre-eminence and power; or to persons of other descriptions whose fortunes have been interesting to the human passions, have, in turn, divided mankind into parties, inflamed them with mutual animosity, and rendered them much more disposed to vex and oppress each other than to co-operate for their common good. So strong is this propensity of mankind to fall into mutual animosities, that where no substantial occasion presents itself, the most frivolous and fanciful distinctions have been sufficient to kindle their unfriendly passions and excite their most violent conflicts. But the most common and durable source of factions has been the various and unequal distribution of property. Those who hold and those who are without property have ever formed distinct interests in society. Those who are creditors, and those who are debtors, fall under a like discrimination. A landed interest, a manufacturing interest, a mercantile interest, a moneyed interest, with many lesser interests, grow up of necessity in civilized nations, and divide them into different classes, actuated by different sentiments and views. The regulation of these various and interfering interests forms the principal task of modern legislation, and involves the spirit of party and faction in the necessary and ordinary operations of the government.

No man is allowed to be a judge in his own cause, because his interest would certainly bias his judgment, and, not improbably, corrupt his integrity. With equal, nay with greater reason, a body of men are unfit to be both judges and parties at the same time; yet what are many of the most important acts of legislation, but so many judicial determinations, not indeed concerning the rights of single persons, but concerning the rights of large bodies of citizens? And what are the different classes of legislators but advocates and parties to the causes which they determine? Is a law proposed concerning private debts? It is a question to which the creditors are parties on one side and the debtors on the other. Justice ought to hold the balance between them. Yet the parties are, and must be, themselves the judges; and the most numerous party, or, in other words, the most powerful faction must be expected to prevail. Shall domestic manufactures be encouraged, and in what degree, by restrictions on foreign manufactures? These are questions which would be differently decided by the landed and the manufacturing classes, and probably by neither with a sole regard to justice and the public good. The apportionment of taxes on the various descriptions of property is an act which seems to require the most exact impartiality; yet there is, perhaps, no legislative act in which greater opportunity and temptation are given to a predominant party to trample on the rules of justice. Every shilling with which they overburden the inferior number, is a shilling saved to their own pockets.

It is in vain to say that enlightened statesmen will be able to adjust these clashing interests, and render them all subservient to the public good. Enlightened statesmen will not always be at the helm. Nor, in many cases, can such an adjustment be made at all without taking into view indirect and remote considerations, which will rarely prevail over the immediate interest which one party may find in disregarding the rights of another or the good of the whole.

The inference to which we are brought is, that the CAUSES of faction cannot be removed, and that relief is only to be sought in the means of controlling its EFFECTS.

*Selected Excerpts from the Federalist Papers*

If a faction consists of less than a majority, relief is supplied by the republican principle, which enables the majority to defeat its sinister views by regular vote. It may clog the administration, it may convulse the society; but it will be unable to execute and mask its violence under the forms of the Constitution. When a majority is included in a faction, the form of popular government, on the other hand, enables it to sacrifice to its ruling passion or interest both the public good and the rights of other citizens. To secure the public good and private rights against the danger of such a faction, and at the same time to preserve the spirit and the form of popular government, is then the great object to which our inquiries are directed. Let me add that it is the great desideratum by which this form of government can be rescued from the opprobrium under which it has so long labored, and be recommended to the esteem and adoption of mankind.

By what means is this object attainable? Evidently by one of two only. Either the existence of the same passion or interest in a majority at the same time must be prevented, or the majority, having such coexistent passion or interest, must be rendered, by their number and local situation, unable to concert and carry into effect schemes of oppression. If the impulse and the opportunity be suffered to coincide, we well know that neither moral nor religious motives can be relied on as an adequate control. They are not found to be such on the injustice and violence of individuals, and lose their efficacy in proportion to the number combined together, that is, in proportion as their efficacy becomes needful.

From this view of the subject it may be concluded that a pure democracy, by which I mean a society consisting of a small number of citizens, who assemble and administer the government in person, can admit of no cure for the mischiefs of faction. A common passion or interest will, in almost every case, be felt by a majority of the whole; a communication and concert result from the form of government itself; and there is nothing to check the inducements to sacrifice the weaker party or an obnoxious individual. Hence it is that such democracies have ever been spectacles of turbulence and contention; have ever been found incompatible with personal security or the rights of property; and have in general been as short in their lives as they have been violent in their deaths. Theoretic politicians, who have patronized this species of government, have erroneously supposed that by reducing mankind to a perfect equality in their political rights, they would, at the same time, be perfectly equalized and assimilated in their possessions, their opinions, and their passions.

A republic, by which I mean a government in which the scheme of representation takes place, opens a different prospect, and promises the cure for which we are seeking. Let us examine the points in which it varies from pure democracy, and we shall comprehend both the nature of the cure and the efficacy which it must derive from the Union.

The two great points of difference between a democracy and a republic are: first, the delegation of the government, in the latter, to a small number of citizens elected by the rest; secondly, the greater number of citizens, and greater sphere of country, over which the latter may be extended.

The effect of the first difference is, on the one hand, to refine and enlarge the public views, by passing them through the medium of a chosen body of citizens, whose wisdom may best discern the true interest of their country, and whose patriotism and love of justice will be least likely to sacrifice it to temporary or partial considerations. Under such a regulation, it may well happen that the public voice, pronounced by the representatives of the people, will be more consonant to the public good than if pronounced by the people themselves, convened for the purpose. On the other hand, the effect may be inverted. Men of factious tempers, of local prejudices, or of sinister designs, may, by intrigue, by corruption, or by other means, first obtain the suffrages, and then betray the interests, of the people. The question resulting is, whether small or extensive republics are more favorable to the election of proper guardians of the public weal; and it is clearly decided in favor of the latter by two obvious considerations.

In the first place, it is to be remarked that, however small the republic may be, the representatives must be raised to a certain number, in order to guard against the cabals of a few; and that, however large it may be, they must be limited to a certain number, in order to guard against the confusion of a multitude. Hence, the number of representatives in the two cases not being in proportion to that of the two constituents, and being proportionally greater in the small republic, it follows that, if the proportion of fit characters be not less in the large than in the small republic, the former will present a greater option, and consequently a greater probability of a fit choice.

In the next place, as each representative will be chosen by a greater number of citizens in the large than in the small republic, it will be more difficult for unworthy candidates to practice with success the vicious arts by which elections are too often carried; and the suffrages of the people being more free, will be more likely to center in men who possess the most attractive merit and the most diffusive and established characters.

It must be confessed that in this, as in most other cases, there is a mean, on both sides of which inconveniences will be found to lie. By enlarging too much the number of electors, you render the representatives too little acquainted with all their local circumstances and lesser interests; as by reducing it too much, you render him unduly attached to these, and too little fit to comprehend and pursue great and national objects. The federal Constitution forms a happy combination in this respect; the great and aggregate interests being referred to the national, the local and particular to the State legislatures.

The other point of difference is, the greater number of citizens and extent of territory which may be brought within the compass of republican than of democratic government; and it is this circumstance principally which renders factious combinations less to be dreaded in the former than in the latter. The smaller the society, the fewer probably will be the distinct parties and interests composing it; the fewer the distinct parties and interests, the more frequently will a majority be found of the same party; and the smaller the number of individuals composing a majority, and the smaller the compass within which they are placed, the more easily will they concert and execute their plans of oppression. Extend the sphere, and you take in a greater variety of parties and interests; you make it less probable that a majority of the whole will have a common motive to invade the rights of other citizens; or if such a common motive exists, it will be more difficult for all who feel it to discover their own strength, and to act in unison with each other. Besides other impediments, it may be remarked that, where there is a consciousness of unjust or dishonorable purposes, communication is always checked by distrust in proportion to the number whose concurrence is necessary.

Hence, it clearly appears, that the same advantage which a republic has over a democracy, in controlling the effects of faction, is enjoyed by a large over a small republic,—is enjoyed by the Union over the States composing it. Does the advantage consist in the substitution of representatives whose enlightened views and virtuous sentiments render them superior to local prejudices and schemes of injustice? It will not be denied that the representation of the Union will be most likely to possess these requisite endowments. Does it consist in the greater security afforded by a greater variety of parties, against the event of any one party being able to outnumber and oppress the rest? In an equal degree does the increased variety of parties comprised within the Union, increase this security. Does it, in fine, consist in the greater obstacles opposed to the concert and accomplishment of the secret wishes of an unjust and interested majority? Here, again, the extent of the Union gives it the most palpable advantage.

The influence of factious leaders may kindle a flame within their particular States, but will be unable to spread a general conflagration through the other States. A religious sect may degenerate into a political faction in a part of the Confederacy; but the variety of sects dispersed over the entire face of it must secure the national councils against any danger from that source. A rage for paper money, for an abolition of debts, for an equal division of property, or for any other improper or wicked project, will be less apt to pervade the whole body of the Union than a particular member of it; in the same proportion as such a malady is more likely to taint a particular county or district, than an entire State.

In the extent and proper structure of the Union, therefore, we behold a republican remedy for the diseases most incident to republican government. And according to the degree of pleasure and pride we feel in being republicans, ought to be our zeal in cherishing the spirit and supporting the character of federalists.

*PUBLIUS*

# FEDERALIST NO. 51

### James Madison

To what expedient, then, shall we finally resort, for maintaining in practice the necessary partition of power among the several departments, as laid down in the Constitution? The only answer that can be given is, that as all these exterior provisions are found to be inadequate, the defect must be supplied, by so contriving the interior structure of the government as that its several constituent parts may, by their mutual relations, be the means of keeping each other in their proper places. Without presuming to undertake a full development of this important idea, I will hazard a few general observations, which may perhaps place it in a clearer light, and enable us to form a more correct judgment of the principles and structure of the government planned by the convention.

In order to lay a due foundation for that separate and distinct exercise of the different powers of government, which to a certain extent is admitted on all hands to be essential to the preservation of liberty, it is evident that each department should have a will of its own; and consequently should be so constituted that the members of each should have as little agency as possible in the appointment of the members of the others. Were this principle rigorously adhered to, it would require that all the appointments for the supreme executive, legislative, and judiciary magistracies should be drawn from the same fountain of authority, the people, through channels having no communication whatever with one another. Perhaps such a plan of constructing the several departments would be less difficult in practice than it may in contemplation appear. Some difficulties, however, and some additional expense would attend the execution of it. Some deviations, therefore, from the principle must be admitted. In the constitution of the judiciary department in particular, it might be inexpedient to insist rigorously on the principle: first, because peculiar qualifications being essential in the members, the primary consideration ought to be to select that mode of choice which best secures these qualifications; secondly, because the permanent tenure by which the appointments are held in that department, must soon destroy all sense of dependence on the authority conferring them.

It is equally evident, that the members of each department should be as little dependent as possible on those of the others, for the emoluments annexed to their offices. Were the executive magistrate, or the judges, not independent of the legislature in this particular, their independence in every other would be merely nominal.

But the great security against a gradual concentration of the several powers in the same department, consists in giving to those who administer each department the necessary constitutional means and personal motives to resist encroachments of the others. The provision for defense must in this, as in all other cases, be made commensurate to the danger of attack. Ambition must be made to counteract ambition. The interest of the man must be connected with the constitutional rights of the place. It may be a reflection on human nature, that such devices should be necessary to control the abuses of government. But what is government itself, but the greatest of all reflections on human nature? If men were angels, no government would be necessary. If angels were to govern men, neither external nor internal controls on government would be necessary. In framing a government which is to be administered by men over men, the great difficulty lies in this: you must first enable the government to control the governed; and in the next place oblige it to control itself. A dependence on the people is, no doubt, the primary control on the government; but experience has taught mankind the necessity of auxiliary precautions.

This policy of supplying, by opposite and rival interests, the defect of better motives, might be traced through the whole system of human affairs, private as well as public. We see it particularly displayed in all the subordinate distributions of power, where the constant aim is to divide and arrange the several offices in such a manner as that each may be a check on the other that the private interest of every individual may be a sentinel over the public rights. These inventions of prudence cannot be less requisite in the distribution of the supreme powers of the State.

But it is not possible to give to each department an equal power of self-defense. In republican government, the legislative authority necessarily predominates. The remedy for this inconveniency is to divide the legislature into different branches; and to render them, by different modes of election and different principles of action, as little connected with each other as the nature of their common functions and their common dependence on the society will admit. It may even be necessary to guard against dangerous encroachments by still further precautions. As the weight of the legislative authority requires that it should be thus divided, the weakness of the executive may require, on the other hand, that it should be fortified. An absolute negative on the legislature appears, at first view, to be the natural defense with which the executive magistrate should be armed. But perhaps it would be neither altogether safe nor alone sufficient. On ordinary occasions it might not be exerted with the requisite firmness, and on extraordinary occasions it might be perfidiously abused. May not this defect of an absolute negative be supplied by some qualified connection between this weaker department and the weaker branch of the stronger department, by which the latter may be led to support the constitutional rights of the former, without being too much detached from the rights of its own department?

If the principles on which these observations are founded be just, as I persuade myself they are, and they be applied as a criterion to the several State constitutions, and to the federal Constitution it will be found that if the latter does not perfectly correspond with them, the former are infinitely less able to bear such a test.

There are, moreover, two considerations particularly applicable to the federal system of America, which place that system in a very interesting point of view.

*First.* In a single republic, all the power surrendered by the people is submitted to the administration of a single government; and the usurpations are guarded against by a division of the government into distinct and separate departments. In the compound republic of America, the power surrendered by the people is first divided between two distinct governments, and then the portion allotted to each subdivided among distinct and separate departments. Hence a double security arises to the rights of the people. The different governments will control each other, at the same time that each will be controlled by itself.

*Second.* It is of great importance in a republic not only to guard the society against the oppression of its rulers, but to guard one part of the society against the injustice of the other part. Different interests necessarily exist in different classes of citizens. If a majority be united by a common interest, the rights of the minority will be insecure. There are but two methods of providing against this evil: the one by creating a will in the community independent of the majority that is, of the society itself; the other, by comprehending in the society so many separate descriptions of citizens as will render an unjust combination of a majority of the whole very improbable, if not impracticable. The first method prevails in all governments possessing an hereditary or self-appointed authority. This, at best, is but a precarious security; because a power independent of the society may as well espouse the unjust views of the major, as the rightful interests of the minor party, and may possibly be turned against both parties. The second method will be exemplified in the federal republic of the United States. Whilst all authority in it will be derived from and dependent on the society, the society itself will be broken into so many parts, interests, and classes of citizens, that the rights of individuals, or of the minority, will be in little danger from interested combinations of the majority. In a free government the security for civil rights must be the same as that for religious rights. It consists in the one case in the multiplicity of interests, and in the other in the multiplicity of sects. The degree of security in both cases will depend on the number of interests and sects; and this may be presumed to depend on the extent of country and number of people comprehended under the same government. This view of the subject must particularly recommend a proper federal system to all the sincere and considerate friends of republican government, since it shows that in exact proportion as the territory of the Union may be formed into more circumscribed Confederacies, or States oppressive combinations of a majority will be facilitated: the best security, under the republican forms, for the rights of every class of citizens, will be diminished: and consequently the stability and independence of some member of the government, the only other security, must be proportionately increased. Justice is the end of government. It is the end of civil society. It ever has been and ever will be pursued until it be obtained, or until liberty be lost in the pursuit. In a society under the forms of which the stronger faction can readily unite and oppress the weaker, anarchy may as truly be said to reign as in a state of nature, where the weaker individual is not secured against the violence of the stronger; and as, in the latter state, even the stronger individuals are prompted, by the uncertainty of their condition, to submit to a government which may protect the weak as well as themselves; so, in the former state, will the more powerful factions or parties be gradually induced, by a like motive, to wish for a government which will protect all parties, the weaker as well as the more powerful. It can be little doubted that if the State of Rhode Island was separated from the Confederacy and left to itself, the insecurity of rights under the popular form of government within such narrow limits would be displayed by such reiterated oppressions of factious majorities that some power altogether independent of the people would soon be called for by the voice of the very factions whose misrule had proved the necessity of it. In the extended republic of the United States, and among the great variety of interests, parties, and sects which it embraces, a coalition of a majority of the whole society could seldom take place on any other principles than those of justice and the general good; whilst there being thus less danger to a minor from the will of a major party, there must be less pretext, also, to provide for the security of the former, by introducing into the government a will not dependent on the latter, or, in other words, a will independent of the society itself. It is no less certain than it is important, notwithstanding the contrary opinions which have been entertained, that the larger the society, provided it lie within a practical sphere, the more duly capable it will be of self-government. And happily for the **republican cause**, the practicable sphere may be carried to a very great extent, by a judicious modification and mixture of the **federal principle.**

*PUBLIUS*

# Madison

NAME: _____

SECTION: _____

DATE: _____

1. Define the term "factions" and explain why they have been called the brief disease of popular government.

   _____
   _____
   _____
   _____
   _____
   _____
   _____

2. James Madison says that of the two traditional methods of curing the mischiefs of factions, the first, removing its causes, was in vain. Explain how his second option, controlling its effects, might be accomplished.

   _____
   _____
   _____
   _____
   _____
   _____
   _____

3. Explain why Madison preferred a republic to a so-called "pure democracy."

   _____
   _____
   _____
   _____
   _____

4. Federalist Paper 51 argues that in part the personal motives of government officials must be made to serve the checks and balance system. How does Madison propose that this be done?

___

5. According to Madison, what does the size of a nation have to do with its ability to sustain democratic government?

___

**Group Exercise:** Pick two ideas shared by all group members. Then, choose one idea for which there is no consensus. Next, write two laws on them telling people how to act. Note which idea requires more time and effort to finalize.

**Individual Project:** Identify and describe three inventions which have created new interest groups and factions in the U.S. since the Madisonian Era. Briefly describe new political clashes resulting from these inventions.

# The Constitutional Setting

## Louis Fisher*

Constitutional law texts have a disconcerting habit of evading discussions about the meaning of "constitutionalism." With little introduction, they plunge into an examination of individual court rulings. They provide few signposts to guide the reader in recognizing the characteristics that distinguish a constitutional system from other forms of government.

Constitutionalism is more than a shorthand expression for a constitution and the case law that accompanies it. To be worthy of the name, a constitution embodies a philosophy of government, an understanding between public officials and the people. The purpose of government is to promote the commonweal and protect individual rights, and toward that end a constitution simultaneously grants and limits power.

### The Elements of Constitutionalism

The main elements of constitutionalism are found in Bolingbroke's definition, written in 1733: "By constitution we mean, whenever we speak with propriety and exactness, that assemblage of laws, institutions and customs, derived from certain fixed principles of reason, directed to certain fixed objects of the public good, that compose the general system, according to which the community hath agreed to be governed." Governmental behavior is guided not only by laws, but also by institutions and customs, and legal principles must be set forth in a written document. Even the "unwritten" constitution of England—an amalgam of major enactments, minor statutes, judicial decisions, custom and convention, and parliamentary debates—is secured by publishing the fundamental principles for all to see: Magna Carta, the Habeas Corpus Act, the Petition of Right, and the Act of Settlement.

"Fixed principles of reason," Bolingbroke's second criterion, cannot be defined with any exact meaning and application. At the very least the concept eliminates political regimes that act in an arbitrary, irrational, and capricious manner. Constitutionalism cannot exist, even in the presence of a constitution, if the principles and standards of behavior are matters of whim for those in authority.

The American concept of "due process of law" depends on reasonableness. Courts strike down statutes when they exhibit the "vice of vagueness" (as in loyalty oaths). Citizens should not have to guess at the meaning of a law. Similarly, courts insist that legislative investigations relate to a legislative purpose. Questions during committee interrogations must be pertinent and relevant. When the judiciary finds that legislators have chosen a "rational basis" for carrying out, for example, the commerce power, the court's examination is at an end.

Fixed principles of reason, as a constitutional standard, invokes the idea of natural law, "higher law," or *jus gentium*, which the Roman jurist

---

* Copyright © 1979 from *The Constitution Between Friends* by L. Fisher. Reprinted with permission of St. Martin's Press, Inc.

Gaius called "that law which natural reason established among all mankind." Natural law is given concrete meaning in a scene from Sophocles's *Antigone*. One of Antigone's brothers, Polyneices, joined in a military attack on the city of Thebes. Among the defenders was his brother. Both men, meeting face to face in battle, were killed. The regent of Thebes, Creon, issued an edict ordering Polyneices's body to rot on the battlefield. Antigone defied the proclamation and buried her brother. When asked by Creon if she chose flagrantly to disobey his law, Antigone responds:

> *Naturally! Since Zeus never promulgated*
> *Such a Law. Nor will you find*
> *That justice publishes such laws to man below.*
> *I never thought your edicts had such force*
> *They nullified the laws of heaven, which,*
> *Unwritten, not proclaimed, can boast*
> *A currency that everlastingly is valid;*
> *An origin beyond the birth of man.*

Even Haemon, son of Creon, tells his father that he is "at loggerheads with open justice!" The chorus uses just eight words to express the issue of constitutionalism: "Where might is right there is no right."

In one of the first examples of judicial review, in Dr. Bonham's Case of 1610, Justice Coke announced that when an act of Parliament was "against common right and reason, or repugnant, or impossible to be performed the common law will controul [sic] it and adjudge such act to be void." Common right and reason, Edward S. Corwin concluded, meant something fundamental and permanent: "it is higher law."

The natural law doctrine enters American constitutionalism by way of John Locke's Second Treatise on Civil Government (1690). Locke believed that people living in the state of nature were governed by a law of nature, which obliged everyone to behave in a certain manner. Reason, "which is that law, teaches all mankind who will but consult it, that being all equal and independent, no one ought to harm another in his life, health, liberty or possessions." But humanity, biased and ignorant, failed to study the law of nature. When called upon to judge in their own cases, people punished others too harshly and excused their own transgressions. The result was that "inconveniences" (Locke's mild term) developed in the state of nature, creating the need for a common, unbiased judge to handle disputes.

Although Locke regarded the legislative power as supreme, it could not be arbitrary. The purpose of the legislature was to preserve life, liberty, and fortune. If it became destructive of this end, people would find themselves in a condition worse than the state of nature. Under such circumstances the people were at liberty to dissolve the government and establish a new legislature.

The Lockean influence carries over directly into the Declaration of Independence. The opening sentence explains that the rupture with England was necessary so that Americans might "assume among the Powers of the earth, the separate and equal station to which the Laws of Nature and of Nature's God entitle them." The idea of constitutionalism, emphasizing individual liberties and Locke's philosophy of government, appears in the very next paragraph:

> *We hold these truths to be self-evident, that all men are created equal, that they are endowed by their Creator with certain unalienable Rights, that among these are Life, Liberty, and the pursuit of Happiness. That to secure these rights, Governments are instituted among Men, deriving their just powers from the consent of the governed; That whenever any Form of Government becomes destructive of these ends, it is the Right of the People to alter or to abolish it, and to institute new Government.*

These sentiments lead to Bolingbroke's last two elements of constitutionalism: (1) government is directed to certain fixed objects of public good; and (2) the community gives its consent to be governed. Both points are consistent with Locke, who held that the legislature's power, "in the utmost bounds of it," was limited to the public good of the society. The executive's emergency power (the prerogative) was "nothing but the power of doing public good without a rule."

The principle of public consent and popular control is implicit in Locke's belief that human rights existed prior to government. If government fails to protect those rights the people can change the government. In this sense the *public's* interpretation of natural law—as developed over a period of time—becomes the ultimate test of the legitimacy of civil law. The community can never agree to be governed by tyrannical or arbitrary regimes. It never loses control over the government it creates. While regimes of that nature may exist, even supported by a written constitution, they are not constitutional forms of government.

The conviction that individuals retain certain rights, never to be surrendered to government, was basic to other political philosophers. Spinoza believed that no man's mind can possibly lie wholly at the disposition of another, for "no one can willingly transfer his natural right of free reason and judgment, or be compelled so to do." Any government attempting to control minds was, by definition, tyrannical. It was an abuse of sovereignty to seek to prescribe what was true or false, or what opinions should be held by men in their worship of God. "All these questions," to Spinoza, "fall within a man's natural right, which he cannot abdicate even with his own consent."

## Sutherland and Friedrich: Modern Views on the Elements of Constitutionalism

These elements of constitutionalism, discussed centuries ago, parallel the principles we follow (or should follow) today. Arthur E. Sutherland, in a major study published in 1965, emphasized the "freedom of men, acting through an organized majority, to control their own political and economic fate." This principle rejects hereditary rule, divine right of kings, and rule by elites. Sutherland also holds that government, to remain righteous and just, must create institutions to correct its own injustices. Or, as Madison cautioned in Federalist 51: "In framing a government which is to be administered by men over men, the great difficulty lies in this: you must first enable the government to control the governed; and in the next place oblige it to control itself."

Sutherland recognizes that his second principle jars with the first. Governmental action may be unjust even if willed by a majority of the people. Judicial officers, less vulnerable to majoritarian pressures, may declare invalid any governmental action that is inconsistent with standards of constitutional justice. This proposition is not the same as "government by judiciary." Charles Evans Hughes reached too far with his injunction: "We are under a Constitution, but the Constitution is what the judges say it is. . . ." The Supreme Court is a coequal, not superior, branch. In his inaugural address in 1861, President Lincoln denied that constitutional questions could be settled solely by Supreme Court rulings. If governmental policy upon "vital questions affecting the whole people is to be irrevocably fixed by decisions of the Supreme Court . . . the people will have ceased to be their own rulers. . . ." Constitutionalism is not entirely what the judges say it is.

In many instances justices conclude that Congress is a more appropriate forum for the determination of conflicts between individual rights and governmental action. Moreover, Congress frequently passes legislation that has the effect of modifying a previous decision of a court. Because of the "political question" doctrine, many important constitutional issues are left to Congress and the president. Even when the courts intervene they often regard as authoritative a set of practices already established by legislators and executive officials. Still other questions never reach the courts because of problems of jurisdiction, mootness, standing, ripeness, and other conditions for adjudication.

Sutherland points to three other criteria of constitutionalism. First, there must be fundamental equality before government. While human beings are not identical, the standard of equality serves to eliminate artificial and arbitrary inequalities, such as discriminatory treatment on the basis of race, sex, or religion. Second, the fundamentals of the constitutional system must be reduced to a written statement, either a concise constitution, as in America, or the fragmented, cumulative written record of England. As a final element, Sutherland depends on structure to restrain government: dividing power between the nation and the states, and then again within the central government (creating separate executive, legislative, and judicial bodies).

To Carl Friedrich this division of power cuts across two planes: functionally (separation of powers) and spatially (federalism). The doctrine of separated powers has been heavily attacked in the twentieth century, first for impeding the flow of power to public administrators (who supposedly possessed expertise not found among legislators), and secondly for interfering with the demand for centralized authority during World War II. Friedrich warned that "Many who today belittle the separation of powers seem unaware of the fact that their clamor for efficiency and expediency easily leads to dictatorship. . . ."

# THE DOCTRINE OF SEPARATED POWERS

The abuse of power by recent presidents, particularly Lyndon Johnson and Richard Nixon, generated some conventional and convenient arguments about the separation doctrine. Opponents of presidential power claimed that the framers distrusted government (especially the executive) and attempted to fashion an instrument of checks and balances to prevent tyranny. While the framers did indeed construct a system designed to restrain power, that was only part of their intention. It would be inaccurate and a disservice to their labors at the Philadelphia convention to believe that they created a document primarily for the purpose of obstructing and hampering the operation of government.

It is important to understand the practical forces that led to the creation of separated branches. Our structure of government owes its existence to the experiences of the framers, not the theory of Montesquieu or precedents borrowed from England. The framers used Montesquieu selectively, adopting what they knew from their own experience to be useful and rejecting what they knew to be inapplicable. The product was more theirs than his. Having served in public life for many years, both in the colonies and in the fledgling republic, they knew firsthand the practical duties and problems of running a government. They were continuously and intimately involved in the mundane, down-to-earth matters of conducting a war and laying the foundation for a more perfect inion. Their close familiarity with the classics in history and government, combined with the daily experience of public office, marked their special genius. It gave them vision without becoming visionaries.

British history, while valuable for the study of private and individual rights, is of marginal interest for the study of executive-legislative relationships in America. Questions of executive privilege, impoundment, and the war power cannot be resolved by harkening back to British practices. The Supreme Court made this valid observation in 1850:

> [I]n the distribution of political power between the great departments of government, there is such a wide difference between the power conferred on the President of the United States, and the authority and sovereignty which belongs to the English crown, that it would be altogether unsafe to reason from any supposed resemblance between them, either as regards conquest in war, or any other subject where the right and powers of the executive arm of the government are brought into question.

It is said that powers are separated to preserve liberties. But separation can also destroy liberties. The French constitutions of 1791 and 1848 represented ambitious efforts to erect a rigid and dogmatic separation of powers. The first document produced the reign of Napoleon Bonaparte; the next effort led to the Second Empire.

Instead of indiscriminately championing the virtues of the separation doctrine, we should remember that it can satisfy a number of objectives, not all of them worth seeking. The framers of the American Constitution did not want a political system so fragmented in structure, so divided in authority, that government could not function. Justice Story pointed out in his *Commentaries* that the framers adopted a separation of power but "endeavored to prove that a rigid adherence to it in all cases would be subversive of the efficiency of the government, and result in the destruction of the public liberties." His observation has been underscored by others. Justice Jackson correctly identified the multiple goals that motivated the framers: "While the Constitution diffuses power the better to secure liberty, it also contemplates that the practice will integrate the dispersed powers into a workable government. It enjoins upon its branches separateness but interdependence, autonomy but reciprocity."

Had this understanding prevailed in the 1960s and 1970s, we might have been spared some of the stark, corrosive confrontations between president and Congress. More recently, in *Buckley v. Valeo* (1976), the Supreme Court noted that the framers recognized that a "hermetic sealing off of the three branches of Government from one another would preclude the establishment of a Nation capable of governing itself effectively."

This conclusion is driven home by studying the political climate in which the framers produced their document. If they wanted weak government, if they wanted it shackled and ineffective, they could have retained the Articles of Confederation. They decided against this, for very good reason. The framers had labored under a weak government from 1774 to 1787, and deliberately rejected that model in favor of stronger central powers. Consciously, at the national level, they vested greater powers in an executive.

The distrust of executive power in 1776—against the king of England and the royal governors—was tempered by two developments in the following decade. Americans discovered that state legislative bodies could be as oppressive and capricious toward individual rights as executive bodies. Also, many delegates to the Continental Congress watched with growing apprehension as the Congress found itself incapable of discharging its duties and responsibilities. Support began to grow for an independent executive, in large part for the purpose of assuring efficiency.

This interpretation challenges a famous dissent by Justice Brandeis, who claimed that the separation of powers doctrine was adopted *not* for efficiency but to preclude the exercise of arbitrary power. Brandeis's dictum, invoked regularly by those who urged legislative reassertion in the 1960s, is a half-truth. The historical record is clear and persuasive that the inefficiency of the Continental Congress convinced the framers of the need for a separate and independent executive.

The practical source of the separation doctrine is generally overlooked or ignored. Much more satisfying, emotionally if not intellectually, is the belief that the Constitution was pounded into shape from abstract principles, with the name of Montesquieu leading the list of theorists. Gladstone reinforced this impression by describing the American Constitution as the most wonderful document ever "struck off at a given time" by the mind of man. But the framers did not create out of whole cloth the document that guides us today. They were alert to the excesses and injustices committed by state legislators. They were sensitive, very sensitive, to the demonstrated ineptitude of the Continental Congress, which had to administer and adjudicate while trying to legislate. One branch of government performed all the tasks.

Because of the repeated failings of the Congress, it soon began to delegate power—first to committees, then to boards staffed by people from outside the legislature, and finally, in 1781, to single executive officers. These events occurred prior to the Philadelphia convention. The Constitution marked a continuity with political developments already underway. John Jay, after serving as secretary of foreign affairs under the Continental Congress, remained in office in the Washington administration until Thomas Jefferson could take his place. Henry Knox was secretary of war under the Continental Congress and under President Washington. Because of this orderly transition it has been said that the Constitution did not create a system of separated powers; rather, a system of separated powers created the Constitution.

Several delegates to the ratifying conventions objected to the fact that the branches of government—legislative, executive, and judicial—had been intermingled instead of being kept separate. "How is the executive?" demanded one irate delegate at Virginia's ratifying convention. "Contrary to the opinion of all the best writers, blended with the legislature. We have asked for bread, and they have given us a stone." This outcry enlisted some support, but not much. By the time of the Philadelphia convention the doctrine of separated powers had been modified to allow for checks and balances. One contemporary pamphleteer called the separation doctrine, in its pure form, a "hackneyed principle" and a "trite maxim." Madison devoted several of his *Federalist* essays to the need for overlapping powers, claiming that the concept was superior to the impracticable partitioning of powers demanded by some of the Antifederalists.

The system of checks and balances is not a contradiction to the separation doctrine. The two are complementary. Without the power to withstand encroachments by another branch, a department might find its powers drained to the point of extinction. The Constitution allocated separate functions to separate branches, but "parchment barriers" were not dependable. It was necessary, Madison concluded in Federalist 51, that "ambition must be made to counteract ambition," while in Federalist 48 he warned: "unless these departments be so far connected and blended as to give to each a constitutional control over the others, the degree of separation which the maxim requires, as essential to a free government, can never in practice be duly maintained."

The case for a strict separation of powers was tested in the form of an amendment to the Constitution. Three states—Virginia, North Carolina, and Pennsylvania—wanted to add a separation clause to the national bill of rights. The proposed language read as follows: "The powers delegated by this constitution are appropriated to the departments to which they are respectively distributed: so that the legislative department shall never exercise the powers vested in the executive or judicial[,] nor the executive exercise the powers vested in the legislative or judicial, nor the judicial exercise the powers vested in the legislative or executive departments." Congress rejected this proposal, as well as a substitute amendment to make the three departments "separate and distinct."

Although powers are not separated in a pure sense, it does not help to characterize the federal government as a "blend of powers." The branches have distinctly different responsibilities, practices, and traditions. A certain distance between the branches is preserved by Article I, Section 6 of the Constitution, which prohibits members of either house from holding appointive office. Congress is prohibited from reducing the compensation of the president and members of the judiciary. The Speech or Debate Clause was designed to protect legislators from executive or judicial harassment.

Any occupant of the White House, after a short time in office, appreciates the degree to which an institutional separation exists, whether Congress is in the hands of the president's party or the

opposition party. That is as it should be. The president does not share with Congress his pardoning power, nor does Congress share with the courts its taxing and appropriations powers (although the judiciary is participating in the outer fringes). In 1974 the Supreme Court highlighted the separation that exists in the federal government by stating that the judicial power vested in the federal courts by Article III of the Constitution "can no more be shared with the Executive Branch than the Chief Executive, for example, can share with the Judiciary the veto power, or the Congress share with the judiciary the power to override a Presidential veto." Even in administrative agencies that discharge executive, legislative, and judicial duties, those tasks are kept separate. Someone who prosecutes a case, for example, would not be called upon to render a decision on the dispute.

## The Durability of the Separation Doctrine

Has the balance among political institutions, as fashioned by the framers, failed to meet the test of time? Have events overtaken theory? Tocqueville, quoting with approval a passage from Jefferson, believed that the "tyranny of the legislature" in America would continue for a number of years before being replaced by a tyranny of the executive. Yet presidential power, after cresting with Abraham Lincoln, subsided in the face of a determined and resurgent Congress. Writing in 1885, Woodrow Wilson believed that Congress had become the dominant branch. He said that the Constitution of 1787 was a form of government in name rather than in reality, "the form of the Constitution being one of nicely adjusted, ideal balances, whilst the actual form of our present government is simply a scheme of congressional supremacy."

Two decades later, glancing with covetous eyes at the White House, Wilson predicted that the president "must always, henceforth, be one of the great powers of the world . . . We have but begun to see the presidential office in this light; but it is the light which will more and more beat upon it . . ." The new wellspring of presidential power, according to his analysis, was the burden of international responsibilities thrust upon the United States. The Great Depression of the 1930s, joined with the personal qualities of Franklin D.

Roosevelt, gave further impetus to executive power.

The reputation of Congress plummeted with such swiftness that Samuel P. Huntington, in an influential study published in 1965, suggested that unless Congress drastically altered its mode of operation it should abandon its legislative role and concentrate on serving constituents and overseeing the agencies. The condition of Congress appeared to deteriorate even further, for in 1968 Philip B. Kurland charged that it did not have the "guts to stand up to its responsibilities." Congress was prostrate, the president transcendent. Kurland invited us to visit the "sickbed of another constitutional concept—the notion of separation of powers." Not only was the patient diseased, the affliction seemed terminal. Theoretically a cure was possible, but Kurland saw no grounds for optimism. To him the patient had lost the will to live.

These dire predictions suggest that the imbalance between president and Congress is chronic and permanent. At no time, however, has either branch been as all-powerful or as defective as critics maintained. Congress, though its particular lifestyle may offend our tastes, is alive and well. The political system has shown a capacity for self-correction. Two presidents, testing the limits of their power during the 1960s and 1970s, were driven from office. Congress, flexing its muscles during this time of reassertion, ran into barriers erected by the courts. In 1976 the Supreme Court ruled against the Federal Election Commission because Congress had staked out a role for itself in the appointment of four of the commission's six members. The court held this procedure contrary to the separation doctrine. Congress could not both legislate and enforce.

The separation doctrine, subjected to ridicule for much of the twentieth century, still retains vitality. A longer view of American history provides room for confidence. Senator George Wharton Pepper offered this sound perspective: "[I]f the geometers of 1787 hoped for perfect peace and if the psychologists of that day feared disastrous conflicts, history, as so often happens, has proved that hopes were dupes and fears were liars. There has not been perfect peace; but the conflicts have not proved disastrous."

## IMPLIED POWERS

In civics courses we are taught that the American Constitution is one of limited and enumerated powers. This is satisfactory only if we stay inside the classroom. Once we venture out and observe the actual workings of government, we must confront and resolve a perplexing array of powers that are not expressly stated. They parade under asserted names: implied and inherent, incidental and interred, aggregate, powers created by custom and acquiescence, and delicate "penumbras," "interstices," and "glosses" that add strange and new qualities to the Constitution. Whatever the name the result is identical: the conferral of a power that is neither expressly stated in the Constitution nor specifically granted by Congress.

The "genius and spirit of our institutions are hostile to the exercise of implied powers." Thus spake the Supreme Court in 1821. After making the appropriate gesture it proceeded to deal amicably with these hostile forces. It was utopian, said the court, to believe that government could exist without leaving the exercise of discretion somewhere. In this particular case the court recognized that Congress possessed powers not expressly granted by the Constitution: the power to issue warrants to compel a party's appearance and the power to punish for contempt.

If a constitution is intended to limit power, and if we admit powers that are not expressly stated, can government be kept within bounds? Let the imagination run to far corners and the answer is No. But let "experience be our guide" (the framers' preference), and the prospect is more reassuring. The American Constitution cannot survive purely on the basis of express powers or "strict constructionism," a phrase made popular by the Nixon administration.

The debate in 1789 on the Bill of Rights settled the need to grant implied powers to government. Members of the First Congress proposed that the Tenth Amendment be so worded that all powers not "expressly delegated" to the federal government would be reserved to the states. Madison immediately objected, insisting that it was impossible to limit a government to the exercise of express powers. There "must necessarily be admitted powers by implication, unless the Constitution descended to recount every minutiae [sic]." After elimination of "expressly" the Tenth Amendment was adopted with this language: "The powers not delegated to the United States by the Constitution, nor prohibited by it to the States, are reserved to the States respectively, or to the people."

Chief Justice Marshall cited this debate when he ruled on the implied power of Congress to establish a United States Bank, even though not expressly permitted by the Constitution. Marshall observed that there was no phrase in the document which (like the Articles of Confederation) "excludes incidental or implied powers; and which requires that everything granted shall be expressly and minutely described." A constitution represented a general structure, not a detailed instruction manual:

> *A constitution, to contain an accurate detail of all the subdivisions of which its great powers will admit, and of all the means by which they may be carried into execution, would partake of the prolixity of a legal code, and could scarcely be embraced by the human mind. It would, probably, never be understood by the public. Its nature, therefore, requires, that only its great outlines should be marked, its important objects designated, and the minor ingredients which compose those objects, be deduced from the nature of the objects themselves.*

In interpreting the Constitution it is important to remember that government is created to carry out certain functions required for the people. A number of essential activities find no ready reference in the Constitution. As Marshall remarked: "All admit, that the government may, legitimately, punish any violation of its laws; and yet, this is not among the enumerated powers of Congress."

The theory of implied powers was treated to an extended debate in 1793 after President Washington issued what is now known as the Neutrality Proclamation. His administration was subjected to bitter attacks, particularly from those who sympathized with France. Alexander Hamilton, writing under the pseudonym "Pacificus," denied that the proclamation had been issued without authority. Hamilton derived the power to issue proclamations from the general clause of Article II of the Constitution: "the executive Power shall be vested in a President of the United States of America." He believed that it was unsound to limit the executive power to the particular items enumerated in subsequent sections. They should not derogate from the "comprehensive grant" of power in the general clause, "further than as it may be coupled with express restrictions or limitations." With the exception of the Senate's participation in the appointment of officers and in the making of treaties, and Congress's power to declare war and to grant letters of marque and reprisal, all other executive powers were lodged solely in the President.

Jefferson, outraged by this doctrine, wrote to Madison: "For God's sake, my dear Sir, take up your pen, select the most striking heresies and cut him to pieces in the face of the public." Madison produced five articles under the name "Helvidius," charging that Hamilton's reading of the Constitution must be condemned "as no less vicious in theory than it would be dangerous in practice." The expansive interpretation of executive power would mean that "no citizen could any longer guess at the character of the government under which he lives; the most penetrating jurist would be unable to scan the extent of constructive prerogative."

Madison indulged in hyperbole, as did Hamilton. We could scarcely expect much else in the supercharged political atmosphere of 1793, heightened as it was by the intense rivalry between Hamilton and Jefferson in the cabinet. But the issue they raised was to remain active. By the end of the nineteenth century the issue of implied powers for the president reached the Supreme Court in the case of *In re Neagle* (1890). Justice Stephen Johnson Field, serving as circuit justice in California, had his life threatened by two malcontents. David Neagle, a United States deputy marshal, was assigned to ride circuit to offer protection. One morning during breakfast, Field was assaulted by David Terry, one of the malcontents. Neagle, after identifying himself, shot and killed Terry. No statute authorized the president to appoint a deputy marshal for the purpose of protecting a Supreme Court justice traveling in his circuit.

The court, split six to two, upheld the assignment of Neagle and his immunity from state law. His attorney acknowledged that there was no single specific statute making it a duty to furnish protection to a Supreme Court justice. To the attorney, however, whatever was "necessarily implied is as much a part of the Constitution and statutes as if it were actually expressed therein." Justice Miller, announcing the opinion for the court, agreed:

> *In the view we take of the Constitution of the United States, any obligation fairly and properly inferrible from that instrument, or any duty of the marshal to be derived from the general scope of his duties under the laws of the United States, is "a law" within the meaning of this phrase.*

The two dissenting justices did not dispute the proposition that "whatever is necessarily implied in the Constitution and laws of the United States is as much a part of them as if it were actually expressed." Nor did they question the propriety of Neagle's action. But they related implied powers to this clause in Article I which augments the powers of Congress: "Congress shall have power . . . to make all laws which shall be necessary and proper for carrying into execution the foregoing powers, and all other powers vested by this Constitution in the government of the United States, or in any department or officer thereof." Finding no such law, and believing that the United States government was powerless to try and punish a man charged with murder in this offense, they would have had Neagle placed in the custody of the sheriff of San Joaquin, California, to be tried by the courts of that state.

Theodore Roosevelt and William Howard Taft, debating the boundaries of presidential authority, appear to have held diametrically opposed positions on implied power. Roosevelt asserted that it was the president's right and duty to do "anything that the needs of the Nation demanded, unless such action was forbidden by the Constitution or by the laws." His argument follows the one presented in Hamilton's "Pacificus" writings. Taft maintained that the president

*can exercise no power which cannot be fairly and reasonably traced to some specific grant of power or justly implied and included within such express grant as proper and necessary to its exercise. Such specific grant must be either in the Federal Constitution or in an act of Congress passed in pursuance thereof.*

Use of the words "express" and "specific" appears to put Taft in the camp of those who believe in enumerated powers. But it is clear that he recognized the need for implied powers—powers that can be "fairly and reasonably traced" or "justly implied." He even adds to the Constitution a necessary-and-proper clause for the president. When Taft's study is read in full, it is evident that he adhered to a generous interpretation of executive power: incidental powers to remove officers, inferable powers to protect the lives and property of American citizens living abroad, powers created by custom, and emergency powers (such as Lincoln's suspension of the writ of habeas corpus during the Civil War). Summing up, Taft said that executive power was limited "so far as it is possible to limit such a power consistent with that discretion and promptness of action that are essential to preserve the interests of the public in times of emergency, or legislative neglect or inaction."

# FISHER

NAME: _____
SECTION: _____
DATE: _____

1. List Bolingbroke's elements of constitutionalism.

   _____
   _____
   _____
   _____
   _____
   _____
   _____

2. Explain briefly whether the doctrine of Separation-of-Powers is compatible with the doctrine of Checks and Balances.

   _____
   _____
   _____
   _____
   _____
   _____
   _____

3. List and define at least six types of powers that are not explicitly written in the constitution.

   _____
   _____
   _____
   _____
   _____
   _____
   _____

4. How has the doctrine of Judicial Review been used to strengthen the Constitution of the U.S.A.?

_____
_____
_____
_____
_____
_____
_____

5. Name and describe three historical events that led to the modification of the Framers' constitutional system.

_____
_____
_____
_____
_____
_____
_____

**Group Exercise:** Review the present Constitution of the U.S. and recommend a change. Why do you want it changed?

**Individual Project:** Select a recent newspaper article which reports on a current constitutional issue and explain your opinions on it.

# American Voting Behavior: Partisanship Turnout, and Types of Elections

## David W. Winder

Electoral behavior, the way citizens vote in elections, is a very important aspect of politics in countries which have democratic forms of government. Currently in the United States, the way we vote on election day determines our officeholders and shapes the quality of the government. When the election takes place, voters choose members of the Congress, the president (through the electoral college), governors, members of state legislatures, mayors, city council members, and other public officials. So elections are crucial in charting the course which government will follow at the national, state, and local levels in America. Elections are also a key aspect of politics and government in Western European countries such as Great Britain and France, and the other North American countries, Canada and Mexico.

In this selection, we will look at changes in American electoral behavior in the period covering the mid-1950s through the mid-1990s. Voting turnout (the share of the electorate voting on election day), partisan choice (the party which voters choose), and types of American elections will be covered.

The 1996 election was an interesting race, with incumbent President Bill Clinton facing his Republican challenger, former senator Bob Dole. This election followed the contest in 1992, in which Clinton won the presidency by defeating the Republican incumbent, George Bush, and the third candidate, Ross Perot. Since Clinton campaigned in 1992 on a promise to improve the economy, one theme of his 1996 campaign was to claim credit for the economy's improvement and increase in jobs. In the 1996 race, Al Gore ran for reelection as Clinton's vice-president, and Jack Kemp was chosen by Dole to contend for the vice-presidency. Kemp, as former Secretary of Housing and Urban Development, brought with him a concern for poverty and urban issues which could appeal to minority voters. Kemp's experience as a professional football quarterback brought interest to the ticket, and Elizabeth Dole's high-profile background, which also included a cabinet position as Secretary of Transportation under President Reagan, drew attention to the Republicans. Hillary Rodham Clinton served as an active first lady and was often a "lightning rod" for Republican criticism. In examining partisan choice, voter turnout, and types of elections, we will look at the 1992 and 1996 presidential elections to provide interesting examples.

## PARTISANSHIP

Partisanship refers to the voter's attachment to a political party. The concept of partisanship called "party identification" was developed in a classic book on American electoral behavior, *The American Voter*. This book, written by Angus Campbell and others, focused on the 1952 and 1956 elections, and both of these contests featured a victory by World War II hero Dwight Eisenhower (a Republican) over the Democrat, Adlai Stevenson. The authors view party identification as a psychological identification with (or attachment to) one party or the alternative party. To measure party identification, voters were asked if they viewed themselves as Democrats, Republicans, or independents. Types of party identification ranged from strong Republicans to strong Democrats, also including types which identified more weakly with either party and independents. During the 1950s, there were generally about 13 percent strong Republicans and 22 percent strong

Democrats in the electorate, so that there was a core of loyalists ready to vote for each party in national elections with the Democrats holding an advantage.

Before discussing party identification further, we should briefly consider a topic which comes up in relationship to the parties: the role of ideology in politics. Political ideology has been defined by Janda, Berry, and Goldman, as "a consistent set of values and beliefs about the proper purpose and scope of government." Common ideologies in America provide the basis to divide citizens into three groups based on political beliefs: liberals, moderates, and conservatives. Liberals form an ideological group which tends to favor more government action to solve social and economic problems, and they are more supportive of non-traditional lifestyles such as newer roles for working women and gay rights. Conservatives favor less government activity and are less supportive of alternative lifestyles. Moderates fall somewhere in between liberals and conservatives in these areas.

Considering party identification in a comparative way, it is important to realize that in many other democracies voters have a choice of more than two major parties with which they may identify. In addition they have the possible choice to consider themselves to be independents. Based on information presented by Gallagher, Laver, and Mair, in Britain the Conservative, Labour, Liberal, and Social Democratic parties all won at least 10 percent of the vote in elections during the 1980s. Conservatives, led by Margaret Thatcher (an imposing political figure and close ally of Ronald Reagan), controlled most of the seats in the British parliament throughout the 1980s. In France, four parties achieved at least a ten percent vote in the 1980s, and the French selection of parties includes stronger "leftist" parties, namely the Communist and Socialist parties. Many Americans would welcome a chance to choose between more than two major party candidates, whom they see as dull and similar.

In addition to the voter's party identification, two other factors are generally held to affect the voter's choice of a candidate to vote for: candidate image and issue positions. Thus a voter in 1996, faced with the choice between Dole, Clinton, and Perot, could simply follow the party attachment and choose the candidate (Dole or Clinton) who matched his or her party. As an alternative, the image of the candidates might be the deciding factor. For example, some citizens might be attracted to what they see as Dole's more solid character, based on his heroic military service in World War II and his achievements in government despite a physical disability. These voters might be turned off by Clinton's rumored extra-marital affairs and lack of military service in the Vietnam War period, or by Perot's "waffling" on his candidacy in 1992. In terms of issues, other voters might be drawn to Clinton's record of economic success, his plans to make post-secondary education more available to push the economy ahead, and his proposed "children's programs" (such as adoption tax credits). They might see Dole's and Perot's prospects for economic success as being weak. So voters are primarily drawn to vote for a candidate not only by party but also by the images of those running for office or the issues which arise in the campaign.

Party identification has been chosen by political scientists such as Luttbeg and Gant (in their book *American Electoral Behavior 1952–1992*) as the most important of the three factors in shaping peoples' votes. Some scholars, though (for example Nie and his co-authors), stress the rising importance of issues in influencing voters' choices.

Party identification and voters' choices divide along group lines. The traditional view is that Democratic support has been from a broad collection of groups which have voted together since the 1930s, the New Deal coalition. Dunham discusses this coalition, arguing that it was made up of southerners, city dwellers, the poor, African Americans, Jews, Roman Catholics, and members of unions. This coalition liked the domestic social programs of the Democratic party, such as government activity to improve the economy. The major change in this picture is that some of the New Deal coalition defected during the Reagan and Bush elections in the 1980s, leaving primarily the African Americans, city dwellers and lower-income groups as the core of Democratic support. President Clinton appealed to some of the defectors in 1992 with his unified all-Southern ticket (Al Gore is from Tennessee) and his social programs, including a national service plan to provide for a college education to be paid back with government service in occupations such as teacher or policeman. He also campaigned in person on his bus tours and appeared in new forums on television, such as Larry King's talk show and MTV. Was his campaign successful in reuniting the old coalition from the 1930s? He had some success in doing so, and this will be discussed in the final section on types of elections.

The most striking trend in party identification is the growth in independent voters between the 1950s and the 1990s. In this period the pure "independent" category grew from 8 percent in 1956 to 12 percent in 1992, as is reflected in figures presented by Luttbeg and Gant. If we include weak identifiers (leaning Democratic and leaning Republican categories) in the total independent category, the growth was from 23 percent to 38 percent over the same span of years.

What could account for this great growth in independent voters? One answer is to look at the other categories to see that both parties lost strength among their strong party identifiers between 1956 and 1992. From the 1950s to the 1990s, the growth in independent voters happened at the expense of the strong party identifiers from the Democrats and Republicans.

The 1994 congressional elections provide an example of the more recent vulnerability of the traditionally strong Democratic party in the electorate. Davidson and Oleszek, in their book *Congress and Its Members*, note that in 1994 the Republicans gained control of both chambers of Congress for the first time in four decades. Although the party of the president usually loses seats in the off-year election (the non-presidential election year), the Democrats' losses in 1994 were unusually heavy. Their losses were particularly great in the South, a region in which whites voted Republican for House seats by almost a two-to-one margin.

What changes go along with the rise of the independent voters? Part of the explanation for the importance of the non-partisan voters is youth. As Dunham shows, in the 1980s the age group most dominated by independents was the 22–25 year-olds. Ticket-splitting, voting for more than one party on election day, has become more common over the past forty years. A voter may choose to split his or her ticket by choosing Republicans for president, congressman, and county commissioner and then picking Democrats for governor, senator, and city councilman. Campaigns have come to rely more on the candidate's appeal and advertising conveyed over the electronic media and less on the party's structure. One of Ronald Reagan's great political strengths was that, with his speaking ability and personality, he was seen on television by many as the "great communicator."

## VOTING TURNOUT

Voting turnout is the percentage of those persons who are legally eligible to vote who actually do vote on election day. Turnout varies by the type of election, with more voters showing up and casting ballots in presidential election years

than when the presidential election is not held. Voting is viewed by many people in our society as an important act of citizenship. In a democratic form of government, reasonably high voting turnout levels indicate citizen interest in and involvement with the process of politics and government. So lower voting turnout levels are a cause for concern. Turnout in U.S. presidential elections has recently been in the 50–55 percent range, and this turnout level ranks the United States below nearly all Western European nations.

Although the United States has low voting participation, the nation has remained politically stable over most of its history. The lack of interest in and disenchantment with politics and government for some people suggested by low voting turnout is a bothersome reality but not a threat to security for the American political system.

Individual characteristics such as education, race, and age are related to voter turnout. Those with lower education vote at a lower rate than do those who are more educated. African Americans vote at a lower rate than do whites, but this gap has narrowed. Regarding the age factor, the youngest adults have the lowest rate of voting turnout.

Once again turning to a theory of democracy, many see an ideal democracy as one in which voters turn out at a high percentage rate to support their parties and candidates in a competitive election. In view of this theory, the trend in American elections since 1960 is quite disappointing. According to election statistics presented by Ross, the turnout in presidential election years in this recent period has declined from a high of 63 percent in 1960, the year John Kennedy was elected, to 50 percent in 1988. After rising again into the percentage range of the mid-fifties in 1992, turnout declined to a level around the 50 percent figure again in 1996. The 1960 election, which Kennedy narrowly won, was an exciting one highlighted by television debates in which Kennedy presented an attractive image and scored points with voters, as opposed to Nixon's grim, unshaven appearance. In election years when the president does not run, turnout has been as low as 35 percent in 1978, which is just above one-third of the electorate.

Why has U.S. voting turnout decreased over the last four decades? It is easier to observe that turnout has declined than to explain why this decline has happened. One explanation is that certain changes in the legal requirements to vote have aimed to make the system more democratic and to provide adults a fair opportunity to vote. However, an unintended consequence has been lower turnout levels. For example, the Twenty-sixth Amendment to the U.S. Constitution (ratified in the 1970s) required states to make eighteen years of age the requirement for voting. This change allowed more young voters, who have lower turnout rates, to enter the pool of eligible voters. Another relevant action, ratification of the Twenty-fourth Amendment in the 1960s, prohibited poll taxes from being charged on voters. Allowing more poor people to vote, while commendable, increases the share of less educated people in the electorate. Again, the less educated are less likely to vote.

A likely cause of declining voting turnout is the rising share of independent voters. Data presented in *American Electoral Behavior 1952–1992* shows that from the 1950s to 1992 strong party identifiers maintained their levels of turnout. In contrast, turnout rates for pure independents have declined on election day. This trend is understandable, since independent voters are generally less interested in political campaigns. We can compare them to the sports fans who don't care much about either of two teams playing for a football championship and who don't attend the game, while the die-hard rooters for the two teams will have more enthusiasm and will show up at the game, even in snow or rain.

Voting turnout in the United States is low in comparison with other Western democracies, and U.S. turnout is generally declining (with the recent exception of 1992). While it is clear that voting turnout has generally declined, political scientists have had a difficult time trying to establish definitely the reasons for the decline, although many ideas have been proposed.

## TYPES OF ELECTIONS

The two elections of the 1990s showed major similarities and certain differences. In both cases, the younger Democrat Bill Clinton defeated an older Republican presidential candidate who had many years of service in Washington, D.C. in various capacities. The age factor received particular attention in 1996, with Bob Dole already in his seventies. In both election years, the "character issue" shadowed Bill Clinton. In 1996 Clinton's associates were being prosecuted in connection with the "Whitewater" matter, a top advisor (Dick Morris) resigned following a sex scandal, and continuing questions were raised about Clinton's character. Both in 1992 and 1996, the Democrat pushed for social programs or tax policies to encourage social outcomes. In 1996, for example, Clinton argued for tax breaks for businesses which hire former welfare recipients and for funding a program to improve children's reading skills.

In terms of contrasts, Clinton's role as a candidate reversed between the two elections. He ran as a challenger to an incumbent president in 1992, and then he ran on his record as an incumbent in 1996. For the Republicans, Bush stressed foreign policy and military aspects in 1992, while Dole proposed a 15 percent tax cut in 1996. In focusing on a particular election for the discussion of three types of elections, we will mainly deal with the 1992 race which included the interesting dimension of a third presidential candidate who showed unusual strength at the polls.

Ross Perot made a big issue out of the large budget deficits in 1992, attacked politics-as-usual in Washington, and called for major changes in government which he compared to "cleaning out the barn." The most surprising thing about the election was the strong showing by Perot, who gained 19 percent of the popular vote, a figure which is unprecedented in modern elections for a candidate not nominated by a major party. Some may see Perot's success as one more indication of a period of dealignment, a time in which parties are not very important and many voters are ticket-splitters.

In *The American Voter*, the following three types of presidential elections are identified: maintaining, deviating, and realigning elections. In a maintaining election, the existing pattern of party identification shapes the vote, so that the party with the most identifiers wins the election. We can compare this type to a favored team winning a sports event. Like an upset in sports, a deviating election is one in which the basic pattern of party loyalty remains without much change, but the impact of the candidates and issues causes the majority party to lose. After such an election, voting returns to normal. Finally, in the rarer realigning election, the basic pattern of party loyalty changes in a lasting way. For example, Campbell et al. point out that the Great Depression of the 1930s was such a shock that it caused groups hit hardest economically to move from the Republican to the Democratic party in the realigning elections of the 1930s. This resulted in landslide victories for the Democrat, Franklin D. Roosevelt, who proposed social welfare programs in his New Deal.

Before placing the election of 1992 into one of the three types, it's important to point out the uniqueness of this election. Although the Democratic and Republican candidates for president finished well ahead of the independent Perot (Clinton received 43 percent and Bush won 37 percent of the vote), the 19 percent showing by Ross Perot is highly unusual in modern times. Technically, Perot was not a "third party" candidate, since his supporting organization, United We Stand, was not organized in party form for the 1992 election. The wealthy businessman did run on the Reform party ticket in 1996. As is shown in Table 1, the only other candidates not from the major parties to win more than a minimal 2 percent of the vote since 1956 were George Wallace in 1968 with 14 percent and John Anderson in 1980 with 7 percent. The Wallace vote occurred in a period of social upheaval in the 1960s, following the height of the civil rights movement and during the Vietnam conflict, events which may account for that departure from the usual two-party races. Perot's significant share of the vote in 1992, big enough to swing any election shown in Table 1, highlights and emphasizes the importance of independent voters and ticket-splitters as a key to winning modern presidential elections. The general tendency for candidates who lack the endorsement of a major party to fail to retain their support over time is shown by Perot's lower share of the vote in 1996.

How does the 1992 election fit into one of the three types of presidential races: maintaining, deviating, or realigning elections? First, consider the matter of party identification. As Janda and his co-authors point out, "The Democrats' status as the majority party has also lessened over time. Nevertheless, most Americans today still identify with one of the two major parties, and there are still more Democrats than Republicans." Since the young Democratic ticket was victorious, one key characteristic of a maintaining election held true: the party with more identifiers among the nation's voters won the election. It's also true, of course, that the whole idea of the importance of party identification is compromised when almost one-fifth of the electorate chooses a businessman who ran for president without a major party's support.

Next, we should look at the behavior of groups to see if they mostly "stayed at home," voting with their previous party ties. In 1992 most groups voted for the party that they had always supported for president since the Carter-Ford election in 1976 or even earlier. These groups might be compared to a young fellow at a party who "danced with the girl who brought him there," faithful to his initial choice. Based on information presented by Ross, African Americans,

## TABLE 2 PRESIDENTIAL ELECTIONS: 1956–1996

| Election Year | Democratic Candidates | Republican Candidates | Other Candidates | Dem. % | Rep. % | Other % |
|---|---|---|---|---|---|---|
| 1956 | Stevenson<br>Kefauver | Eisenhower<br>Nixon | | 42.0 | 57.4 | |
| 1960 | Kennedy<br>Johnson | Nixon<br>Lodge | | 49.7 | 49.5 | |
| 1964 | Johnson<br>Humphrey | Goldwater<br>Miller | | 61.1 | 38.5 | |
| 1968 | Humphrey<br>Muskie | Nixon<br>Agnew | Wallace<br>LeMay | 42.7 | 43.4 | 13.5 |
| 1972 | McGovern<br>Shriver | Nixon<br>Agnew | | 37.5 | 60.7 | |
| 1976 | Carter<br>Mondale | Ford<br>Dole | | 50.1 | 48.0 | |
| 1980 | Carter<br>Mondale | Reagan<br>Bush | Anderson<br>Lucey | 41.0 | 50.7 | 6.6 |
| 1984 | Mondale<br>Ferraro | Reagan<br>Bush | | 40.6 | 58.8 | |
| 1988 | Dukakis<br>Bentsen | Bush<br>Quayle | | 45.6 | 53.4 | |
| 1992 | Clinton<br>Gore | Bush<br>Quayle | Perot<br>Stockdale | 43.0 | 37.4 | 18.9 |
| 1996 | Clinton<br>Gore | Dole<br>Kemp | Perot<br>Choate | 49.9 | 41.4 | 8.6 |

*Sources.* For 1956–1992 data source is *America Votes 20* by R. M. Scammon and A.V. McGillivray, 1993, Washington: Congressional Quarterly; for 1996 data source is *New York Times*, November 7, 1996, sec. B, p. 5.

*Note.* Presidential candidates are listed above vice-presidential candidates. Only candidates receiving more than 2 percent of the vote are included.

Latinos, Jews, those in the poorest category of income, and Democratic identifiers all voted for Clinton, just as they had for Carter and every Democrat for president since 1976. Whites, white Protestants, the richest two income categories, and Republican identifiers remained faithful to the Republican ticket in 1992, as they had each time since 1976. A couple of swing groups, Catholics and Eastern voters, went for Carter in 1976, voted Republican in the three elections in the 1980s, and returned to Clinton in 1992. They are more like the person who came to the dance with his partner, enjoyed a flirtation with another dancer, and went home with their original partner.

The group evidence also supports the view that the 1992 election was basically a maintaining election. Most of the major groups voted for the party that had claimed their loyalty for more than fifteen years, and the 1992 election best fits a maintaining election among the three election types.

In the 1996 election the "gender gap," involving the contrast between the voting preferences of men and women as groups of voters, was very prominent. This difference has its roots in the elections of the 1980s. In 1996 the "gender gap" was important, with Bill Clinton receiving a support level among female voters that was ten percentage points higher than his rate of support from men. Clinton's vague campaign theme of building "a bridge to the twenty-first century" took on a much more specific form in his positions on issues favoring women and children. Clinton built on his pro-choice position on abortion when he signed the family leave bill. He made various proposals in the 1996 campaign which appealed to women: expanding family leave, more health insurance for children, and a variety of tax deductions and other measures to invest in education and make it more widely accessible. Much of Bob Dole's 1996 campaign was built on his proposal for a large tax cut and the "character issue" (contrasting his virtues with doubts about Bill Clinton's character), but these issues lacked a specific appeal to women voters.

One lesson that jumps off the page in Table 2 for the Democrats is that a Southerner who is more moderate than much of the party has the best chance to win the presidency. Three out of the four Democratic presidents since 1956 have been Southerners (Johnson, Carter, and Clinton), and the latter two were more moderate than the liberal wing of the Democratic party. Clinton stands out as the only Democrat in this period to win two presidential elections. By contrast, the four Republicans who won were more varied in terms of the geographic regions and ideologies.

## Conclusion

This selection has focused on changing American electoral behavior from the 1950s to the 1990s. In discussing voting behavior over this period, several key points (which follow) have been made:

1. The independents' share of the electorate grew, while the percentages of strong identifiers from both parties decreased.
2. There has been a general decline in voting turnout.
3. Ross Perot won an unusually large share of the vote (19 percent) in 1992, for a candidate without ties to a major party. The size of the Perot vote shows numerical strength and the pivotal role which independents and ticket-splitters can have in the electorate.
4. Among the three major varieties of elections described in *The American Voter*, the 1992 election best fits the maintaining type.
5. Southerners had the best chance among Democratic nominees to win the presidency.

Some observers see the trends toward less party identification and lower turnout as bad signs for the health of American politics. The 1992 election showed more drama and excitement than other recent elections and a temporary increase in voting turnout, although turnout fell again in 1996. However we view the changes, elections remain at the heart of the democratic process and ultimately determine the quality of American national government.

# Winder

NAME: _____

SECTION: _____

DATE: _____

1. Define voter turnout, and explain its importance in maintaining popular government.

2. Does the American system of two-party elections tend to increase or decrease the intensity of partisanship, as compared to multi-party systems? Explain your answer.

3. Has voter turnout increased, decreased, or remained the same in recent years? Why?

4. Describe each of the various types of elections in the United States.

_____
_____
_____
_____
_____
_____
_____

5. Several factors have been described as influencing people's votes; which do you think is the most important and why?

_____
_____
_____
_____
_____
_____
_____

**Group Exercise:** Convene and poll the group members' opinions on any six issues. Then, poll members on the intensity of opinions. To what extent are any members willing to take time off from work to vote on these issues? Why?

**Individual Project:** Write a brief essay explaining whether or not you support same-party control over both Congress and the White House.

# Partners in Power: Federalism in the U.S.

## Richard T. Saeger

Does anybody really care about state government? The news media don't cover it, which may explain why most Americans can't identify the names of their state legislators. Most do know who their governor is, however, although sometimes they confuse the name of the governor with the name of one of their U. S. Senators. When asked which level of American government is most responsive to their concerns, people pick state government last after federal and local.

Republicans in the 104th U.S. Congress (1995–1997) vowed to return power to the states, and in a real sense, they succeeded with welfare reform, reform of unfunded mandates, etc. Bob Dole, the Republican nominee for President in 1996, campaigned with a laminated copy in his coat pocket of the Tenth Amendment to the U.S. Constitution: "The powers not delegated to the United States by the Constitution, nor prohibited by it to the States, are reserved to the states respectively, or to the people."

## The Doctrine of National Supremacy

Former Senator Dole's interpretation of these words is that the only powers that the national government has are those that the Constitution of the United States specifically gives it. Thus, the national government can declare war, borrow money, establish post offices, create federal courts, coin money, naturalize citizens, and a whole host of other things, but it can't, or at least it shouldn't, provide welfare, get involved with education, raise the drinking age, or set speed limits. For Dole, the Constitution envisions a fairly clear division between federal and state powers. But that's not the way the U.S. Supreme Court has seen it for most of our history as a nation.

Early on (1801–1835), when John Marshall was Chief Justice of the U.S., the high court's philosophy was one of national supremacy, which argued that whenever a question arose concerning the proper repository of a power, it was always to be resolved in favor of the national government. Thus, the "elastic clause," which gives Congress the power to make all necessary and proper laws, was interpreted to give the Congress power to establish a national bank, despite the Constitution's silence on that issue, and the interstate commerce clause, which gives Congress the power to regulate interstate commerce was construed to apply to intrastate commerce as well as commerce between and among the states.

## The Doctrine of Dual Federalism

When Roger Taney replaced John Marshall, more than the Chief Justiceship changed. Taney, like Bob Dole, believed that the Tenth Amendment imposed restrictions on federal power. The only powers that the national government possessed under this new philosophy of "dual federalism" were those specifically granted by the express language of the Constitution. That was interpreted to mean that the national government could not regulate child labor, could not provide health, education, and welfare benefits, except in a very limited manner, could not, in short, do anything that was not specifically granted by the Constitution. And while that began to change early in this century, especially with the passage of the 16th Amendment to the U.S Constitution in 1913, the Amendment which allowed Congress to impose a tax on incomes, dual federalism had certainly not ended by the time of the Great Depression in the 1930s.

President Herbert Hoover had the dubious honor of presiding when the stock market "Crash" of 1929 occurred. Hoover took a few measures to alleviate the economic suffering that followed in the wake of the collapse of the market, and he regretted that he could not do more. But his hands were tied, he said, by the Constitution. What needed to be done, needed to be done by the national government, but the doctrine of dual federalism prohibited the national government from intruding on the powers of the states. The states—and the local governments—may have had the powers, but they lacked the money to enact and implement programs to alleviate the hardships resulting from the Depression. Failing to appreciate the pain that the President felt at his inability to do what he knew needed to be done, the electorate sent Hoover "packing" in the election of 1932.

Franklin Delano Roosevelt was elected overwhelmingly, vowing to try anything to get the country moving again, and if "anything" didn't work, he'd try something else. Supported by a Democratic Congress and an electoral mandate from the people, this new Democratic President began this first of his four terms with a barrage of legislation sent to Congress. His record of activity in the first 100 days is paralleled only by Lyndon B. Johnson's. FDR actually submitted bills to the Congress in the morning that he signed into law in the afternoon of the same day.

His New Deal—the name given to this alleviative legislative package—was going to save the nation.

But much of this new law hit a snag. The Supreme Court, a majority of whose members had been appointed by previous Republican Presidents (except for the two terms of Woodrow Wilson, Republicans had controlled the White House since 1897), continued to adhere to the philosophy of dual federalism. Programs that expanded the national government's role in areas such as agriculture, education, health, welfare, transportation, etc. were, in the minds of these justices, clearly beyond the purview of the national government, and, therefore, unconstitutional. They might be necessary programs, but only the states and localities, which were still broke, could legally undertake them.

## THE DOCTRINE OF COOPERATIVE FEDERALISM

Following an even more overwhelming electoral victory in 1937—FDR carried 46 of the 48 states, losing only Maine and Vermont—the President proposed to Congress what has come to be known as his "infamous" court-packing plan. For every justice over the age of 70, Roosevelt proposed to appoint another justice. Complaining about those "nine old men" on the Supreme Court, the President planned to "pack" the Court with his own appointees, six of them in all, for a total of 15 on the High Court. Although the Congress was generally sympathetic to the President on most matters, it refused to go along with this obvious "power grab." Nonetheless, the Court itself saw "the hand writing on the wall." Gradually its philosophy changed, and a more expansive role for the national government opened. Dual federalism was out; "cooperative" federalism was in.

As political scientist Morton Grodzins (1961) has suggested, dual federalism invites comparison to a layer cake, because the layers—the national and state governments—are fairly clearly delineated just like the layers in a cake. Cooperative federalism—which involves the cooperation of the national, state, and local governments, as well as the private sector—is analogous to a marble cake, with all of the elements swirled throughout; it's difficult to determine where one level's responsibility ends and another one's begins.

## FISCAL FEDERALISM

Because it takes money to implement programs, cooperative federalism has become synonymous with fiscal federalism. Fiscal federalism implies that the national government is particularly adept at generating revenue (although it runs a deficit every year, and has since 1969, the national government through the Internal Revenue Service of the Department of the Treasury is nonetheless a magnificent money machine currently raising close to one and one-half trillion dollars a year). However effective it may be at raising money, the national government is regarded as somewhat less effective at administering the programs it funds. Thus, state and local governments as well as the private sector receive funds from the national government to carry out its programs. These funds may be granted to the

subnational government in a variety of ways. Currently, most grants are either categorical or block grants, although from 1972 to 1986, some were in the form of general revenue sharing, which was money granted to the states and the localities to be used for fairly unrestricted purposes, and for which the subnational governments did not have to apply. In other words, it was regarded by the state and local governments as "manna from heaven." Largely for that reason it was not always allocated in the most responsible manner—e.g., a town in Vermont spent their entire annual check for uniforms for the municipal band, even though they didn't have a municipal band.

Categorical grants are grants to state and local governments for specific purposes. The subnational government must apply for the grants, and the national government attaches stipulations to its largesse. For example, the local government might have to comply with rules of the Environmental Protection Agency, rules of the Department of Labor, and a host of other rules and regulations that might absorb a significant portion of the money granted. Thus, state and local governments would much prefer block grants, which are much less cumbersome.

Block grants are made to the states and are made for general purposes. The states determine how the money will be spent and who will spend it; the states, in other words, establish the rules and regulations. It's up to Congress and the President to determine whether federal money will be in the form of categorical grants or block grants. Democratic Presidents and Congress members prefer categorical grants, because they tend to trust the national government to do the right thing in terms of protecting the civil rights and well-being of the "downtrodden," who are, of course, disproportionately, the Democratic party's constituents. Republicans, on the other hand, have a tendency to trust the states to do the right thing. They believe that the states are better able to determine what their problems are and better able to fashion solutions to those problems than a government far away in Washington, D.C. Hence, Republicans favor block grants that go directly to the states.

## CREATIVE FEDERALISM

From 1964 to 1971 the number of federal grants increased more than tenfold, from 51 to 530 (Nice, 53). Most of these grants were so-called "project" grants, a type of categorical grant which accounts for about 80% of all grants, and which requires an elaborate application procedure by the local government. Project grants, as the name implies, are earmarked for particular projects. Of course, Lyndon B. Johnson was president during much of this time (1963–1969), and his administration was one of the most active in history. Associated with that administration is still another variant of federalism, known as "creative federalism."

According to David C. Nice:

> *Creative federalism envisioned a partnership of national, state, and local governments as well as the private sector. Together they would develop new solutions and, when necessary, new organizations to attack society's ills. In this view, the private sector could provide new ideas and additional resources. If existing government organizations proved to be inadequate, new governmental bodies could be created.*

The Great Society of LBJ, which was a series of programs not just to alleviate society's ills but to cure them, embodied this concept of creative federalism, and many of these new grants were made in conjunction with the Great Society.

## NEW FEDERALISM (NIXON-FORD)

But much of the proliferation of grants occurred during the administration of Richard M. Nixon. While Nixon railed against the growth of the national government, he did little to trim it back. His affection for cooperative federalism may have lacked the ardor of his Democratic predecessors, but it was not replaced by a desire to return to dual federalism. Nixon wanted less regulation and less federal intrusion, more state and local discretion and more simplification, but his brand of federalism, while he called it "The New Federalism," had little about it that was truly new. And President Ford, ascending to the presidency upon the resignation of Nixon, largely continued the Nixonian approach.

## NEW FEDERALISM (REAGAN-BUSH)

President Ronald Reagan, however, advanced a "New Federalism" that opened a new area in cooperative federalism. As envisioned by Reagan, it was almost a return to dual federalism. The President proposed to replace virtually all categorical grant-in-aid programs with block grants to the states. His philosophy was that the federal government had become bloated at the expense of the states and much power ought to be returned to the states, where it belonged. But because the House of Representatives was controlled by the Democrats during his first term and both houses fell under Democratic control during his second term, Reagan was unable to prevail. Cooperative federalism survived, and Reagan seemed to lose interest in the subject. His indifference was largely shared by his successor and his vice-president, George Bush.

## NEW FEDERALISM (CLINTON)

Arriving at the White House after five terms as a state governor, Bill Clinton was to many officials of state and local governments the "New Messiah," come to save them from their fiscal woes. But Clinton had fiscal woes of his own, and, when Congress voted down his economic stimulus package, hopes for a new era of federal support for subnational government began to fade. Following the Republican capture of both houses of Congress in 1994, hopes were dashed. By the end of his first term, Clinton had largely capitulated to the New Federalism of his Republican predecessors, favoring block grants to the states to replace the federal role in welfare, food stamps, etc.

## WHITHER FEDERALISM?

Does this signal and end to cooperative federalism? If so, what kind of federalism has replaced it? Indeed, is federalism even a viable arrangement in the waning years of the 20th Century?

In 1985, the U.S. Supreme Court, in reversing the precedent established in the 1970s, held that local governments are required to adhere to federal minimum wage requirements (*Garcia v. San Antonio Metropolitan Transit Authority* 105 S.Ct. 1005). In and of itself, this is not all that significant a case. The ramifications, however, are far-reaching. What the Supreme Court was establishing in *Garcia* was a new form of national supremacy. In essence, the Court was saying that the Tenth Amendment is all but meaningless. The only thing that protects the states from being run roughshod over is the fact that they are guaranteed representation in Congress. In effect, the states are reduced to the status of interest groups, competing with one another and with other interest groups to protect their powers.

But ten years later, the Court reduced the power of the national government *vis-à-vis* the states by holding that the power to regulate commerce applies to commerce, such as a gold mine in Alaska (*United States v. Robertson*), not to noncommercial activities, such as possession of guns near schools (*United States v. Lopez*). And that same year (1995), the justices came within one vote of what critics charged was tantamount to reinstalling the Articles of Confederation (*U.S. Term Limits v. Thornton*). With the decision to turn welfare over to the states in 1996, as well as to let the states set their own speed limits, and with other moves to devolve power to the states promised by the still Republican led 105th Congress, it appears that the states are enjoying a level of attention that has escaped them for most of this century. How long this new importance continues depends largely on how well the states perform. If they are creative and attack problems effectively, if they are responsible and treat their citizens equitably, if they demonstrate that they are up to the task, a new era in the history of federalism may have dawned. However, what is fairly certain is that it won't last forever. As Beer, one of federalism's foremost scholars observed, "The American federal system has never been static. It has changed radically over the years, as tides of centralization and decentralization have altered the balance of power and the allocation of functions among the different levels of government."

The recent history of performance by the states bodes well for their continued success as vital partners in the American political process. While states have been slow to write new constitutions to replace long outmoded ones (Georgia is the one exception, having written its most recent constitution in 1982), many states have nonetheless revised their constitutions by amendment. States have actually taken the lead from the national government in the area of rights protection. Although the rights of defendants have been restricted, equal rights for women, environmental rights, privacy rights, and victims' rights have been extended by constitutional revision.

Long a laughingstock, state legislatures have recently gained a modicum of respect. Most states now have annual sessions, and many have increased the pay and the staffs of their state lawmakers. Several of the larger states have adopted the idea of full-time legislatures, although there is still much resistance from a public that believes in citizen (read amateur) legislators.

At one time, two-year terms for governors was the norm. Today, virtually all the states have moved to four-year terms with reeligibility to be elected to at least one additional term. And governors are relatively well-paid, with a median salary around $80,000. And their powers have been increased. All but the governor of North Carolina have veto power, and 44 have the item veto power that Congress recently gave the president. While most governors must share power with other independently elected executives, the number of such executives has been declining steadily.

The state judiciaries have improved as well. Most states select all or some of their judges in a system that combines appointment by the governor and election by the people. This is considered superior to either of the elements that compose it in that the nominees for judgeships come from a professional nominating commission. And more and more states are moving to unified court systems, with all courts falling under the direction of the highest court in the state. This leads to increased judicial efficiency.

Although many states are in dire need of revamping their revenue systems, most have come a long way in recent years toward developing sources of revenue to provide them with the means to meet the growing fiscal needs associated with growing responsibilities. Lotteries, other forms of legalized gaming, user fees, sales taxes on services, not just on commodities, have been just some of the sources the states have tapped.

And states are no longer notorious for their corruption. Occasionally a scandal is uncovered, but the days of patronage, vote-selling, and riotous behavior that once were associated with state government are largely relics of the past.

The states are as vibrant and as vital as they've ever been. That is not to say that state government has eclipsed national government; that certainly hasn't happened yet. But it is to say that the partnership has become more equal. Thus, it looks like the flexibility that has so long characterized the American political system ensures that federalism will remain the system's most distinguishing feature. It may be true that we have become much more homogeneous a people as our union has matured, but we still have differences. I was born in Pennsylvania, educated in Virginia and Ohio, and currently live and work in Georgia. I also pay taxes in Georgia, vote in Georgia, serve on juries in Georgia, and cheer for the Braves and the Falcons. The state and its government are important to me. It provides the roads I drive on, the schools my children attend, the parks I visit, the police protection I need, indeed the job that I hold. The national government provides defense, social security, medicare, and a variety of programs and protections that I've come to rely on. The idea of divided power among the national, state, and local governments is so thoroughly ingrained in us Americans that the possibility of our doing away with such a division is no more real than the possibility of doing away with Congress or the presidency. We are likely to remain always partners in power.

# Saeger

NAME: _____

SECTION: _____

DATE: _____

1. What was Chief Justice John Marshall's philosophy of Federalism?

   _____
   _____
   _____
   _____
   _____
   _____
   _____

2. Describe the role the Supreme Court has played in the evolution of the relationship between the Federal Government and the States.

   _____
   _____
   _____
   _____
   _____
   _____
   _____

3. Describe four types of grants in aid and show how each either strengthens or weakens State Government.

   _____
   _____
   _____
   _____
   _____
   _____

4. Explain how "fiscal federalism" has led to a new type of political relationship called "Co-operative Federalism."

___

5. Describe some of the areas in which State Governments have taken the lead in establishing new policies and programs.

___

**Group Exercise:** Convene the group and discuss the 10th Amendment to the Constitution. Should States have complete control over the wages and working conditions of State employees? Why, or why not?

**Individual Project:** Select and explain a recent newspaper article dealing with the issue of National/State Government relations. What is your opinion?

*Chapter Four*

# PUBLIC LAW

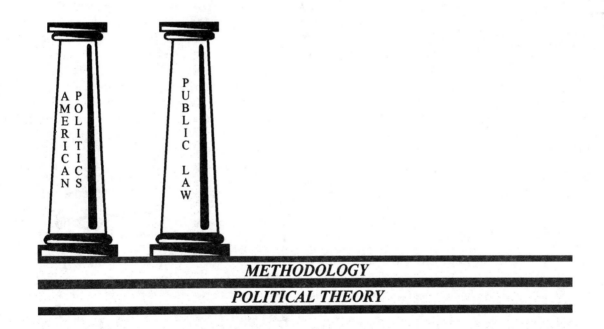

# Federalist Paper Number 78

## Alexander Hamilton

We proceed now to an examination of the judiciary department of the proposed government.

In unfolding the defects of the existing Confederation, the utility and necessity of a federal judicature have been clearly pointed out. It is the less necessary to recapitulate the considerations there urged as the propriety of the institution in the abstract is not disputed; the only questions which have been raised being relative to the manner of constituting it, and to its extent. To these points, therefore, our observations shall be confined.

The manner of constituting it seems to embrace these several objects: 1st. The mode of appointing the judges. 2nd. The tenure by which they are to hold their places. 3rd. The partition of the judiciary authority between different courts and their relations to each other.

*First.* As to the mode of appointing the judges: this is the same with that of appointing the officers of the Union in general and has been so fully discussed in the two last numbers that nothing can be said here which would not be useless repetition.

*Second.* As to the tenure by which the judges are to hold their places: this chiefly concerns their duration in office, the provisions for their support, the precautions for their responsibility.

According to the plan of the convention, all judges who may be appointed by the United States are to hold their offices *during good behavior*; which is conformable to the most approved of the State constitutions, and among the rest, to that of this State. Its propriety having been drawn into question by the adversaries of that plan is no light symptom of the rage for objection which disorders their imaginations and judgments. The standard of good behavior for the continuance in office of the judicial magistracy is certainly one of the most valuable of the modern improvements in the practice of government. In a monarchy it is an excellent barrier to the despotism of the prince; in a republic it is a no less excellent barrier to the encroachments and oppressions of the representative body. And it is the best expedient which can be devised in any government to secure a steady, upright, and impartial administration of the laws.

Whoever attentively considers the different departments of power must perceive that, in a government in which they are separated from each other, the judiciary, from the nature of its functions, will always be the least dangerous to the political rights of the Constitution; because it will be least in a capacity to annoy or injure them. The executive not only dispenses the honors but holds the sword of the community. The legislature not only commands the purse but prescribes the rules by which the duties and rights of every citizen are to be regulated. The judiciary, on the contrary, has no influence over either the sword or the purse; no direction either of the strength or of the wealth of the society, and can take no active resolution whatever. It may truly be said to have neither FORCE nor WILL but merely judgment; and must ultimately depend upon the aid of the executive arm even for the efficacy of its judgments.

This simple view of the matter suggests several important consequences. It proves incontestably that the judiciary is beyond comparison the weakest of the three departments of power; that it can never attack with success either of the other two; and that all possible care is requisite to enable it to defend itself against their attacks. It equally proves that though individual oppression may now and then proceed from the courts of justice, the general liberty of the people can never be endangered from that quarter; I mean so long as the judiciary remains truly distinct from both the legislature and the executive. For I agree that "there is no liberty if the power of judging be not separated from the legislative and executive powers." And it proves, in the last place, that as liberty can have nothing to fear from the judiciary alone, but would have everything to fear from its union with either of the other departments; that as all the effects of such a union must ensue from a dependence of the former on the latter, notwithstanding a nominal and apparent separation; that as, from the natural feebleness of the judiciary, it is in continual jeopardy of being overpowered, awed, or influenced by its coordinate branches; and that as nothing can contribute so much to its firmness and independence as permanency in office, this quality may therefore be justly regarded as an indispensable ingredient in its constitution, and, in a great measure, as the citadel of the public justice and the public security.

The complete independence of the courts of justice is peculiarly essential in a limited Constitution. By a limited Constitution, I understand one which contains certain specified exceptions to the legislative authority; such, for instance, as that it shall pass no bills of attainder, no *ex Post facto* laws, and the like. Limitations of this kind can be preserved in practice no other way than through the medium of courts of justice, whose duty it must be to declare all acts contrary to the manifest tenor of the Constitution void. Without this, all the reservations of particular rights or privileges would amount to nothing.

Some perplexity respecting the rights of the courts to pronounce legislative acts void, because contrary to the Constitution, has arisen from an imagination that the doctrine would imply a superiority of the judiciary to the legislative power. It is urged that the authority which can declare the acts of another void must necessarily be superior to the one whose acts may be declared void. As this doctrine is of great importance in all the American constitutions, a brief discussion of the grounds on which it rests cannot be unacceptable.

There is no position which depends on clearer principles than that every act of a delegated authority, contrary to the tenor of the commission under which it is exercised, is void. No legislative act, therefore, contrary to the Constitution, can be valid. To deny this would be to affirm that the deputy is greater than his principal; that the servant is above his master; that the representatives of the people are superior to the people themselves; that men acting by virtue of powers may do not only what their powers do not authorize, but what they forbid.

If it be said that the legislative body are themselves the constitutional judges of their own powers and that the construction they put upon them is conclusive upon the other departments it may be answered that this cannot be the natural presumption where it is not to be collected from any particular provisions in the Constitution. It is not otherwise to be supposed that the Constitution could intend to enable the representatives of the people to substitute their will to that of their constituents. It is far more rational to suppose that the courts were designed to be an intermediate body between the people and the legislature in order, among other things, to keep the latter within the limits assigned to their authority. The interpretation of the laws is the proper and peculiar province of the courts. A constitution is, in fact, and must be regarded by the judges as, a fundamental law. It therefore belongs to them to ascertain its meaning as well as the meaning of any particular act proceeding from the legislative body. If there should happen to be an irreconcilable variance between the two, that which has the superior obligation and validity ought, of course, to be preferred; or, in other words, the Constitution ought to be preferred to the statute, the intention of the people to the intention of their agents.

Nor does this conclusion by any means suppose a superiority of the judicial to the legislative power. It only supposes that the power of the people is superior to both, and that where the will of the legislature, declared in its statutes, stands in opposition to that of the people, declared in the Constitution, the judges ought to be governed by the latter rather than the former. They ought to regulate their decisions by the fundamental laws rather than by those which are not fundamental.

This exercise of judicial discretion in determining between two contradictory laws is exemplified in a familiar instance. It not uncommonly happens that there are two statutes existing at one time, clashing in whole or in part with each other and neither of them containing any repealing clause or expression. In such a case, it is the province of the courts to liquidate and fix their meaning and operation. So far as they can, by any fair construction, be reconciled to each other, reason and law conspire to dictate that this should be done; where this is impracticable, it becomes a matter of necessity to give effect to one in exclusion of the other. The rule which has obtained in the courts for determining their relative validity is that the last in order of time shall be preferred to the first. But this is a mere rule of construction, not derived from any positive law but from the nature and reason of the thing. It is a rule not enjoined upon the courts by legislative provision but adopted by themselves, as consonant to truth and propriety, for the direction of their conduct as interpreters of the law. They thought it reasonable that between the interfering acts of an equal authority that which was the last indication of its will should have the preference.

But in regard to the interfering acts of a superior and subordinate authority of an original and derivative power, the nature and reason of the thing indicate the converse of that rule as proper to be followed. They teach us that the prior act of a superior ought to be preferred to the subsequent act of an inferior and subordinate authority; and that accordingly, whenever a particular statute contravenes the Constitution, it will be the duty of the judicial tribunals to adhere to the latter and disregard the former.

It can be of no weight to say that the courts, on the pretense of a repugnancy, may substitute their own pleasure to the constitutional intentions of the legislature. This might as well happen in the case of two contradictory statutes; or it might as well happen in every adjudication upon any single statute. The courts must declare the sense of the law; and if they should be disposed to exercise WILL instead of JUDGMENT, the consequence would equally be the substitution of their pleasure to that of the legislative body. The observation, if it proved anything, would prove that there ought to be no judges distinct from that body.

If, then, the courts of justice are to be considered as the bulwarks of a limited Constitution against legislative encroachments, this consideration will afford a strong argument for the permanent tenure of judicial offices, since nothing will contribute so much as this to that independent spirit in the judges which must be essential to the faithful performance of so arduous a duty.

This independence of the judges is equally requisite to guard the Constitution and the rights of individuals from the effects of those ill humors which the arts of designing men, or the influence of particular conjunctures, sometimes disseminate among the people themselves, and which, though they speedily give place to better information, and more deliberate reflection, have a tendency, in the meantime, to occasion dangerous innovations in the government, and serious oppressions of the minor party in the community. Though I trust the friends of the proposed Constitution will never concur with its enemies in questioning that fundamental principle of republican government which admits the right of the people to alter or abolish the established Constitution whenever they find it inconsistent with their happiness; yet it is not to be inferred from this principle that the representatives of the people, whenever a momentary inclination happens to lay hold of a majority of their constituents incompatible with the provisions in the existing Constitution would, on that account, be justifiable in a violation of those provisions; or that the courts would be under a greater obligation to connive at infractions in this shape than when they had proceeded wholly from the cabals of the representative body. Until the people have, by some solemn and authoritative act, annulled or changed the established form, it is binding upon themselves collectively, as well as individually; and no presumption, or even knowledge of their sentiments, can warrant their representatives in a departure from it prior to such an act. But it is easy to see that it would require an uncommon portion of fortitude in the judges to do their duty as faithful guardians of the Constitution, where legislative invasions of it had been instigated by the major voice of the community.

But it is not with a view to infractions of the Constitution only that the independence of the judges may be an essential safeguard against the effects of occasional ill humors in the society. These sometimes extend no farther than to the injury of the private rights of particular classes of citizens, by unjust and partial laws. Here also the firmness of the judicial magistracy is of vast importance in mitigating the severity and confining the operation of such laws. It not only serves to moderate the immediate mischiefs of those which may have been passed but it operates as a check upon the legislative body in passing them; who, perceiving that obstacles to the success of an iniquitous intention are to be expected from the scruples of the courts, are in a manner compelled, by the very motives of the injustice they meditate, to qualify their attempts. This is a circumstance calculated to have more influence upon the character of our governments than but few may be aware of. The benefits of the integrity and moderation of the judiciary have already been felt in more States than one; and though they may have displeased those whose sinister expectations they may have disappointed, they must have commanded the esteem and applause of all the virtuous and disinterested. Considerate men of every description ought to prize whatever will tend to beget or fortify that temper in the courts; as no man can be sure that he may not be tomorrow the victim of a spirit of injustice, by which he may be a gainer today. And every man must now feel that the inevitable tendency of such a spirit is to sap the foundations of public and private confidence and to introduce in its stead universal distrust and distress.

That inflexible and uniform adherence to the rights of the Constitution, and of individuals, which we perceive to be indispensable in the courts of justice, can certainly not be expected from judges who hold their offices by a temporary commission. Periodical appointments, however regulated, or by whomsoever made, would, in some way or other, be fatal to their necessary independence. If the power of making them was committed either to the executive or legislature there would be danger of an improper complaisance to the branch which possessed it; if to both, there would be an unwillingness to hazard the displeasure of either; if to the people, or to persons chosen by them for the special purpose, there would be too great a disposition to consult popularity to justify a reliance that nothing would be consulted but the Constitution and the laws.

There is yet a further and a weighty reason for the permanency of the judicial offices which is deducible from the nature of the qualifications they require. It has been frequently remarked with great propriety that a voluminous code of laws is one of the inconveniences necessarily connected with the advantages of a free government. To avoid an arbitrary discretion in the courts, it is indispensable that they should be bound down by strict rules and precedents which serve to define and point out their duty in every particular case that comes before them; and it will readily be conceived from the variety of controversies which grow out of the folly and wickedness of mankind that the records of those precedents must unavoidably swell to a very considerable bulk and must demand long and laborious study to acquire a competent knowledge of them. Hence it is that there can be but few men in the society who will have sufficient skill in the laws to qualify them for the stations of judges. And making the proper deductions for the ordinary depravity of human nature, the number must be still smaller of those who unite the requisite integrity with the requisite knowledge. These considerations apprise us that the government can have no great option between fit characters; and that a temporary duration in office which would naturally discourage such characters from quitting a lucrative line of practice to accept a seat on the bench would have a tendency to throw the administration of justice into hands less able and less well qualified to conduct it with utility and dignity. In the present circumstances of this country and in those in which it is likely to be for a long time to come, the disadvantages on this score would be greater than they may at first sight appear; but it must be confessed that they are far inferior to those which present themselves under the other aspects of the subject.

Upon the whole, there can be no room to doubt that the convention acted wisely in copying from the models of those constitutions which have established *good behavior* as the tenure of their judicial offices, in point of duration; and that so far from being blamable on this account, their plan would have been inexcusably defective if it had wanted this important feature of good government. The experience of Great Britain affords an illustrious comment on the excellence of the institution.

*Publius* (Alexander Hamilton)

# Hamilton

Name: _____
Section: _____
Date: _____

1. Define the terms "judicial independence" and "good behavior" and explain why there was so much resistance to these ideas.

   _____
   _____
   _____
   _____
   _____
   _____

2. Alexander Hamilton says that the judicial branch was the least dangerous to liberty of the three branches of government. Explain his argument.

   _____
   _____
   _____
   _____
   _____
   _____

3. Hamilton asserted that when there was a clash between two statutes or laws, it was "the province of the court to liquidate and fix their meaning and operation." What has this come to mean in today's terminology?

   _____
   _____
   _____
   _____
   _____
   _____

4. If the people have the right to alter or abolish the constitution, why should judges have fortitude in their role as constitutional guardians?

_____
_____
_____
_____
_____
_____
_____

5. According to Hamilton, it was inevitable that the legal records would grow to be of considerable size. How does this impact upon arguments about lifelong appointments to the Judiciary?

_____
_____
_____
_____
_____
_____
_____

**Group Exercise:** Pick a very controversial legal or constitutional issue and discuss the advantages and disadvantages of permanent appointments for judges. Should the judges always follow popular opinions? Why?

**Individual Project:** Locate, identify, and describe a contemporary legal journal article about judicial tenure. Is there still a great deal of controversy over this issue? Why, or why not?

# Constitutional Interpretation: Distinctions without Differences

## Clyde Willis

### Introduction

Article III of the U.S. Constitution places the judicial power of government in the Judicial Branch. This constitutional power, not unlike judicial power everywhere, as defined by the Constitution itself includes the command that judges decide "cases and controversies." This process of deciding cases is described by Carl Brent Swisher as follows: a court "determines the facts involved in particular controversies brought before it, relates the facts to the relevant law, [and] settles the controversies in terms of the law." It is just that simple. Yet, it may not be quite so simple after all.

One aspect of judicial decision making that belies simplicity is one of the most contentious issues of contemporary political and legal debate. It is the role of judicial interpretation: the extent to which judges can or should be restricted in their role as "interpreters of the law." The debate revolves around whether or not judges should, or can for that matter, apply the law in either an objective or subjective manner. For in applying the law, judges must invariably interpret the law. Thus, the argument: can or should judges interpret the law objectively, or is the process inherently or unavoidably subjective?

### The Subject-Object Dichotomy

The problematic relationship of judges and legislators is by no means a recent phenomenon. Throughout most of history, judges have been considered capable of treating the laws enacted by others in an objective manner. For example, Plato describes the role of judges through a dialogue between the Younger Socrates and the Eleatic Stranger in *The Statesman*. The Stranger asked: "Do [judges] do anything but decide the dealings of people with one another to be just or unjust in accordance with the standard which they receive from the King and legislator . . . not perverted by . . . any sort of favor or enmity . . . contrary to the appointment of the legislator?" "No; their office is such as you describe," the Younger Socrates replies. Later the Code of Justinian instructs the jurist as follows: "if anything shall seem doubtful, let it be referred by the judges to the Imperial Throne and it shall be made plain by Imperial Authority, to which alone is given the right both to establish and to interpret the laws."

More recently and closer to home we find the counsel of Montesquieu, a venerable political philosopher who had a significant impact on political and legal philosophy in the United States. Montesquieu flatly stated: "judges are no more than the mouth that pronounces the words of the law, mere passive beings, incapable of moderating either its force or rigor." Following Montesquieu's admonition, political and legal theory in the United States has been consumed for over two centuries in establishing the fountain of objectivity whereby the subjectivity of judicial officers can be—or at least should be—eliminated from the decision making process.

### Objectivism

Certainly, from at least the latter part of the nineteenth century through the middle of the twentieth century, objectivism, or formalism as it has been called, has been the dominant explanation for judicial interpretation of authoritative texts. Formalism, in very brief terms, holds that rules or principles of law, whether derived from or embodied in the texts of constitutions, statutes or cases, determine the outcome of disputes by controlling or dictating a judge's decision. With formalism one can supposedly take the rule as a major premise, place the immediate factual situation beside it as the minor premise, and deduce the result without fear of contradiction. This is what is commonly referred to as the legal syllogism.

A classic statement of the objectivist goal of passive judges applying the law is found in the opinion of Justice Roberts in *United States v. Butler*, 297 U.S. 1, 56 S.Ct. 312, 80 L.Ed. 477 (1936). Roberts argued that "the judicial branch has only one duty: to lay the article of the Constitution which is invoked beside the statute which is challenged and to decide whether the latter squares with the former . . . neither approv[ing] nor condemn[ing] any legislative policy."

There are two corollaries to the formalist's belief that rules control judges. One is that conclusions are predictable and certain. Second, is the belief that judicial decisions result from the logical operation of the argument uninfluenced by the judge's subjectivism. The net result of formalism, then, is a legal system in which formal rules, as the embodiment of principles of human conduct, rather than subjective judges control the decision-making process. Hence, the aphorism: a nation of law, not of men.

## SUBJECTIVISM

A counter movement arose during the early part of the twentieth century against the objectivism of formalism. This movement which spanned various philosophical and scholarly categories is known as behavioralism in political science and realism in law. While these two groups had differences, they shared a common attitude toward formalism. Each believed that the actual behavior of judges and the results of judicial decision making belied the essential theory of formalism. To the behavioralists-realists, the reality of judicial decision-making was what judges did with the rules in concrete, factual situations, not some theory about how rules were supposed to control judges. According to Rumble:

> The advocates of "realistic jurisprudence" demonstrated the limitations of established rules as means to determine decisions in most cases doubtful enough to be litigated, contested, and appealed; they opened juristic eyes to the often unpredictable and subjective character of the process by means of which the facts of a case are determined.

Subjectivists, especially the more radical elements, argue that due to the dominating influence of personal subjectivity, certainty and uniformity are totally lacking in judicial principles. The legal philosopher Roscoe Pound argued that some skeptical realists even believe that law "is only what judges and officials do, motivated by their prejudices and individual inclinations . . . they insist on the non-rational element in judicial and administrative action as reality, and the rational element as illusion."

A more moderate version of this subjectivism can be found in the dictum of Justice Blackmun in *Garcia v. San Antonio Metro. Transit Authority*, 469 U.S. 528, 105 S.Ct. 1005, 83 L.Ed. 2d 1016 (1985). While acknowledging the mandate of specific language in the Constitution, Justice Blackmun stated "it is equally true, however, that the text of the Constitution provides the beginning rather than the final answer to every inquiry . . . for behind the words of the constitutional provisions are postulates which limit and control."

Following Justice Blackmun's statement, the focus of our concern must turn toward those postulates that are not part of the rule that nevertheless limit and control not only the decision making process, but how the legal text is interpreted in the first place. Are these postulates Blackmun speaks of located in the realm of objectivity or subjectivity? The issue is joined thusly: is there an external, objectively existing reality outside the judge that controls judicial decision making in general and judicial interpretation in specific?

## THE MEESE-BRENNAN DEBATE

The search for the answer to the issue of objectivity versus subjectivity and the actual attributes of judicial interpretation and decision making can be undertaken through the recent debate between two prominent public officials: a former Associate Justice on the United States Supreme Court and a former United States Attorney General. In July 1985, then U.S. Attorney General Edwin Meese III, characterizing many recent Supreme Court opinions as "bizarre," called for "a return to an objective jurisprudence of Original Intention." Meese's fulmination was quickly met in October of that year by then sitting Associate Justice William Brennan. Brennan, rejecting the hermeneutics of original intention and similar process-based techniques regarding constitutional interpretation, advocated an approach to interpreting the text which must account for the existence of substantive value choices, and must accept the ambiguity inherent in the effort to apply them to modern circumstances. This initial exchange was followed with a speech by each antagonist setting forth at some length their respective positions.

At first glance, there seems to be a radical distinction between Meese and Brennan respecting their approaches to judicial interpretation. Meese argues for what he calls "a jurisprudence that seeks fidelity to the Constitution—a jurisprudence of original intention." He derides those who view the Constitution as a "charter for judicial activism on behalf of various constituencies," indicating those who suggest that "constitutional interpretation be guided by such standards as whether a public policy 'personifies justice' or 'comports with the notion of moral evolution' or confers 'an identity' upon our society or as consistent with 'natural ethical law' or is consistent with some 'right of equal citizenship.'"

Meese's jurisprudence of original intention holds that the "further afield interpretation travels from its point of departure in the text, the greater danger that constitutional adjudication will be like a picnic to which the framers bring the words and the judges the meaning." While he acknowledges that not all constitutional provisions are "exactingly specific," Meese insists that any interpretative outcome must nevertheless be firmly rooted in the literal language of the document. Rejecting what many call the "spirit" of the Constitution in favor of its words, Meese describes his interpretative approach as follows:

> *Where the language of the Constitution is specific, it must be obeyed. Where there is a demonstrable consensus among the Framers and ratifiers as to a principle stated or implied by the Constitution, it should be followed. Where there is ambiguity as to the precise meaning or reach of a constitutional provision, it should be interpreted and applied in a manner so as to at least not contradict the text of the Constitution itself.*

In short, Meese's argument maintains that the Constitutional text provides an objective, authoritative mechanism that can dictate the interpretative process if judges will set aside their subjective values and submit to its mandate. It is, as Meese puts it, simply "a jurisprudence faithful to our Constitution."

Justice Brennan took the opposing position in short order. He began his speech by stating:

> *Like every other text worth reading, [the Constitution] is not crystalline. The phrasing is broad and the limitations of its provisions are not clearly marked. Its majestic generalities and ennobling pronouncements are both luminous and obscure. This ambiguity calls forth interpretation, the interaction of reader and text.*

Brennan argues that interpretation is inevitable and that there is nothing inherent in the interpretative process that requires one to adhere to original intention, or, for that matter, any particular position. Brennan's statements recall a declaration by Chief Justice John Marshall in the famous case of *Gibbons v. Ogden*, 22 U.S (9 Wheat.) 1, 6 L.Ed. 23 (1824). Responding to an argument that the Court accept a particular interpretative approach regarding Congressional power as stated in the Constitution because it was **the** correct approach, Marshall stated: "It has been said that these powers ought to be construed strictly. But why ought they to be so construed? Is there one sentence in the constitution which gives countenance to this rule [of interpretation]?" Marshall opined that there is no such rule commanding one interpretative approach or another in the Constitution, or anywhere else for that matter. He went on to argue that the words of the Constitution must be read or interpreted in light of the objects to be served by the Constitution. Put differently, there is a transcendent purpose supporting the constitutional text which must not be lost in the interpretation.

Brennan argues, and Marshall supports, the proposition that the appropriation of any one interpretative position is just as political or subjective as any other. In Brennan's opinion, if we want to remain faithful to the purpose of the Constitution, "an approach to interpreting the text must account for the existence of these substantive value choices." Accordingly, the ultimate interpretative standard is: "What do the words of the text mean in our time." Brennan believes that the Constitution was established to create a new society, rather than maintain the status quo. Therefore, the "interpretative process must account for the transformative purpose of the text." In short, Brennan rejects Meese's objectivist position as one that "feigns self-effacing deference to the specific judgments of those who forged our original social compact. But in truth it is little more than arrogance cloaked as humility."

## Distinctions without Differences

While the distinctions between Meese's position and Brennan's position are becoming more and more the topic of discussion in legal and political circles, they may also be seen as distinctions without differences. What is truly significant about both positions is not their distinguishing features, but the fact that both seek to validate value choices outside the constitutional text: Meese in the history of Eighteenth Century politics—even inquiring into the psyche of the Framers, Brennan in the milieu of contemporary politics. Each position employs the dictum of Justice Blackmun that the constitutional text is simply the beginning. The distinctions crumble under this glaring non-difference.

What separates Meese and Brennan is not the role of subjectivity *per se*, but rather how the subjectivity that enables judges to choose differently among a wide array of legal principles and factual scenarios presented in each case are employed. Just as the facts of any case do not come in only one mode of appearance, the rules that are applicable in any given situation are not singular: there are different versions of the facts and there are different, but equally valid, applicable laws which can be applied to the facts. The focus must be on how subjectivity plays in viewing the facts and selecting the applicable law.

Both Meese and Brennan have differing subjective viewpoints which give each differing views of the facts and different views of which legal principles are applicable. The debate between them should not be over some technical-sounding interpretative methodology, but over the substance of their subjective viewpoints regarding what kind of society we should have—those "postulates which control and limit." In short, the argument is over ends, not means.

## The Role of Subjectivity

In order to understand the role of subjectivity in the interpretative process that both Meese and Brennan are engaged in, there must be a close examination of the component parts of a judicial decision, particularly the role of subjectivity. There is a very good reason that Meese as well as Brennan employ a subjective element in interpreting legal texts. It is simply impossible to do otherwise. In fact, it is impossible to interpret or decide anything without subjectivity. The three components which bear focus are: a set of empirical facts that can have many versions, none of which is **the** true version; numerous abstract legal principles, any one of which can be validly applied to any set of facts depending on the desired outcome; and human subjectivity which perceives and manifests goals in society.

In order to illustrate these three components with a familiar example, take something as simple as a vase. While it may at first seem that a vase *qua* vase is quite simple, it really is not. In hermeneutical terms the vase provides a good analytical analogy for use here. To arrive at the decision that a vase is a vase requires the three components of decision making: empirical facts, transcendental or abstract concepts, and human subjectivity or intentionality.

The empirical facts of a vase, or an object, are identified as glass, tin, metal, or whatever. These characteristics exist in the objective world. We do not literally reconfigure the physical components of a vase. Neither can we determine its essence or true nature—at least in human terms—by simply focusing on its physical qualities. In order to view the vase as a vase, we must also have a transcendental notion or idea of a vase, as something that can be used to hold cut flowers, for instance. This "vaseness," if you will, is an abstract, transcendental concept, one of several ways an empirical object can be used or understood.

Even given the physical facts and the concept of vaseness, the determination that the object is a vase is still not, however, completed. Many objects that can be used as a vase can also be used as a bookend, a pitcher, an icon, or a pictograph as well. In other words, there are many available abstract ideas of how the same empirical object may be used. What determines the object's use is our subjectivity, our subjective intentionality.

We select the concept and apply it to the object depending on how we wish to use the object. Whether the object is a vase, bookend, pitcher, icon, or pictograph is controlled in part by what we as subjects intend for the object. The very object that might appear to me in a shop as a vase may well appear to someone else as an icon or pictograph, depending on what our individual and collective (i.e., community) subjective intentions are. In short, what exists in the realm of mind and matter is irrelevant or meaningless apart from a human's lived or subjective experience.

This is not to say that human subjectivity can make anything of something. For subjectivity cannot rearrange the empirical facts of an object willy nilly. The physical components of an object will remain the same physical components. While abstract ideas are limited only by the boundaries of our imagination, empirical objects are much less amenable to fluctuations of human subjectivity. A tin object may be a vase, an icon, or a pictograph; but it will always be tin and probably never be understood as an bookshelf.

## THE COMPONENTS OF JUDICIAL DECISION MAKING

The process of deciding that an object is a vase is implicated by analogy in the interpretation of legal texts. It can be illustrated though examination of a typical problem decided by the United States Supreme Court. Take the issue of whether the Fair Labor Standards Act is applicable to state and local governments. In 1938 Congress enacted the Fair Labor Standards Act (FLSA) which imposed certain imitations on private employers such as a minimum wage and a maximum workweek without overtime pay. In 1941 the FLSA was upheld by the Court in *U.S. v. Darby* as a valid regulation under the Commerce Clause. In 1974 the FLSA was amended by Congress to bring state and local governmental entities within its provisions.

The National League of Cities, along with certain cities and states, brought suit against the Secretary of Labor to have the application of FLSA to their governmental units set aside as violative of the Constitution. The League maintained that as applied to state and local government FLSA was not a valid exercise of Congressional power to regulate interstate commerce. This position was based upon the claim that the regulation infringed the rights of states under the Tenth Amendment and that it contravened the over-arching concept of Federalism which the League claimed must be taken into account when Congress employs the Commerce Clause to regulate state governmental activities.

Supporting the regulation, the government took the position that Congress was regulating interstate commerce under the Commerce Clause as defined over the years by Supreme Court decisions. Since the action was within the expressed powers of Congress and since valid laws of the national government are the Supreme Law of the Land, contrary activity by state and local governments must therefore yield.

The analysis of how the Court arrived at its conclusion focuses on the three aspects of inter-

pretation mentioned above, namely, the empirical facts, abstract concepts, and human subjectivity. The facts are rather simple: state and local government employ people to perform a wide variety of tasks at a cost to the taxpaying public; the national government has enacted a regulatory scheme which requires most of the state and local governments to alter their wage and hour programs in a manner that appears unduly burdensome to state and local administrators due mainly to the lack of a revenue or tax base with which to fund such requirements. The various abstract legal principles contained in the Constitutional text are also quite straightforward: the Commerce Clause, the Supremacy Clause, and the Tenth Amendment. There is also the relevant concept of Federalism which is not explicitly stated in the text of the Constitution.

Now, if the judicial task is simply to engage the mechanical process as described by Justice Roberts and allow objective principles to dictate the factual outcome by controlling the justices' decision, what would be the result? First, we would simply identify the significant portion of the Constitution, simply lay the Constitutional provision alongside the facts, the amended FLSA as applied to state and local governments, and simply see if the statute squares with the Constitution. The problem is that we cannot arrive at a decision by any such method.

For one thing, the facts are not straightforward. The justices could not agree on a version of the facts. While those that joined Justice Rehnquist's majority opinion concluded that the facts indicated FLSA as amended placed an undue burden on state and local governments, Justices Brennan, White, and Marshall believed the facts manifested no such situation.

Moreover, the justices could not agree which constitutional provision was applicable to the facts. On the one hand, the justices that saw the facts as constituting an undue burden on state and local governments selected the Tenth Amendment and a particular version of the concept of Federalism as applicable law. On the other hand, the dissenting justices, seeing the facts otherwise, selected the Commerce Clause, the Supremacy Clause, and another version of Federalism as applicable. Thus, the facts were not self-evident, and the question of which laws were applicable was just as problematical; even more difficult than what the law meant in the first place.

Thus, formalism as a means-based methodology is an inadequate explanation of how judges decide cases. The fact that in *National League of Cities v. Usery* five justices decided to reject the FLSA as valid while four voted to uphold it as constitutionally permissible demands that another component be added to the explanation. Moreover, how could we explain without subjectivity what the Court did nine years later when it revisited the problem in *Garcia v. San Antonio Metropolitan Transit Authority* and overturned *National League of Cities v. Usery*? In *Garcia* five justices voted to uphold the power of Congress to regulate wage and hour conditions of state and local employees, four voted to disallow the regulation.

It is obvious that the justices had different subjective notions of the social and political ends that were to be served by the Constitution *vis à vis* the congressional enactments. The fact that justices among themselves and as representative of the public differed as to the preferred "postulates which [ultimately] limit and control," does not mean that those postulates do not exist and play a significant role in judicial decision making. It means that something else is at work in the process of decision making; something else that begs to be explained and understood.

The words of the Constitution are not empirically existing, objective facts. They are the symbols for highly sophisticated socio-political concepts. They are idealistic abstractions which transcend the empirical facts. Moreover, there are not just one or two, or even three that can apply in these cases. Both sides called upon one powerful concept that is not even set out in the Constitution: the concept of Federalism. Indeed, in *National League of Cities* the Court relied more heavily on the abstract notion of Federalism than any specific provision of the Constitution.

The fact that a Court's decision usually turns more on **which** valid constitutional principle to apply rather than what any particular principle means is simply lost on those who subscribe to objectivism. The empirical facts are just as problematical. We come to see and appreciate the facts in a way that is influenced by what we are looking for. When we are predisposed to see facts a certain way, we usually do. This is what is called prejudice, the ability to pre-judge. Without prejudice or the ability to anticipate what experience means, we are lost in a sea of nihilism. The task is not to reject prejudice out-of-hand, but to examine its validity and replace it with other understandings and expectations when they better serve legitimate personal and community ends.

What influenced the justices in *National League of Cities* and *Garcia* was their prejudice which is based on their subjective intentionality, their individual and collective notions of what ends are valid for the political community. No process-driven method can dictate this. It must come from an arduous and continuing process of developing one's goals for social and political society. One must subject their own subjective biases and intentionality to critical scrutiny as well as that of others; else one becomes what passes in the vernacular, as "narrow-minded."

## Conclusion

One can follow the example of Justice Brennan who delved into his own subjectivity in his speech before the guests at the symposium. Brennan grappled with his version of human dignity that informs his subjective intentionality and provides him direction in interpreting—selecting—the facts and the law. He dialogued in public with his own subjectivity as well as his "role in seeking out the community's interpretation of the constitutional text," in what is essentially a public enterprise.

Or one can follow the example of Attorney General Meese who's ends of political society may be just as valid or even more desirable than Justice Brennan's. But if we hide behind the notion that means dictate ends, that subjectivity and prejudices have been set aside, we will not be able to know each other, much less engage each other in debate about community.

The subjective factor in judicial interpretation must become manifest if we are to achieve a true political community of free individuals. We must refuse to conceal our prejudices regarding the ends of society. We must be concerned by results rather than process, ends not means. We must follow the lead of those who are willing to put their prejudices "at risk" in a public enterprise. This is all that we can ask of others; this is what we must ask of ourselves.

# WILLIS

NAME: _____

SECTION: _____

DATE: _____

1. Formalism has been called the legal syllogism. What are its major and minor premises?

2. The so-called "behavioral revolution" had an impact on legal scholars as well as political scientists. Did it improve the image of judges as passive "mouths of the law"?

3. What was the significance of the two cases of *National League of Cities v. Usery* and *Garcia v. San Antonio Metropolitan Transit Authority*?

4. Willis argues that legal prejudice is necessary because the alternative is nihilism. What is nihilism?

5. Should we maintain an official mask of objectivity or should the subjectivity of law be acknowledged? Why, or why not?

**Group Exercise:** Compare the two cases, *National League of Cities versus Usery* and *Garcia versus San Antonio Metropolitan Transit Authority*. What do these cases tell us about Supreme Court reasoning?

**Individual Project:** Consult reference books and explain what is meant by the phrase: "hermeneutics of original intention."

# THE HISTORY OF MAINSTREAM LEGAL THOUGHT

## Elizabeth Mensch*

The most corrosive message of legal history is the message of contingency. Routinely, the justificatory language of law parades as the unquestionable embodiment of Reason and Universal Truth; yet even a brief romp through the history of American legal thought reveals how quickly the Obvious Logic of one period can become the silly formalism of another, or how easily Enlightened Modern Policy can, from another perspective, be perceived as irresponsible judicial meddling. The account that follows is a short, and necessarily superficial, summary of the major changes that have taken place in American legal thought since the onset of the nineteenth century. There will be no attempt to examine the complex causes of those changes, nor their relation to the social and economic contexts within which they have, of course, occurred. The goal is more limited: to describe the legal consciousness of distinct (although overlapping) periods of American legal thought. Since the effort is to reconstruct the world-view of those who have been most directly concerned with making, explaining, and applying legal doctrine, many theorists who have written on the fundamental questions of jurisprudence are not included. This is an account of conventional, and therefore often wholly unreflecting and unconscious, legal consciousness.

## PRE-CLASSICAL CONSCIOUSNESS (1776–1885)

During the disruptive and potentially radical period that immediately followed the Revolution, elite American jurists devoted themselves to reestablishing legal authority. As the embodiment of reason and conduct, law seemed to offer the only source of stability in a nation that otherwise threatened to dissolve into the chaotic, leveling passions of a people now so dangerously declared to be sovereign.

In a flowery vocabulary drawn largely from the natural-law tradition, late-eighteenth and early-nineteenth-century legal speakers made extravagant claims about the role of law and lawyers. Law was routinely described as reflecting here on earth the universal principles of divine justice, which, in their purest form, reigned in the Celestial City. For example, the single most popular legal quotation, for rhetorical purposes, was taken from the Anglican theologian Hooker: "Of law no less can be acknowledged, than that her seat is the bosom of God; her voice harmony of the world."

Similarly, lawyers portrayed their own professional character as the embodiment of republican virtue; ideally, within each well-educated lawyer reason had subdued the unruly passions, and that triumph rendered the lawyer fit to consecrate himself to the service of law, as a "Priest at the temple of justice." In this role the lawyer/priest was to act, not as an instrument of his client's unbridled will, but as a voice for the interests of the whole community. As advisor and guardian, he would attempt to elicit elevated rather than base motives in his clients, guiding them to promote a social order consistent with those universal principles that were ordained by God and most clearly understood by lawyers.

This special trusteeship meant that lawyers played a crucial political role in the new democracy, where principle and legal right constantly faced the threat of mass assault. Leaders of the bar often described lawyers as sentinels, placed on the dangerous outposts of defense, preserving the virtue of the republic from the specifically democratic threats of irrational legislation and mob rule. Not surprisingly, many nineteenth-century

---

* From *The Politics of Law*, Pantheon Book, 1992, pages 18–39. Reprinted by permission of D. Kairys.

jurists cited with satisfaction de Tocqueville's observation that the legal profession constituted a distinctively American aristocracy, providing order in an otherwise unstable democracy.

The universal principle that seemed to require the most zealous protection was the sanctity of private property. With something approaching paranoia, leading American jurists explained that the redistributive passions of the majority, if ever allowed to overrun the barrier of legal principle, would sweep away the nation's whole social and economic foundation. Thus Joseph Story, upon his inauguration as professor of law at Harvard, announced that the lawyer's most "glorious and not infrequently perilous" duty was to guard the "sacred rights of property" from the "rapacity" of the majority. Only the "solitary citadel" of justice stood between property and redistribution; it was the lawyer's noble task to man that citadel, whatever the personal cost. "What sacrifice could be more pure than in such a cause? What martyrdom more worthy to be canonized in our hearts?

The ornate legal rhetoric of the period obscured a number of dilemmas deep at the core of early American legal theory. First, despite the rhetorical appeal to natural law as a source of legitimacy, most jurists readily conceded that natural law alone was too indeterminate to guide judicial decision making in specific cases. Natural law provided divine sanction but yielded few concrete rules or results. Moreover, pure natural-law theory could lead in unwanted directions. The notion of natural reason upon which it rested, for example, could be translated to mean the natural reason of the sovereign people—Thomas Paine's common sense—rather than the reason of trained lawyers. That suggested precisely the unlimited popular will, which most jurists feared. Furthermore, the moral content of natural-law theory often led in contradictory directions. One key example was the right to property; while a Lockean natural-law tradition asserted the sanctity of private property, an even older (and alarmingly popular) natural-law tradition questioned the morality of all social and economic inequality.

Most early nineteenth-century lawyers were thus ready to concede that the most immediate, practical source and definition of law was to be found in positive law—not statutes, which were feared because of their origin in unpredictable representative assemblies—but the complex, ancient forms of the English common law. The legitimacy of those forms was said to derive not from universal moral principle but from custom and long usage. It was the extraordinary technicality of the common law that provided lawyers with their claim to expertise and served, by its very artificiality, to distinguish legal reasoning from the "common-sense" reason of the general populace. Moreover, common-law rules, however quirky, seemed able to supply the certainty and formal realizability impossible to find in the vague morality of natural law.

The precise relation between natural-law and common-law forms was inevitably problematic. Occasionally, it was announced that the common law and natural law were simply identical, but that claim was inherently implausible. Many technical rules of the common law seemed purely whimsical, obviously rooted exclusively in the English legal tradition, and often derived from the history of feudal property relations, which Americans had explicitly repudiated. Some rules had already been declared wholly inapplicable to the New World, where they had been modified, in quite various ways, in each of the colonies; even in England there had been obvious changes within the supposed changelessness of the common law. Thus, it was hard to argue that each common-law rule was an expression of immutable, universal truth.

The potential conflict between natural-law conceptions and the common-law tradition, as well as between contradictory assertions within natural law, was obscured in the early nineteenth century by a surprisingly self-confident belief that one would always reach a just conclusion by employing two techniques of legal reasoning: liberality of interpretation and implication. By the first, judges and treatise writers meant a willingness to interpret technical common-law rules—which were still unquestioningly assumed to form the bulk of the law with a flexible, progressive American spirit and, in particular, with concern for commercial utility. Lord Mansfield in England, who had often drawn on civil law to modify rigid common-law rules in the name of commercial good sense, was often cited as an example to be followed by enlightened American decision makers.

This notion of utility became a key mediating concept in liberal interpretation. It suggested that one did not have to choose *between* a strict, rigid adherence to common-law technicalities and the less certain demands of substantive justice, nor between commercial utility and the moralistic claims of traditional natural law. Instead, it was common to cite utility as a justification for departing from common law rules, often on the claim that the common law itself, properly understood by liberal judges like Mansfield, had always allowed for utilitarian change; and then to further explain that in the form of commercial "reasonableness," utility was implicit in natural reason and therefore in the whole natural-law and civil-law tradition. Thus, modern departures from common-law rules could be seen as both consistent with the long "changing changelessness" of the common-law tradition and also as evidence of the common law's link to natural reason and universal principle.

The technique of implied intent, also basic to early nineteenth century legal thought, performed a similar function. Routinely, judges appealed to the intent of the parties as a basis for decision making, which coincided with the increased use of contract imagery in judicial opinions. The emphasis on implied intent did not, however, necessarily evidence concern with the actual, subjective intent of individual parties; instead, it represented a fusion of subjective intent with socially imposed duty. Legal thinkers self-confidently assumed that they could find the "law" within the obligations inherent in particular social and commercial relations, obligations which, it could be claimed, parties intended to assume when they entered the relationship.

For example, in his important treatise on contract law, Parsons devoted over 90 percent of the pages to a description of various types of parties (e.g., agents, guardians, servants) and relational contexts (e.g., marriage, bailment, service contracts, sale of goods). Each category represented a social entity with its own implicit duties and reasonable expectations. A party entering into a particular relationship would be said to have intended to conform to the standards of reasonable behavior that inhered in such a relationship. Specific rules could then be defended or modified depending upon whether they promoted the principles and policies basic to that relationship (encouraged transactions in goods, promoted honorable dealing between merchants, etc.). Subjectivity and free will were thus combined with the potentially conflicting imposition of objective, judicially created obligations; and both notions were integrated into the amorphous blend of natural law, positive law, morality, and utility, which made up the justificatory language of early nineteenth-century law.

Despite the confidence with which early nineteenth-century judges invoked liberality and implied intent, the conceptual mush they made of legal theory posed serious problems for the emerging liberal conception, in constitutional law, of a sovereignty limited by private legal rights. Public law thinking was dominated by the Lockean model of the individual rightholder confronting a potentially oppressive sovereign power. Within that world-view, there ideally existed a realm of pure private autonomy, free from state intrusion. It was a realm in which individuals owned property protected from the encroachment of others and made self-willed, freely bargained for choices. Of course there was also a legitimate public realm, comprised of state and federal institutions entrusted with maintaining public order and serving clearly to delineate public functions. Nevertheless, the public realm and the private were vacuum-bounded: in other words, they were conceived as wholly separate, in-or-out categories that could allow for no blurring or intermeshing. It was, in effect, the vacuum boundary between public and private that jurists of the early nineteenth century promised to guard with such everlasting zeal.

Yet, in order to justify protecting private rights from public power, it was necessary to conceive of the private as purely private. This demanded, in turn, a fully rationalized structure of private law which, in theory, did no more than protect and facilitate the exercise of private will and which could also give concrete, objective content to the private rights supposedly protected by the Constitution. The loose hodgepodge of conflicting premises that made up early nineteenth-century private law was insufficient for that purpose, and the great thrust of nineteenth-century legal thought was toward higher and higher levels of rationalization and generalization. Eventually, that process produced a grandly integrated conceptual scheme that seemed, for a fleeting moment in history, to bring coherence to the whole structure of American law, and to liberal political theory in general.

## CLASSICAL LEGAL CONSCIOUSNESS (1885–1935)

The nineteenth century's process of legal rationalization resulted in the abstraction of law from both particularized social relations and substantive moral standards. By the "rule of law" classical jurists meant quite specifically a structure of positive, objective, formally defined rights. They viewed the legal world not as a multitude of discrete, traditional relations but as a structure of protected spheres of rights and powers. Logically derivable vacuum boundaries defined for each individual her own sphere of pure private autonomy while simultaneously defining those spheres within which public power could be exercised freely and absolutely.

This conception of social action as the exercise of absolute rights and powers within bounded spheres extended to all possible relations: in a way inconceivable to the early nineteenth century, the relation of private parties to each other was seen as deeply analogous to the relation of private parties to states, of states to each other and to federal powers, etc. In every instance of dispute, the key legal question was whether the relevant actors had stayed within their own protected sphere of activity or had crossed over the boundary and invaded the sphere of another. To the classics, freedom *meant* the legal guarantee that rights and powers would be protected as absolute within their own sphere, but that no rightholder/powerholder would be allowed to invade the sphere of another.

In that classical scheme, the utterly crucial task of boundary definition was assigned to the judiciary. Necessarily, this task required objectivity and impartiality. Other actors were free, within their own spheres, to exercise unbridled will in pursuit of their particular (subjective) moral, political, or economic goals. In contrast, the judicial role of boundary finding required the exercise of reason—a reason now conceived, however, not as embodying universal moral principles and knowledge of the public good but strictly as the application of objective methodology to the task of defining the scope of legal rights. Upon the supposed objectivity of that method hinged the liberal faith that the rule of law resolved the conflict between freedom as private, civil right and freedom as public participation in a democracy.

The supposed judicial objectivity upon which the classical structure depended was based in turn upon the intersection of constitutional language and an increasingly generalized, rationalized conception of private law. First, jurists pointed out that by enacting the Constitution, the sovereign American people had unequivocally (and wisely) adopted a government premised on private rights and strictly limited public powers. Thus, while it was certainly the exalted function of the judiciary to protect private rights from uncontrolled public passion, this function required merely the application of positive constitutional law—there was no painful choice to be made between positive law and natural rights.

Second, and of prime importance, the objective definition given to rights protected by the Constitution could be found within the common-law tradition, which had been wonderfully cleansed of both messy social particularity and natural-law morality. Classical jurists claimed that as a result of an enlightened, scientific process of rationalization, the common law could now properly be understood as based upon a few general and powerful—but clearly positivised—conceptual categories (like property and free contract), which had also been incorporated into the Constitution as protected rights. All of the specific rules of the common law (at least the "correct" rules) were said to be deduced from those general categories. For example, Williston's monumental treatise on contracts assumed that from the general principle of free contract one could derive the few central doctrines around which the treatise was organized—offer and acceptance, consideration, excuse, etc.—and from the logic of those central doctrines one could derive all of the specific rules that made up the law of contracts. Those rules could then be applied, rigidly and formally, to *any* particular social context; in fact, failure to do so would be evidence of judicial irrationality and/or irresponsibility. Moreover, because every rule was based upon the principle of free contract, the logical coherence of a contract doctrine, correctly applied, ensured that private contracting was always an expression of pure autonomy. With no small amount of self-congratulation, classical jurists contrasted their conceptualization of private autonomy to Parson's description of contract law as something to be found within numberless particular social relations. In retrospect, Parsons could be viewed as naive and unscientific.

The new rationalization of common law meant that the old conflict between formally realizable "rules" and substantive "justice" seemed resolved. Common-law rules were no longer a quirky relic from the English feudal past. Instead, they were both an expression and a definition of rights, and of course the protection of rights constituted the highest form of justice. Furthermore, as integrated into the constitutional law structure, the rationalization of private law meant that the boundary between the realm of private autonomy and the realm of public power could be objectively determined by reference to specific common-law doctrine.

The notorious case of *Coppage v. Kansas* provides a clear example of the classical approach. In that case the Kansas state legislature had passed a statute outlawing yellow-dog contracts (i.e., contracts in which workers agreed not to engage in union activities). The question was whether this was a reasonable exercise of police power (i.e., fell within the bounded sphere of public power) or whether it constituted an invasion of private contract right, a right considered implicit in the even more general category of liberty protected by the Fourteenth Amendment.

An earlier case, *Adair v. United States*, had declared that a similar federal regulation was invalid; and through the Fourteenth Amendment, the constitutional protection of liberty as against the federal government was made applicable to the states—evidence of the deep analogy now perceived in what were once conceived as quite different relationships. In response to the argument that *Adair* controlled, however, Kansas argued that its statute was designed specifically to outlaw contracts formed under coercion. Since workers had no realistic choice but to accept the terms obviously imposed by employers, the agreement to sign yellow-dog contracts was not an expression of freedom, and it was no violation of liberty to regulate a "choice" that was never freely made. The Court refused to accept that argument, not because it denied the obvious inequality between workers and employers, but because freedom of contract as a legal category had to be defined objectively, which meant according to common-law doctrine. Since the common law had excluded economic pressure from its definition of duress as a legal excuse for nonperformance of contracts, then *by definition* yellow-dog contracts were not formed under duress and were therefore freely entered. It then followed logically that the statute constituted an invasion of liberty protected by the Constitution.

Cases like *Coppage* are now commonly cited as representing a judiciary determined to impose its own economic biases on the country. This both trivializes the underlying power of the classical conceptual scheme and, more significantly, trivializes the importance of the realist assault that revealed its incoherence. In fact, courts during the classical period described a police power as absolute in its sphere as were private rights in theirs, and they by no means overruled all legislation designed to regulate corporate power. Their key claim was that they could objectively "find" the boundary that separated private from public, and it was that supposed objectivity that gave the appearance of coherence and reality to the legal (and social/political) model of bounded rights and powers. That basic model, although in bankrupt form, is with us still, despite the realist challenge that demolished all of its premises. The message the model conveys is that actual power relations in the real world are by definition legitimate and most go unchallenged.

# THE REALIST CHALLENGE (1920–1939)

The realist movement was a part of the general twentieth-century revolt against formalism and conceptualism. As applied to law, that revolt was directed against the whole highly conceptualized classical legal structure. More Specifically and politically, realism was also a reaction against Supreme Court decisions like *Coppage*, which had invalidated progressive regulatory legislation favored even by many business leaders.

Some of the realists confined their attack to the relatively mild suggestion that legal thought should be more in accord with changing times and public sentiment. That meant recognizing the growing importance of government—especially administrative agencies—in an advanced industrial economy. Thus judges should defer to legislators on economic issues, and law students should prepare themselves to be policy makers in the new regulatory state. Meanwhile, in private law, enlightened, progressive judges should be willing to sacrifice rigid adherence to the logic of doctrine for the sake of doing a more common-sense and overtly policy-oriented "justice" within the particular context of each case.

The best of the realist critique, however, cut so deeply into the premises of American legal thought that no amount of enlightened policy-making and informed situation sense could ever really put Humpty Dumpty together again. Chiefly, the realists undermined all faith in the objective existence of "rights" by challenging the coherence of the key legal categories that gave content to the notion of bounded public and private spheres. Traditionally, legal discourse had justified decisions by making reference to rights; an opinion, for example, would set out as a reason for finding the defendant liable that she had invaded the property rights of the plaintiff—or, similarly, would justify declaring a statute unconstitutional by saying that it violated the right of property. Yet, as the realists pointed out, such justifications are inevitably circular. There will be a right if, and *only* if, the court finds for the plaintiff or declares the statute unconstitutional. What the court cites as the *reason* for the decision—the existence of a right—is, in fact, only the *result*.

Moreover, in every dispute, both sides' interests or goals can be asserted and formulated in terms of rights. In a nuisance case, for example, one party's "right" to complete security from the other's invasion (as in the form of industrial pollutants, noise from animals, or whatever) can be countered by an equally coherent "right" to complete freedom to use property as one chooses. Thus, instead of a preexisting right that compels a particular result, there are, in fact, conflicting (and contradictory) rights between which the court must always choose. It is that legal *choice* which then determines the result and forms the so-called right.

This attack upon the logic of rights theory was closely linked to an attack upon the logic of precedent. The realists pointed out that no two cases are ever exactly alike; there will always be some difference in the multitude of facts surrounding them. Thus, the "rule" of a former case can never simply be applied to a new case; rather, the judge must *choose* whether or not the ruling in the former case should be extended to include the new case. That choice is essentially a choice about the relevancy of facts, and those choices can never be logically compiled. Given shared social assumptions, some facts might seem obviously irrelevant (e.g., the color of socks worn by the offeree should not influence the enforceability of a contract), but decisions about the relevance of other distinguishing facts are more obviously value-laden and dependent on the historical context (e.g., the relative wealth of the parties).

That dilemma does not vanish when the "law" to be applied comes not from cases but from the language of statutory or constitutional provisions, or the language of a private contract. There was a time when words were thought to have a fixed, determinate content, a meaning partaking of objective Platonic forms. In the absence of a belief in Platonic intelligible essences, however, no interpretation or application of language can be logically required by the language itself. Words are created by people in history, and their definition inevitably varies with particular context and with the meaning brought to them by the judges who are asked to interpret them. That act of interpretation is, in every instance, an act of social choice.

Thus, the realists claimed that the effort of the nineteenth century to cleanse law of messy social particularity and moral choice was inevitably a failure. There was *no such thing* as an objective legal methodology behind which judges could hide in order to evade responsibility for the social consequences of legal decision making. Every decision they made was a moral and political choice.

Furthermore, the realists understood, as had the classics, that the whole structure of the classical scheme depended upon the coherence of private law and the public/private distinction. Thus, the realists spent little time attacking the methodology of constitutional law and concentrated instead upon undermining the coherence of the key private-law categories that purported to define a sphere of pure autonomy. For example, Morris Cohen's essay "Property and Sovereignty" pointed out that property is necessarily public, not private. Property *means* the legally granted power to withhold from others; as such, it is created by the state and given its only content by legal decisions that limit or extend the property owner's power over others. Thus, property is really an (always conditional) delegation of sovereignty, and property law is simply a form of public law. Whereas the classics (and liberal theorists generally) had drawn a bright line separating (private) property from (public) sovereignty, Cohen simply collapsed the two categories.

Hale made a similar point about the supposed private right of free contract: state enforcement of a contract right represents, like property, a delegation of sovereign power. Moreover, he also pointed out, coercion, including legal coercion, lies at the heart of every "freely" chosen exchange. Coercion is inherent in each party's legally protected threat to withhold what is owned; that right to withhold creates the right to force submission to one's own terms. Since ownership is a function of legal entitlement, every bargain is a function of the legal order. Thus, there is no "inner" core of free, autonomous bargaining to be protected from "outside" state action; the inner and outer dissolve into each other.

Potentially, that collapse of spheres carried with it the collapse of the whole structure of American legal thought. Realism had effectively undermined the fundamental premises of liberal legalism, particularly the crucial distinction between legislation (subjective exercise of will) and adjudication (objective exercise of reason). Inescapably, it had also suggested that the whole liberal, world view of (private) rights and (public) sovereignty mediated by the rule of law was only a mirage, a pretty fantasy that masked the reality of economic and political power.

Since the realists, American jurists have dedicated themselves to the task of reconstruction; indeed, the realist message was so corrosive that many of the most influential realists evaded the full implications of their own criticism and quickly sought instead to articulate a new justification for legal reasoning's old claim to objectivity and legitimacy. That effort seemed especially crucial after the rise of fascism in Europe: If the liberal model of legally protected private rights was mere illusion, then where could one look for protection against totalitarian statism? Nevertheless, the modern search for a new legitimacy, however earnest, was destined always to have a slightly defensive tone; after realism, American legal theorists had, as it were, eaten of the tree of knowledge, and there could be no return to the naive confidence of the past.

## ATTEMPTS AT MODERN RECONSTRUCTION (1940–PRESENT)

During the 1940s, Laswell and McDougal at Yale followed out the implications of realism by announcing that since law students were destined to be the policymakers of the future, Yale should simply abandon the traditional law school curriculum and teach students how to make and implement policy decisions. Their simultaneously antidemocratic and antilegalist message was a bit jarring; most of the major post-realist reconstructors of American legal thought have been somewhat more restrained. Indeed, much of the reconstruction has consisted of simply conceding a number of key realist insights and then attempting to incorporate those insights into an otherwise intact doctrinal structure. What were once perceived as deep and unsettling logical flaws have been translated into the strengths of a progressive legal system. For example, the indeterminacy of rules has become the *flexibility* required for sensible, policy-oriented decision making; and the collapse of rights into contradiction has been recast as "competing interests," which are inevitable in a complex, tragic world and which obviously require an enlightened judicial *balancing*. In other words, we justify as legal sophistication what the classics would have viewed as the obvious abandonment of legality.

The most elaborate attempt to resurrect the legitimacy of the whole American lawmaking structure can be found in the extraordinarily influential Hart and Sacks legal process materials of the 1950s. Those materials were premised on a vision of American society which, it seemed for a time, offered a viable alternative to the whole classical world view. Hart and Sacks started by explaining that the critical view of law as a "mask for force, providing a cover of legitimacy" for the exercise of political and economic power, was based on "the fallacy of the static pie." According to Hart and Sacks, the "pie" of both tangible and intangible goods was in fact everexpanding, and a primary, shared purpose of social life was to keep the pie growing.

Within the Hart and Sacks description of American society, the essentially private actors who shared the goal of expansion also shared a belief in the stability afforded by the institutional settlement (by law) of the few disputes that were likely to arise, and more specifically in the particular distribution of functions that was set out in the American Constitution; that distribution was itself designed to ensure both the maximization of valid human wants and a "fair" (although not necessarily equal) distribution of tangible and intangible goods.

The effect was to postulate not particular substantive rights but rather a shared social value in the *process* by which rights were defined—a shared value in distinct institutional competencies. That implied, in turn, a differentiation of the processes by which judges, in contrast to legislators and administrators, reached decisions. According to Hart and Sacks, judges had the competence to settle questions that lent themselves to a process of "reasoned elaboration"—that could, in other words, be justified by reference to general, articulated standards which could be applied in all like cases: that process was to be contrasted with the "unbuttoned discretion" enjoyed by legislators. Presumably, it was the judiciary who decided which questions lent themselves to this process of reasoned elaboration.

The shift from an emphasis on substance to an emphasis on process seemed for a time to satisfy the realist critique of substantive rights; but of course it still rested on the distinction between reasoned elaboration and discretion, which in turn rested on the availability of principled, objective, substantive categories to which judges could make reference. More generally, it also rested on the complacent, simplistic assumption that American society consisted of happy, private actors maximizing their valid human wants while sharing their profound belief in institutional competencies. That may have reflected the mind-set of many in the 1950s, but by the end of the 1960s it seemed oddly out of touch with reality.

Another response to the collapse of clear conceptual categories has been less self-consciously articulated than Hart and Sacks', but pervades modern case law. The prevailing pattern is to accept as inevitable and "in the nature of things" the absence of vacuum-bounded categories. Instead, the boundaries between categories are portrayed as fluid, or "live," meaning that many particular examples will occupy a mushy middle position, which includes attributes of two nonetheless distinct categories. Thus, the collapse of spheres is not total, and the goal is to deal comfortably with a world made up largely of middle positions.

This livening up of boundaries cuts across all doctrinal lines. For example, the traditional rule of jurisdiction was that a state court could exercise jurisdiction only over a defendant who was within the borders of the state; the line was as clear as the state's boundary marker. That straightforward "in or out" conception has now given way to a conception that recognizes "presence" as often a middle ground, sort-of-in sort-of-out notion, to be determined by standards of "fair play and substantial justice" and by a "balance" of the interests of the relevant parties and forums. Similarly, whereas classical doctrine had drawn a clear line, at the moment of formation, between contract and no contract, modern reference to reliance breaks down that clarity by recognizing a sort-of contract prior to formation, based on one party's reasonable reliance on the other's precontract negotiating promises, the same notion also breaks down the once sharp contract/tort distinction (i.e., obligations agreed to by the parties as distinct from obligations imposed by law), since reliance is the basis of neither a recognized tort nor a fully contractual cause of action.

At this point in time it would be hard to state any pair of categories still legally conceived as vacuum-bounded. Even life/death and male/female have been treated by courts as live-bounded, as in the *Karen Quinlan* case and cases involving parties who have undergone sex transformations. Similarly, in the landmark abortion case, *Roe v. Wade,* the Supreme Court recognized a woman's abortion decision as protected by the right to privacy during the first trimester, as legitimately subject to public power during the last trimester, and during the middle trimester as partly private but also subject to some limited public control. Notably, however, courts have still refused to recognize a live boundary between capital and labor.

Closely paralleling the emergence of live rather than vacuum boundaries has been the breakdown of the deep sense of analogy and uniformity that once characterized classical thought. Private-law categories such as property or contract were then thought to have fixed meanings that did not vary with differences in context; that uniformity was conceived to be crucial to the ideal of rationality and formal equality. Now, however, it is common to concede that rights may vary depending upon status and relationship. As Justice Robert Jackson explained in *United States v. Willow River Power Company,* simply because a particular water-flow level might constitute property as between two private parties, that did not necessarily mean that the same flow constituted property as between a private party and the federal government.

Despite the breakdown of vacuum boundaries and uniform, generally applicable categories, modern American legal thought continues to be premised on the distinction between private law and public law. Private law is still assumed to be *about* private actors with private rights, making private choices, even though sophisticated judges tend quite frankly to refer to public policy when justifying private-law decision making. Similarly, the major post-realist reconstructors of private-law theory, like Edward Levi and Karl Llewellyn, acknowledged the necessary role of policy choice in legal decision making but described judicial choices as still specifically "legal" because judges worked within a long-established judicial tradition, which exerted a steadying (if not precisely "logical") constraint. By training, judges acquire a "craft-consciousness," which leads them to respond to new situations through a "reworking of the heritage" rather than through unguided impulse. The result is neither unbridled choice nor inflexible formalism but "continuity with growth" and "vision with tradition." The new private-law heroes were therefore not the rigorous Willistonians, who refused to acknowledge the role of social change in shaping law, but (once again) Mansfield in England, America's own preclassical nineteenth-century judges, and, in more recent times, Benjamin Cardozo.

As an example of enlightened decision making, Levi described with admiration Cardozo opinion in *McPherson v. Buick Motors Company.* There, Cardozo had modified the classical privity of contract rule (according to which a manufacturer's liability for personal injuries due to a defective product extended only to those with whom he had directly entered a contract) in order to hold Buick liable for a "foreseeable" injury to a party not in privity. As justification, Cardozo had specifically referred to changes in automobile retailing practice because of which only retailer middlemen, and rarely consumers, directly contracted with manufacturers. Under the privity rule, consumers would almost always be left unprotected when defective cars caused injuries, an "anomalous" result, Cardozo's said, which he did not want to reach.

Cardozo also justified his decision by referring to the category of "abnormally dangerous" products, which had evolved as an exception to the privity rule and to the standard of "foreseeability" upon which Cardozo claimed the exception was based. Using the notion of foreseeability,

Cardozo masterfully suggested that his decision was a reasoned application of past doctrine, not simply a result-oriented exercise of judicial policy choice. Nevertheless, the skilled craft of the opinion obscured rather than solved the key realist point: for every rule there is bound to be a counterrule, *because* the choice to be made is always between the contradictory claims of freedom and security. In their extreme form here, that would mean freedom as complete absence of manufacturer liability versus consumer security as manufacturer liability for all injuries caused by use of his product. Within legal logic there is no reason for drawing the line at any particular point, and recasting the problem as one of a supposedly neutral public policy does not resolve the dilemma. Trite, conventional policy arguments can always be made for *either* freedom or security.

As with policy, modern private-law thinking has both conceded and evaded the inevitability of value choice in legal decision making. The great post-realist treatise writers, Corbin on contracts and Prosser on torts, appeal at least as often to presumably neutral, shared standards of substantive "justice" and "reasonableness" as they do to fixed rules; but the vocabulary of modern treatises is still the vocabulary of classical doctrine—questions of justice emerge within discussions of offer and acceptance, the elements of a cause of action in negligence, etc. The message is that we can advance beyond the silly stage of formalism while still retaining the basic structure and premises of classical thought. Both Prosser and Corbin, however, leave unresolved the old conflict between formal realizability and general standards of substantive justice; and neither explains where, within liberalism's supposed subjectivity of values, one is to find a source for objective standards of justice.

The most sophisticated version of private-law reconstruction can be found in the Sales Article of the Uniform Commercial Code—essentially Llewellyn's revamping of traditional contract law. Like Corbin and Prosser, Llewellyn relied on standard doctrine for most of his vocabulary, but he also sought to replace a formalistic application of rules with standards of good faith and reasonableness. Those standards were to be known not as the abstract universals of natural law but through a judicial understanding of actual intent and reasonable expectations within each specific fact situation and within the customs and usages of specific trades. This was Llewellyn's famous "situation-sense" which, he insisted, was distinctly "legal" because it drew on the legal tradition of craft, reason, and principle, and at the same time saw (universal) reason as embodied within the particularity of specific commercial practice.

Llewellyn's "singing reason," as he perhaps unfortunately termed it, has already raised methodological problems. The facts of particular customs or situations tend to elude objective judicial determination; some courts have simply refused to hear all of the conflicting testimony with which they are confronted. The choice as to relevancy, of course, remains a *choice;* and even if objectively "known," the precise role of custom and usage in relation to traditional rules is still problematic. It is commonly said, for example, that custom and usage can be used to interpret contracts but not to create them; yet it is unclear why the line should be drawn at that point, or whether the distinction is even an intelligible one. Equally problematic is the precise relation between reason and custom—a problem as old as the coexistence of a natural-law and a (supposedly customary) common-law tradition. Without standards of reasonableness *outside* existing practice, singing reason is simply ratification of the status quo—the "is" automatically becomes the "ought." Yet absent a fully developed natural-law theory, the source of any such normative standard remains unavailable. Moreover, taking custom and usage as a source of legal standards does not really avoid the problem of self-referencing, which was inevitable in rights theory, since social practice and reasonable expectations are, like "free" bargains, in large measure a *function* of the legal order. The wholly spontaneous custom and usage is rare, if it exists at all; thus, by reflecting "custom," the law in large measure reflects only itself, and the nagging problem of legitimacy reemerges.

The hodgepodge of policy, situation-sense, and leftover doctrine that now makes up the indeterminate body of private law provides scant basis for a rationalization of constitutional rights; and the search for some coherent foundation for rights analysis, particularly for judicial review, has been the preoccupation of modern constitutional law theorists. That search has led to two distinct branches in constitutional law thought. The first is based on a model of deference to legislative bodies, while the second is based on various attempts to formulate affirmative, substantive bases for constitutional rights.

During the New Deal, the Supreme Court virtually abandoned to the legislature the field of economic regulation, once subject to invalidation under the categories of property and free contract. Deference in that area, however, left unresolved the fate of other supposed constitutional rights. For some theorists, deference simply became the preferred model for all cases. Alexander Bickel, for example, created a new category, somewhere between general principle and mere expediency, which he called prudence. A prudent Supreme Court would avoid judicial review by using procedural grounds (e.g., problems of ripeness or standing) to justify a refusal to reach the merits. The Court could thereby avoid both the criticism that it stood in the way of the democratic majority (the basic argument against judicial review) and the criticism that it legitimated, by finding constitutional, action that seemed to violate fundamental rights. One of Bickel's examples was the notorious *Korematsu* case, where the Supreme Court upheld the detention of all Japanese Americans living on the West Coast in holding camps during World War II. Bickel argued that the Court should have dodged the question rather than label the detention and its underlying statute constitutional. The exercise of such prudence would have gained the trust of the country and placed the Court in the position of "teacher" in the public discussion of values. Then, when a time of *real* crisis to the Constitution arose, the court would have been in a position to act on principle, with the backing of the people.

Bickel's "passive virtues" inevitably represent something of a retreat from the juristic model of rights and sovereignty. The person in a concentration camp is presumably not comforted with the knowledge that her case has been prudently decided on procedural rather than constitutional grounds; and a Court unprepared to make hard decisions in such a case is in a weak position to then hold out legal rights as the ultimate protection against totalitarianism. Bickel maintained that the prudent Court could still act when the dictator's troops came marching down Massachusetts Avenue, but his claim rang a bit hollow.

Moreover, the Bickel approach of deference to the legislative process, while on the surface the most obvious answer to the claim that judicial review is undemocratic, evades questions about the nature of our particular form of representation. The American legislative model is not, under our constitutional structure, itself a model of pure, participatory, consensualism; its particular form is not more unquestionably democratic or legitimate than is judicial review. *Both* are part of a total constitutional structure, as interpreted by past legal decision making. In fact, an attack on any single part of that structure inevitably calls into question the legitimacy of the whole structure. Also, Hale's critique of free choice in the market can be applied to the political process (the marketplace of ideas) as well. So-called free political choice takes place within a system of legally protected economic power, which is a function of past legal decision making and which profoundly affects outcomes in the political decision-making process. The Court, by suddenly avoiding judicial review, cannot escape responsibility for the social decisions that are made.

Alternatively, other theorists have sought a more affirmative defense of constitutional rights. Herbert Wechsler, for example, advocated a return to "general" and "neutral" principles as the only sound basis for judicial review. He complained, for example, that in the *Brown* case the Court rested its decision on sociological fact rather than on constitutional principle. Yet he also acknowledged that the only available, general principle that seemed to cover the case was "freedom of association," which quickly confronts an equally neutral and general but contradictory principle barring forced association. As he conceded, at the level of pure, ahistorical generality there was no logical resolution; yet the necessary move to greater particularity raises the dilemma of necessarily illogical choice—somewhere between abstract, transcendental generality and ad hoc, "unprincipled" case-by-case decision making. The choice is bound to appear arbitrary.

The most recent attempts to derive a substantive basis for fundamental constitutional rights have vacillated between a more or less veiled reliance on natural-law theory (David Richards, Kenneth Karst, Lawrence Tribe), and recourse to a model, only somewhat more sophisticated than Hart and Sacks', of shared American values (Harry Wellington, Michael Perry). John Ely, criticizing both approaches, has attempted to take a stand somewhere between the assertion of affirmative substantive rights and complete deference. He has postulated instead a supposedly value-neutral "participation-oriented, representation-reinforcing" standard for judicial review. Drawing on Justice Harlan Fiske Stone's suggestion, Ely argues that the judiciary should actively scrutinize only that legislation (1) "which restricts those political processes which can ordinarily be expected to bring about repeal of undesirable legislation," or (2) which is based on "prejudice against discrete and insular minorities." Yet this approach too rests on a conception of substantive values—the value of participation within this particular form of representative structure and the "badness" of prejudice as opposed to all those other values which the legislature would be left free to implement. As in the Hart and Sacks materials, the nagging problem of asserting objective, substantive values within a system premised on a pluralistic subjectivity of values inevitably reemerges.

Currently, perhaps the most influential attempt to provide a general, legitimating rationale for American legal decision making has been through a blending of legal theory and free-market economic theory. Scholars within the law and economics movement have happily embraced the realist view that legal language, which purports to be about preexisting rights, simply obscures what courts do. Their claim is that, in fact, American judges have succeeded, with surprising consistency, in mimicking those solutions that would be reached through unimpeded market exchange, solutions that can therefore be described as most efficient (least costly). Furthermore, shifting from the descriptive to a normative claim, they argue that efficiency provides a neutral, objective standard for judicial decision making, unlike obviously value-laden rights analysis.

The most frequently cited "rule" that emerges from the law and economics literature—the Coase theorem—is that courts should simply assign any "right" in question to the party who would find it worthwhile to purchase that right if it were assigned to the other party and if transaction costs were zero. By definition, any other result would be costly in that it would either give the right to the party for whom it had less value—a failure of exchange equilibrium—or else lend to unnecessary exchange transaction costs in order to achieve equilibrium. While law and economic theorists concede that in some cases the application of the Coase theorem might lead to unwanted distributional consequences, those should be ignored by judges. Distribution is essentially a political question that should be left to legislation, and judges should confine themselves to applying the objective, neutral exchange calculus.

Most of those who are used to assuming that law is really "about" rights find the instrumental tone of the law and economics literature startling; indeed, the assertion that the common law has traditionally served to mimic the market under the guise of protecting rights sounds starkly Marxist. On another level, however, most current law and economics theory represents neoconceptualism strikingly similar to the classical conceptualism successfully undermined by the realists. The law and economics model is the model of free, value-enhancing exchange, yet as Hale

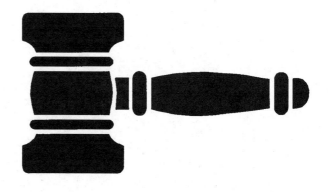

*Judgment of Time*

pointed out with reference to free contract theory, market exchanges are in fact a function of the legal order; the terms of so-called free bargains (and, taken collectively, the supposedly objective market price) are determined by the legally protected right to withhold what is owned. Exchange "value" (and "costs") is a function of that right, so that the rationale of exchange is ultimately as circular and self-referencing as the rationale for legal rights. The legitimacy of every exchange calculus depends upon the legitimacy of prior legal decisions: it neither establishes that legitimacy nor evades the problem of intimacy by a purported ahistorical objectivity. Similarly, judges cannot escape responsibility for the distributional consequences of legal decisions. The exchange calculus cannot be divorced from the question of distribution, since exchange is a function of the existing distribution of legal entitlement, and every new legal decision (including those that rigorously apply the law and economics approach) will inevitably affect subsequent distribution and, in turn, affect subsequent exchanges, costs, values, etc. Like the older spheres of private and public, questions of market exchange and of distribution simply collapse into each other.

Nevertheless, despite all of their fairly obvious intellectual incoherences, the various efforts to reconstruct American legal thought continue daily, filling numberless volumes of case reports and law reviews. Presumably, they still play the role Rousseau identified: "The strong is never strong enough to be always the strongest, unless he transforms strength into right, and obedience into duty."

# MENSCH

NAME: _____

SECTION: _____

DATE: _____

1. In the brand new republic, lawyers were praised as the embodiment of Republican virtue. Why was this a change from the colonial period?

2. What universal principle seemed to require the most zealous protection under the new legal system? Why?

3. Did the classical legal consciousness try to create a ground structure of protected spheres of rights and power, or merely try to increase its own political power?

4. What impact did the so-called "Behavioral Revolution" have on the classical legal consciousness? What was the new theory of jurisprudence called?

_____
_____
_____
_____
_____
_____
_____
_____

5. Explain Mensch's conception of "vacuum bounded" categories and "live bounded" categories.

_____
_____
_____
_____
_____
_____
_____
_____

**Group Exercise:** Contemporary legal theorists have attempted to stabilize the judicial function by offering two new approaches: legislative deference and formulation of constitutional rights. Which does the group favor, and why?

**Individual Project:** Consult a professional journal and select and identify an article on legal theory. Which school of thought does the author favor?

# JUDICIAL REVIEW

## Sarah Ellerbee

Judicial review is the legal concept which states that courts have the power to declare actions of the political branches of government—legislative and executive—unconstitutional. The doctrine allows acts of the latter to be defined as legally unacceptable and therefore unenforceable. All state and national courts may exercise this authority, though a final decision is usually made by the highest state or federal (national) court. Though the United States Constitution does not specifically grant it the authority, the Supreme Court asserted the power of judicial review in the famous case of *Marbury v. Madison* (1803). The doctrine rests upon several assumptions, including one which sees the Constitution as the supreme law, that acts of public officials contrary to the Constitution are null and void, and that the judiciary is the chief guardian of the Constitution. The primary method of altering the meaning of the Constitution historically has been through the use of judicial review. Of fundamental importance is the fact that major changes in the political system have taken place without the expressed approval of the American voting public. The exercise of judicial review inevitably puts it into direct conflict with the ultimate democratic concept of popular sovereignty. Judicial review allows members of the judiciary, and the Supreme Court in particular, sweeping authority to decide the meaning of the Constitution and to act as final arbiter of questions involving the powers of both national and state government officials. What further complicates matters is the fact that the Constitution is silent about who should have the last word in disagreements over matters of interpretation. During the last two centuries, approximately 1200 state and local laws and at least 131 federal statutes have been declared unconstitutional by the Supreme Court. Though these cases are but a small percentage of the total number of laws passed, any declaration of unconstitutionality will inevitably deter similar legislation in the future. For this reason, the doctrine remains a major source of legal controversy that will never be fully resolved.

## HISTORY AND BACKGROUND

As with many other ideas that were eventually incorporated into our American political system, the roots of judicial review are found in British legal theory. The belief that courts could nullify a legislative act is several hundred years old and said to originate in the remarks of Chief Justice Edward Coke in *Dr. Bonham's Case* (1610). In that celebrated case, Coke asserted an almost mystical claim that the English common law was the virtual equal of both Parliament and King, and when actions of either of the latter were found lacking in "common right and reason," the former was properly interpreted (by judges such as himself) to be superior and dominant. Similarly, during the final years leading to the American Revolution, colonials often asserted the primacy of the same common law over English political acts, most notably by James Otis in the legal attack against Parliament's authorization of writs of assistance. During the post-revolutionary period, under the Articles of Confederation, there were no national courts although judges in at least six states challenged enactments of their legislatures, thereby lending credence to the belief in judicial review as legitimate, legal doctrine. The underlying issue surrounding its use, however, is whether an independent judiciary would be as attentive to the rights of citizens as one more directly accountable to popular control. The state judiciary was never given an explicit power of judicial review and therefore it was questionable whether judges could invalidate an act of the legislature. The rather limited number of precedents for judicial review among the states during the period provides little assurance that it was perceived as a logically necessary feature of government created by a written constitution, as many later contended. Indeed, it is not well established that most delegates to the Convention at Philadelphia had significant prior experience with or knowledge of the doctrine.

It was with this somewhat questionable or limited knowledge of judicial review that delegates in Philadelphia proposed to discuss the constitutional powers of the new national courts. Article III, Section One, of the Constitution provides "The judicial Power of the United States, shall be vested in one supreme Court, and in such inferior Courts as the Congress may from time to time ordain and establish." Section Two of the Article extends national judicial power to "all Cases . . . arising under this Constitution, the laws of the United States, and Treaties . . . to Controversies to which the United States shall be a Party, — to Controversies between two or more States; between a State and Citizens of another State; —between citizens of different States. . . ." Unresolved constitutional questions that may arise because of contradictory rulings among the highest of the thirteen states were addressed by adoption of the Supremacy Clause in Article Six. Judicial review of presidential and congressional acts, then and now, however, remains controversial. It is frequently noted by some observers, for example, that the absence of any specific grant of judicial review is hardly conclusive in establishing the true intentions of the Framers.

It is only in the aftermath of the Philadelphia Convention, within state convention debates over ratification of the Constitution, that one can find contemporaneous statements involving controversy over the doctrine of judicial review. Writing in a local newspaper entitled *The New York Journal and Weekly Register*, Robert Yates questioned the potentially unbridled power that had been proposed for the Supreme Court. Yates' statements are most noteworthy because of his longstanding disagreements with Alexander Hamilton that began when both served in the Constitutional Convention as delegates from the state or New York. The latter's response to such questions is located in *The Federalist Papers* and No. 78 is usually considered a quintessential statement and justification for the doctrine of judicial review. In it he professes not to suppose ". . . a superiority of the judicial to the legislative power. It only supposes that the power of the people (whose will the Constitution embodies) is superior to both." According to Hamilton, when judges exercise this power they claim no supremacy, but rather merely express the will of the people. The ultimate quandary surrounding use of the doctrine, of course, is that when the Court invokes judicial review the topics examined are invariably of major importance. Following the ratification of the Constitution in 1789 and prior to 1803, few cases concerning judicial review arose and those that did were inconclusive as to their results.

## MARBURY V. MADISON

The first assertion of judicial review against an act of Congress was made by Chief Justice John Marshall's opinion in *Marbury v. Madison* (1803). The political and social fabric of the controversy is a fascinating backdrop upon which to consider the exercise of the doctrine.

The men who dominated the Convention at Philadelphia and the United States government in the period at the close of the eighteenth century were nationalists, persons sympathetic to the idea of a strong and vigorous nation led by a strong and vigorous national government. It is reasonable to assume that most would have been supportive of the idea of judicial review even where no evidence can be found to link them to the doctrine. Their opponents in the Democratic-Republican party of Thomas Jefferson were not so inclined. When political parties emerged during the second administration of President George Washington, the nationalists affiliated with what became known as the Federalist party—the major source of organized opposition to Jefferson and his followers. Jefferson's defeat of the Federalists in the election of 1800 (and the hard feelings that resulted) created the circumstances that led to the Marbury decision.

After the Federalists lost control of both the presidency and Congress to their bitter enemies they sought to influence future events through last-minute judicial appointments. Indeed, the Chief Justice of the Supreme Court who wrote the majority decision was the most important beneficiary, and major participant behind the creation of these "midnight" appointments. The outgoing Congress created numerous judicial positions with opportunities for new appointments. The Federalist secretary of state was none other than John Marshall who, having received a large number of signed judicial commissions from President John Adams, was expected to deliver them before the expiration of the president's term of office. Marshall did his best to deliver the commissions to confirm the new judicial appointments. But whereas Marshall could easily see to his own appointment others were less fortunate and many lesser appointees failed to receive their commissions. Among them was William Marbury, a Federalist who had been assigned a position as justice of the peace for the District of Columbia. Whether he intended to do so or not, Marshall left the delivery of Marbury's appointment to his successor, James Madison. Angered by the self-serving actions of the Adams administration, Jefferson ordered Madison not to transmit seventeen undelivered Federalist commissions. Marbury sued.

What Marbury expected to receive from a sympathetic Supreme Court controlled by Federalists was a writ of mandamus, a court order requiring Madison to deliver the commissions to Marbury and his fellow would-be justices of peace. The writ was a legal remedy written into the Judiciary Act of 1780, legislation made necessary by the fact that the Philadelphia Convention could only agree to very minimal provisions for a national court. The nominal and immediate problem was political in nature, a patronage dispute between Federalists and Jeffersonians; the more serious and consequential problem was a constitutional crisis of the greatest magnitude. Marshall knew full well that Jefferson would not obey an order of the Court that favored Marbury. The legitimacy of the Court was at risk and perhaps that of the entire political system, also—after all, the new national government had yet to establish any firm measure of popular acceptance. If Jefferson's strong states rights view of the political system had prevailed, it is hard to imagine what the national government's powers would be today. Indeed, every state in the union would challenge the legitimacy and authority of the national government prior to the Civil War. Marbury's case exhibited the potential to destroy all that had been accomplished at Philadelphia.

Recognizing the problems Marbury's case presented, Marshall sought a solution that would protect the role of the Supreme Court within the context of separation of powers while simultaneously avoiding Jefferson's effort to ferment a constitutional crisis. His solution was noteworthy not only for its cleverness, but because in doing so Marshall created a foundation for a Supreme Court with the power necessary to deal with those of the political branches of government. Marbury was entitled to his position and certainly within his right to seek a writ of mandamus in order to receive the commission, said Marshall; he could not, however, receive his commission from the Supreme Court. The legislation which granted the Court authority to issue the writ of mandamus was incompatible with Article III of the Constitution. Congress had overstepped its bounds. The Court could not enforce legislation, wrote Marshall, that is in conflict with the Constitution which is the fundamental or highest law. It was the central function of the Supreme Court, moreover, to interpret and protect this law against those who would disobey it, whoever the parties may be. Marshall thereby expanded the Court's powers while limiting them to what he saw as the proper scope of its authority; judicial review to determine the ultimate meaning of the constitution. An angry Jefferson could do little because Marshall had given him nothing to challenge or any orders to refuse. What Marshall had done simultaneously was scold his opponents about the nonperformance of their constitutional duties while asserting his authority and that of his judicial colleagues.

## THE TANEY COURT

Whereas Chief Justice Marshall had done much to establish the doctrine of judicial review as the foundation for the authority of the Supreme Court, little was in fact done to exercise that authority for almost fifty years following 1803. It was not until 1857, in the notorious Dred Scott decision, that the Court chose to exercise its power of judicial review for a second time. The importance of the case as it relates to the American political system is not only that it declared slaves to be property, but that it allowed Chief Justice Roger Taney to enlarge Marshall's view of judicial review into one of judicial supremacy. Marshall had been willing to assert the supremacy of the national government over the states, but when it came to claims of judicial supremacy over coordinate branches of the national government, he had cautiously steered away from such assertions. Taney displayed no such caution or scruples and boldly chose to assert judicial supremacy over actions of the Congress and presidency. (In fairness to Taney, however, it should be noted that this decision was the only occasion during his tenure of twenty-eight years as Chief Justice that the Supreme Court exercised the power of judicial review to deny an act of Congress.) He claimed Congress had no authority to outlaw slavery in the territories and thus the Missouri Compromise could not stand before the Constitution. What Taney did was invent a judicial veto that made the Supreme Court *primus inter pares* (Latin, "first among equals") among coordinate branches of the national government.

## JUDICIAL REVIEW IN AN INDUSTRIAL AGE

The Civil War launched the age of industrialization in America and the national government supported it with actions favoring economic growth, not unlike the Federalists earlier in the history of the republic. Industrial developments in transportation and communications required a favorable exercise of national power and centralization of authority to guide a truly national economy. The response of the Court, reminiscent of the Marshall era, was to invoke national power over contracts and commerce. In 1877, the Court pushed aside state regulations contrary to national legislation of the telegraph industry. In 1886, the Court laid the groundwork for preemption in *Wabash, St. Louis & Pacific Railway v. Illinois* when it denied state regulation of railroad rates. By the turn of the century, the Court could be found upholding national regulation in such diverse areas as meat-packing, lotteries, poached game, food and drugs, liquor, oleomargarine, narcotics, prostitution and white slavery, and phosphorous matches.

But the Supreme Court was not committed to national dominance of the states, preferring instead a "dual federalism" in which the state and national governments were seen to operate in separate spheres of authority and jurisdiction. The Court also made clear that there existed constitutional limits on both spheres. During this period, for example, judicial review was used to overturn a law of Congress regulating lamplight oil because it was seen to intrude upon the police powers of the states. A combine of sugar companies controlling ninety percent of the American market, moreover, was found not to be in violation of the Sherman Anti-Trust Act because it had not been engaged in commerce (only in "production"). In 1879, the Court employed judicial review to overturn national legislation protecting trademarks and in 1895 it rejected a federal tax on income from land because it was not fairly apportioned (according to population) among the states. Probably the high point of Court efforts to curb national economic regulation in this period can be found in *Hammer v. Dagenhart* (1920). Because of increasing public concern, Congress sought to abolish child labor by outlawing the interstate sale of products made by children. But because "products" resulted from "production" rather than commerce, said the Court, the national government lacked constitutional regulatory authority. Indeed, the justice writing the opinion said it would be the death of federalism itself if such a law was allowed to stand. In regard to social and political issues, the Court was also more receptive to the authority of the states. In the *Slaughterhouse Cases* (1873) and the *Civil Rights Cases* (1883), it sharply limited the scope of national political power over states with narrow interpretations of the Civil War Amendments, specifically the Fourteenth Amendment.

## THE GREAT DEPRESSION AND THE NEW DEAL

In spite of the Wall Street crash of 1929 and the Great Depression, the Supreme Court remained wedded to a view of national power that limited economic regulation, private property, and a market economy. Franklin Roosevelt and his New Deal program of national recovery came to Washington with a commitment to social and economic change. His solutions were often unconventional or nontraditional and certainly without precedent in more than a few instances. The problem was that political pressures caused by the Great Depression had elected Franklin Roosevelt, not members of the Supreme Court. They were already there. The justices became increasingly disenchanted with the president's programs and by 1937 had all but halted the New Deal. Angered by the Court's opposition, Roosevelt attempted to "pack" the judiciary with a series of new appointees who would hold greater sympathy for his legislative efforts. Although he failed to enlarge the judiciary in such a blatantly partisan manner, he nonetheless won out over his opposition on the Court. By 1940, he was able to appoint five new justices and when he did so, he replaced them with men friendly to the New Deal. Judicial review ceased to be a constitutional obstacle and weapon of opposition wielded by the Supreme Court.

## JUDICIAL REVIEW IN THE MODERN WORLD

Following the conclusion of the Second World War, the Supreme Court again began to energetically exercise its power of judicial review to limit actions by coordinate branches of national government. Under the leadership of Chief Justice Earl Warren (1953–1969), for example, it overturned nineteen acts of Congress. Although Chief Justice Warren was considered more of a judicial activist, his successor presided over a Court that far outdistanced him in limiting actions of the Congress. During the tenure of Chief Justice Warren Burger, the Court used the doctrine of judicial review to overturn more cases than under the leadership of any other chief justice in the history of the United States. Between the years 1969 and 1986, the period of Burger's service, the Supreme Court overturned thirty-two acts of Congress. The Burger Court attacked congressional actions in areas of the law involving gender classification, election financing, judicial salaries, and granting eighteen-year-olds the right to vote in state elections. The same Court also struck down the "legislative veto," a statutory device employed by Congress to control actions of the executive branch.

Nor was the presidency spared the lash of judicial review. In *United States v. Nixon* (1974), the Court reaffirmed its commitment to judicial supremacy when it ordered a president to surrender evidentiary materials that would damage his political career. President Nixon obeyed the order, thereby affirming the Supreme Court as the ultimate source of constitutional authority.

## JUDICIAL REVIEW IN A DEMOCRATIC SOCIETY

Since a constitution is a delegation of the power of the people which is supposed to limit the authority of political institutions created by them, it follows that when those institutions exceed the boundaries of that constitution, their exercise of that power is not legitimate. The necessarily ambiguous nature of written constitutions leads inevitably to disagreements about their meanings. It then becomes the province of a court to determine when such a violation has taken place and to declare the law invalid as it applies to the parties in the case before the court. This reasoning is clearly articulated by Alexander Hamilton in Federalist No. 78. Hamilton's defense of judicial review assumes clear standards for definition of when such a violation has occurred and what the intentions of the people are. The exercise of judicial review by the Supreme Court has raised the dilemma of the substitution of the Court's will for that of the people.

One viewpoint concerning this dilemma is that the exercise of judicial review is not necessarily an antidemocratic feature of representative government. Proponents of this idea such as Louis Fisher assert that "the Constitution establishes a limited republic, not a direct or pure democracy." In our system of government, they argue, there exist many layers of representation and any number of restraints that filter popular sentiment. Judicial review, therefore, should be understood as just another function of one of three coordinate branches of government that is employed to restrain the other two. Fisher points out that there exist a variety of limits on public choice and that the government is no less democratic because of them. He cites, for example, the presence of age limits on the public's right to vote, term limits on the presidency, the undemocratic representation of the states in the federal Senate, filibusters, bicameralism, checks and balances of all kinds. There also exists evidence that in some instances the unelected judiciary has strengthened democratic principles through the use of judicial review. In decisions affecting reapportionment and the right of association, for example, the Court has expanded the rights of citizens by allowing a greater number of people to participate in the political process.

An opposing view often favored by "strict constructionists" is articulated rather clearly by former Supreme Court nominee, Judge Robert Bork: "When the judiciary imposes upon democracy limits not to be found in the Constitution, it deprives citizens of a right that is found there, the right to make the laws to govern themselves." Bork's view is that an unelected judiciary in possession of life tenure often acts without a mandate from the people and, indeed, often makes decisions in spite of them or contrary to their will. In his view, the Constitution remains a controlling document, one that limits, above all other persons, the judges themselves. Bork's position is rooted in the idea that a problem has arisen because today's judges have chosen to ignore the original intentions of the Framers. Without the presence of limitations imposed by the latter, judges are left with the impression they are free to substitute their own moral or political values and free to decide cases according to the moment. As a result, legislatures and politically elected executives are at a loss how to regain the ground they have lost to the judiciary. Impeachment, constitutional amendments and threats to "pack" are too slow, cumbersome, or have been demonstrated failures unable to satisfactorily control judges. An uncomfortable extension of the argument that the doctrine of judicial review makes judges the ultimate protector of the rights of the people—rather than their own elected public officials—is that democracy is somehow unprincipled and unworthy, also. What makes Bork's viewpoint questionable and difficult to accept is his lack of appreciation for the power of legislative and executive authority. When judges act in a manner that is intolerable or otherwise unacceptable to the public, elected officials have every right and opportunity to retaliate under the Constitution. There is nothing in our fundamental law that prevents the Congress and president from passing statutory limitations on the Court's abuse of the power of judicial review. Judicial appointments remain firmly and completely in the hands of the public's leaders and representatives. Nor has it been demonstrated that the members of the Supreme Court are insensitive to public opinion. President Roosevelt's court packing scheme did have its intended effect. As recently as 1996, it should be noted, a judicial appointee of President Clinton rather quickly changed his opinion when subjected to public scrutiny and criticism from the public and its elected officials. Judge Bork and those who share his view do possess a valid argument when they chastise judges who would recklessly impose their personal preferences for those of the Framers. Democratic government is at risk when judges behave in such a manner, but it has also been protected by that same judiciary on a number of occasions when publicly-elected officials have lacked the courage to defend the Constitution.

# ELLERBEE

NAME: _____
SECTION: _____
DATE: _____

1. Identify the basic major assumptions of the doctrine of Judicial Review.

   _____
   _____
   _____
   _____
   _____
   _____
   _____

2. If John Marshall's decision in Marbury v. Madison had been different, would the federal system have been endangered?

   _____
   _____
   _____
   _____
   _____
   _____
   _____

3. If Roger Taney's decision in *Dred Scott* had been different, would the federal system have been endangered?

   _____
   _____
   _____
   _____
   _____
   _____

4. If the Age of Industrialization was marked by a judicial preference for dual federalism, with limits on both the state and federal spheres, what theoretical label would you call it?

___

5. What Chief Justice used Judicial Review to overturn the most acts of Congress? Did this strengthen or weaken the court?

___

**Group Exercise:** Discuss the role of the courts in the forming of the American Nation. On balance, has it helped or hindered the creation of a unified country and people?

**Individual Project:** Select and identify a recent example of some issue of Judicial Review. In your opinion, did the court go too far? Why, or why not?

*Chapter Five*

# Public Administration

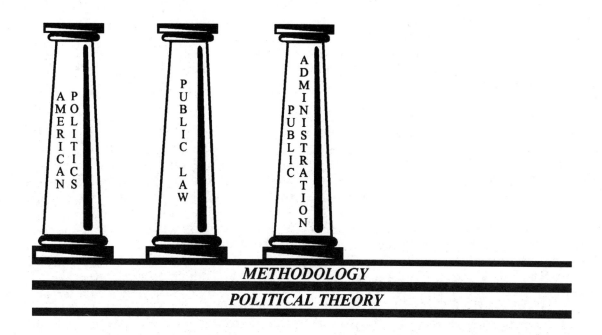

# Concerning the Secretaries of the Prince

## Niccolò Machiavelli*

The choice of servants is of no little importance to a prince, and they are good or not according to the discrimination of the prince. And the first opinion which one forms of a prince, and of his understanding, is by observing the men he has around him; and when they are capable and faithful he may always be considered wise, because he has known how to recognize the capable and to keep them faithful. But when they are otherwise one cannot form a good opinion of him, for the prime error which he made was in choosing them.

There were none who knew Messer Antonio da Venafro as the servant of Pandolfo Petrucci, Prince of Siena, who would not consider Pandolfo to be a very clever man in having Venafro for his servant. Because there are three classes of intellects: one which comprehends by itself; another appreciates what others comprehend; and a third which neither comprehends by itself nor by the showing of others; the first is the most excellent, the second is good, the third is useless. Therefore, it follows necessarily that, if Pandolfo was not in the first rank, he was in the second, for whenever one has judgement to know good or bad when it is said and done, although he himself may not have the initiative, yet he can recognize the good and the bad in his servant, and the one he can praise and the other correct; thus the servant cannot hope to deceive him, and is kept honest.

But to enable a prince to form an opinion of his servant there is one test which never fails; when you see the servant thinking more of his own interests than of yours, and seeking inwardly his own profit in everything, such a man will never make a good servant, nor will you ever be able to trust him; because he who has the state of another in his hands ought never to think of himself, but always of his prince, and never pay any attention to matters in which the prince is not concerned.

On the other hand, to keep his servant honest the prince ought to study him, honoring him, enriching him, doing him kindnesses, sharing with him the honors and cares; and at the same time let him see that he cannot stand alone, so that many honors may not make him desire more, many riches make him wish for more, and that many cares may make him dread changes. When, therefore, servants, and princes towards servants, are thus disposed, they can trust each other, but when it is otherwise, the end will always be disastrous for either one or the other.

## How Flatterers Should Be Avoided

I do not wish to leave out an important branch of this subject, for it is a danger from which princes are with difficulty preserved, unless they are very careful and discriminating. It is that of flatterers, of whom courts are full, because men are so self-complacent in their own affairs, and in a way so deceived in them, that they are preserved with difficulty from this pest, and if they wish to defend themselves they run the danger of falling into contempt. Because there is no other way of guarding oneself from flatterers except letting men understand that to tell you the truth does not offend you; but when every one may tell you the truth, respect for you abates.

Therefore a wise prince ought to hold a third course by choosing the wise men in his state, and giving to them only the liberty of speaking the truth to him, and then only of those things of which he inquires, and of none others; but he ought to question them upon everything, and listen to their opinions, and afterwards form his own conclusions. With these councilors, sepa-

---

\* Excerpted from: Machiavelli, N. (1908) *The Prince*. (Trans. W. K. Marriott). New York: E. P. Dutton & Co.

rately and collectively, he ought to carry himself in such a way that each of them should know that, the more freely he shall speak, the more he shall be preferred; outside of these, he should listen to no one, pursue the thing resolved on, and be steadfast in his resolutions. He who does otherwise is either overthrown by flatterers, or is so often changed by varying opinions that he falls into contempt.

I wish on this subject to adduce a modern example. Fra Luca, the man of affairs to Maximilian, the present emperor, speaking of his majesty, said: He consulted with no one, yet never got his own way in anything. This arose because of his following a practice the opposite to the above; for the emperor is a secretive man—he does not communicate his designs to any one, nor does he receive opinions on them. But as in carrying them into effect they become revealed and known, they are at once obstructed by those men whom he has around him, and he, being pliant, is diverted from them. Hence it follows that those things he does one day he undoes the next, and no one ever understands what he wishes or intends to do, and no one can rely on his resolutions.

A prince, therefore, ought always to take counsel, but only when he wishes and not when others wish; he ought rather to discourage every one from offering advice unless he asks it; but, however, he ought to be a constant inquirer, and afterwards a patient listener concerning the things of which he inquired; also, on learning that any one, on any consideration, has not told him the truth, he should let his anger be felt.

And if there are some who think that a prince who conveys an impression of his wisdom is not so through his own ability, but through the good advisers that he has around him, beyond doubt they are deceived, because this is an axiom which never fails: that a prince who is not wise himself will never take good advice, unless by chance he has yielded his affairs entirely to one person who happens to be a very prudent man. In this case indeed he may be well governed, but it would not be for long, because such a governor would in a short time take away his state from him.

But if a prince who is not experienced should take counsel from more than one he will never get united counsels, nor will he know how to unite them. Each of the counsellors will think of his own interests, and the prince will not know how to control them or to see through them. And they are not to be found otherwise, because men will always prove untrue to you unless they are kept honest by constraint. Therefore it must be inferred that good counsels, whencesoever they come, are born of the wisdom of the prince, and not the wisdom of the prince from good counsels.

# MACHIAVELLI

NAME: _____

SECTION: _____

DATE: _____

1. Machiavelli describes three classes of intellects in public servants; which of these do you think might describe the lad in the Plato article on learning or remembering?

   _____
   _____
   _____
   _____
   _____
   _____
   _____
   _____

2. One bit of advice on evaluating public servants is that they ought not to put their own personal interests before the State's interest. Briefly relate this advice to Willis' article on constitutional interpretation and objectivity.

   _____
   _____
   _____
   _____
   _____
   _____
   _____

3. Should all public servants offer advice to the chief executive? Why, or why not?

   _____
   _____
   _____
   _____
   _____

4. Why should the ruler of a state be careful to avoid surrounding him or herself with flatters?

_____
_____
_____
_____
_____
_____
_____

5. Machiavelli suggests that people will always pursue their own interests in opposition to the interests of the ruler. Is he being too cynical? Why, or why not?

_____
_____
_____
_____
_____
_____
_____

**Group Exercise:** Discuss the question: Is Machiavelli relevant today? Should a president heed any of his advice? Whose advice should a president heed? Anyone?

**Individual Project:** Do you personally ever use flattery instead of truth in your business relationships? What is your justification for it?

# WHAT IS PUBLIC ADMINISTRATION?

## *Herbert A. Simon, Donald W. Smithburg, and Victor A. Thompson*\*

## INTRODUCTION

In its broadest sense, **administration** can be defined as the activities of groups cooperating to accomplish common goals. The following pages of this chapter are designed to give the reader a view of the subject matter that we propose to treat and of our general approach to it. After exploring further the nature of administration, we shall delimit the specific field of public administration and point out some of the similarities and differences between public and business administration.

Next, we will survey briefly the growth of organizations and the resulting demand for expert and efficient governmental service. We will see how this led, in turn, to programs of research and training in public administration. The final section of the chapter will set forth some fundamental distinctions between the "scientific" and the "practical" (i.e., "advice-giving") approaches to administrative theory. It will explain why this book emphasizes the underlying sociological and psychological phenomena involved in administrative behavior rather than specific rules and "know-how" for manipulating human beings in organizational situations.

## THE NATURE OF ADMINISTRATION

We have defined administration as cooperative group behavior. The term administration is also used in a narrower sense to refer to those patterns of behavior that are common to many kinds of cooperating groups and that do not depend upon either the specific goals toward which they are cooperating or the specific technological methods used to reach these goals. For example, the two men rolling the stone could have used various techniques in accomplishing their purpose. They might have merely pulled and shoved the stone in some manner. Or they could have used a pole or a steel bar as a lever. They might have fastened a rope to it, with a pulley attached to the nearest tree. They might have broken the stone with sledge hammers and then carried away the fragments. The methods of moving the stone are legion.

However, administration in the more restricted sense is not basically concerned with the technological methods selected. It is concerned with such questions as **HOW** the method was chosen, how the two men moving the stone were selected and induced to cooperate in carrying out such a task, how the task was divided between them, how each one learned what his particular job was in the total pattern, how he learned to perform it, how his efforts are coordinated with the efforts of the other.

## THE NATURE OF FORMAL ORGANIZATION

Any activity involving the conscious cooperation of two or more persons can be called organized activity. However, in modern society cooperative activity is carried on within a much more formal structure than the one just described. Participants have tasks assigned to them; the relationships between participants are ordered in such ways as to achieve the final product with a minimum expenditure of human effort and material resources. Thus, by **formal organization** we mean a planned system of cooperative effort in which each participant has a recognized role to play and duties or tasks to perform. These duties

---

\* "What is Public Administration" by Simon, Smithburg and Thompson. From *Public Administration*. Copyright 1950. Reprinted by permission of Transaction Publishers; all rights reserved.

are assigned in order to achieve the organization purpose rather than to satisfy individual preferences, although the two often coincide.

## The Universality of Administration

Since administration is concerned with all patterns of cooperative behavior, it is obvious that any person engaged in an activity in cooperation with other persons is engaged in administration. Further, since everyone has cooperated with others throughout his life, he has some basic familiarity with administration and some of its problems. The boys' club, the fraternity, the church, the political party, the school, and even the family require administration to achieve their goals.

Most persons, while they are engaged in administration every day of their lives, seldom deliberately set out to consider the ways in which the cooperative activities of groups are actually arranged; how the cooperation could be made more effective or satisfying; what the requirements are for the continuance of the cooperative activity. In most of the simpler organizational situations in life—the family, for example—there are traditional and accepted ways of behaving that are gradually acquired during childhood and that are seldom the objects of conscious attention or planning. Like Moliere's hero who had talked prose all his life without knowing it, most persons administer all their lives without knowing it.

The governmental organizations are more complex than these everyday administrative situations we are familiar with. The difficulties of securing effective cooperative action in performing large and intricate tasks become so great that they force themselves upon the attention. Traditional, customary ways of behaving no longer suffice, and cooperation becomes conscious and requires planning. The **"rules of the road"** that govern family life and the relations among family members are informal, carried around in the heads of parents and children. The rules of the road that govern the relations among the employees of a government agency may fill ten volumes of a looseleaf "**Administrative Manual.**"

If large-scale organizations are to accomplish their purposes; if the extremely complex interrelationships of an industrial era are not to break down, organizational life—its anatomy and its pathology—needs to be understood. Those who participate in and operate the formal organizations through which so much of our society's activity is channeled must know what makes cooperation effective and what hampers it. Either through experience or through formal education,

or both, they must study administration. Our concern is with the formal study of **public** administration.

## PUBLIC ADMINISTRATION

By public administration is meant, in common usage, the activities of the executive branches of national, state, and local governments; independent boards and commissions set up by Congress and state legislatures; government corporations; and certain other agencies of a specialized character. Specifically excluded are judicial and legislative agencies within the government and non-governmental administration.

## GOVERNMENTAL AND NON-GOVERNMENTAL ADMINISTRATION

It has been customary in this country to make a sharp distinction between governmental and non-governmental administration. In the popular imagination, governmental administration is "bureaucratic"; private administration is "business-like"; governmental administration is political; private administration is non-political; governmental administration is characterized by "red-tape"; private administration is not. Actually, the distinction is much too sharp to fit the facts. As we shall see in the course of this book, large-scale public and private organizations have many more similarities than they have differences. It is possible, therefore, in examining the activities of public administration to use the results of research carried on in private business. In actual administration there is often a greater difference between small and large organizations than there is between public and private ones. For example, the differences in organizations and in administrative problems between a hospital with 1000 beds and one with 50 beds will be far greater than the differences that result from the fact that one hospital is privately owned and the other publicly owned.

Many of the same skills are required in public and private administration. A statistician might transfer from a large insurance company to the Bureau of Labor Statistics in Washington and find his tasks almost identical. He possesses skills that can be used by a great many organizations, public or private. Similarly, a doctor performing an appendectomy will use the same technique whether he is employed in an Army hospital or in private practice. General Dwight Eisenhower left the Army to become president of Columbia University. Two more different organizations would be hard to imagine. Yet it is likely that the administrative problems of the two organizations are sufficiently similar so that he had little difficulty in making an adjustment to this new position.

## DIFFERENCES BETWEEN PUBLIC AND PRIVATE ADMINISTRATION

While the similarities between governmental and non-governmental organizations are greater than is generally supposed, some differences nevertheless exist. Most often these are differences in degree rather than in kind. For example, both governmental and non-governmental organizations are usually based on law. Activities of a government agency are usually authorized by statute or executive order, based on some statutory or constitutional authority. All corporations and a good many other non-governmental organizations operate under a legal charter. The officers of both types of organizations are legally required to carry out their activities within the law. However, the duties and responsibilities of the public administrator will usually be described by law in much greater detail than those of his private counterpart, and there will usually be greater possibilities for holding him accountable in the courts for the discharge of these duties in a lawful manner. For example, a corporation can ordinarily authorize its officers and employees to make purchases for it under any procedure the board of directors sees fit to approve. A public purchase, however, must usually satisfy numerous legal requirements with respect to advertising for bids, letting the contract to the lowest responsible bidder, authorizing the expenditure, and so forth. . . .

The public administrator may be the subject of Congressional criticism or investigation. . . . The extensive Congressional hearings to establish responsibility for the Pearl Harbor disaster are a good example. The private administrator may also be the subject of investigation, but he is much less likely to be, and then usually only in cases where his business is subject to public regulation. With the increasing scope of governmental regulation of business, however, his chances of being the object of public investigation are growing rapidly.

The private administrator is often given much more latitude in interpreting the relationship between his organization and the general welfare than is the public administrator. It is accepted that the former is in business primarily to further his private ends; the latter is expected to serve the public interest, and it is considered unethical for him to use the advantages of his position for personal gain. In 1947, governmental employees who speculated in the grain market were objects of public censure, even in cases where they possessed no "inside" information that gave them special advantage. Of course, the price and production policies of business may also be scrutinized when it is felt that they impinge upon the public welfare.

## The Growth of Administration

When the fifty-five Founding Fathers met in Philadelphia to write the Constitution, the United States consisted of about four million people living on the eastern seaboard, most of them east of the Allegheny Mountains. The great proportion of the population were farmers and most of them were relatively self-subsistent. . . . Modern frills like running water, paved roads, labor unions, large corporations, sewage systems, telephones, electric lights, airplanes, automobiles, movie theaters, atom bombs, all of which require some public supervision of their use, were unheard of. In that earlier kind of simple social structure government was limited in cost, specialization, and number of employees.

The growth of population, the very growth in size of the United States, and, particularly, advances in technology have changed the picture. Many things that could have been handled in Revolutionary times without public authority must now be handled by governments. Many problems that could then be solved by the spontaneous cooperation of neighbors now require the highly organized cooperation of professional specialists.

## Efficiency as a Goal

Advocacy of efficiency in the performance of governmental tasks was, in good part, a taxpayers' movement. Governmental inefficiency was expensive; it tended to raise taxes. Therefore, even those who violently opposed the extension of governmental activities to new areas were insistent on having efficiency in those activities that were deemed necessary.

Intellectually, both the efficiency and anti-patronage movements were made possible by assuming an almost air-tight distinction between "policy" and "administration." It was assumed that the legislatures and the elected officials would lay out the policies, and the administrative officials would merely carry them out. In the first place, on this assumption, only the elected officials need be politically responsible. Administration could, without loss of democracy, be entrusted to "neutral" civil servants selected under civil service procedures. In the second place, these civil servants would not then be responsible for formulating policies but only for carrying them out without waste of public funds—that is, as efficiently as possible.

Most theorizing about public administration, and most of the administrative principles proposed by the writers on the subject, have accepted this assumption that efficiency is the criterion by which the administration of government agencies is to be judged.

### *Recommendations of "Good Practice"*

There are several reasons why a study of administration should begin with the objective analysis of organization behavior rather than with rules on "how to be a successful executive" or "how to organize a government agency." The first reason is that practical rules simply do not exist which can be applied in an automatic or mechanical fashion to actual organization problems. Practical administrators find that formal principles of administration are of far less importance to them than an ability to size up an administrative situation—to understand the psychological processes at work—and then apply common sense once the situation is thoroughly understood. At the present stage of knowledge, administrative theory is of far more practical use in diagnosing situations than in prescribing suitable courses of action.

A second reason is that the practice of administration involves skills—skills that have become thoroughly incorporated in the administrator's personality—rather than mere intellectual knowledge. Rules as to how one ought to behave are of no use unless the actual ability to behave according to the rules has been learned and practiced. Formal training will be of greater help in developing the skills of administration if it concentrates upon an understanding of the reasons behind the rules than if it emphasizes the learning of specific rules that cannot possibly cover the whole wide range of situations that will be encountered in practice.

A third reason for avoiding a "how-to" approach in the study of administration has already been mentioned. Practical recommendations for organization action always depend upon the values of the person making the recommendation. For example, a person primarily interested in doing a job efficiently may make a recommendation different from that of a person interested in doing the job so as to preserve democratic responsibility, and different again from a person interested in doing it in a manner that will interfere as little as possible with the property or other rights of the individuals. . . .

No knowledge of administrative techniques then, can relieve the administrator from the task of moral choice—choice as to organization goals and methods and choice as to his treatment of the other human beings in his organization. His code of ethics is as significant a part of his equipment as an administrator, as is his knowledge of administrative behavior, and no amount of study of the "science" of administration will provide him with this code.

# Simon, Smithburg, and Thompson

NAME: _____

SECTION: _____

DATE: _____

1. Define public administration.

   _____
   _____
   _____
   _____
   _____
   _____
   _____
   _____

2. List and describe reasons for the contemporary growth of public administration.

   _____
   _____
   _____
   _____
   _____
   _____
   _____
   _____

3. Compare and contrast public and private administration.

   _____
   _____
   _____
   _____
   _____
   _____
   _____
   _____

4. Explain why the study of public administration needs to focus on the analysis of organizations instead of on rules on how to be a good administrator.

___

5. Why have growth of population and advances in technology led to an increased need for cooperation among professional specialists?

___

**Group Exercise:** Imagine that you have to design the public organization of the future. Discuss: Would you increase or decrease the power of government bureaucrats?

**Individual Project:** Look for a contemporary newspaper article on bureaucracy. Is it positive or negative in its depiction of public administration?

# Legal, Political, and Managerial Approaches to Public Administration

## David H. Rosenbloom*

### INTRODUCTION

[P]ublic administration contains three relatively distinct approaches that grow out of different perspectives on its functions. Some have viewed it as a managerial endeavor, similar to practices in the private sector. Others, stressing the "public-ness" of public administration, have emphasized its political aspects. Still others, noting the importance of sovereignty, constitutions, and regulation in public administration, have viewed it as a distinctly legal matter. Each of these approaches tends to stress different values and procedural and structural arrangements for the operation of public administration, each views the individual citizen in a remarkably different way, and each adopts a different perspective on how to develop knowledge. It is very important to bear in mind that these approaches are embedded in our political culture. They reflect the constitutional separation of powers and assignment of functions to different branches. The managerial approach is associated with the executive branch's interest in faithful execution or implementation of the law. The political approach is associated with legislative policymaking concerns. The legal approach focuses on government's adjudicatory function and commitment to maintaining constitutional rights (the "**blessing of liberty**" and the rule of law).

Once we have presented the gist of these three approaches to public administration, we will have completed our definitional discussion. Then we can turn to an explanation of how each of these approaches is present in the various central activities of contemporary public administration.

### THE MANAGERIAL APPROACH

Those who define public administration in managerial terms and take a businesslike approach to it tend to minimize the distinctions between public and private administration. In their view, public administration is essentially the same as big business and ought to be run according to the same managerial principles and values. This outlook is strongly entrenched in some segments of American society and is frequently found among elective political leaders who tend to resent the political influence exercised by civil servants. It is unusual for a presidential campaign not to stress the candidates' purported abilities to "**manage**" the "**huge**" federal bureaucracy and to make it more efficient.

But the roots of the managerial approach go back much farther. It was the nineteenth-century civil service reformers who first promoted the approach as a means of organizing the public service. The reformer's chief complaints were that political patronage appointments to the public service at all levels of government led to corruption, inefficiency, and the emergence of a class of politicians—"**spoilsmen**"— as they were frequently called—who were fundamentally unfit to lead the nation. In fact, one well-known historian of the 1850s insisted that the federal service had become staffed by the nation's "**refuse**" (garbage). In the reformer's view, "What civil service reform demand[ed], [was] that the business part of government shall be carried on in a sound businesslike manner." In order for it to become businesslike, it had to become nonpolitical. Consequently, appointments were to be made on the basis of "merit" and "fitness" rather than political partisanship. Many reformers thought that public

---

* D. Rosenbloom, *Public Administration*, 3ed, pp. 15–32. McGraw-Hill Companies. Reprinted by permission of the publisher.

employees should be prohibited from taking an active part in electoral politics, other than voting. Once politics was rejected as the basis for hiring and firing public administrators, the reformers believed that the selection and tenure of public servants could be based on their efficiency and performance.

In order to sustain this logic, the reformers had to insist that the vast majority of public administrators had no legitimate political or policymaking functions. Much of their thinking and the logic of the managerial approach depended on the existence of a dichotomy between politics and administration. This aspect of the managerial approach was most influentially put forward by Woodrow Wilson, who in the 1880s could be counted among the strong supporters of civil service reform. In Wilson's well-known words, "Administration lies outside the proper sphere of politics. Administrative questions are not political questions." Rather, they are managerial questions, for as Wilson expressed it, public administration is "a field of business."

Just as politics involves certain values, such as representativeness, so does business or management. Wilson was also influential in his straightforward articulation of these: "It is the object of administrative study to discover, first, what government can properly and successfully do, and secondly, how it can do these proper things with the utmost possible efficiency and at the least possible cost either of money or energy." In other words, according to the managerial approach, public administration is to be geared toward maximizing effectiveness, efficiency, and economy.

The advocacy of businesslike public administration eventually became the orthodox or classical view of how the public service should be run. Managers, not politicians, were to be in control, and efficiency was to be considered the ultimate "good," the "axiom" number one in the value scale of administration. Politics was to be eliminated because it produced inefficiency. Moreover, despite the growing regulatory activities of the public service, law was deemphasized because, as Leonard White's influential *Introduction to the Study of Public Administration* (1926) contended, "the study of administration should start from the base of management rather than the foundation of law, and is therefore more absorbed in the affairs of the American Management Association than in the decisions of the courts." In fact, from the 1910s to the 1940s, a worldwide "scientific management" movement based on the work of Frederick Taylor, developed and advocated the premise that effective, efficient management could be reduced to a set of scien-

tific principles. In the view of critics of this approach, the net result in terms of administrative values was that:

> *the "goodness" or "badness" of a particular organizational pattern was a mathematical relationship of "inputs" to "outputs." Where the latter was maximized and the former minimized, a moral "good" resulted. Virtue or "goodness" was therefore equated with the relationship of these two factors, that is, "efficiency" or "inefficiency." Mathematics was transformed into ethics.*

Wastefulness, through inefficiency, was considered immoral.

## THE POLITICAL APPROACH

The political approach to public administration was perhaps most forcefully and succinctly stated by Wallace Sayre:

> *Public administration is ultimately a problem in political theory: the fundamental problem in a democracy is responsibility to popular control; the responsibility and responsiveness of the administrative agencies and the bureaucracies to the elected officials (the chief executives, the legislators) is of central importance in a government based increasingly on the exercise of discretionary power by agencies of administration.*

This approach grew out of the observations of scholars, such as Paul Appleby, that public administration during the New Deal and World War II was anything but devoid of politics. Appleby considered administration to be a "**political process**," and numerous others have since called attention to the extent to which public administrators participate in public policymaking. Unlike the origin of the managerial approach, which stressed what public administration ought to be, the political approach developed from an analysis of an apparent practical reality.

Once public administration is considered a political endeavor, emphasis is inevitably placed on a different set of values than those promoted by the managerial approach. Efficiency, in particular, becomes highly suspect, because it has little to do with the larger questions of government....

The political approach to public administration stresses the values of representativeness, political responsiveness, and accountability through elected officials to the citizenry. These are viewed as crucial to the maintenance of constitutional democracy, and it is considered necessary to incorporate them into all aspects of government, including public administration.

One can find many examples of governmental reforms aimed at maximizing the political values of representativeness, responsiveness, and accountability within public administration. For instance, the Federal Civil Service Reform Act of 1978 sought representativeness by making it "the policy of the United states . . . to provide a . . . Federal work force reflective of the Nation's diversity" by endeavoring "to achieve a work force from all segments of society." The Federal Advisory Committee Act of 1972 sought to make use of advisory committees more representative. It declares that such committees "are frequently a useful and beneficial means of furnishing expert advice, ideas, diverse opinions to the Federal Government" and requires that "the membership of advisory committee(s) . . . be fairly balanced in terms of the points of view represented. . . ." Earlier, the poverty and model cities programs of the 1960s sought to use citizen participation as a means of promoting political responsiveness in administrative operations. In addition, the quest for responsiveness has blended into a wide variety of attempts to promote the accountability of public administrators to the public and their elected officials, including the use of "**sunshine**" and "**sunset**" provisions.

It is important to note that the values sought by the political approach to public administration are frequently in tension with those of the managerial approach. For instance, efficiency in the managerial sense is not necessarily served through sunshine regulations that open aspects of public administration to public scrutiny and can dissuade public administrators from taking some course of action, though they may be the most efficient. They can divert time and resources from program implementation to the deliverance of information to outsiders. Consultation with advisory committees and "citizen participants" can be time-consuming and costly. Since it is not chosen by merit alone, a socially representative public service may not be the most technically competent or efficient one. Accountability has a price.

As Marven Bernstein reported long ago, "Many officials complain that they must spend so much time preparing for appearing at Congressional hearings and in presenting their programs before the Bureau of the Budget and other bodies that often leaves little time for directing the operations of their agencies." Managerial effectiveness is often difficult to gauge, of course, but federal managers have long complained that their effectiveness is hampered by the large congressional role in public administration and the need to consult continually with a variety of parties having a legitimate concern with their agencies' operations.

## LEGAL APPROACH

In the United States, the legal approach to public administration historically has been eclipsed by the other approaches, especially the managerial. Nevertheless, it has a venerable tradition and has recently emerged as a full-fledged way of defining public administration. It views public administration as applying and enforcing the law in concrete circumstances. As such, it is infused with legal and adjudicatory concerns.

This approach is derived primarily from three interrelated sources. First is administrative law. As early as 1905, Frank Goodnow, a leading contributor to the development of public administrative theory, published a book entitled *The Principles of the Administrative Law of the United States*. He defined administrative law as "that part of the law which fixes the organization and determines the competence of the authorities [that] execute the law, and indicates to the individual remedies for the violation of his rights."

A second source of the legal approach has been the movement toward the **judicialization** of public administration. Judicialization is the tendency for administrative processes increasingly to resemble courtroom procedures. Judicialization falls within the purview of Goodnow's definition of administrative law but tends to concentrate heavily on the establishment of procedures to safeguard individual rights....

Thus, judicialization brings not only law but legal procedure to bear on administrative decision making. Agencies begin to function more like courts, and consequently legal values come to play a greater role in their activities. In 1991, thirty-one federal agencies employed 1,090 administrative law judges (ALJs). Another twelve agencies "borrowed" ALJs under a program operated by the Office of Personnel Management. Seventy-one per cent of all ALJs were employed by the Social Security Administration.

Constitutional law provides a third source of the contemporary legal approach to public administration. Since the 1950s, the federal judiciary has virtually redefined the procedural, equal protection, and substantive rights and liberties of the citizenry *vis-à-vis* public administrators. An old distinction between rights and privileges, which had largely made the Constitution irrelevant to individuals' rights regarding the receipt of governmental benefits, met its demise. There was also a vast expansion in the requirement that public administrators afford constitutional procedural due process, such as trial-like hearings, to the specific individuals whose governmental benefits, such as welfare or public education, were terminated through administrative action. A new stringency was read into the Eighth Amendment's prohibition of cruel and unusual punishment. Wholly new rights, including the rights to treatment and rehabilitation, were created, if not fully ratified by the Supreme Court, for those confined to public mental health facilities. The right to equal protection was vastly strengthened and applied in a variety of administrative matters ranging from public personnel recruitment systems to the operation of public schools and prisons....

The constitutional law affecting public administration is continually changing as the judiciary applies the Constitution to new situations and revises its interpretations of older ones. Some rights that have not yet been established will be declared; the scope of others will be reduced. But constitutional law, and therefore the courts, will continue to define the rights of individuals *vis-à-vis* public administrative activity.

The legal approach to public administration emphasizes the rule of law. It embodies several central values. One is **procedural due process**, which is hard to define precisely because it has long been recognized that this value cannot be confined to any single set of requirements or standards. Rather, the term stands for the value of fundamental fairness and is viewed as requiring procedures designed to protect individuals from malicious, arbitrary, erroneous, capricious, or unconstitutional deprivation of life, liberty, or property at the hands of government. A second value concerns individual **substantive rights** and **equal protection** of the laws as embodied in evolving interpretations of the Bill of Rights and the Fourteenth Amendment. In general, the judiciary views the maximization of individual rights and liberties as a positive good and a necessary feature of the United states political system. Breaches of these rights may be tolerated by the courts when, on balance, some essential governmental function requires their abridgement. However, the usual presumption is against the government in such circumstances; consequently, judicial doctrines place a heavy burden on official administrative action that infringes upon the substantive constitutional rights of individuals. Third, the judiciary values **equity**, a concept that, like due process, is subject to varying interpretation. However, in terms of public administration in general, equity stands for the value of fairness in the **result** of conflicts between private parties and the government. Equity includes the power to dispense with the harsh application of the law where it would be inappropriate. It militates against arbitrary or invidious treatment of individuals and enables the courts to fashion remedies for individuals whose constitutional rights have been violated by administrative action. Additionally, the legal approach values constitutional integrity and opposes efforts to take shortcuts, such as legislative veto, to get around the strict application of constitutional procedures.

One of the major features of the values of the legal approach to public administration is the downgrading of the cost-effectiveness reasoning associated with the managerial approach. The judiciary is not oblivious to the costs of its decisions, but its central focus tends to be on the nature of the individual's rights, rather than on the costs to society of securing those rights. This is especially evident in cases involving the reform of public institutions. As one court said, "Inadequate resources can never be an adequate justification for the state's depriving any person of his constitutional rights.

## Conclusion: Public Administration Reconsidered

Public administration is an extremely complex endeavor. It embodies at least the three major approaches just discussed. Each of these approaches emphasizes values, organizational arrangements, views of individuals, and intellectual orientations that are at odds with those of the other two approaches. The public administrator is called upon to be a manager, policymaker, and constitutional lawyer. He or she is stuck between the proverbial rock and a hard place when called upon to act in a fashion that will integrate three approaches that may defy successful integration. This is one reason why politicians and the society in generally have become so critical of bureaucracy. It is virtually impossible to satisfy all the managerial, political, and legal/constitutional demands placed upon public agencies and public administrators.

# ROSENBLOOM

NAME: _____

SECTION: _____

DATE: _____

1. Identify and describe the three major perspectives on the functioning of the public sector agencies.

2. Is there any identifiable difference between "administration" and "management"? Explain your answer.

3. Should public administration focus on efficiency or representation? Which does the political approach favor?

4. The legal approach to public administration is based on three major sources. Identify these and describe them.

_____
_____
_____
_____
_____
_____
_____

5. Describe some of the tensions and contradictions between the three approaches to public administration.

_____
_____
_____
_____
_____
_____
_____

**Group Exercise:** Discuss the topic of hiring staff for public agencies. Should politicians be able to control the bureaucracy through appointments?

**Individual Project:** Find and identify a law review journal article that favors more legal control over public administration. Also find a business management article with an opposing suggestion. Which do you find more persuasive? Why?

# Performance in Public Administration: Measuring Government Efficiency and Effectiveness

## *Robert T. Aldinger*

## Introduction

Public administrator, author, and educator Paul Appleby told us that public administrators are very much involved in the political process of formulating and implementing public policy. And because of this role, one could characterize public administration as the action part of government, the means by which the purposes and goals of government are realized. As public administrators strive to reach agency goals, they often have to attempt to measure performance levels in their organizations. However, deciding on reliable and valid measures of performance is difficult and open to challenge regardless of the yardsticks used.

In this chapter we will examine some traditional methods of measuring performance and then look at a popular process called Total Quality Management (TQM). One objective of this chapter is to demonstrate how difficult it can be to determine how well—or how poorly—public organizations are functioning.

To begin, a traditional approach public and private organizations have used to measure performance is probably familiar to you: counting and evaluating outputs. Shortcomings in this method have encouraged decision makers to find better ways to evaluate performance and improve output, shifting focus from an output orientation to one focused on process and customer service through a comprehensive approach of TQM. Let's begin by briefly reviewing the standard performance measurement method.

## Measuring Performance the Traditional Way

Traditionally, performance measures for both public and private organizations focused on counting and evaluating outputs. For example, automobile manufacturers tracked the number of cars they sold, the profits they made, and their share of the automobile market—and compared these outputs to those of their competitors. A public hospital counts the number of patients treated or the size of their staff as indicators of their output. Typically, in both public and private organizations, higher output indicated more success than lower output, particularly if they were produced most efficiently, meaning that the ratio between outputs over inputs is high relative to competitors.

## Public versus Private Goods

Business enterprises usually produce tangible goods and target them to a particular "customer." The common indicators such as number of sales and profit indicate the efficiency and success of the company. Government agencies, however, usually provide goods and services that don't generate income, much less a profit. Their "**product**" is typically a "**public good**," one where potential customers cannot be easily excluded from enjoying the benefits which are often provided to a large population without reference to who pays the cost, such as in national defense, public roads, and the like. Unlike the **"customers"** in the public sector, managers' in the private sector typically know who their specific customers are: those who pay for the goods or services the company produces.

Therefore, while companies commonly target their outputs for a specific market or set of customers and measure their marketing success in sales and profits, public agencies, on the other hand, often have a wide range of direct and indirect customers, and cannot rely on sales records or profit charts to measure success. To complicate public managers' dilemma, they also have to be aware of the political aspects of very interested non-customers, such as the court system, media, interest groups, legislatures, each with their own reasons for monitoring how well government agencies are doing their jobs—and can prove their successes. This is a complex arena where public administrators must meet both managerial goals (efficiency, effectiveness) and satisfy political concerns of responsiveness and representativeness. One method, and probably the one used most widely in government, for managers to indicate how well their organizations are achieving their goals is Management by Objectives (MBO).

## MANAGEMENT BY OBJECTIVES

MBO originated in the private sector in the 1920s, but became widely implemented in the business world throughout the 1950s and 1960s. It was institutionalized in the federal government under the Nixon administration's second term to induce agencies to set out specific objectives and periodically report back to management the progress they were making toward achieving those objectives. Through 1975, the Office of Management and Budget required federal agencies to submit their objectives with fiscal year budget estimates.

While the program became less of a requirement in the federal government after the end of the Nixon administration, MBO continues to be used in the "most important federal departments," many state agencies, and over 60 percent of U.S. cities. Thus, MBO, in various forms, continues its impact on government management. In fact, today MBO systems are more widespread in government than ever, although agencies have given new names to their MBO-type systems, such as "goals planning systems," and "performance tracking systems."

However, in the last two decades, a host of organizations in the U.S. have shifted emphasis

from "bean counting" the number of outputs to examining quality of service or product. The focus on quality serves as the basis for the approach known as Total Quality Management (TQM). In fact, one of the major tenets of TQM is the elimination of output-oriented performance measurements such as MBO. Now let's concentrate on TQM. We'll start with a brief history, then offer some pros and cons of the approach.

## THE EMERGENCE OF "TOTAL QUALITY MANAGEMENT"

TQM was originally developed by an American statistician, W. Edwards Deming, in the 1940s. While TQM has gained favor in the U.S. over the last two decades, its roots are found in post-World War II Japan, where Deming's approaches were adopted much more enthusiastically than in his native country. The Japanese began their recovery from the war by gearing up their industries. In order to compete with the industrial giants in the U.S., Japanese manufactures enthusiastically adopted Deming's approach. Deming recalled that during the 1940s, "management in America had no idea what was happening. . . . I realized that nothing would happen in Japan unless management learned something about statistical techniques and how to manage them." And the leaders of Japanese industry listened and followed Deming's teachings.

Japanese automobiles and electronics began outperforming and outselling American products, prompting U.S. business leaders to examine the techniques they and their competitors were using. Thus, while U.S. companies were capable of producing large quantities of goods, consumers were buying those made in Japan. The difference, observers of Japanese industries concluded, was the focus of TQM on delivering quality products to the customer versus the American styled output-oriented approach.

## TOTAL QUALITY MANAGEMENT AS A SHIFT IN FOCUS

Federal Quality Institute describes TQM this way: a strategic, integrated management system for achieving customer satisfaction. It involves all managers and employees and uses qualitative methods to improve continuously an organization's processes. And customer satisfaction is directly linked to their perception of the quality of the product. What do we mean by quality?

One way of looking at **"quality"** is as an **"implied contract"** between the manufacturer and the customer—a promise of superior performance, durability, satisfaction. The end result of the organization's output should be a sale to a satisfied customer. And, again most importantly, the customer is the ultimate determiner of quality, and this perception will guide the customer's preferences in selecting products and services. As Deming stated, "quality should be aimed at the needs of the consumer, present and future. Quality begins with the intent, which is fixed by management." But quality is more than just the tangible product, the notion of quality, according to this perspective, is ingrained in the organization itself—as a part of the organization's culture.

## TQM AS AN ORGANIZATIONAL CULTURE

The quick answer is to shift focus from monitoring and evaluating the piecemeal outputs to an examination of the processes throughout the management and production process. And that means a focus and emphasis on quality throughout the organization. How do we do this? Dr. Deming's fourteen points referred to as the "Principles of TQM" (Table 3) lay out the framework.

As these points indicate, first and foremost, the customer is the ultimate determiner of quality; if the product does not provide the customers with the performance they wish, then the quality test has been flunked. And quality should be built into the product early in the production process—upstream rather than being added on at the end. It seems a simple enough concept, certainly one which business can evaluate based on sales, profits, and other traditional yardsticks. But there are difficulties in applying this approach to the public sector, where management efficiency and political demands are often competing, if not conflicting.

## DIFFICULTIES WITH APPLYING TQM TO THE PUBLIC SECTOR

With recurring battles over annual budgets and the short tenure of political appointees, one difficulty in maintaining enthusiasm for developing a TQM culture of quality is the length of time

**TABLE 3: DEMING'S FOURTEEN *POINTS* OF *MANAGEMENT***

1. Create constancy of purpose toward improvement of product and service.
2. Adopt the new philosophy.
3. Cease dependence on inspection; achieve quality by building quality into the product from scratch
4. Stop awarding business on the price tag alone. Instead, minimize the total cost and move toward a single supplier for any item, on a long-term relationship of loyalty and trust.
5. Improve the system of production and service, to improve quality, productivity, and decrease costs.
6. Institute training on the job.
7. Institute leadership to help people and machines do a better job. Overhaul supervision of management and supervision of production workers.
8. Drive out fear, so that everyone may work effectively for the company.
9. Break down barriers between departments.
10. Eliminate slogans and exhortations.
11. Eliminate work standards (quotas), management by objectives, numbers, or numerical goals. Substitute leadership.
12. Remove barriers that rob workers and managers of their right to pride in workmanship.
13. Institute a vigorous program of education and self-improvement.
14. Put everybody in the company to work to accomplish the transformation.

*Source:* Deming, W. E. (1986). *Out of the Crisis*. (Cambridge, Mass.: Massachusetts Institute of Technology), pp. 23–24.

it takes to instill TQM values and processes into an organization. Most experts agree that it takes six to twelve years for a quality management effort to affect an organization's culture; and that's if it's done right and has significant resources committed to it. And the process of TQM is never completed, it's a continuous process.

Even if time were not restricted, the technical knowledge and understanding required to apply TQM may not be present.

"Doing it right" means using the requisite statistical techniques upon which TQM is based. TQM techniques are based on statistical models and interpreting the results depends heavily on precise measurement of results to gauge improvement. Swiss observes: "Total quality management requires adaption for use in the public sector because it is very much a product of statistical quality control and industrial engineering, and almost all of its early applications were for assembly-line work and other routine processes." And for government agencies geared to producing continuous services, as opposed to piecemeal widgets off an assembly line, applying statistical techniques to services is not customary nor familiar to many bureaucrats.

Another restriction public managers may find when implementing TQM in their organization is the cost in terms of time and other resources? Relative to MBO, TQM is expensive and time-consuming to implement. Experts estimate that TQM takes up to 15 percent of a staff's time on a regular basis, not including supplemental training. And it requires across-the-board involvement, because, as we already noted, TQM relies on what may be a cultural change to the way the organizations looks at performance. That means everyone in the organization needs to be involved, not just top-line management. TQM requires that every job and every activity in the enterprise be part of the transformation. No one is exempt.

## TQM in Operation: the Downside

Despite these constraints, as one observer noted, TQM is "spreading like wildfire" in the public sector, even though it was developed by Deming for private manufacturing business, not government—in fact, Deming, expressed doubts that it could be applied successfully in the public sector.

In spite of the difficulties present in implementing TQM, by the mid-1980s many U.S. corporations began to encourage quality through integrated, multifaceted systems. But successful implementation in public agencies has not been easy. Most agencies haven't achieved notable results; many, in fact, haven't achieved any measurable results at all.

One reason is that support for TQM in government is wide, but thin. GAO found that in 68 percent of agencies that reported starting quality-improvement efforts, only about 13 percent of employees were actually involved in TQM activities. Even so, there have been notable successes for TQM in government.

### TQM in Operation: the Up-side

Notable successes for TQM in the public sector indicate what it takes to implement this process originally designed for the assembly line and market place. Posner and Rothstein contend that while it must be adapted to the complexity of government, "TQM does a great job of helping a department decentralize control and identify its customers.

Postmaster General Marvin Runyon, head of America's biggest service organization, the 700,000 peopled Postal Service, took reins in July 1993, turning the organization upside down. Shoop quotes Runyon:

*We still have people in departments with fewer employees who are trying to do all the same work. . . . Now we're trying to convince them that some of the work isn't really necessary. We get reports we don't really need, we get the same report from two areas. You need to look and see what big parts of work you can take to the process. And how long will this take? Runyon concludes, We've got a very, very autocratic system at the Postal Service. . . . We're getting it changed, but that takes time. It could take three years to get where we ought to be with our culture.*

Is cultural change possible in such large, bureaucratic organizations? Perhaps no other group of organizations is viewed as more bureaucratic than the U.S. military. Yet the U.S. Air Force has made notable strides in promoting quality management. The Air Force Combat Command (ACC) published its key areas for quality: decentralization, empowerment and ownership, measurement, training, and leadership. Vice President Gore visited Langley Air Force Base, headquarters for ACC, in 1994. He stated that ACC's organizational units, called "wings," used internal competition in constructive ways by developing a set of performance measures, with each wing receiving feedback on where they were ranked vis-à-vis every other wing according to these measures. Gore stated, "One of Washington's most promising reinvention stories comes from the Air Combat Command."

Many other public organizations and systems have achieved notable success with TQM and continuous improvement. The Internal Revenue Service reports (IRS) that each IRS office is currently focusing its efforts toward being certified by the IRS as a total quality organization. The IRS experiences an overwhelmingly favorable reaction to the quality process assessments, and most important, first- and mid-level managers sensed that their voices were being heard. Many truly believed they were, for the first time, a part of the quality process. Further, public school systems and the Forest Service have implemented TQM. Other large federal agencies have jumped on the TQM band wagon, including the U. S. Air Force, the U. S. Navy, and the U.S. Forest Service. In fact, hundreds of federal agencies in DoD and on the domestic side have shifted their focus to quality and customer service. And the feeling in many areas is that TQM is here to stay.

## THE FUTURE OF TQM IN PUBLIC MANAGEMENT

TQM has met with mixed reactions and success in the public sector. Osborne notes that "the significant problems involved with the translation of TQM into the government sector have less to do with the applicability of the central concepts of TQM, e.g., the concepts of customer and work process . . . than with its political culture and the unmet needs of an unlimited supply of customers that creates real problems for the application of TQM." This point is evident in research on adapting TQM methods in a wide variety of institutions, including those in the public educational system, as well as implementing those processes in routine agency processes, such as personnel performance evaluations. Yet, even in the presence of these problems, it would be a mistake to believe that TQM cannot be successfully integrated into the government organization.

But TQM does require adaption for the demands of managing in the public sector, particularly in consideration of the political, managerial, legal constraints which distinguish public agencies from private sector organizations. One way to accommodate these considerations is to recognize and incorporate these constraints in the list of other factors, with related guidelines and parameters, as a **"contingency"** strategy, rather than relying on any single, one-best-way model.

Some of the factors that may temper the way TQM is implemented in a particular agency are: how specific and precise are the policies you will evaluate; what are the values held and promoted by the organization; what are the technical capabilities of those involved in the process, do you know the characteristics and number of customers served; and are you aware of (and have any control over) the environment in which the organizations operate (political, managerial, and legal factors). Even with an understanding of these factors, as we have indicated, TQM does not promise quick results and great cost savings. With other management approaches, such as "reengineering," have emerged to challenge TQM as the next management revolution, supporters of TQM are many and the list is growing.

## Conclusion

This section has tried to give you some insight into the difficulties of measuring performance in public agencies. We've reviewed some of the shortcomings of the "output" oriented approach in government organizations. Then we highlighted Management by Objectives as a major method still in use for evaluating performance. The main thrust of this piece is to introduce you to what many consider a quantum change in philosophy as well as technique for improving the production and processes of public agencies. While there is a growing list of organizations that are implementing this methodology, the jury is still out on the future of TQM. Perhaps the key word that will determine the ultimate success or failure of TQM in public agencies is commitment. And in the public environment where managers balance managerial, political, and legal constraints continually, the question is: commitment from whom and for how long?

One might pessimistically suggest that the demands imposed by the complexity, costs, and commitment required to sustain TQM are too great for managers operating in the public sector. The obvious alternative, should we fail to adopt a qualitative-process approach is to evaluate performance the old-fashioned way: count beans. It's easy, it's quick, even if it doesn't tell us much. But that hasn't been much of a roadblock to management techniques in the past, nor will it probably be in the future.

# ALDINGER

NAME: _____

SECTION: _____

DATE: _____

1. Describe the two major approaches to measuring performance in public sector organizations.

_____
_____
_____
_____
_____
_____
_____
_____

2. Why isn't "bean counting" always considered to be a sufficient means of assessing the performance of a government agency?

_____
_____
_____
_____
_____
_____
_____
_____

3. What are some of the difficulties of applying TQM to the public sector?

_____
_____
_____
_____
_____
_____
_____
_____

4. Why does TQM's potentiality as a "contingency" strategy make it more appealing to managers in the modern world?

5. What do you think is going to be the future for TQM. Will it be as successful as MBO?

**Group Exercise:** The IRS has won several awards for TQM achievements. Do you favor a more customer oriented IRS?

**Individual Project:** Look at Deming's fourteen points of management and identify those which may be difficult to apply in a federal system of government.

# Part Three

# FIELDS WITH A GLOBAL EMPHASIS

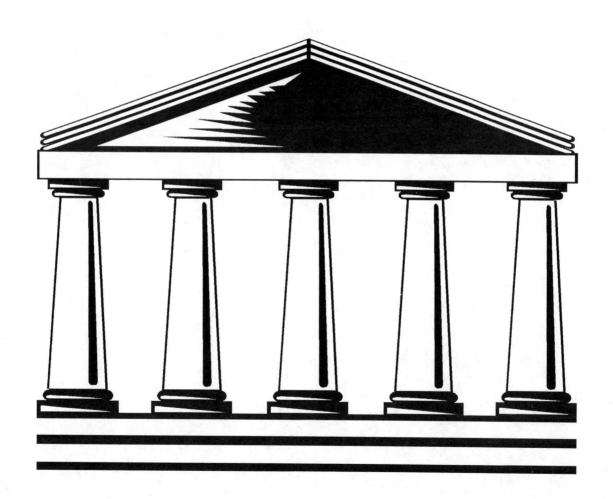

*Chapter Six*

# COMPARATIVE POLITICS

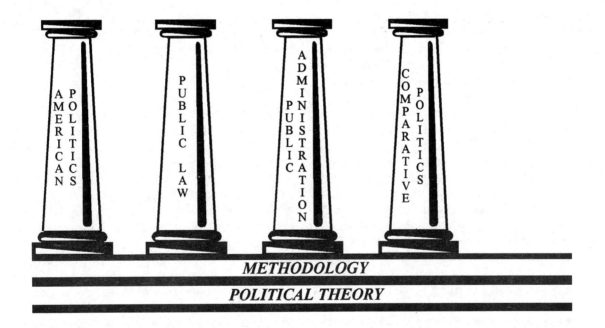

# The Varieties of the Main Types of Constitutions

## Aristotle*

The reason why there are many forms of government is that every state contains many elements. In the first place we see that all states are made up of families, and in the multitude of citizens there must be some rich and some poor, and some in a middle condition; the rich are heavy-armed, and the poor not. Of the common people, some are husbandmen, and some traders, and some artisans. There are also among the notables differences of wealth and property—for example, in the number of horses which they keep, for they cannot afford to keep them unless they are rich. Besides differences of wealth there are differences of rank and merit, and there are some other elements which were mentioned by us when in treating of aristocracy we enumerated the essentials of a state. Of these elements, sometimes all, sometimes the lesser and sometimes the greater number, have a share in the government. It is evident then that there must be many forms of government, differing in kind, since the parts of which they are composed differ from each other in kind. For a constitution is an organization of offices, which all the citizens distribute among themselves, according to the power which different classes possess, for example the rich or the poor, or according to some principle of equality which includes both. There must therefore be as many forms of government as there are modes of arranging the offices, according to the superiorities and the differences of the parts of the state.

There are generally thought to be two principal forms: as men say of the winds that there are but two—north and south, and that the rest of them are only variation of these, so of governments there are said to be only two forms—democracy and oligarchy. For aristocracy is considered to be a kind of oligarchy, as being the rule of the few, and the so-called constitutional government to be really a democracy, just as among the winds we make the west a variation of the north, and the east of the south wind. About forms of government this is a very favorite notion. But in either case the better and more exact way is to distinguish, as I have done, the one or two which are true forms, and to regard the others as perversions,

*Aristotle*

whether of the most perfectly attempted mode or of the best form of government: we may compare the severer and more overpowering modes to the oligarchical forms, and the more relaxed and gentler ones to the democratic.

It must not be assumed, as some are fond of saying, that democracy is simply that form of government in which the greater number are sovereign, for in oligarchies, and indeed in every government, the majority rules; nor again is oligarchy that form of government in which a few are sovereign. Suppose the whole population of a city to be 1300, and that of these 1000 are rich, and do not allow the remaining 300 who are poor, but free, and in all other respects their equals, a share of the government—no one will say that this is a democracy. In like manner, if the poor were few and the masters of the rich who outnumber them, no one would ever call such as government, in which the rich majority have no share of office, an oligarchy. Therefore we should rather say that democracy is the form of government in which the free are rulers, and oligarchy in which the rich;

---

* Excerpted from: Aristotle. (1905). *Politics* (Trans. Benjamin Jowett). Oxford: Clarendon Press, Book IV, Chpts. 3–10.

it is only an accident that the free are the many and the rich are the few. And yet oligarchy and democracy are not sufficiently distinguished merely by these two characteristics of wealth and freedom. Both of them contain many other elements, and therefore we must carry our analysis further, and say that the government is not a democracy in which the freemen, being few in number, rule over the many who are not free. Neither is it a democracy when the rich have the government because they exceed in number. But the form of government is a democracy when the free, who are also poor and the majority, govern, and an oligarchy when the rich and the noble govern, they being at the same time few in number.

I have said that there are many forms of government, and have explained to what causes the variety is due. Why there are more than those already mentioned, and what they are, and whence they arise, I will now proceed to consider, starting from the principle already admitted, which is that every state consists, not of one, but of many parts. If we were going to speak of the different species of animals, we should first of all determine the organs which are indispensable to every animal, as for example some organs of sense and the instruments of receiving and digesting food, such as the mouth and the stomach, besides organs of locomotion. Assuming now that there are only so many kinds of organs, but that there may be differences in them—I mean different kinds of mouths, and stomachs, and perceptive and locomotive organs—the possible combinations of these differences will necessarily furnish many varieties of animals. (For animals cannot be the same which have different kinds of mouths or of ears.) And when all the combinations are exhausted, there will be as many sorts of animals as there are combinations of the necessary organs. The same, then, is true of the forms of government which have been described; states, as I have repeatedly said, are composed, not of one, but of many elements. One element is the food-producing class, who are called husbandmen; a second, the class of mechanics who practice the arts without which a city cannot exist;— of these arts some are absolutely necessary, others contribute to luxury or to the grace of life. The third class is that of traders, and by traders I mean those who are engaged in buying and selling, whether in commerce or in retail trade. A fourth class is that of the serfs or laborers. The warriors make up the fifth class, and they are as necessary as any of the others, if the country is not to be the slave of every invader. For how can a state which has any title to the name be of a slavish nature? The state is independent and self-sufficing, but a slave is the reverse of independent. And as the soul may be said to be more truly part of animal than the body, so the higher parts of states, that is to say, the warrior class, the class engaged in the administration of justice, and that engaged in deliberation, which is the special business of political common sense—these are more essential to the state than the parts which minister to the necessaries of life. Whether their several functions are the functions of different citizens, or of the same—for it may often happen that the same persons are both warriors and husbandmen—is immaterial to the argument. The higher as well as the lower elements are to be equally considered parts of the state, and if so, the military element at any rate must be included. There are also the wealthy who minister to the state with their property; these form the seventh class. The eighth class is that of magistrates and of officers; for the state cannot exist without rulers. And therefore some must be able to take office and to serve the state, either always or in turn. There only remains the class of those who deliberate and who judge between disputants; we were just now distinguishing them. If presence of all these elements, and their fair and equitable organization, is necessary to states, then there must also be persons who have the ability of statesmen. Different functions appear to be often combined in the same individual; for example, the warrior may also be a husbandman, or an artisan; or, again, the counsellor a judge. And all claim to possess political ability, and think that they are quite competent to fill most offices. But the same persons cannot be rich and poor at the same time. For this reason the rich and the poor are regarded in an especial sense as parts of a state. Again, because the rich are generally few in number, while the poor are many, they appear to be antagonistic, and as the one or the other prevails they form the government. Hence arises the common opinion that there are two kinds of government—democracy and oligarchy.

I have already explained that there are many forms of constitution, and to what causes the variety is due. Let me now show that there are different forms both of democracy and oligarchy, as will indeed be evident from what has preceded. For both in the common people and in the notables various classes are included; of the common people, one class are husbandmen, another artisans; another traders, who are employed in buying and selling; another are the seafaring class, whether engaged in war or in trade, as ferrymen or as fishermen. To the classes already mentioned may be added day-laborers, and those who, owing to their needy circumstances, have no leisure, or those who are not of free birth on both sides; and there may be other classes as well. The notables again may be divided according to their wealth, birth, virtue, education, and similar differences.

Of forms of democracy first comes that which is said to be based strictly on equality. In such a democracy the law says that it is just for the poor to have no more advantage than the rich; and that neither should be masters, but both equal. For if liberty and equality, as is thought by some, are chiefly to be found in democracy, they will be best attained when all persons alike share in the government to the utmost. And since the people are the majority, and the opinion of the majority is decisive, such a government must necessarily be a democracy. Here then is one sort of democracy. There is another, in which the magistrates are elected according to a certain property qualification, but a low one; he who has the required amount of property has a share in the government, but he who loses his property loses his rights. Another kind is that in which all the citizens who are under no disqualification share in the government, but still the law is supreme. In another, everybody, if he be only a citizen, is admitted to the government, but the law is supreme as before. A fifth form of democracy, in other respects, the same, is that in which, not the law, but the multitude, have the supreme power, and supersede the law by their decrees. This is a state of affairs brought about by the demagogues. For in democracies which are subject to the law the best citizens hold the first place, and there are no demagogues; but where the laws are not supreme, there demagogues spring up. For the people becomes a monarch, and is many in one; and the many have the power in their hands, not as individualism but collectively. Homer says that 'it is not good to have a rule of many,' but whether he means this corporate rule, or the rule of many individuals, is uncertain. At all events this sort of democracy, which is now a monarch, and no longer under the control of law, seeks to exercise monarchical sway, and grows into a despot; the flatterer is held in honor; this sort of democracy being relatively to other democracies what tyranny is to other forms of monarchy. The spirit of both is the same, and they alike exercise a despotic rule over the better citizens. The decrees of the demos correspond to the edicts of the tyrant; and the demagogue is to the one what the flatterer is to the other. Both have great power;—the flatterer with the tyrant, the demagogue with democracies of the kind which we are describing. The demagogues make the decrees of the people override the laws, by referring all things to the popular assembly. And therefore they grow great, because the people have all things in their hands, and they hold in their hands the votes of the people, who are too ready to listen to them. Further, those who have any complaint to bring against the magistrates say, 'let the people be judges'; the people are too happy to accept the invitation; and so the authority of every office is undermined. Such a democracy is fairly open to the objection that it is not a constitution at all; for where the laws have no authority, there is no constitution. The law ought to be supreme over all, and the magistracies should judge of particulars, and only this should be considered a constitution. So that if democracy be a real form of government, the sort of system in which all things are regulated by decrees is clearly not even a democracy in the true sense of the word, for decrees relate only to particulars.

These then are the different kinds of democracy.

Of oligarchies, too, there are different kinds:— one where the property qualification for office is such that the poor, although they form the majority, have no share in the government, yet he who acquires a qualification may obtain a share. Another sort is when there is a qualification for office, but a high one, and the vacancies in the governing body are filled by co-optation. If the election is made out of all the qualified persons, a constitution of this kind inclines to an aristocracy, of out of a privileged class, to an oligarchy. Another sort of oligarchy is when the son succeeds the father. There is a fourth form, likewise hereditary, in which the magistrates are supreme and not the law. Among oligarchies this is what tyranny is among monarchies, and the last-mentioned form of democracy among democracies; and in fact this sort of oligarchy receives the name of a dynasty (or rule of powerful families).

These are the different sorts of oligarchies and democracies. It should however be remembered that in many states the constitution which is established by law, although not democratic, owing to the education and habits of the people may be administered democratically, and conversely in other states the established constitution may incline to democracy, but may be administered in an oligarchical spirit. This most often happens after a revolution: for governments do not change at once; at first the dominant party are content with encroaching a little upon their opponents. The laws which existed previously continue in force, but the authors of the revolution have the power in their hands.

# ARISTOTLE

NAME: _____

SECTION: _____

DATE: _____

1. What are the two major forms of government, as described by Aristotle?

   _____
   _____
   _____
   _____
   _____
   _____
   _____

2. If Aristotle compares countries like one compares species of animals, by looking at similarities and differences, is this approach similar to any of the approaches described in the chapter on methodology? Explain your answer.

   _____
   _____
   _____
   _____
   _____
   _____
   _____

3. What are the different forms of democracy described by Aristotle? Does the U.S. fit into his model?

   _____
   _____
   _____
   _____
   _____
   _____

4. Aristotle compares flatterers to demagogues. Do you agree? Why or why not?

_____
_____
_____
_____
_____
_____
_____

5. If, as Aristotle says, city states have different types of governments because they contain different types of people, is there any ideally best type of government?

_____
_____
_____
_____
_____
_____
_____

**Group Exercise:** Assess the focus and tone of Aristotle's article on Constitutions. Do you agree that the work has a modern ring to it?

**Individual Project:** Compare Aristotle to Machiavelli. Who do you find to be more helpful? Why?

# The European Union in Transition: From Independent Nation-States to a United States of Europe?

## Carol Glen

The European continent has experienced dramatic and sudden change in recent years. The fall of the Berlin wall, the re-unification of Germany, and the disintegration of previously intact nation-states have all contributed to new and more unstable trends that have still to reach their full fruition. The most dramatic political changes continue to be felt in Eastern and Central Europe, as governments struggle to transform authoritarian political systems into democracies, and convert command based economies into free market systems. However, longer term political transformations are also underway in Western Europe. Countries that once faced each other as enemies in war are now solid allies. Peace, democracy, and cooperation between states, characterize the latter half of the 20th century in Western Europe, as they did not characterize the first.

One significant development that has contributed to the stability and cooperation between many of the countries in Europe has been the formation and growth of the European Union (E.U.). Founded by six countries in 1958 as the European Economic Community (EEC), the E.U. now incorporates a population of 366 million in 15 countries, and stretches geographically from the Arctic circle to the Mediterranean Sea. The goal of the E.U. is to promote political cooperation and economic integration among its member states. Economic integration refers to the removal of barriers to trade and other economic activity among countries, for the purpose of economic growth. The E.U. has moved further than any other group of countries in this direction. It is currently creating a single market in which goods, services and people can move freely, and proposals for the establishment of a single currency are now being implemented. Because the E.U. has become larger, stronger and more integrated than most could have imagined during the early days of its formation, some have begun to wonder how far the organization might extend. Are we witnessing an embryonic United States of Europe which will someday develop into a federal system of government like the U.S., or is this scenario too unrealistic given the recent history of the continent, and the unwillingness of European governments to give up power? The answer to this question will obviously only be known in the long term, but by looking at the E.U.'s recent history, and by examining the interests of its member governments, we can assess the possibility that Europe will become unified in the near future.

## THE ORIGINS AND GROWTH OF THE EUROPEAN UNION

The impetus for creating a community of European nations emerged from the devastation and economic upheaval caused by World War II. Although a Pan-European Union movement had been active earlier in the century, it took the brutalities of two major wars, both started on European soil, to bring concrete proposals for a united Europe to the table. The political rationale for establishing a community rested initially on a desire for peace. It was hoped that the creation of such an organization would promote cooperation among countries that had been enemies in war only a few years earlier, and would prevent future conflicts from occurring. In addition, to the most optimistic observers, a prosperous and unified Europe would become strong enough to some day take its place beside the superpowers as an equal participant on the world stage. Political motivations were a large part of the initial impetus of the European Economic Community, but as its name suggests, the founding fathers envisaged economic growth to be the key to peace and prosperity. An economically strong Europe in which every nation shared would be a peaceful Europe. However, from the beginning there was some dispute as to how the twin goals of peace and prosperity would be achieved.

On one side of the argument were federalists such as Altiero Spinelli, the leader of the European Federalist Movement and a member of the Italian Parliament, who called for a quick and dramatic shift to a united Europe. Spinelli proposed that this could be achieved through the establishment of a constitutional convention, similar to the Philadelphia Convention of 1787, which would take responsibility for writing a European constitution, and for creating a European federal government. The convention would gain its legitimacy by being democratically elected, and by being recognized as a representative voice of European public opinion. Spinelli believed that only mass public support for federalism could pressure national governments to relinquish sovereignty to a new central institution. In the United States of Europe which Spinelli envisaged, each country would have political representation at the federal level, but each would be subject to the collective decisions of the entire polity. For the federalists, only a dramatic solution such as this one could ensure the future peace and stability of Europe.

On the other side of the argument were the functionalists, epitomized by French diplomat and civil servant Jean Monnet. In contrast to federalist solutions, Monnet maintained that it was unrealistic to expect sovereign nations to give up political power in order to create a new and unfamiliar form of government. Rather, he argued, the road to European integration would be smoother and more successful if it were gradual. The functionalist vision of European unity was therefore a bottom-up approach, European governments could build trust slowly by cooperating in specific, essentially non-political, or technical areas. As cooperation succeeded in one policy area, it would create momentum for further cooperation that would "spill-over" to other policy areas. Gradually, over time, governments would become increasing willing to give up, or at least pool, their sovereignty in a common supra-national decision-making institution.

Federalist proposals proved to be too bold for either governments or public to accept, but Monnet's more cautious approach did find some success. Monnet's vision greatly influenced proposals for the establishment of a European Coal and Steel Community (ECSC) which were officially presented in 1950 by Robert Schuman, the French Foreign Minister. The ECSC was to be primarily a technical mechanism for stabilizing the price and production of coal and steel, but would also require the establishment of a High Authority as a forum for joint decision-making. Schuman initially directed his proposals toward Germany in the hope that the ECSC could become a vehicle for Franco-German reconciliation. From the French perspective, the ECSC might help to contain Germany by preventing any secret buildup of arms. From the German perspective, the ECSC presented a much needed opportunity to re-build its reputation only a few years after the end of WWII. Recognizing the joint benefits that could be gained from such an organization, both countries decided to go ahead with the establishment of the ECSC in 1951, and were joined by Belgium, Luxembourg, Netherlands, and Italy. The other leading European power at the time Britain was invited to join, but suspicious of longer term federalist intentions, refused.

The ECSC proved to be an immediate success both in terms of its economic and its political goals. Within five years of its founding, negotiations began between the same group of counties to extend cooperation beyond coal and steel production. This was finally achieved in 1958 with the signing of the Treaty of Rome, which created two new organizations: the European Atomic Energy Community, (EURATOM) and the European Economic Community (EEC). The former was created to regulate the peaceful uses of atomic energy, and the latter to create a customs union which would remove internal tariffs and quotas, and establish a common external tariff among member states. Of the two organizations, the EEC was the more successful, growing in both size and scope over the years. The ECSC and EURATOM merged with the EEC in 1967 creating a common set of institutions which became known as the European Community (EC). One year later, the EC successfully reached its goal of completing a customs union, slightly ahead of schedule.

Despite these early successes, the development of the EC was not without its political controversies, rooted largely in competing visions of which future path the organization should take. In particular, French president Charles de Gaulle came into conflict with other members over his insistence that political power remain firmly in the hands of national governments. Although de Gaulle believed that the EC could be a useful economic organization, he drew the line at giving up national political power to supra-national institutions. This dispute came to a head in 1965 in what became known as the "empty chair crisis" when de Gaulle refused to participate in meetings until he received guarantees that his wishes could not be over-ridden by a majority vote. In effect, de Gaulle demanded that member governments be given veto power over issues deemed vital to national interests. After holding out for months, member governments reached agreement in the Luxembourg Compromise which gave in to de Gaulle's demands. During the same period, the French president was also instrumental in thwarting British attempts to join the EC. Britain had initially refused to become part of the ECSC or the EEC, but altered its position after witnessing the success of these organizations. The British government submitted two membership applications, one in 1963 and one in 1967, but both were blocked by de Gaulle who believed that the British view of the future of Europe was very different from his own. It was only after de Gaulle's death that the British membership application was accepted. Along with Ireland and Denmark, Britain joined the EC in 1973, raising its membership total to nine countries.

The first membership expansion of the EC did not end the organizations problems, however. Instead, it coincided with the beginning of a long and severe economic recession that further hampered integration attempts. As governments faced economic and political difficulties at home they became increasingly unwilling to expend time or energy searching for collective European solutions. At the same time, the EC was faced with a number of internal disagreements, including disputes over Britain's budgetary contributions, and over subsidies to European farmers. For many observers during the 1970s and early 1980s the European Community had been halted in its tracks. Spill-over was not occurring, and despite another increase in membership with Greece joining in 1981, the organization was quickly becoming irrelevant.

But the EC did not fade away. To the surprise of many, the mid 1980s brought a new flurry of activity and cooperation among members states which culminated in the accession of two new members, Spain and Portugal in 1986, and the signing of two important documents. The first was the Single European Act signed in 1985 which was an agreement to create a common market by 1992 so that goods, capital, and people could move freely across borders. The second was the ratification in 1993 of the Treaty on European Union (TEU), also known as the Maastricht Treaty. The TEU changed the name of the EC to the European Union and promoted further integration by expanding the breadth of policies over which member governments would cooperate. The TEU laid out a time-table for European monetary union (EMU), and added two new 'pillars' of cooperation that includes foreign policy and defense, and immigration and policing policy. The mid 1990s also witnessed the E.U. expand its membership for the fourth time, incorporating Austria, Finland and Sweden in 1995.

There is still some debate as to why the EC became so quickly revitalized during the mid 1980s, but most seem to agree that it was the result of a combination of both domestic and international factors. In particular, explanations have tended to focus on three influences: (1) the relatively poor performance of European economies in the years prior to 1985 which encouraged business and government elites to look for ways to improve European competitiveness; (2) the similar economic policy perspectives adopted by governments in Britain, France and Germany; and (3) the role played by the European Commission under the leadership of Jacques Delors who worked diligently to re-launch the integration process.

## INSTITUTIONS OF THE EUROPEAN UNION

The E.U. has a government structure similar to that found in many national political systems consisting of legislative, executive and judicial branches, but it does not operate like a country. It does not have its own military, it does not have independent tax raising powers, and its power is much more limited than that enjoyed by national governments. On the other hand, the E.U. has a broader and more firmly established system of government than any other international organization. It can pass laws that legally bind member governments, and its Commission has diplomatic representation around the world. The work of the E.U. is conducted in four main bodies and two advisory committees, which are both intergovernmental and supra-national in nature. The principal intergovernmental institutions are the European Council and the Council of the European Union. The main supra-national institutions are the European Commission, the European Parliament and the European Court of Justice. The key difference between the intergovernmental and the supra-national bodies is that in the former, members act according to national interests, whereas in the latter members are obligated to act in the interests of the E.U. as a whole.

## EUROPEAN COUNCIL

The European Council has been described as Europe's most exclusive club. It is comprised of the heads of government of all of the E.U. member countries and meets twice per year to provide strategic direction for future E.U. policy. The Treaty of Rome made no mention of the European Council, rather it grew out of a series of summit meetings which were first held during 1974, on the initiative of French president Giscard d'Estang. Although European Council directives still carry no legal force, because of its composition, no major E.U. policy initiatives will be taken without its approval.

### *Council of the European Union*

The other major intergovernmental institution is the Council of the European Union, formerly the Council of Ministers. This body consists of 15 representatives from each of the member states, but its composition varies depending on the topic under discussion. Foreign Ministers of each country attend all General Meetings, but if the topic is, for instance, agriculture, then ministers responsible for agriculture in each country would attend. The Council is the principle decision-making body of the E.U. and has both executive and legislative powers. It adopts legislation submitted to it by the Commission, and sets guidelines as to how laws are to be implemented. Each member country sends only one minister to Council meetings, but voting is weighted according to population size in order to give larger countries more influence. More populous countries such as Germany and France receive ten votes each, whereas a small country such as Luxembourg, receives only two votes. On important matters, such as membership applications and treaty issues, voting must be unanimous for legislation to pass, on less important issues a "qualified majority," (70% of total votes) will be sufficient. To ensure fair representation the presidency of the Council rotates every 6–months on an alphabetical basis.

## Commission of the European Communities

The Commission sits at the heart of the E.U. and has been called the "engine of the community" since this is where policy initiatives begin. The Commission has the exclusive right to initiate legislation, administer the community budget, ensure that treaty obligations are being fulfilled, and it is also the bureaucracy of the organization. The Commission is comprised of 20 Commissioners appointed for 4 year terms by member governments. Once appointed, Commissioners become responsible for administering a particular policy area such as external affairs, agriculture, or transportation. Although these are similar functional divisions to those found in the Council of the European Union, Commissioners are required to represent the interests of the E.U. as a whole rather than individual member governments. The Commission is headed by a President elected by E.U. governments for two year terms, renewable once. Like the rest of the Commission the president takes an E.U.-wide perspective on policy. In recent years this position has become increasingly visible and influential, due in large part to the work of Jacques Delors who headed the Commission through much of the 1980s. Delors has been given at least some of the credit for the passage of the Single European Act in 1985, which helped to re-energize the Community.

## European Parliament

If the Council of the European Union represents the interests of member governments, and the Commission represents the organizational interests of the E.U., then the European Parliament (EP) represents the interests of the people. Since 1979 direct elections to the EP have been held in each country every five years, with the last taking place during June of 1994. Currently, the EP is comprised of 626 Members of the European Parliament (MEP's), with seats being allocated to each country on the basis of population, but with MEP's having just one vote. The EP's organizational structure is divided into nine political groupings, and voting occurs along party/ideological lines rather than according to nationality. Two groups presently make up more than half of all EP members: the European Socialists (217 members), and the Christian Democrats (172 members). The power of the EP varies considerably from one policy area to the next, but in general it is responsible for debating legislation sent to it by the Commission, and suggesting amendments which are then sent to the Council of the European Union for approval. Although the powers of the EP were increased with the passage of the Single European Act and the TEU, for most legislation, the EP cannot override the wishes of the Council of the European Union. This apparent weakness of the EP, the only directly elected institution in the E.U., has led many to argue that the E.U. suffers from a "democratic deficit."

## European Court of Justice

The European Court of Justice (ECJ) acts as the supreme court of the E.U., its highest legal authority. It is comprised of 15 judges and 9 Advocates General appointed by member governments for six year terms. The task of the ECJ is to interpret E.U. law and settle disputes among E.U. institutions, and between governments and individuals. Over the years, the ECJ has become an important supra-national institution. Through the strict application of law, and by setting legal precedents, the ECJ ensures that each member country adheres to its treaty obligations. Since E.U. law takes precedence over national law, the ECJ can also impose fines on member states that violate existing statutes.

## Economic and Social Committee and the Committee of Regions

In addition to the legislative, executive and judicial branches of government discussed above, the E.U. also has two advisory bodies: the Economic and Social Committee and the Committee of Regions. The Economic and Social Committee (ESC) was established under the Treaty of Rome as a means of incorporating organized economic interests into the decision-making process. It is comprised of 222 representatives from European labor unions, employers association and other interest groups, and gives policy advice to other E.U. institutions. More recently, the TEU added another body, the Committee of Regions (COR). The COR is comprised of 222 representatives from local and regional governments, and gives policy advice on regional development issues. Like the ESC, the COR can act only in an advisory capacity, however its significance lies in the fact that this is the only E.U. institution that gives formal recognition to representatives from subnational governments, whose opinions may, or may not, coincide with those at the national level.

# MEMBER STATE INTERESTS AND EUROPEAN UNITY

From the previous review of E.U. institutions, it is clear that member governments still play a dominant role. The E.U.'s intergovernmental institutions have relatively more power than its supra-national institutions, so it is not unreasonable to conclude that the future direction of the E.U. will continue to be shaped by the interests of its dominant member states. The governments of these states however, do not all view the European Union in the same way. Some are highly supportive wishing to see the E.U.'s policy prerogatives expanded, while others are more inclined to seek cooperation over a narrower range of policy. This breadth of opinion and support is well represented in the views of the E.U.'s three largest and most influential countries: Germany, France and the United Kingdom, whose positions are briefly outlined below.

## *Germany*

Germany has long been a supporter of the integration process in Europe. It was one of the original signatories of the Treaty of Rome which established the European Economic Community in 1958, and it continues to be the major driving force behind further integration today. For more than 35 years, European integration has served German economic and political interests well. The initial creation of a customs union and then a common market, provided German industry with a large and prosperous market for its products. Taking advantage of this market helped propel Germany from post-war devastation to economic superpower in only a few years. At the same time, the E.U. allowed Germany to achieve this transformation without becoming overly threatening to its neighbors. Such a dramatic increase in German economic strength might have been viewed with a great deal more suspicion had Germany not become so closely allied with other European powers through the E.U.

The current German government, led by Helmut Kohl, is among the most fervent supporters of European integration. Kohl successfully engineered the re-unification of Germany, and sees the German federal system of government as a loose model for the long-term future of Europe. The principle short-term goal of the Kohl government is the creation of a single European currency by the end of the century. Even if this can only be achieved by a few countries, the German position holds that a single currency should be introduced in a 'hard core' of countries first, probably Germany, France, the Netherlands, Belgium and Luxembourg, with others following later if their economies meet certain economic criteria, and if they wish. This arrangement would in effect establish a "multi-speed" Europe, with some countries proceeding further along the path toward European unity than others.

## *France*

French attitudes toward European integration have undergone a dramatic reversal since the De Gaulle presidency, shifting from a strongly nationalistic position to one which is more accommodating and supportive of the process. Much of this turn-around can be attributed to Francois Mitterand, who was president of France from 1981 to 1995. Mitterand played a major role in the Community's re-vitalization during the 1980s, and he became a key player in the negotiations that led to the Single European Act (SEA) and the Treaty on European Union. At the same time, another Frenchman Jacques Delors, who presided over the European Commission during much of the 1980s, has also been given credit for helping to make the SEA and the TEU become reality.

Despite this general shift in orientation, French government opinion has remained consistent in viewing the E.U. as an effective mechanism to counter German influence on the continent. Mitterand's support for the TEU can be attributed, at least in part, to a desire to bind Germany closer to its western allies following that country's re-unification. It can also be attributed to a French desire to reduce German control over European monetary policy. The TEU which Mitterand strongly supported, establishes a system of European Central Banks which will take over the fiscal coordination role previously enjoyed by the German Bundesbank. Decisions in this new system will be made collectively, and France will be assured a significant voice.

Today, the French government, like the German government, is supportive of European integration, albeit for different reasons. The current French President, Jacques Chirac, is committed to the full implementation of the TEU, and pledges to adopt the single currency by the 1999 deadline. The main difference between the French and German positions seems to be over how far integration should proceed. German government officials have been much more willing than French officials to discuss the possibility of a federal system of government for Europe's future.

## *United Kingdom*

Britain has been the most reluctant of the "big three" member states. Its focus has traditionally been more transatlantic than continental, and it is the only E.U. member to have had its membership application initially vetoed. Added to that, once Britain did gain entry, its government spent several years quarrelling with other member states in an attempt to lower British contributions to the E.U. budget. Despite this general reticence however, successive governments have acknowledged that continued E.U. membership is a preferable option to going it alone.

In its relations with other E.U. members and with E.U. institutions, the UK continues to stress the importance of national sovereignty. British governments have rejected attempts to erode national power in favor of supra-national institutions, and have refused to consider a 'federalized' Europe as an option. This reluctance to commit to a more integrated Europe has led British governments to opt out of many of the obligations agreed by other member states. Britain, for instance, opted out of the Social Chapter of the TEU, which would have required that U.K. labor regulations be aligned with those of its continental partners. Britain has also refused to commit to the adoption of a single European currency, although this is not yet completely out of the question.

Given the British record in the E.U., it is perhaps not surprising that the UK government has been frequently accused, by its European allies, of being deliberately obstructionist in negotiations. This may be the case, but often these disputes are rooted in different conceptions of what the European Union is, and what it should become. For Britain, the E.U. is first and foremost an intergovernmental organization in which European allies cooperate to enhance the security and prosperity of each member state. For some other members however, the E.U. as it exists today is simply a stepping stone to something much more elaborate. It is the irreconcilability of these two views that produces disagreement.

## A UNITED EUROPE?

The E.U. has come a long way since its early days. It has not met the high expectations of the early federalists, but neither has it become a European super-state, as feared by some nationalists. Today, the E.U. is both an intergovernmental and supra-national organization, although the balance is clearly tipped toward the former. If Europe is to one day become united then it will have to overcome a number of major obstacles, not the least of which is the reluctance of its own member governments. At present there is simply insufficient support for such a proposition to succeed.

There are also a few more practical difficulties that could stand in the way of further integration. The E.U. is almost certainly going to expand its membership in the near future. Thirteen countries have already applied, and the next expansion could come by the end of the decade. With 28 members, and in the absence of major institutional reform, it will become increasingly difficult for member countries to reach the type of agreements necessary to move the process forward. Finally, the role of European public opinion cannot be ignored. Traditionally, European publics have been viewed as passive in the integration process, knowing little, and caring even less. This perception was dramatically challenged however, during the ratification process for the Treaty on European Union. Despite support for the treaty among Danish political leaders, the electorate initially rejected it in a national referendum. This event, plus a very slim vote of approval in France, indicated that in some cases political leaders had pushed policy beyond public desire. It is therefore conceivable, if not likely, that all of these factors will combine to make the road to European unity very difficult. This is not to say that the integration process will come to a complete halt, only that it will likely proceed in the same irregular, piecemeal fashion as before.

# GLEN

NAME: _____

SECTION: _____

DATE: _____

1. Describe the tensions and pressures which led to the founding of the EEC.

   _____
   _____
   _____
   _____
   _____
   _____
   _____
   _____

2. Compare and contrast the two major proposed routes for the creation of a United States of Europe.

   _____
   _____
   _____
   _____
   _____
   _____
   _____
   _____

3. Compare and contrast the federal structure of the United States with the structure of the European Union (E.U.).

   _____
   _____
   _____
   _____
   _____
   _____
   _____
   _____

4. What is the main opposition within the E.U. to complete political unification of its member states?

___

5. What is the role of the advisory commissions in E.U.? Does the U.S. have similar institutions?

___

**Group Exercise:** Structures of government have recently demonstrated dual tendencies of joining together (E.U.) and breaking up (U.S.S.R). Does this have any relationship to future developments in the U.S.? If so, what?

**Individual Project:** Locate and identify some recent information about developments in the E.U. Is it optimistic about unification? Why or why not?

# Democratization and Structural Adjustment Programs in Africa: Failures and Successes of Two Development Strategies

## Napoleon Bamfo

Since the mid-1980s, most African nations have participated in or been directly affected by programs of structural adjustment and democratization. The two strategies have become the prescription for development which the World Bank and the International Monetary Funds have recommended and promoted in several developing nations. Nations, particularly those in Africa, have been persuaded to agree that unless they started radical economic reforms and encouraged free political activity, they would have limited success at development. In the past four decades or so, only a handful of African nations have been successful at maintaining democracy and sustaining economic growth. The two strategies have been touted as providing better alternatives in removing the bottlenecks that have stifled economic growth and political development on the continent.

In the *World Development Report, 1989,* the World Bank defined structural adjustment as programs that use changes in fiscal programs, monetary, and sectoral policies, in regulations, and in institutions to alter relative prices and the level of spending and thereby redirect economic activity. Generally, the prescription for adjustment that was recommended for each nation was tailor-made to fit that nation's particular needs. Yet, since most African states have similar economies, the recommendations made for most nations have looked strikingly similar. In every African nation, the central government plays the dominant role in economic decision making. Moreover, the bulk of the population is engaged in subsistence farming, which is the primary economic activity. Most states have a one-crop dominated export sector; therefore, they are vulnerable to the instability generally associated with the prices of export crops. Industrialization forms a relatively small part of most economies; hence, wages are small. Structural adjustment programs, therefore, have been designed to reduce the dominant role of the state in economic decision making, to increase agricultural and industrial production, and to improve the general economic welfare of the people. They have included downsizing the public sector by the laying off of civil servants. Other strategies promoted have involved fiscal adjustment through the devaluation of currencies, and the development of human capital through education and training. Adjustment programs also have encouraged decentralization, reduction of bureaucratic red-tape, and greater administrative accountability. Governments have been encouraged to increase the producer price of agricultural commodities paid to local farmers to encourage them to increase productivity.

The other strategy for development is democratization, which is aimed at reforming political systems away from their traditional bent toward authoritarianism. Governments that have embarked on democratic reform have not given any supernal meaning to it. In practical terms, it has come to signify a publicly announced time-table for the drafting and promulgation of a new constitution, lifting the ban on political party activity, conducting general elections, and establishing the rule of the victorious party. To symbolize a break with the past, newly adopted constitutions have guaranteed individual freedoms, including due process of law, the release of political prisoners, and a free press.

# A Checkered Political and Economic Past

What triggered economic and political reform programs in Africa has been the disappointing outcome of nations in their political and economic development efforts. Although Africa is a continent rich in raw materials, cultivable land, and potential energy resources, the economic performance of most states has been disappointing. Nearly every African nation has experienced problems arising from declining productivity, changing tastes, changes in terms of trade, and rising expectations. During the mid-1980s, conditions in the sub-Saharan region had so badly deteriorated that the World Bank declared the region as one that faced the most serious developmental crisis in the world.

Since the early 1980s, per capita food production on the continent has been declining. A UNDP report in 1990 revealed that 31 of the world's 42 poorest nations with per capita national income of less than $500 were located in Africa. This has been a serious cause for concern because of the nearly threefold increase in population growth, from 280 million in 1960 to 753 million in 1995, according to Bulatao and Associates. In the early 1960s when several African nations became independent, they placed their developmental emphasis on the production of cash crops for export. Today, national economies have become heavily dependent on the production of one or two primary commodities for export, most of them agricultural. Because of hard economic times, nations have failed to invest sufficiently in the education of their ever-growing young population. According to a UNDP report, the average literacy rate in sub-Saharan Africa in 1985 was the lowest in the world, with only 45 percent of the population over 15 years being able to read and write. Politically, African states have not fared well either. From the late 1950s to 1995, nearly every state had been hit by a military coup d'etat. Since Africans liberated themselves from colonial domination in the early 1960s, most of the new states have been unable to sustain any tradition of democracy. Departing colonial powers had hoped that the rudimentary democracies they had established, involving multi-party elections and elected parliaments, would last. However, no sooner had they left the shores of the continent than a series of political setbacks begin to neutralize the great optimism the people had felt about their newly-acquired independent status. During the first decade of independence, incumbent civilian administrations, realizing how difficult it was to maintain national unity and promote economic growth, began to find scapegoats for their failed policies. They passed repressive laws under which political opponents were arrested for misdemeanors. To consolidate political power, administrations began proscribing opposition parties. On the few occasions multi-party elections were allowed, they were often rigged in favor of incumbents. Ex-president Nyerere of Tanzania defended one-partyism, arguing that traditional African families had always lived according to the basic principles of *Ujamaa*, which required members to live together and work together. Some heads of states like Kamuzu Banda of Malawi and Kwame Nkrumah of Ghana went so far in conferring life-presidencies on themselves. Other anti-democratic activities like detention without trial and censorship of the media were rampant.

It was the military which dealt the most devastating blow to African nations' attempts to establish democracies. According to Peter Esterhuysen, ever since the first military coup was staged in post-independent Africa in Benin in 1963, nearly ninety have been successfully staged. The latest was staged in Niger in May 1996. For two and one-half decades, African politics was punctuated not only by coups, but counter-coups, political assassinations, and the disappearance of political opponents. In their over-zealousness to correct what they perceived to be blatant maladministration, military officers often resorted to initiating populist programs such as the confiscation of property and the delivery of street justice. However, such programs were short-lived and usually backfired. As close relatives became victims, such heavy-handed attempts at changing society soon hit home at the civilian population whom the military was trying to impress.

# Implementation

Developmental strategists have always assumed an inextricable link between political stability and economic development. Consequently, in the early 1980s, the World Bank implored African nations to combine programs of economic restructuring with political liberalization. In Rostow's seminal work, The *Stages of Economic Growth*, he argued that democracy was a necessary precondition for economic development. In

*The Downward Spiral,* Sandbrook and Baker explained the factors that had contributed to Africa's unimpressive development efforts and attributed the failure of nations to raise people's living standards to the widespread decay of their political systems. They observed of African nations that as their economies deteriorated, so did political stability because whenever people experienced hard economic times, they wanted change, no matter how that change was accomplished. In his study of Zambian politics in the mid to late 1980s, Zuckerman affirmed this linkage between economics and politics. Deteriorating economic conditions in Zambia during the 1980s led to the electoral defeat in 1991 of Kenneth Kaunda, the nation's political leader for twenty-seven years.

From the beginning, African governments gave uneven consideration to the World Bank's proposal to combine economic liberalization and political reform. Since several nations were already facing hard economic times, their initial fascination was for programs that would promote economic growth. Several nations already were indebted to the IMF, so it was relatively easy for the IMF and the World Bank to impose stringent conditions on their loans and force nations to adhere strictly to the prescriptions they suggested for economic reform. Ghana, Tanzania, Nigeria, Benin, and Cote d'Ivoire, among others, which had heavy debt burdens were among the first to undertake reform. In a study of structural adjustment programs in Kenya and Cote d'Ivoire, Jennifer Widner laid out some of the broad patterns involved in the process. They included infrastructural improvement, educational improvement, and the sale of public enterprises to private citizens. Export promotion also was high of the list on the programs of restructuring, a process which was aimed at stabilizing commodity prices on behalf of farmers. These reform efforts usually set in motion a series of layoffs and pay cuts, but reduced the opportunities which took money away from taxpayers and gave it to unproductive government employees.

African nations embraced democratization shortly after economic restructuring had begun. Tanzania and Benin pioneered that effort. In 1985, president Nyerere, the long-term ruler of Tanzania, voluntarily relinquished his presidency to his vice-president. In Benin, president Kerekou, facing an economic crisis, renounced his Marxist-Leninist belief and agreed to hold multi-party elections. Meanwhile, the birth of democracy in Eastern Europe following the fall of the Berlin Wall in late 1989, precipitated this political change. The year 1990, therefore, began with a great deal of optimism among African nations to resuscitate their democratic institutions and processes. The release of Nelson Mandela from prison in early 1990 by apartheid South Africa added to this euphoria among nations. Soon after Mandela's release, the last apartheid regime promised to hold free elections that would involve all races, focus attention on human rights, cooperatively participate in Africa's development, and abandon South Africa's long-term policy of trying to subdue neighboring countries. Meanwhile on the rest of the continent, one autocratic leader after the other voluntarily committed themselves to a time-table for reform or were coerced to do so. The World Bank added to this pressure by indicating its reluctance to reschedule short and long-term loans of nations that did not liberalize their political institutions.

## SUCCESSES AND SETBACKS

Some ignoble setbacks and remarkable successes have characterized Africa's politics since the early 1990s. As 1990 drew to a close, there was little to show for its democratization effort. Just before the year ended, a successful military coup was launched in Chad, while the civil war in Liberia that had started in 1989, raged on. Only Namibia had held multi-party elections. By contrast, 1991 was an improvement as three nations, Zambia, Sao Tome, and Cape Verde, held multi-party elections. More significantly, two dictators, Ethiopia's Mengisthu Haile Mariam and Siad Barre of Somalia were forced to flee from office. During 1992, six nations became democratic. In 1993, Africa's youngest nation, Eritrea, declared itself independent. In 1994, eight nations held multi-party elections, excluding the elections in Togo and Zaire where military leaders who had ruled since the mid-1960s, successfully stymied the opposition.

Table 4 compares Africa's political situation before and after 1989. By the end of 1989, out of a total of fifty-two nations, only twelve could be classified as democratic, according to the criteria of multi-party activity and general elections. Sixteen nations were either being ruled by single parties or the military. However, between 1990 and 1994, twelve more nations had become democratic, with others intending to become so. Only two nations were being ruled by single parties while the military ruled in ten. By the end of 1996, forty out of fifty-two African nations could be

## Table 4 Regime Change (Before 1990 and After)

| Regime type | Before 1990 | After 1990 | % change |
|---|---|---|---|
| military | 33 | 12 | −64 |
| single party | 11 | 5 | −54.5 |
| democratic | 10 | 37 | +270 |
| total undemo | 44 | 17 | −61 |
| total demo | 10 | 37 | |

*Source:* Adapted from Pieter Esterhuysen, *Africa at a Glance,* 1992. Pretoria: Africa Institute of South Africa, p. 53. and *New African Yearbook, 1995–96,* 1995. 10th ed. Edison: Hunter.

classified as democratic. Twelve nations were in different phases of autocracy or military rule. By the end of 1996, the number of nations that were classified as democratic had improved by two hundred seventy per cent over those thus classified by the end of 1989. Those classified as undemocratic had declined by sixty-one percent. Generally, incumbents who put their leadership on the line in multi-party elections won, although, in all cases, opposition parties complained of massive rigging of election results.

An unanticipated set-back to political reform has been the civil wars that sprung up at several places including Liberia, Somalia, and Sierra Leone. While the causes of these wars might be deeply-rooted in those nations' social and political history, the birth of the democratic movement appeared to have encouraged dissatisfied groups to express their displeasure with the central government openly and violently. Minor disputes have escalated into full-blown ethnic conflagrations that have become difficult to stop. Aryittey has argued that most civil wars being fought in Africa have arisen from the eagerness of dissatisfied groups to rid themselves of what they consider incompetent and oppressive dictatorships. The most gruesome of these civil wars unquestionably has been the one between the Tutsi and Hutu tribes in Rwanda. The war was rekindled in 1994, following the assassination of the presidents of Rwanda and Burundi when their plane was shot down. The resulting chaos led to an orgy of ethnic killing between the two tribes. Easy availability of arms has led to the deaths of over half a million civilians and created a horde of refugees who poured into neighboring countries to escape the fighting.

The inclination among military officers to forcibly assume political power and tenaciously hang on to it, still persists. Between 1990 and 1996, twelve military take-overs were successfully carried out in twelve nations. Moreover, archetypes of authoritarianism such as Mouamar Gaddafi of Libya and Mobutu Sese Seko of Zaire, continue to rule. Also there has been flagrant negation of promises for political reform by military leaders in Nigeria and Togo. In 1993, the Nigerian military government nullified the results of presidential and parliamentary elections in which so much time and resources had been invested. Despite protestations by local and international observers, this decision was never reversed. Paul Adams referred to Nigeria as "Africa's next pariah," and recalled that a string of military regimes is to blame for severely crippling the country's economic, social, and political development. Since 1990, the outcomes of most popular elections have been challenged for electoral fraud by unsuccessful political parties and candidates. In Egypt and Algeria, for example, ruling governments have had to do battle with fundamentalist Islamic movements that have been plotting their overthrow. The wanton destruction of life and property in those nations has posed a threat to national stability. The 1990s is becoming notorious for the proliferation of bloody ethnic conflicts. The ethnic wars have wrought great devastation in terms of the lives lost, property destroyed, and people displaced.

Structural adjustment, as a development model, has not enjoyed popular support because of the economic hardship it has brought on people. Consequently, individual governments have been reluctant to fully implement all the recommendations the World Bank and the IMF made for recovery. The findings of a World Bank's study of adjustment programs in seven African nations in 1991 indicated that the implementation of adjustment policies in those countries had been uneven, mixed, and intermittent. The devaluation of currency which had accompanied most adjustment programs had precipitated inflation, deterioration in the terms of trade, and the lowering of living standards. Only few outcomes of economic adjustment have been positive. However, the World Bank believes that economic growth in Africa can only proceed with consistent and unfettered program implementation. In 1994, a World Bank report on the progress of adjustment in 29 sub-Saharan African nations warned that unless they increased investment in human capital and infrastructure, and showed a stronger commitment to good governance, the region would not be able to quickly restore economic growth and development. Even in those nations where adjustment appeared to have been successful, it had been difficult to sustain economic growth for long periods of time. In 1986, when Egypt adjusted the producer price of five major crops, it made a positive impact on the welfare of individual crop producers. However, by 1995 the Egyptian economy was beginning to experience sagging productivity in agriculture.

## Conclusion

Most African nations entered the fourth decade of independence hopeful that the recent democratic processes they had embarked upon would last. Before 1989, the political landscape of the continent was littered with coups, counter-coups, insurrections, and despotic rulers who steadfastly refused to relinquish power. On the other hand, the 1990s have seen a dramatic change among leaders to make political systems open and more participatory. In several nations, the interminable ban on political party activity has been lifted, general elections held, and opposition newspapers allowed to circulate. By the end of 1996, the number of African governments professing to be practicing democracies was the highest it had ever been since the early 1960s. Important victories that have been won include the dramatic ascension of Nelson Mandela to the presidency of South Africa as well as the relinquishing of white rule in Namibia. In 1993 and 1994, peace finally returned to Mozambique and Angola respectively, after several years of civil war.

Yet this renewed attempt toward democratic reform has not been an unmitigated success. There have been setbacks along the way, and accounts of the intrigue and ineptitude that characterized African politics in the past are being reported. Political events in Africa during the 1990s are ample proof of the topsy-turvy nature of the progress and the frustrations inherent in democratic institutional building on the continent. Some age-old rivalries still continue. In practical terms, political reform has not translated into improving the quality of life of the average citizen. Democracy cannot succeed if the chronic economic problems the continent faces are not resolved.

Simply counting the gains of democratic reform in terms of the number of countries that currently are practicing it may not do justice to the invaluable experience Africans have gained from the process. It is impossible to quantify the satisfaction people derive from voting, feeling that their opinion counts, and enjoyment of relative peace under the rule of law. To consolidate these gains, African nations must continually address fundamental questions about civic culture. How can a largely uneducated populace appreciate the complex relationships that have to be maintained among the central government, local governments, and ethnic groups. Citizens would have to understand their rights and responsibilities under the law, and how to preserve traditional customs and practices in the face of strong modernizing influences. Above all, governments need to adopt a common sense approach in their effort at political and economic development. They need to use resources wisely and make a greater commitment to raising educational standards. Democracy can only be sustained by a literate population that enjoys a reasonable degree of economic prosperity.

# BAMFO

NAME: _____
SECTION: _____
DATE: _____

1. Identify some of the problems facing African States today.

   _____
   _____
   _____
   _____
   _____
   _____
   _____
   _____

2. What are some of the linkages between economic development and political stability?

   _____
   _____
   _____
   _____
   _____
   _____
   _____

3. Describe the role of the World Bank in promoting economic development in Africa.

   _____
   _____
   _____
   _____
   _____
   _____
   _____

4. What has been the effect of centralized authoritarian rule on attempts to re-structure African economies?

___

5. Although initial democratization of most of the newly created African States lapsed into authoritarian rule, recent efforts have been more successful. Describe some of the factors in this transition.

___

**Group Exercise:** Compare and contrast the political experiences of the African Nations with the experiences of America after the Revolutionary War.

**Individual Project:** Compare the problems of Sub-Saharan Africa with the problems of unrest in the Balkan Mediterranean countries.

# Elections and Electoral Reform in Comparative Perspective

## Malcolm Punnett

An *election* is a means of choosing between candidates, normally for some office or title, by means of votes. An *electoral system* is the set of rules for conducting an election. Elections can be between individuals who have no group, faction or party affiliation. Political parties play such a fundamental role in modern politics, however, that political scientists invariably regard elections as contests between parties. Thus D. W. Rae describes an electoral system as: "The laws which govern the process by which electoral preferences are articulated as votes *and* by which these votes are translated into distributions of governmental authority (typically parliamentary seats) among the competing political parties."

Elections are not necessarily competitive. An election may be a formal process that merely confirms a result that has been achieved by other means, as with the endorsement of a single candidate through an 'election' in a totalitarian regime. Equally, a nominally competitive election can be so one-sided as to be largely meaningless, as when a party is so dominant that its candidates are virtually assured of success in particular constituencies. Political science discussions of elections, however, generally assume *competitive* elections. Indeed, North American and European concepts of democracy tend to regard the operation of 'free' and 'competitive' elections (rightly or wrongly) as the litmus test of when a country can be justifiably described as being 'democratic.'

As well as determining which individuals and parties will hold high office, the electoral process confers an elected legitimacy on the victors' subsequent exercise of power. An election provides an opportunity for people to demonstrate their partisan allegiance, even if they cannot directly affect the outcome of the contest. For many people, voting is the only form of partisan activity in which they indulge. Electoral systems have a symbiotic relationship with party systems. Parties seek to put in place electoral systems that will serve their ends: once in place, electoral systems help to shape party systems by the manner in which they reflect parties' electoral strength.

Clearly, however, there are distinct limits to the value of electoral systems as democratic devices. Elections that are held on one particular day at four or five-year intervals, with large numbers of electors choosing not to participate, are a slim basis for claims to democracy. Fortunately, elections are only one of the links between government and people: interest groups provide another form of representation that is available constantly (not just in election months). The harshest critics of 'electoral democracy' would say that elections provide a legitimizing facade behind which power is distributed and exercised in a far from democratic way. Despite their limitations, however, elections are central to modern concepts of democracy and their features, strengths and weaknesses have to be assessed.

## Electoral Systems

Elections are rarely simple but degrees of complexity may be noted. A contest between two candidates for a single office (as in most elections for the post of Governor of Georgia) does not require complicated voting procedures. The electors vote for one or the other of the candidates and the candidate with the most support wins. If three or more candidates enter a contest, however, difficulties immediately arise. The leading candidate may secure a plurality of votes (more than any other single candidate) but may not have an overall majority (more than all the other candidates combined). In face of such a possibility those who design the electoral system have to decide whether 'a plurality is enough' or whether the process has to be refined so as to produce a candidate with an overall majority.

Different issues arise when the contest is not between individuals for a single office, but is between political parties competing for representation in a legislature (as in elections to the United States Congress). In particular, the relationship between each party's total share of votes and its total share of seats in the legislature becomes an issue. The electoral architects have to decide how strenuously the electoral system should seek to produce a proportional outcome in which each party's total share of seats reflects its total share of votes.

Further complications are involved when the contest is not only to elect a legislature but is also, indirectly, a contest to determine which party or parties in the legislature will form the government (as in the case of elections in all Parliamentary-Cabinet systems). The issue then arises of whether the principal objective of the electoral process should be to produce a) a legislature that is closely representative of electoral opinion, or b) a legislature in which the largest party is overrepresented in order to increase its chances of forming a government.

The possible differences between electoral systems are vast, but three principal variables can be identified. First, how are votes cast? How many votes does each elector have, and is voting 'categorical' (with the elector indicating a single choice) or 'preferential' (with the voter listing the candidates in order of preference)? Second, how are constituencies structured? Are they single-member or multi-member constituencies, or is the election conducted as a national contest without territorial divisions? Third, in the case of party contests, how are votes translated into seats? Particularly, how seriously does the process seek to give parties seats in the legislature in proportion to the electoral votes they receive? This issue of proportionality was debated at length by Jeffersonians and Hamiltonians in the United States in the 1900s and dominates much of the contemporary discussion about electoral systems beyond the United States.

Among the several hundred electoral systems that are currently in operation throughout the world, an initial distinction can be drawn between disproportional, proportional and majority systems. Disproportional (or 'weighted' systems) are deliberately skewed, in the interests of 'strong' single-party government, to give the winning party more seats in the legislature than it has earned in votes. Thus in Romania between the wars, if a party received 45 per cent of the seats in the legislature it was rewarded with additional seats to give it an overall majority. In one of Argentina's post-war electoral systems the party that attracted most votes received two-thirds of the seats in the legislature. Such systems, however, are relatively rare, partly because it is now difficult to argue in favor of such *a deliberately* 'unfair' basis for an electoral system, but also because some majority systems conveniently achieve disproportional outcomes without specifically setting-out to do so.

Majority (or 'neutral') systems have neither proportional nor disproportional objectives. The basic assumption behind these systems is that the election is a collection of individual constituency contests rather than an overall national contest: the relationship between each party's total share of votes and seats is incidental. Among majority systems there is a distinction between 'plurality' and 'overall majority' systems. A plurality system requires merely that the winner receives more votes than any other single candidate: he is required to be first past the post, but the post is not set at any particular percentage of votes.

With the plurality system that is currently used in elections to the United States Congress and the British House of Commons, the country is divided into single member constituencies; the elector casts a vote for his choice of candidate; the candidate that receives the most votes wins, regardless of the percentage of votes he has received. In each country the system took root before national party systems had developed: elections were essentially local contests between individuals, and usually just two individuals. Categorical voting was thus logical as the means of choosing between candidates, and 'a party's national share of the vote' was a meaningless concept. In the United States a Congressional election remains, largely, a collection of local contests. In Britain, however, the historical logic of the majority system has been overtaken by the modern reality of a general election as a national contest between the government party, the alternative-government party and various other smaller parties.

An overall majority system requires that the winner receives more votes than all the other candidates combined. This can be achieved through a succession of ballots, or through a second (or 'run off') ballot that is confined to the top two candidates from the first ballot. Multiple ballots were at one time a feature of American Presidential Nominating Conventions, but they are less practical in national elections. The more practical second-ballot system has been used in France for the greater part of the last hundred years, where it has had the effect of offering the voter a multi-party first-ballot contest and a two-party second-ballot contest.

An overall majority can also be achieved through the Alternative Vote system (also known, more descriptively, as 'preferential voting in single-member constituencies'). With this system the voter is required to rank the candidates in order of preference; if no candidate achieves an overall majority of first preferences, the bottom candidate is eliminated and his ballot papers are re-distributed according to the second preferences on them; the process is repeated until a candidate emerges with an overall majority. The Alternative Vote achieves much the same effect as a multiple ballot contest but it requires the voter to indicate his successive preferences at one time, in anticipation of the outcome of the first count. The system has been used in elections to the Australian House of Representatives for over seventy years and is used in the Republic of Ireland in by-elections to the Dail. An important variable is whether or not the voter is required to indicate a full list of preferences for his vote to be valid: formerly in Australia he was obliged to do so but currently in Australia and in Ireland he is not.

## *Proportional Representation*

Proportional systems seek to achieve as close a relationship as possible between each party's votes and seats. There are many routes to this end but the national party list system offers the most direct means of achieving a proportional outcome. Each party submits a national list of candidates and the elector votes for one of the lists, as in a national referendum. Each party receives seats in the legislature in accordance with its share of the total vote: with 40 per cent of the votes a party would be entitled to 160 seats in a 400–seat legislature, and the top 160 candidates on its list would be elected. Various formulae can be used to determine the precise share of seats each party receives. To prevent the flooding of the legislature with a multiplicity of very small parties, the system can be modified by the imposition of a minimum number (or 'threshold') of votes that a party must achieve before it is entitled to any seats. The Netherlands operates its national list system with a 0.67 per cent threshold, Israel has a 3 per cent threshold and Portugal a 4 per cent threshold.

The national party list system is simple to operate and is readily understood (which is not always the case with electoral systems). It fits the logic of a modern election as a national contest between political parties. It has three major disadvantages, however. First, as the order in which candidates are ranked in the list is vital to their chances of election, those who determine the rank order are able to affect the prospects of particular elements in the party (moderates or extremists, men or women, majorities or minorities). Some list systems allow voters to indicate preferences within the list they are supporting (as in Austria and Belgium), but this rarely operates satisfactorily. Second, it is necessarily a contest between national parties, which excludes independents and puts at a disadvantage regionally-strong but nationally-weak groups. The system can be modified to operate with a series of regional lists, but such refinements can limit the overall national proportionality. Third, as it dispenses with territorial constituencies and treats the whole country as a single entity, the system is unattractive to those who favor the creation of a close relationship between an elected representative and a discrete territorial constituency.

The German 'additional member' system achieves a proportional outcome while retaining features of the single-member constituency system. The German legislature is composed of two types of member—'constituency' members, elected in single-member constituencies, and 'general' members, elected in a party list. A German elector casts one vote to elect a candidate in a single member constituency and another vote for a party list of candidates. When the results of the constituency section emerge, seats in the general section are distributed between the parties so that each party's *overall* representation in the legislature is in proportion to its share of the vote in the general section of the ballot. Thus, assuming a 400 seat legislature, a party that wins 110 of the 200 seats in the constituency section and receives 40 per cent of the votes in the general section, will be awarded 50 'additional members' from its list of candidates to raise its total representation to 40 per cent of the whole legislature.

The system is easier to operate than it is to describe. It achieves a nationally proportional outcome while retaining the concept of territorial representation through single-member constituencies. While it combines many of the merits of proportional and single-member systems, it also has some of their defects. It operates with a 5 per cent threshold, which weakens its claim to be proportional, and many criticize the basic concept of having two classes of representative in the legislature. Nevertheless, while once unique to Germany, it has become more popular in the last twenty years and has been adopted, in modified forms, in many of the new democracies of southern and east-central Europe.

The Single Transferable Vote (STV) system provides another means of achieving a proportional outcome while preserving the voters' ability to vote for individual candidates. In an STV election, voters in multi-member constituencies rank candidates in order of preference. To secure election a candidate has to achieve a quota of votes (usually, the total number of votes that have been cast divided by the number of seats). Once a candidate has reached the quota, any additional votes he may have are 'surplus to requirements' and can be transferred to other candidates on the basis of the second preferences marked on them. The process is repeated until all the seats have been filled. The system is used in the Republic of Ireland and Malta, and in Australia for elections to the Senate.

STV was initially designed to give the voter a wide choice of candidates, rather than specifically as a means of achieving proportional representation, but it does generally produce a fairly close relationship between the parties' votes and seats. As the elector votes for a number of individual candidates he can place independents or minor party candidates high in his preferences. The degree of proportionality in the system depends to a great extent on the size of the constituencies that are used. With seven-member constituencies the outcome can be highly proportional, but with just three-member constituencies there can be pronounced disproportional distortions. At the same time, of course, the larger the constituency, and thus the greater the number of candidates, the more complex the voter's task.

## Leaping in the Dark

When the British Conservative government extended the vote to working-class electors in 1867, Disraeli warned that "No doubt we are making a great experiment and taking a leap in the dark." He was correct, and the Conservatives were heavily defeated in the first election fought under the new franchise. Any electoral reform is to some extent a 'leap in the dark,' but despite the unpredictable consequences of change, electoral processes are constantly under review. In Athens, in the fourth-century BC, changes were often made to the manner in which the ruling Council of 500 was selected. Over the last hundred years issues that have preoccupied electoral reformers have been the gradual extension of the franchise: the desirability of the secret ballot; the frequency with which elections should be held; the size and bases of territorial constituencies; the means of recording votes and counting them. Currently in the United States, important issues are the control of electoral finances and the representation of minorities.

In countries with multi-party systems, a persistent issue is the desirability of proportional representation, but attitudes on the issue vary from country to country (and from party to party within the same country). While New Zealand has recently adopted an electoral system that will produce a closer relationship than formerly between the parties' votes and seats, Japan has reformed its electoral system in an effort to increase the chances of the winning party receiving a disproportionately large share of parliamentary seats. In Israel, where the commitment to the principle of proportional representation is well-entrenched, a reform issue is the precise manner in which votes are translated into seats.

When a new Constitution is devised, and 'first principles' are under review, wholesale changes in the electoral system may be made. The electoral system that was introduced in 1948 by the West German 'Basic Law' differed significantly from the system that had been used prior to the Nazi period. The electoral system adopted for the Fifth French Republic in 1958 was different from that of the Fourth Republic, which in turn had been different from that of the Third Republic. Where the constitution is of long standing, as in the United States, the opportunity for such wholesale electoral change does not occur. Rather, electoral reform comes through a process of 'disjointed incrementalism'—piecemeal change over an extended period. Such incremental change may be stimulated by a new political fashion. In a number of countries in the 1970s, for example, the voting age was lowered from 21 to 18, not as a result of concerted international pressures, but because of the simultaneous acceptance in a number of countries of a new conventional wisdom that adulthood commenced at 18.

Constitutional constraints are often placed in the way of changes in electoral laws in an effort to limit their manipulation by self-serving incumbents. Even in Britain, where the Constitution is exceptionally flexible, a Bill to extend the period between elections beyond the established five year maximum would have to be approved by the House of Lords—the only type of legislation to which the Lords can still apply a veto. Normally, the self-interest of those in power will militate against change. By definition, those currently in office have prospered under the established, unreformed, electoral process and have a vested interest in its preservation. Parties that were eager for a 'fairer' electoral system often lose their enthusiasm for reform when the 'unfair' system brings them to power. Incumbents are sometimes tempted to make 'adjustments' to the electoral system in an attempt to increase their chances of re-election, but the consequences of change can be unpredictable. In 1986 the French Socialist Government made substantial changes in the electoral system because they assumed that their chances of re-election would be thereby improved. Whatever might have happened under the old system, however, the reformed system failed to produce the re-election of the Socialists. The Conservative government that came to power proceeded to restore the old system—only to be defeated when the restored system was next used.

It is clear that there is no 'ideal' electoral system against which actual systems can be measured. Rather than asking 'What is the best electoral system?' constitution-makers and electoral reformers have to ask 'What sort of outcome do we want to achieve and what is the best means of achieving that?' In some cases the priority will be to identify the party or candidate with most support; in others it will be to identify the 'least unpopular' candidate; in yet others the most important consideration may be to achieve a precise relationship between parties' votes and seats.

While these are reasonable priorities within a democratic system, they may be mutually incompatible, and electoral reformers have to assess their relative importance when proposing change. How the priorities of the electoral system will be perceived will depend on the Constitutional and cultural assumptions of a country or regime. In the Netherlands, where there is a strong commitment to electoral fairness and equality in face of the country's cultural diversity, the production of a representative legislature is the major requirement from the electoral system. In Australia, in contrast, where stable government based on a disciplined legislature is regarded as particularly desirable, unfair and disproportional outcomes are tolerated with a shrug of the shoulders.

Those who adopt, or adapt, electoral systems are obliged to make basic value-judgements about the relative importance of considerations such as fairness, simplicity, administrative convenience and proportionality. Above all, those who devise electoral systems in Parliamentary systems have to ask not only 'What sort of an electoral system do we want?,' but also 'What sort of *government* do we want?' Electoral systems that give a close relationship between votes and seats invariably produce legislatures in which no party has an overall majority of seats, and such legislatures spawn coalition governments that seek to govern through consensus. Systems that distort the relationship between votes and seats normally produce legislatures in which one party does have an overall majority of seats, and that party governs as a single-party government on the basis of majority rule. The relative merits of 'majoritarian single-party government' and 'consensual coalition government' are, however, beyond the scope of this essay.

# PUNNETT

NAME: _____

SECTION: _____

DATE: _____

1. Why are elections sometimes viewed as either largely meaningless, or a facade for totalitarian regimes, or simply too uncompetitive?

   _____
   _____
   _____
   _____
   _____
   _____
   _____

2. What are the three main types of electoral systems?

   _____
   _____
   _____
   _____
   _____
   _____
   _____

3. Describe some of the differences between British and American electoral systems.

   _____
   _____
   _____
   _____
   _____
   _____

4. Describe the functioning of the "alternative vote" system in Australia.

_____
_____
_____
_____
_____
_____
_____

5. Is there an "ideal" electoral system? Why, or Why not?

_____
_____
_____
_____
_____
_____
_____

**Group Exercise:** Consider the variety of electoral systems in the world and suggest which, if any, could be instituted in the U.S. to make it more democratic.

**Individual Project:** Pick a country and explain how its civic culture is related to its electoral system.

*Chapter Seven*

# INTERNATIONAL RELATIONS

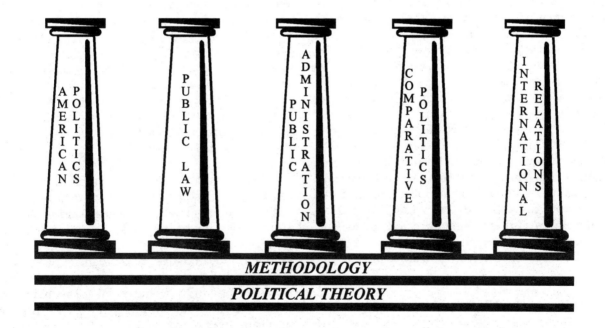

# INQUIRY INTO THE LAWFULNESS OF WAR

## Hugo Grotius*

After examining the sources of right, the first and most general question that occurs, is whether any war is just, or if it is ever lawful to make war. But this question like many others that follow, must in the first place be compared with the rights of nature. Cicero in the third book of his Bounds of Good and Evil, and in other parts of his works, proves with great erudition from the writings of the Stoics, that there are certain first principles of nature, called by the Greeks the first natural impressions, which are succeeded by other principles of obligation superior even to the first impressions themselves. He calls the care, which every animal, from the moment of its birth, feels for itself and the preservation of its condition, its abhorrence of destruction, and of every thing that threatens death, a principle of nature. Hence, he says, it happens, that if left to his own choice, every man would prefer a sound and perfect to a mutilated and deformed body. So that preserving ourselves in a natural state, and holding to every thing conformable, and averting every thing repugnant to nature is the first duty.

But from the knowledge of these principles, a notion arises of there being agreeable to reason, that part of a man, which is superior to the body. Now that agreement with reason, which is the basis of propriety, should have more weight than the impulse of appetite; because the principles of nature recommend right reason as a rule that ought to be of higher value than bare instinct. As the truth of this is easily assented to by all men of sound judgement without any other demonstration, it follows that in inquiring into the laws of nature the first object of consideration is, what is agreeable to those principles of nature, and then we come to the rules, which, though arising only out of the former, are of higher dignity, and not only to be embraced, when offered, but pursued by all the means in our power.

This last principle, which is called propriety, from its fitness, according to the various things on which it turns, sometimes is limited to a very narrow point, the least departure from which is a deviation into vice; sometimes it allows a wider scope, so that some actions, even laudable in themselves, may be omitted or varied without crime.

The general object of divine and human laws is to give the authority of obligation to what was only laudable in itself. It has been said above that an investigation of the laws of nature implies an inquiry, whether any particular action may be done without injustice: now by an act of injustice is understood that, which necessarily has in it any thing repugnant to the nature of a reasonable and social being. So far from any thing in principles of nature being repugnant to war, every part of them indeed rather favors it. For the preservation of our lives and persons, which is the end of war, and the possession or acquirement of things necessary and useful to life is most suitable to those principles of nature, and to use force, if necessary, for those occasions, is no way dissonant to the principles of nature, since all animals are en-

---

* Excerpted from: Grotius, H. (1901). *The rights of war and peace* (Trans. A. C. Campbell). New York: M. W. Dunne.

dowed with natural strength, sufficient to assist and defend themselves.

Now right reason and the nature of society which claims the second, and indeed more important place in this inquiry, prohibit not all force, but only that which is repugnant to society, by depriving another of his right. For the end of society is to form a common and united aid to preserve to every one his own. Which may easily be understood to have obtained, before what is now called property was introduced. For the free use of life and limbs was so much the right of every one, that it could not be infringed or attacked without injustice. So the use of the common productions of nature was the right of the first occupier, and for any one to rob him of that was manifest injustice. This may be more easily understood, since law and custom have established property under its present form. Tully has expressed this in the third book of his Offices in the following words, "if every member could have separate feeling, and imagine it could derive vigor from engrossing the strength of a neighboring part of the body, the whole frame would languish and perish. In the same manner if every one of us, for his own advantage, might rob another of what he pleased, there would be a total overthrow of human society and intercourse. For though it is allowed by nature for every one to give the preference to himself before another in the enjoyment of life and necessaries, yet she does not permit us to increase our means and riches by the spoils of others." It is not therefore contrary to the nature of society to provide and consult for ourselves, if another's right is not injured; the force therefore, which inviolably abstains from touching the rights of others, is not unjust.

The observation that all war is not repugnant to the law of nature, may be more amply proved from sacred history. For when Abraham with his servants and confederates had gained a victory, by force of arms, over the four Kings, who had plundered Sodom, God approved of his act by the mouth of his priest Melchisedech, who said to him, "Blessed be the most high God, who hath delivered thine enemies into thine hand."(Gen. XIV 20) Now Abraham had taken up arms, as appears from the history, without any special command from God. But this man, no less eminent for sanctity than wisdom, felt himself authorized by the law of nature.

Proofs of what has been advanced, may be drawn also from the consent of all, especially, of the wisest nations. There is a celebrated passage in Cicero's speech for Milo, in which, justifying recourse to force in defense of life, he bears ample testimony to the feelings of nature, who has given us this law, which is not written, but innate, which we have not received by instruction, hearing or reading, but the elements of it have been engraved in our hearts and minds with her own hand: a law which is not the effect of habit and acquirement, but forms a part in the original complexion of our frame: so that if our lives are threatened with assassination or open violence from the hands of robbers or enemies, any means of defense would be allowed and laudable. He proceeds, reason has taught this to the learned, necessity to the barbarians, custom to nations, and nature herself to wild beasts, to use every possible means of repelling force offered to their bodies, their limbs and their lives. Caius and Lawyer says, natural reason permits us to defend ourselves against dangers.

This principle is founded on reasons of equity, so evident, that even in the brute creation, who have no idea of right, we make a distinction between attack and defense.

From the law of nature then which may also be called the law of nations, it is evident that all kinds of war are not to be condemned. In the same manner, all history and the laws of manners of every people sufficiently inform us, that war is not condemned by the voluntary law of nations. Indeed Hermogenianus has said, that wars were introduced by the law of nations, a passage which ought to be explained somewhat differently from the general interpretation given to it. The meaning of it is, that certain formalities, attending war, were introduced by the law of nations, which formalities were necessary to secure the peculiar privileges arising out of law. From hence a distinction, which there will be occasion to use hereafter, between a war with the usual formalities of the law of nations, which is called just or perfect, and an informal war, which does not for that reason cease to be just, or agreeable to right. For some wars, when made upon just grounds, though not exactly conformable, yet are not repugnant to the law. By the law of nations, says Livy, provision is made to repel force by arms; and Florentinus declares, that the law of nations allows us to repel violence and injury, in order to protect our persons.

# GROTIUS

NAME: _____

SECTION: _____

DATE: _____

1. Grotius asks if any Wars are just. What is his answer? Explain.

2. Should civilized peoples follow the rules of instinct or of reason in deciding to go to war?

3. What kinds of historical authority does Grotius rely upon to justify his philosophy of War?

4. What is the distinction between formal wars and informal wars?

_____
_____
_____
_____
_____
_____
_____

5. Do Grotius' arguments have the same tone, the same emotional impact, as do Machiavelli's arguments? Explain in full.

_____
_____
_____
_____
_____
_____
_____

**Group Exercise:** Convene the group and discuss the Vietnam War. How might Grotius have classified America's involvement?

**Individual Project:** Compare Grotius' quotation from Cicero on the feelings of Nature with Plato's depiction of Socrates's conception of remembering. What is the linkage?

# OBLIGATION AND POST WORLD WAR II ORDER AND STATE ACTION

## Marc G. Pufong

This section examines the dynamic of post World War II order and state actions, specifically how they contribute to our understanding of the current state of obligation under international law. The central question in this examination is whether prevailing international legal principles on obligation have been able to deter state hostilities within the current world order. Instances of contemporary state conduct such as Iraq's aggression over Kuwait and the hostilities and civil war that ensued in the former Republic of Yugoslavia are used here as samples to illustrate state action.

## CURRENT ORDER

Following the post World War II United Nations Charter order, contemporary international society has been based on a community-centered law rooted on the existence of a general will and global public policy interests. This order has been radically different from the state-centered international legal order based on sovereign consent upon which the 1648 Westphalia order was premised. The latter principle (i.e., state-centered order) relied heavily on domestic order as opposed to community-centered international order. As structured, the post war U.N. Charter embodies the conception of a new authoritative order for the contemporary international system. However, current state actions/behavior exhibit the continued persistence of both orders. Put differently, in spite of the post World War II U. N. Charter order of universalism and pacifism, the Westphalia international order professing absolute state sovereignty is far from being displaced.

The U. N. Charter order superficially respects or at least contains nothing to contradict the traditional notion of state obligation, one based on "sovereign consent." Note for example that two dominant conceptions of international order are reconciled in Article 2, the provision of the Charter that sets out the Principles that are supposed to control the operation of the UN as an Organization. From the perspective of reconciliation Article 2(1) and 2(7) are particularly relevant. The former [i.e., 2(1)] states that "the Organization shall be based on the principle of sovereign equality of all its members" and the latter 2(7) assert that "nothing contained in the present Charter shall authorize the United Nations to intervene in matters which are essentially within the domestic jurisdiction of any state or shall require the Members to submit such matters to settlement under the present Charter."

Indeed, the U. N. Charter's conception was a modification, in most essential aspects, of the ideas of international society embodied in the defunct League of Nations. The new community of nations, as conceived in the Charter, welcomed de facto as well as de jure regimes without much prospect for behavioral impact. The U. N. Charter also adopted, with modifications, the main critical component of the Westphalia order having bearing on the status of war, the role of national sovereignty, and the degree to which authority and authoritative structures are centralized within the international system. In this view the new U. N. Charter's ideas overlap in many aspects the Westphalia order, but complement it because it centralizes some cooperative activities. It also contradicts the Westphalia order to the extent that community-oriented procedures, laid out in the new Charter, displace the previously sovereignty-oriented procedures. A poignant example of this apparent contradiction [i.e., displacing the previously sovereignty-oriented procedures with community-oriented procedures] is the subsequent insert of the human rights provisions in the Charter and the General Assembly Resolution adopting the Nuremberg Judgment.

The inserts were also essential parts of the new U. N. Charter directing state commitments to respect and foster the new international order following the new community-oriented procedures. For example, on December 10th 1946, the General Assembly unanimously affirmed "the principles of international law recognized by the Charter of the Nuremberg Tribunal and the judgment of the Tribunal." The same Resolution directed the International Law Commission to formulate these principles as part of an overall effort to evolve a codification of "offenses against the peace and security of mankind, or of an International Criminal Code." Thus, what may be viewed as an apparent contradiction, may in part, explain why instruments such as the Universal Declaration of Human Rights, though widely recognized and accepted in theory, have proven to be unworkable, if not unenforceable in practice.

## CURRENT STATE ACTIVITIES AND PRACTICES

How instructive are conducts and practices of states under prevailing international order? The Charter of the United Nations in Article 2(6) claims competence to ensure that states which are not members, as well as members of the United Nations, act in accordance with the principles enumerated in Article 2 so far as may be necessary for the maintenance of "international peace and security." The significance of the point here is that the United Nations claims for itself whatever authority is necessary to establish global peace and security. The Charter embodies the claim and the Organization gives it continuing effect. Article 2(6) is a significant provision (one that carries forward the approach of Article 17 of the League Covenant) because it relies on a treaty instrument such as the Charter to establish the basis for community wide obligatory authority that is extended without consent of non-participating states.

However, contemporary state actions and behavior question both the deterrence effect of U.N. Charter and obligatory propensity of states to the U.N. Charter. The Iraqi aggression over Kuwait and the situation that resulted, and the human rights violations in the former Yugoslavia are typical cases from which to examine state obligation within contemporary legal order. The problem may lie, in part in Article 2(7) of the Charter which continues to uphold the domestic jurisdiction or sovereignty of a state which remains a prime element of the former Westphalia conception. It also may lie in the ambiguity of Article 2(4) and 51 "prohibiting all recourse to use force in relations among states except individual or collective self defense against armed attack." Also note that it says "Nothing in the present Charter shall impair the rights of individual or collective action ... until the Security Council has taken the measures necessary to maintain international peace and security." Suppose that a member state fails to report immediately its exercise of self-defense? Or suppose the Security Council fails to reach any determination or recourse for resolving a particular conflict? While the first question illustrates the Iraq-Kuwait conflict, the second depicts the attitude of the international community toward the ongoing conflict in the former Yugoslavia.

### The Iraq-Kuwait conflict

Self-defense was one of the several versions of Iraq's claim and rationale provided for its 1990 invasion and occupation of the territory of Kuwait and its subsequent annexation. In 1982, Argentina made a similar claim on Malvinas (Falklands) in justifying that the use of force to "recover" the island was self-defense [see Statement of Argentina in U. N. Doc. A/37/PV.51 (Nov. 2, 1982)]. Iraq claimed that Kuwait was a lost Iraqi territory and that its actions were legitimate to recover a territory that was rightfully its own. While the invasion, occupation and annexation of Kuwait were the primary legal issues in the Iraq-Kuwait conflict and were issues to which Iraq deemed to be legally defensible and/or justifiable, it too raised other related "secondary" political issues. Elsewhere, Singer and Waldovsky list these political issues that triggered desert storm as: (a) Iraq's (power) threat to its neighbor and build-up of nuclear weapon, (b) Iraq's potential to control all oil in the Persian Gulf [a unique asset of the world that has been protected from abusive use by the fact that it's always been divided among a number of rival countries], and (c) Iraq persecution of Shiites and Kurds as well as the dreadful treatment of its own citizens (human rights violations). It is important to note however, that Iraq's action was not the first time that a state used force to seek recovery of a territory it claimed as its own. It was the first time however, that the entire territory of a member state of the United Nations was forcibly annexed since the beginning of the new U. N. Charter order in 1945. Though the Security Council acted with unanimity in condemning the invasion, it, however, referred to Articles 39 and 40 of the

Charter, thus bringing the matter under chapter VII and the power of the Council to impose mandatory measures. The Council did so under Resolution 660 which demanded the immediate withdrawal of Iraqi forces and that both countries begin "intensive negotiations to resolve their differences." It is also interesting to note that the Resolution did not specify exactly what those differences to be negotiated were, but presumably they were territorial and financial claims as asserted by Iraq.

Surprisingly, at first the Security Council did not expressly condemn Iraq's invasion of Kuwait as a violation of Article 2(4) nor its Resolution 660 of August 2, 1990. Even Resolution 661, adopted four days after, made no reference to the invasion as an act of aggression. Surely, the Council's initial action, deferring authority to both Iraq and Kuwait, was consistent with the Westphalia "sovereignty-oriented procedural" requirements, even though it soon resorted to "community-oriented procedures" consistent with post war U. N. Charter orders. It did so by bringing the matter under chapter VII of the United Nations Charter, and within the purview of the Security Council's authority. It rejected Iraq's claim of Kuwait as "lost" Iraqi territory as having no legal justification. This point is important because other invading states such as India and Argentina, before Iraq, justified their actions as legal on the grounds that the territory invaded was their own. In the India situation in 1961, India maintained that there was "no legal frontier" between it and Goa because the territory had been under the "illegal domination" of Portugal for 450 years and that consequently the armed takeover by Indian troops was legal.

However, in Iraq's situation, in rejecting its claim and using Article 41 of the Charter, the Security Council imposed sanctions on Iraq. Under Council's Resolution 661 adopted pursuant to Article 41, the Council required all states to ban imports to, and exports from, Iraq and Kuwait. It also banned transfer of funds to Iraq and Kuwait and, in effect, required a freeze on the bank accounts affected. This was followed by yet other resolutions [SC Res. 678, November 29, 1990], adopted pursuant to Article 42, authorizing states cooperating with Kuwait to take all possible means to restore peace and security in Kuwait. It is debatable whether Resolution 678 was needed at all because Article 42 of the U. N. Charter can be invoked only under precise conditions. Article 42 clearly states that "Should the Security Council consider that measures provided in Article 41 would be inadequate, it may take such actions by air, sea, or land forces."

While the Security Council's post fact action was partially effective in obligating Iraq into obeying the rule of law, Iraq's behavior was similar to India's over Goa in 1961 or Argentina's on the Malvinas or Falklands in 1982. This raises serious questions about both the deterrence effect of the U. N. Charter and its obligatory propensity on states. Could the Security Council's actions against Iraq have been any different if Iraq made public its self defense claim prior to invading Kuwait? Perhaps not under prevailing "uni-polar" world order, with one superpower, as opposed to the previous "bipolar" order, with the US and USSR as superpowers. Indeed, in India's invasion situation of Goa in 1962, under the former bipolar world order, the USSR effectively vetoed the draft resolution that was favored by a majority in the Security Council who condemned India's action and requested its withdrawal from Goa.

## The Yugoslavia Conflict

The United Nations' Security Council and the European Community's (E.C.) failure to reach any determination or a workable recourse for resolving the conflict between the various nationalist groups in the republics, depicts the ongoing conflict in the former Yugoslavia. The republics and capitals of the former Yugoslavia were: Albania (Tirane), Bosnia and Herzegovenia (Sarajevo), Croatia (Zagreb), Macedonia (Skopje), Serbia or Yugoslavia (Belgrade), and Slovenia (Lubljana). The conflict raised a combination of issues of secession (division of the republics of the former Yugoslavia state), aggression (Croats and Serbian-controlled Yugoslavia strife to maintain or forge new internal borders to safeguard Serbian communities from the other republic through the policies of "ethnic cleansing"), and massive abuse of the civilian population (human rights violations).

Initially, the key issue in the conflict was whether the succeeding components of Yugoslavia could be recognized by other democracies, especially the European Community countries and the United States, as sovereign independent nations and thus, be part of the international community. The act of recognition is an important concept in international law that grants legitimacy, and thus, it creates the basis for obligation. According to Von Glahn, recognition is ". . . the acknowledgment of the existence of a new state or a new government in an existing foreign state, coupled with an expression of willingness by the recognized entity or government." Elsewhere, Whiteman also maintains that the act of "recognizing" a new state and/or a new government is "a political act with a legal consequence." The failure of the international community to participate in the original dispute of independence involving Slovenia and Croatia in June 1991 contributed to the state of aggression and the subsequent human rights violations in the former Yugoslavia. What sets of facts explain the development of the conflicts and the ensuing human rights violations in the republics of Croatia and Bosnia-Herzegovina?

a. The conflicts: The Republics of Croatia and Slovenia were the first to unilaterally declare their independence on June 25, 1990 after failing to negotiate either a confederate status or their independence with the federal government of the Socialist Federal Republic of Yugoslavia (SFRY). Bosnia-Herzegovina followed suite in February 29 and March 1, 1992 declaring its independence from SFRY after a successful referendum. SFRY was a post-World War II creation from the previously defunct Yugoslav multinational state created in 1918. The post-World War II Yugoslav Federal Republic in essence, reconciled the tension that existed in the post-war Yugoslav state by dividing the state into six republics under a federal structure, but with a strong central government. This structure was buttressed by a strong one-party rule under the League of Communists of Yugoslavia with the authoritarian leadership of Josip Broz (Marshall) Tito, who ruled SFRY until his death in 1980.

Prior to Tito's death, a new constitution promulgating "decentralization" was ratified in 1974 which gave considerable powers to the republic's administrations. The new powers granted to the republics, in effect, also weakened the authority of the (SFRY). The readily weak federal structure also increased the assertiveness of the republics. The increased nationalist and ethnic tensions in the 1980s also contributed to the demise of the previously one-party rule in Yugoslavia, and in 1990 multi-party competitive elections were successfully held in all six republics. It was precisely after these elections that the republics of Slovenia and Croatia pressed for confederation and, eventually, for succession (independence) in June 25, 1991. The Republic of Yugoslavia, and in particular, Serbia, countered Slovenia and Croatia's declarations with warnings and the threat of invasion and the changing of internal borders to safeguard "Serbian Communities" in Croatia, Slovenia and later, Bosnia-Herzegovina.

b. The human rights violations: The warnings and threats were soon transformed into actual invasion of Slovenia and Croatia which led to several atrocities in war zones (i.e., the tortures, and deliberate and arbitrary killings). The United Nations, the Council on Security and Cooperation in Europe (CSCE), the European Community, and NATO were slow to coordinate an effective response to the conflict. An initial position taken by the international community was to impose an "arms embargo" and to demand "negotiation between Yugoslavia and the component republics to agree on a future arrangement between them." A similar position was also taken when the war escalated into Bosnia-Herzegovina in 1992 between Bosnian Muslims, Bosnian Croats, and Bosnian Serbs. Bosnian Muslims in particular, were terrorized by the brutal policies of "ethnic cleansing" wherein civilians were systematically driven from their homes, put into concentration camps, tortured, raped or simply slaughtered. An accurate account of casualties from the war may never be made, but estimates of the number killed run into the hundred of thousands. U. N. peacekeeping forces were deployed early on in the conflict precisely to maintain and bring a peaceful end to the situation. But, these efforts were in vain. In 1994, NATO organized sporadic military action to enforce the UN-ordered cease-fire at a time when 70 percent of Bosnia-Herzegovina had already been carved up by Serbian and Croatian forces.

Thus, there was inaction as well as slow-to-action by the international community, especially from the European Community and from the United States. However, the initial refusal to accept the credentials for independence (succession) of Slovenia and Croatia, thereby recognizing them as new states within the international community of nations, was viewed by Serbian controlled Yugoslavia as an implicit support of their position (i.e., of a united Yugoslavia Republic). Singer and Wildovsky speak directly to this very issue in the following passage:

*Sometimes as in the former Yugoslavia, doing nothing—that is, refusing to recognize new governments—will help one side. Even neutral-seeming actions, like preventing any weapons from being delivered to the area, often really favor one side. In Yugoslavia, the arms embargo hurt the Croatians and other new states [i.e, Slovenia, Albania, Bosnia- Herzegovina, and Macedonia] and helped Serbia because Serbia already had the former Yugoslav national weapons.*

As noted above, Serbian intervention continued in Bosnia-Herzegovina in and after 1992 to the support of Bosnian Serbs' warring activities and "ethnic cleansing" in the various enclaves of the republic. Even though the United States and the European Community, on April 7, 1992, rushed to recognize the independence of Bosnia-Herzegovina (declared in March 1992), heavy fighting continued throughout. That fighting led to Serbian occupation of roughly 70 percent of the republic. Since the recognition was irrevocable, Serbian actions were viewed as nothing more than a bluff in response to the hastened international recognition. They viewed the quick recognition of Bosnia-Herzegovina as a correction of a previously slow posture of the international community. This of course, triggered their rush to suppress Croatian and Slovenian succession to independence in 1991.

Thus, the halting response of the international community to the war in the former Yugoslavia argued poorly for the ability of international institutions to maintain peace. Simply put, the United Nation's Security Council and the European Community's failure to reach a workable recourse for resolving the conflict between the republics of the former Yugoslavia raises serious questions about traditional notions of sovereignty (sovereign-oriented procedures) and the will of the contemporary global community (with community oriented procedure) under the U. N. Charter and other multilateral instruments.

Finally, how instructive are the above conflicts (Iraq-Kuwait and Yugoslavia v. republics) as test cases for contemporary order or obligation? First, for the purpose of ascertaining state actions and behavior, both conflicts remind us of the axiom: plus ca change, plus ca rest la meme "the more things change, the more they stay the same." States do not behave any differently in the post World War II order than they did before World War II. The triggers of both conflicts examined above are hardly new. The Iraq-Kuwait conflict was a territorial claim, and the conflict in the former Yugoslavia was an ethnic and nationalistic one. Second, for purposes of ascertaining state obligatory propensities, both conflicts teach us that the community oriented procedure of the post World War II U.N. Charter does not conclusively displace the previous post Westphalia sovereign-oriented procedures. Thus, while the aggrieved states in both conflicts (Kuwait, Croatia, Slovenia and Bosnia-Herzegovina) sought help from the international community consistent with the community oriented procedures, the aggressors (Iraq and Serbia-Yugoslavia), exhibited autonomy and rational prerogatives of sovereign conception of statehood where the content of law is the result of voluntary state actions.

In the case of Iraq, and to a lesser extent, that of the former Yugoslavia, the international community has been able to provide only partial answers. Through the use of force, for example, Iraq was compelled to obey the rule of international law to compensate for its aggression. Yet, the questions of justice in other areas of international crime, such as human rights violations and the propriety of forums and/or competence of authority for the administration of justice, are at best unclear. That includes bringing perpetrators of crimes to justice and holding the states, or their instrumentalities (persons), directly liable for their crime.

## Conclusion

Following the analysis presented above, it is possible to understand the significance of international obligations and the indifference expressed by states asserting autonomy, especially those who violate international law. Such violation may include internal state transgressions over its people or an international norm. The examination of state behavior and obligation under international law in the above sections reveal little, and indeed, no perceptual change in state actions. This is true under the post-World War II bi-polar order under the U.N. Charter authority and under the current unipolar power order after the collapse of the former Soviet Union. Clearly, the current state of obligation viewed from contemporary meaning associated with state duty and responsibilities does not deter the increase in state hostilities under current world order as opposed to the previous world order. The Iraqi claim and aggression over Kuwait and the succession and war in the former Yugoslavia discussed above are powerful examples.

Thus, for the purpose of assessing and understanding state action, the community oriented procedure under the U. N. Charter does not conclusively displace the pre-World War II sovereignty-oriented procedures. Indeed, under current world order which professes universality, the Westphalia basis of statehood in which state sovereignty is glorified remains the basis of state interaction. Because the U.N. Charter fails to completely sever the old basis of statehood in its postwar universality environment, state sovereignty remains a significant barrier to justice for those that are concerned about increased internal state affairs inconsistent with rules of the international community.

# PUFONG

NAME: _____

SECTION: _____

DATE: _____

1. Describe the basic differences on war between the Westphalia Treaty of 1648 and the United Nations Charter.

   _____
   _____
   _____
   _____
   _____
   _____
   _____

2. The Westphalia Treaty, the League of Nations, and the United Nations show political evolution in dealing with war and violence. Describe that evolutionary pattern.

   _____
   _____
   _____
   _____
   _____
   _____
   _____

3. Explain how international reaction to the ethnic conflict in the former Yugoslavia supports the contention that the sovereign-oriented procedures of the Westphalia Treaty are still operational.

   _____
   _____
   _____
   _____
   _____
   _____

4. Explain the axiom: "plus ca change, plus ca rest la meme" and relate it to prospects for world peace.

___

5. What obligations do nations have to the international community, and vice-versa, under the U.N. charter?

___

**Group Exercise:** Imagine a hypothetical situation in which minority protestors in the U.S.A. request U.N troops to enforce their civil rights. Is it likely that the U.N. would do so? Why, or why not?

**Individual Project:** Perform some library research and try to ascertain how many countries are currently experiencing U.N. military involvement.

# Technology, Power, and Competitiveness among Developed States

## Robert S. Walters & David H. Blake*

Technology gaps are not exclusive concerns of less developed countries confined to the North-South conflict. Advanced industrial states place great emphasis on their relative technological strength as it affects their growth potential, national security, and political-economic independence. In the mid-1960s, fears of America's seemingly unassailable scientific and technological predominance relative to Europe prompted the French, especially, to politicize this issue. In the decade 1957–1966, the United States devoted over three times the resources to research and development ($158 billion) as did all the industrialized states of Western Europe combined ($50 billion). From 1951 to 1969, scientists in the United States received twenty-one of thirty-eight Nobel prizes in chemistry and twenty-three of forty Nobel prizes in medicine and physiology. Giant American-based multinational firms such as IBM and Kodak were capable of devoting resources to research and development equal in magnitude to the gross sales of their competitors in Europe. Indeed from 1965 to 1970, IBM spent as much on the development of its model 360 computer ($5 billion) as the French government planned to spend on the Force de Frappe, its nuclear deterrent.

Taking note of these and similar developments, Robert Gilpin summarized the French position on the centrality of science and technological capability to leadership in international relations:

> Today Great Power status accrues only on those nations which are leaders in all phases of basic research and which possess the financial and managerial means to convert new knowledge into advanced technologies. In the case of the two superpowers, eminence in science and technology go hand-in-hand, and it appears unlikely that any nation or group of nations can ever again aspire to a dominant role in international politics without possessing a strong, indigenous scientific and technological capability. International politics has passed from the era of traditional industrial nation states to one dominated by the scientific nation states.

The vulnerability of even an advanced industrial state that is dependent upon an ally for foreign sources of technology was revealed when the U.S. government initially prohibited the French purchase of certain IBM computers required for its Force de Frappe on the grounds that the nuclear test ban treaty forbade America's assisting a non-nuclear power to obtain nuclear weapons. In the eyes of the French and numerous other states on the wrong side of the technology gap, the achievement of a greater degree of self-sufficiency in science and technology is a prerequisite for the capacity to forge an independent stance in global political and economic relations.

During the 1980s and 1990s, fears of technological decline in the United States relative to Ja-

---

* Robert S. Walters/David H. Blake, *The Politics of Global Economic Relations*, 4e, © 1992, pp. 178–184. Reprinted by permission of Prentice-Hall, Englewood Cliffs, New Jersey.

*Is the U.S.A. Losing?*

pan, Europe, and the newly industrializing countries of East Asia emerged as a major concern among analysts of American national security and international competitiveness—even though the picture remains very complex. The United States in 1986 still spent more on research and development than the next four largest countries combined (Japan, West Germany, France, and Britain). Yet, the U.S. share of the combined R&D budgets of these five leading states declined from 68 percent in 1966 to 54 percent in 1986. Both West Germany and Japan spend a larger share of their GNP on research and development than the United States, and a larger portion of both German and Japanese R&D has been focused on commercial applications than American R&D, which is more defense oriented. The share of U.S. patents granted to foreigners rose from 30 percent in 1970 to 48 percent in 1986—the highest share of U.S. patents that foreign inventors have ever achieved. Japanese inventors accounted for 21 percent of U.S. patents in 1986.

Most alarming of all has been a dramatic decline in America's trade balance in high-technology manufactures during the 1980s, traditionally a strong point in U.S. trade performance. The United States actually imported more high-technology manufactured goods than it exported in 1986. Japan and the newly industrializing Asian countries have been the major threat in this regard. For a summary of U.S. high-technology trade developments during the 1980s, see Figure 8–1.

These trends have immense impacts on American national security, competitiveness, and international leadership, as noted by Charles Ferguson: "U.S. technological decline in an era of globalized economic activity implies that foreign and national security policy now depends upon economic and technology policy to a degree not seen since the advent of nuclear weapons. The future economic and geopolitical security of the United States will be determined ever more heavily by the fundamental health of its technology-intensive industries." Yet, as trade data in Figure 8–1 indicate, these industries are not faring as well as they used to in the United States.

Ferguson and others attribute this decline to a combination of domestic and international developments. Domestic factors involve shortcomings in U.S. government policies, industrial structures and corporate strategies—including such things as tax and economic policies biased toward consumption; fragmented political and economic structures impeding long-term technological and strategic coordination; research, higher education, trade, and military policies that afford other countries asymmetric access to American science and technology; and entrenchment of outdated manufacturing processes within American industry. International factors include developments in financial markets, the pace of international technology transfers, rises in foreign competition, lower capital costs in other countries, industry structures and corporate strategies abroad that more effectively commercialize new product and process technologies, and the diminishing importance of the U.S. market to the total global demand—Japan is clearly perceived to pose the greatest external threat to American technological leadership.

Concerns such as these have led to numerous conflicts involving technology competition and transfers between the United States and its closest military and economic partners. The Reagan and Bush administrations opposed a Japanese effort to develop and construct a new fighter airplane (FSX) on its own, based on the F-16, and insisted upon a joint U.S.–Japanese project involving American contractors. The Japanese accommodated these demands only to face bitter outcries from Congress that the United States was giving Japan access to American technology that the Japanese would certainly use to develop into a strong future international competitor in civil and defense aviation. The arrangements for joint U.S.–Japanese development and production of the FSX were maintained in 1989 with limits on Japanese access to particularly sensitive U.S. technologies. The conflict created over technology transfers by the United States in connection with the project will accelerate pressures for indigenous Japanese defense production including an aviation industry to compete with American and European firms. Moreover, we can certainly expect more difficulty in the future military cooperation between these allies as issues of technology and competitiveness intrude more directly on defense production in both states.

At the outset of the 1990s all of the advanced industrial states were competing vigorously through public policy and private initiatives for leadership to develop and commercialize important technologies associated with potential high-growth industries in the international economy. Within months after the discovery of new materials with superconducting properties at liquid nitrogen and higher temperatures in 1986, for example, both Japan and the United States launched highly publicized national policies to accelerate the commercialization of new superconductivity technologies with myriad commercial and military applications in areas such as energy (production, storage, and transmission), transportation (magnetic levitation trains, ship propulsion), and medicine (magnetic resonance imaging). Europe, Japan, and the United States were competing at the outset of the 1990s to establish national and international standards for high definition television (HDTV) that will largely determine which countries' industries will assume the lead in the next generation of products for television transmission and reception, computer terminals, and defense-related electronic displays.

Leadership in important dual-use (military and commercial) technologies has assumed such importance for national military and economic security that the United States, as most states, has experimented with new forms of state-industry relations to position its important industries more favorably in the international division of labor. During the 1980s Japanese firms seized the lead in semiconductor manufacturing from the United States "merchant" firms (producers of semiconductors for end-users other than themselves) that pioneered the industry. By the middle of the decade several U.S. government studies "concluded that the nation was falling behind Japan in most of the key process and manufacturing technologies necessary for the production of future generations of semiconductor technology. Indeed, for over five years Japanese producers have been first to the market with new memory chips that represent the next advance in miniaturization." In an electronic age, surrender of technological leadership in semiconductor products and manufacturing processes has important connotations for economic preeminence and defense. Accordingly, with the support of the Defense Department, a consortium of leading U.S. semiconductor firms, chip tooling and materials suppliers pooled resources to advance and disseminate semiconductor manufacturing techniques in an effort to overtake the Japanese–Semeiotic, the Semiconductor Manufacturing Technology Initiative located in Austin, Texas. The results of this effort are not yet clear. However, an active role by the federal government to promote generic process technologies to strengthen the domestic semiconductor industry's competitive position in international commercial markets marks a bold departure from it's traditional noninterventionist role in the civilian economy. In this regard the federal government of the United States is engaged in the same game that Americans criticize Japan's Ministry of Trade and Industry (MITI) for playing. Indeed, its attempting to emulate the Japanese model of close government-business cooperation through state funding for the creation of industrial consortia in critical, high-technology sectors.

The United States, the European Economic Community, and Japan bring different strengths and weaknesses to their competition for technological leadership in the world. Technological innovation is reflected in nations' research, development, production, and distribution capabilities. In very general terms, U.S. strengths lie in research and development as manifested in high funding levels for R&D, the unparalleled research capacity of its universities and national laboratories in basic science, the numerous ties between universities and industry, commercial spillovers from large federal defense and space programs in the postwar period (computers, semiconductors, civil aviation, for example), and the world's largest domestic market.

American industries' weaknesses in technological innovation tend to lie more in production and distribution—in commercializing new scientific discoveries and technologies. Several factors are important in this regard. Research in universities and national laboratories contribute importantly to basic science in the United States, but their research agendas are not driven by considerations of commercialization. The national laboratories, especially, have a poor track record for transferring technology to civilian industry. While the U.S. federal government spends far more on R&D than any other state, over 70 percent of that was directed toward defense in the late 1980's. It is often argued that dual-use technology is spun off to the private sector from defense R&D, but there is a widespread sense that the increasingly specialized nature of defense applications is diminishing the commercial impact of dual-use technologies in the United States. In more commercially relevant, nondefense R&D expenditures as a percent of GNP, the United States ranks forth behind Japan, West Germany, and France.

In both Japan and Germany a higher percentage of national R&D expenditures are derived from business sources than in the United States and the late 1980's witnessed declines in the rate of growth of U.S. corporate funding for research. Xerox and Eastman Kodak, long noted for their vigorous research programs, have sharply curtailed and reorganized their research, especially in basic sciences. Factors inhibiting corporate research spending in the United States relative to Japan and West Germany include greater fragmentation within industries and heavier reliance on equity-based investment requiring more attention to short-term returns on capital. The surge of leveraged buyouts in the United States also inhibits R&D as management looks for ways to cut back on long-term investments to focus on higher immediate returns to stockholders and on generating higher cash flows to service heavy financial debts. The purchase of RCA by General Electric, for example, resulted in less research for both.

Japan's innovative strength has been more in its rapid commercialization of innovative technologies, production, and distribution than in basic science, research, and development. Its "remarkable success, at first with traditional manufacturing and later in the advanced technology sectors, emphasized the application of good engineering to both manufacturing processes and production technology, and the release of high-quality, competitively priced products on world markets. Its capacities in overtaking American firms in automobiles, electronic consumer goods, and semiconductors clearly reflect these strengths. The Japanese have been somewhat less impressive than might be expected from such a technological giant in basic science and the creation of innovative technologies. However, much greater emphasis in Japan is now being placed on these activities, especially as American firms and public officials demonstrate increased reluctance to share technology as they did in the earlier postwar period (witness the FSX episode). This trend is evident in recent increases in R&D budgets in both the private and public sectors; in attempts to strengthen Japan's weak university research structure and to connect it more effectively to high-tech industries and government laboratories through regional "Third Technological Revolution" at the turn of the century.

The science and technology challenge of West Europe, despite the EEC and its high-technology projects such as ESPRIT and RACE, lies in the fact that "the whole of European technology is less than the sum of its (national) parts, many of which are individually impressive." National R&D efforts among the member states of the Common Market are five to six times those at the level of the EEC, but there is relatively little transfer of technology from one country to another. Simply put, unlike both the United States and Japan as technological rivals, Europe is not "technologically unified." The EEC's creation of a single "domestic" market in 1992 will become a pivotal factor in overcoming Europe's competitive disadvantage in the technology race among the advanced industrial states.

Competition for scientific and technological leadership, generally reflecting the neomercantilist orientation to political economy, conditions all aspects of relations among the developed states. Trade balances, competitiveness of important domestic industries, employment levels, international investment patterns, and national economic and military security all are functions of the changing distribution of technological capabilities among the leading states. Technology issues among even the closest economic partners will certainly assume ever larger importance in the international political economy.

# WALTERS & BLAKE

NAME: _____
SECTION: _____
DATE: _____

1. Why is technological sophistication and competency an increasingly important aspect of global political and military power?

   _____
   _____
   _____
   _____
   _____
   _____
   _____
   _____

2. American technological and scientific progress still greatly outperforms all of the other countries in the world, but what new area is beginning to catch up, and why?

   _____
   _____
   _____
   _____
   _____
   _____
   _____

3. Relate some of the recent technologically progressive trends among some of the foreign nations to the T.Q.M. discussion in an earlier chapter. Is there a linkage, and if so what is it?

   _____
   _____
   _____
   _____
   _____
   _____

4. Explain how recent developments in superconductor technology may lead directly to increased tensions between the United States and the nation of Japan.

___

5. What are some of the major strengths and weaknesses of current American technological policies and practices?

___

**Group Exercise:** Consider the weaknesses of the European Union in technological development. What political changes can be suggested that might strengthen the group in that field?

**Individual Project:** Aristotle thought that the Polis was necessary for human development. Perform some library research and find and describe an article that demonstrates that global trade plays the same role today.

# AMERICAN FOREIGN POLICY IN THE POST COLD WAR WORLD

## James W. Peterson

Throughout the 1990s the United States has been at a crossroads in its foreign policy. The end of the Cold War at the conclusion of the 1980s removed the polestar of containment from the firmament of international affairs. For over forty years the foreign policy of American leaders had centered on containing Soviet-led aggression in various parts of the world. Then, in the space of a few short years, communist leaders fell in eight East European countries and in the Soviet Union as well. Whereas there had been nine communist bloc countries as recently as 1988, by 1993 there were twenty-seven non-communist states in the same geographic space. While leading to a collective sigh of relief and even considerable rejoicing among western leaders, this sudden, largely unexpected change also threw U.S. policy and policy makers into a perpetual quandary throughout the decade of the 1990s.

In a sense, the dilemma at the close of the twentieth century is as monumental as the challenge at the end of the nineteenth century. The challenge one hundred years ago was design of a blueprint for getting involved in world affairs. A young, strengthening nation sought outlets and channels for its restless energy. How much power would America be able to exercise in the global political arena? What kinds of objectives would she pursue? How would a move onto the world stage fit with traditional preferences of Americans to focus on domestic affairs and economic priorities? There is a familiar ring in the questions that have recently emerged at the end of the twentieth century. Will the United States see power slip away due to the transformation of the common threat that united the West under American leadership? Will a single objective or set of objectives replace the containment of communism that defined goals so simply in much of the Cold War period? Will continued involvement in international police rescue missions continue to receive support from an American public that is increasingly focused on education, health care, economic, and social questions? While the ring of these questions sound much like their predecessors a century ago, they emerge in new cadences for a nation that has, like Moses and the ancient Hebrew people, wandered about the wilderness of the world arena for too long a time without yet entering the promised land of unblemished success and respect.

Achievement of international objectives in this decade of change has been mixed. On the one hand, the decade opened with an overwhelming success in the Persian Gulf War. After over twenty years of embarrassed frustration and vacillation in the aftermath of Vietnam, Americans felt proud of the careful, considered leadership of President Bush in face of the challenge from Iraq. Americans could see that national interests were involved in the Gulf War in a way that they were not in the Southeast Asian conflict. The President seemed to define objectives in a relatively clear way and took the time both to mobilize public support and to orchestrate global approval through the machinery of the United Nations. It was apparent that the United States achieved a definite victory over a recognizably dangerous foe, and the victory was attained quickly and with a minimum of casualties. On the other hand, the United States fell into the swamp of Somalia in 1992–93. The unclear objectives, unexpected consequences, unnecessary casualties, and lack of public comprehension of the situation all sounded a haunting echo of Vietnam. Had the American leaders learned nothing in the second half of the century? Was the United States doomed to replay continuously the unpleasant, cacophonous tunes of the Cold War?

In trying to come to terms with this series of post-Cold War dilemmas, it is important to pay heed to three sets of related topics. First, what attempts have American leaders made to codify objectives and uncover a replacement for Cold

War-style containment? New enemies have emerged and American power remains at a level close to what it was during the Cold War. Both a Republican and a Democratic President have made serious efforts to develop common themes to pull together the underlying threads of policy. Second, how much have domestic forces and variables affected the process of developing a new foreign policy for the next century? Domestic factors such as public opinion and interest groups deserve attention. The elective mandate which drives the Congress as well as the Presidency injects the separation-of-powers into the practice of foreign policy. The cast of appointed administrators has lengthened in a fashion congruent with their increased status and influence. Third, what kinds of policy themes have recently emerged in the areas with which American leaders must deal on a daily basis? They have been impelled to refashion policies towards a variety of regional theaters with which the United States dealt in the Cold War. They have had to devise new strategies for the deployment of nuclear weapons as well as new perspectives on necessary capabilities. There have been visible, well-publicized forays into the international arena as part of international police actions. In all three of these challenges, the ground rules are different from what they were during the Cold War, and predictable patterns of policy have yet to emerge.

## REDEFINING OBJECTIVES

During the containment era the setting of objectives was not difficult. It was in the application of the objectives that difficulties appeared. The origin of the containment strategy lay in the immediate post-World War II effort to come to terms with a newly expansionist Soviet foreign policy under Stalin. Specifically, President Truman first used containment to justify assistance in 1947 to non-communist forces battling in Greece and Turkey. It was assumed that such assistance would halt Soviet-inspired aggression and might even weaken the capabilities of the Soviet Union. The roll call of places in which American leaders applied the containment strategy has a familiar sound to careful observers of the foreign policy process. It includes the Marshall Plan for Europe in 1948, involvement in the Korean War in the 1950s, imposition of a blockade around Cuba in 1962, the major commitment to Vietnam in the 1964–73 period, and lesser involvements such as Hungary in 1956, the Dominican Republic in 1965, and Grenada in 1983. Central to all those commitments was the assumption that the injection of American military power would help to erode Soviet influence.

With the collapse of communism and the end of the Cold War, containment can no longer provide a clear list of objectives. Several presidential administrations have attempted to come up with a replacement that pertains more directly to the new kinds of challenges in the post-Cold War world. Other voices from within the United States have uttered cries for even different objectives.

In the aftermath of the Gulf War, the Bush Administration bandied about the concept of "New World Order." It is unclear if that concept meant a new set of objectives or a new description of the balance of power. Clearly, the concept spoke to a world in which the American military was the strongest and most effective in the international political arena. With the decline of the Soviet military and the break-up of the Soviet Union, policing operations led by the American military would be needed. At the same time, it was anticipated that other strong leaders like Saddam Hussein might endanger surrounding states. Perhaps a new mission for the American military would be constructing coalitions to restrict them and push them back when they became too aggressive. However, "New World Order" did not really become an effective substitute for containment, for there were after 1991 no obvious successors to the Persian Gulf-type situation. Serbian aggression into Croatia and Bosnia looked similar to some, but the ethnic complexity and lack of an economic stake made a firm American response unlikely.

The Clinton Administration has at times utilized "enlargement" as a unifying concept. It is the American objective in the world to "enlarge" the universe of market economies and countries which protect human rights. There is surface plausibility to this concept as well. It has been in the American interest to help the fledgling new capitalist systems in the former communist world establish their economies on free market principles. Principally, this has meant Russia, but it has also meant some of the more advanced states of East Central Europe. At the same time, there has been an effort to use a variety of tactics to promote protection of human rights. Concern about the excesses of the Bosnian War, about the bloodletting in Rwanda, and about the transfer of power to the black majority in South Africa reflect this priority. In addition, efforts to press China and Cuba to incorporate more protection for human rights have at times been a major concern. At best, "enlargement" provides a common sense explanation of American values but does not really offer the simple guidance and message that containment did.

It may be the case that the global politics have become so decentralized and regionally based that no clear set of objectives will emerge in the near future. It may be the case that American military power will make the country necessary in any policing effort. It may also mean that the United States may have to wait for situations to emerge before defining its objectives. That too may be necessary since there are no obvious arenas in which the United States would seek influence short of a direct threat to its interests. In the short-run a willingness to use force in a defensive, reactive way when individual and national freedoms are threatened may be the most accurate, although cumbersome, substitute for containment.

## DOMESTIC PRESSURES

Domestic pressures have always played a role in the making of U.S. foreign policy. However, during the early Cold War they often yielded to the need to present a united front at home against communist threats in various corners of the globe. This was certainly the case during the formation of NATO in 1949, the mobilization for the Korean War in the early 1950s, the response to the Soviet invasion of Hungary in 1956, and the battle of wits with the Soviet Union over various hot spots such as Berlin and Cuba. The war in Vietnam changed that domestic consensus on foreign policy issues. Many of the key domestic pressure points were sharply critical of administration policy in Southeast Asia in the 1960s and early 1970s. Vietnam seems to have set a pattern in this regard, for well into the 1980s many domestic actors remained active in evaluating and disagreeing with administrative policy. What happened after the end of the Cold War was a simple extension of this pattern of descensus. At the same time, with the Cold War over the stakes were not nearly as high. Thus the division of domestic actors over policy may not have mattered quite as much.

Congress has remained quite willing to challenge administration policy in the post-Cold War period. The period of buildup to the Persian Gulf conflict was one of extended debate between Congress and President Bush over the proper course of action. Figures within Congress were the ones who called for extension of economic sanctions as long as possible. In the end, President Bush presented the issue of war and peace to the Congress. Senate support for use of "all means necessary" came according to a narrow 52–48 vote. It was from the Congress that voices emerged in criticism of the Somali venture in 1993. In fact, key Republican congressional voices became critical of a number of Clinton efforts to inject American military power in a variety of theaters. These included Haiti, Bosnia, and Rwanda. Congressional critics seemed to worry about being sucked into another Vietnam but were also wary about involvement where national interests were not obviously engaged. Economics played a role as well, for Congress was not as interested as the President in increasing trade relations with either China or Cuba.

Public opinion continued to provide a large fence that hemmed in administration policy. The public demanded that policy be clear, and that military commitments be limited. For example, the Dayton Agreement of 1995 included a call for 20,000 American troops to be used as part of the IFOR presence in Bosnia. Due to public pressure, President Clinton promised that the troops would only remain in Bosnia until December 1996. Emerging conflict in Bosnia generated a call for an additional commitment well into 1997. Similarly, public reluctance led to extreme caution being exercised with respect to the refugee crisis in late 1996 in central Africa. Nations affected included Zaire, Burundi, and Rwanda. It would not be fair to conclude that public support for administration policy decreased since the mid-1980s, but it is the case that the public imposes real limits on the nature and execution of policies in various parts of the world.

U.S. elections in the post-1985 period make up another domestic variable that influences American policy. In the 1988 election there was debate over various aspects of the Reagan-Bush foreign policy. In particular, Democrats criticized the failure to bring President Noriega of Panama under control. His connection with the drug trade made him a double challenge to U.S. policy. It is not surprising that President Bush set troops after him within the first year of his administration. While the 1992 election was fought on mainly domestic issues, the 1996 election did include foreign policy messages and topics once again. For instance, after 1993 the Republicans criticized President Clinton for developing no coherent rationale for his policy and continually sounded the theme that the United States should never again grant control of its forces to the United Nations. In fact, this criticism had effect, for the design of

Bosnian policy in the wake of the Dayton Agreement specifically avoided such a situation.

The make-up of the foreign policy bureaucratic team constitutes another domestic factor of significance. Under President Bush there was a relatively close-knit group of key advisors. Their cohesion and apparent agreement on most major matters was probably a consequence of their guidance in the Gulf War crisis. However, even that group included a diversity of perspectives on the question of whether to pursue Saddam Hussein and remove him from power. Under President Clinton there has been even greater division. Secretary of State Warren Christopher has received criticism for playing too passive a role in the various crisis areas in which he has been involved. Secretary of Defense Les Aspin did not mesh very well with Pentagon officials, and his term ended early and abruptly. Both Secretary Christopher and Aspin's successor William Perry left the administration at the conclusion of the first term. Continuing controversy over the role of the CIA kept the spotlight on division and bureaucratic politics within the foreign policy team of the Clinton Administration.

In sum, domestic factors such as Congress, public opinion, key elections, and the foreign policy bureaucracy displayed a pattern of pluralism and conflict in the post-Cold War period. In part, this dissensus was a continuation of the Vietnam-era break-down of domestic consensus. In part, the lack of unanimity on foreign policy within the domestic arena may have reflected the lower profile and fewer stakes involved in the various conflictual spots around the globe.

## POLICY THEMES

Policy themes in a variety of arenas shifted in the period immediately after the Cold War ended. Regional changes, a shifting capabilities mix, and emerging global conflicts accounted for the key differences. While the United States did not succeed in coming up with a unifying doctrine that encapsulated a coherent set of objectives in this new policy setting, the leadership did manage to devise policy adaptations in each of those key areas.

The virtual elimination of the communist threat in many regional theaters led to the necessary adjustment of American policy. In the old communist bloc, nine nation-states gave way to twenty-seven by 1993. This meant that the United States had to develop a more diversified foreign policy. Towards Central Asian newcomers like Azerbaidjan, U.S. policy concerns incorporated oil politics, ethnic unrest, and link-ups with more established powers in the Persian Gulf-Mideast area. This was quite a change from the days when Central Asian areas were lumped under the umbrella of American policy towards the Soviet Union. Towards other countries like the Czech Republic, the U.S. concern became future membership in NATO or even in the European Union.

Policy themes towards other global regions may not have undergone such major transformation but were nonetheless affected. For example, African nations began a series of democratizing efforts. The most dramatic example was South Africa itself. Promotion of democracy and human rights replaced the anti-communism that had characterized American foreign policy towards states such as Angola, Namibia, and Ethiopia. Within Asia China became a power to be reckoned with in the early part of 1996. A focus on the interests of Hong Kong, Taiwan, and Japan in relation to Chinese ambitions replaced the old fixation on Soviet ambitions in East Asian arenas such as North Korea, the Kurile Islands, and Vietnam. Of course, American preoccupation with the Soviet threat in Central America in the early 1980s yielded to an abiding concern about nurturing democratic processes and economic progress in the area. In all of these regional theaters, policy themes which had been secondary became primary with the end of the Cold War.

U.S. military capabilities underwent change as well. In 1991, 1993, and 1995, the Defense Department proposed base cutbacks. This process was painful both for the military and for the communities involved. Personnel cutbacks that would result in a smaller and more streamlined military occurred. Congress and President battled each year over the size of the reduction in the military budget. Congressional Republicans typically desired a smaller cut than did the President, but both agreed on the direction of change. In the nuclear area the main emphasis was on arms control and reduced capabilities. President Bush signed two START agreements with Russia, and when finalized they will mean substantial cutbacks in numbers of weapons. The only issue that held back progress in this area was the complication of the break-up of the Soviet Union. In particular, Russian-Ukrainian conflict over their joint nuclear stockpile made progress difficult with the United States. Further, the real post-Cold War issue in this area became the matter of rogue states like Iraq and North Korea. How could the

United States cope with their ambition to possess nuclear capabilities.

In conclusion, the nature of warfare changed with the end of the Cold War. In a sense, the Cold War division of the globe into a communist camp and a democratic camp bottled up many ethnic and regional tensions that might have resulted in shooting wars. Truly, the end of the "Cold" War led to the outbreak of a number of "hot" wars that took a huge toll in human life and well-being. In addition to the Gulf War, there were major conflicts in Croatia, Bosnia, Rwanda, and Somalia. Conflicts in Georgia, Azerbaidjan, Moldova, and Haiti were minor only because the countries and populations were smaller. Ethnic and nationality tensions bubbled in numerous other cauldrons, including even such "developed" states as Canada and Great Britain. In a sense, the replacement of a psychological war of nerves between two superpowers with a series of actual and potential wars among numerous pairs of states summarizes the essence of change overall in the post-Cold War world. The conflicts were so many and so varied that development of a coherent set of objectives by the United States was an impossibility. In turn, the increasing bitterness and rivalry in world politics brought domestic divisions within the United States to the surface with greater frequency.

# Peterson

NAME: _____

SECTION: _____

DATE: _____

1. Does the fact that in the last five years nine communist countries have devolved into twenty seven non-communist countries support the idea that American foreign policy has been a success?

2. What are some of the major dilemmas facing America's foreign policy makers in the contemporary global political scene?

3. Explain the new foreign policy concept of "enlargement" as a potentially new unifying framework for American planners.

4. Relate Peterson's discussion of changes in domestic consensus on foreign policy to the earlier discussion in Winder's article on electoral realignment. Are these changes good or bad?

___

5. Explain how success in achieving political and policy goals may create a crisis for planners and decision makers.

___

**Group Exercise:** Discuss whether American troops should intervene directly in the many new little "hot wars" now springing up all over the world. Why, or why not?

**Individual Project:** Locate and describe information on the ethnic and nationalistic tensions of Canada and the United kingdom. Should the U.S. intervene in those struggles? Why, or why not?

*Part Four*

# The Integrative Field

*Chapter Eight*

# PUBLIC POLICY

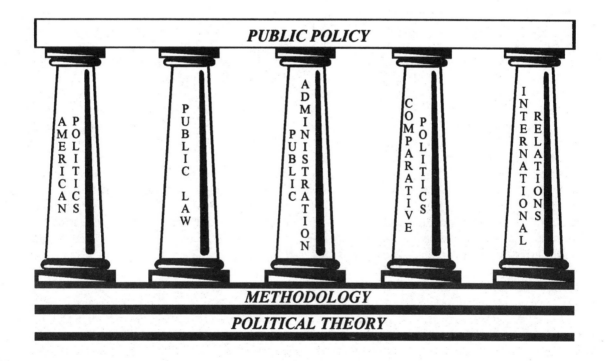

# ANALYZING THE CAUSES OF REVOLUTION

## Aristotle

*[Editor's note: Aristotle explains that Revolutions, based on varying interpretations of justice and equality, lead to conflict, political struggles, and constitutional changes. The objective political scientist is interested in the various methods by which revolutionary threats may be created and/or averted.]*

We have also to consider the particular way in which each constitution is liable to be ruined. In addition we have to discuss policies to preserve the state. We should assume that the reason why there are so many different constitutions is the fact that each is based on a different conception of justice. Democracy arises out of the notion that those who are equal in one respect should be equal in all respects. Oligarchy is based on the notion that those who are unequal in one respect are in all respects unequal (ie: if superior on one, superior in all). All these forms of government have a kind of justice, but in any absolute terms, all are faulty and subject to revolution. This is the reason why either side turns to sedition whenever their share in the government does not accord with their preconceived ideas of justice.

Those who excel in virtue are the most justified in attempting sedition for they alone can with reason claim to be superior; but they are always the last ones to make an attempt. Also, those who possess an advantage of birth regard themselves as entitled to more than an equal share on the ground of their ancestral merit or wealth. Here then arise two fountains of revolution and changes in constitution. These considerations explain two different ways in which constitutional charges may happen: (a) sometimes the dissidents change the constitution, to convert democracy into oligarchy, or oligarchy into democracy; or to elevate them into 'polity' and aristocracy; or, conversely, to degrade these into the lower forms; (b) sometimes the rebels leave the constitution unmolested but try to get the administration into their hands. There is also a change of degree, to make a democracy more or less democratic and to make an oligarchy more or less oligarchic. Everywhere inequality is a cause of revolution, and always it is a desire for equality which rises in rebellion. Finally, a revolutionary party may try to change only a part of the constitution. For example, some writers state that Spartans attempted to abolish the Kingship, and that the Epidaurans created a democratic Council to take the place of the traditional tribal meetings.

Still, democracy seems to be safer and less liable to revolution than an oligarchy. For in oligarchies there is always the double danger of the oligarchical elite falling out among themselves and also with the people; but in democracies there is only the danger of a quarrel with the members of the oligarchic class. No dissention worth mentioning arises among the people themselves. (Greek city-states did not have large multi-ethnic populations or religious conflicts; editors). It should be remarked that a government composed of the middle class more nearly approximates to democracy than to oligarchy, and is the safest of all of the imperfect forms of government.

In dealing with revolution under different governments, there are three causes: (1) psychological motives; (2) goals or objects in view; and (3) the initial occasions. We begin by giving a brief outline of each of them separately. One cause leading to sedition is a state of mind. The universal cause of revolution, inequality, has already been described. Some stir up sedition because of their desire for equality, others because their minds are filled with beliefs of their superiority. Both of these pretensions may or may not have some justification. Inferiors revolt in order that they might become equal, and equals to become superiors. This is the state of mind which creates sedition.

Motives for revolt, the objects which are at stake, are the desire for gain or honor, or the fear of loss and dishonor. The authors of these passions may want to divert punishment, disgrace, or a monetary fine, from themselves or their friends. The occasions and origins of these motives and dispositions, when viewed in one way, may be regarded as seven, and in another as more than seven, because while two of them, avarice and honor, have already been noted, such passions may also be excited by seeing others justly or unjustly receiving such gains or honor. Other causes are insolence, fear, too much influence, contempt, and disproportionate increase in some part of the state. The immediate causes of revolution are particular events or imbalances, such as election intrigues, negligence, non-feasance or dissimilarity of elements in the human composition of a state.

The share that insolence and avarice have in creating revolutions are obvious enough. When the magistrates are grasping and corrupt, the citizens turn seditious—attacking these persons and the constitutional order, giving such persons power. It is evident too what an influence honor exerts and how it is also a cause of revolution. Men who are dishonored and who see others honored rise in rebellion. When the honor or dishonor is undeserved it is unjust, but both may be justifiable, if the honor or dishonor is deserved.

Again, superiority is a cause of revolution when one or more persons have too much influence; out of such a condition a monarchy or oligarchy might arise. Another cause of revolution is fear. Both wrongdoers afraid of punishment and victims anxiously anticipating being wrong may revolt out of fear. For example, in Rhodes the notables were moved to conspire against the people by alarm at the number of law-suits with which they were being threatened. Contempt is also a cause of sedition and insurrection, in oligarchies, when the disenfranchised think themselves strong enough; and in democracies, when the wealthy despise the disorder and anarchy which they see. There are several examples of democracies collapsing from contempt: Thebes, because of misgovernment; Megara, as the result of a military defeat; and Syracuse, as Gelon became tyrant and was a factor at Rhodes, as just mentioned.

Political revolutions also spring from the disproportionate increase of a part of the state. The body of the state is composed of many members and parts, and each must grow proportionately if symmetry is to be preserved. The number of the poor, for example, may become too large in democracies and in 'polities.' If the rich become too numerous, or if properties increase, democracies may turn into oligarchies and dynasties may evolve.

Another cause of sedition and rebellion is a division of the city into different races, especially if they lack a common spirit. Therefore the admission of foreigners into colonies has generally produced a revolution. There are many examples that can be named. The Achaeans teamed up with settlers from Troezen to found the City of Sybaris, but when their numbers increased they turned on their Troezen allies and expelled them.

In addition to racial diversity, disproportionate territory may also be an occasion for sedition. This may occur in states with a territory unsuited for political unity, such as where the inhabitants of a mainland suburb are at discord with the urban inhabitants of an island, or where there is discord between a major city and its harbor area.

Finally, we should look at the immediate causes of revolution found in particular events or imbalances. These include the impact of election intrigues, which may lead to subversion of the constitutional system. On the other hand, wilful negligence may be an occasion for rebellion; and disloyal persons may slip their way into the highest of offices. Another such event may be the neglect of trifling changes. A great change of the whole system of institutions slowly evolves unnoticed if small changes are overlooked. In Ambracia, for example, the property qualification for office, small at first, was eventually reduced to nothing, for they thought that a small qualification was much the same as having none at all. Just as in war, where the dividing line of a ditch, however small it may be, may break a regiment, so every cause of difference, however slight, makes a breach in a city. The greatest opposition is confessedly that of virtue and vice; but next comes that of wealth and poverty. There are other antagonistic elements, greater or lesser, of which one is the difference of territory.

In revolutions the occasions may appear trifling, but great issues are at stake. Trifles are most important when they concern oligarchic rulers. There is an example in the history of Syracuse, where a constitutional revolution arose from a quarrel between two young men, who were both in office, about a love affair. Eventually they drew the whole city population into their quarrel and it divided into serious political factions. In general, when the nobles quarrel, the whole city is involved, as happened in Hestiaea after the Persian War over a family inheritance. We should be on guard against the beginnings of such evils, and should put an end to the quarrels of chiefs and mighty men.

Constitutions may also be changed in either direction, towards oligarchy or democracy, as a

*Aristole*

result of the growth in reputation or power of a government official or magistrates. In Athens, for example, The Council of the Areopagus gained in reputation during the Persian War and the result appeared for a time to be a tightening of the constitution towards oligarchy. But the tide turned because the common people serving in the navy were responsible for the victory of Salamis, and secured for Athens a naval empire the effect which strengthened the cause of democracy. In general it should be remembered that whenever any person or body adds new power to the state they are apt to cause revolutions started either by persons who envy their honors, or due to their refusal to remain on a footing of equality when they feel themselves superior.

Such, on a general view, are the springs and causes of sedition and change in all constitutions. Revolutions also break out when opposing parties, such as the rich and the poor are too equally balanced, especially when there is little or nothing of a middle class to tip the scales; for if either side has a clear preponderance, the other will be unwilling to risk a struggle with the stronger. This is the reason why men of pre-eminent virtue do not, as a rule, attempt to stir up sedition: they are only a few against many.

We may add that political revolutions are accomplished in two ways: sometimes by force, and sometimes by fraud. Force may either be used initially or at a later stage. Fraud, again, is of two kinds: (1) sometimes it is used in the initial stage. In this way a change may be made at the moment with general assent; but those who have made it then have to proceed to keep control. For example, in the revolution of the Four Hundred at Athens they first defrauded the people by an assurance that the Persian King would provide money for the war against Sparta, and then attempted to keep control with force. (2) sometimes, however, an initial act of fraud is followed up afterwards by a similar policy, and control is thus kept with good will and allegiance is retained. Such, on a summary view, are the common causes from which spring constitutional change.

Next we have to consider what means there are to preserve states in general and in particular cases. In the first place, it is evident that if we understand the causes of revolution, we shall also understand how to avoid them and so preserve the state, how opposites create opposites, and destruction is the opposite of preservation. In a well-organized government there is nothing which should be more jealously maintained than the spirit of obedience to law, especially in trifling matters. For if lawlessness creeps in unperceived it will at last ruin the state, just as the constant outlays of small expenditures will in time eat up a fortune.

In the first place, we should guard against the very beginning of change, and in the second place we should guard against the temptation to use fraud to deceive the people, for in the long run such has proven to be useless. Further, we should note that neither oligarchy nor democracy has any special virtue of stability; but both last only when the rulers are on good terms both with the lowest unenfranchised and with the governing classes. Neither should be mistreated, and leading spirits from both should be admitted into the government. The equality attained from democratic institutions is not only just but expedient among numerous elites. For example, the restriction of the tenure of office to six months will allow people of equal station to share them, making it unlikely that demagogues will arise among them.

The relations of a state to its foreign enemies impact on the preservation of the states. A distant enemy is a small threat, and a near enemy makes the government keep the state well in hand. Therefore the ruler who fears for the welfare of the state should invent terrors and bring distant dangers near in order that citizens should remain on their guard. Rulers should also use the laws to control the contentions and quarrels of the nobles and prevent the enlarging of the conflict. A true statesman, unlike an ordinary man, can discern the beginning of evil. Men are easily spoilt, and laws should be used to prevent the disproportionate growth of money, honor or power. The proper remedy for such evil is always to distribute the management of affairs among the opposite elements of the state, giving proper offices of state to both the poor and the rich, and to increase the middle class. Thus an end can be put to those seditious elements seeking revolution on the grounds of inequality.

But above all, special precautions should be taken against rulers stealing the public money. If offices brought no profit, then and only then could democracy and aristocracy be combined, for both nobles and people might have their wishes gratified. In democracies, the rich and their property should be spared, and their incomes protected. In an oligarchy, on the other hand, great care should be taken of the poor, and lucrative offices should go to them. It is also expedient to assign to the less powerful class, an equal share or a preference in all offices except the principal ones. The principal offices should be entrusted chiefly or preferentially to the members of the governing class

# ARISTOTLE

NAME: _____

SECTION: _____

DATE: _____

1. A reading of Aristotle's discussion of revolutionary causes and their characteristics indicates that some are classified as "elevating" and progressive and others are classified as being "degrading." How would you classify the American revolution? Why?

   _____
   _____
   _____
   _____
   _____
   _____

2. What are Aristotle's three main causes of revolution? What is the relationship between these causes and his conception of "motives" for revolting?

   _____
   _____
   _____
   _____
   _____
   _____

3. Why are political scientists interested in methods by which revolutionary trends may be created or averted?

   _____
   _____
   _____
   _____
   _____
   _____

4. Aristotle seems to indicate that an expansion of the Polis to include a larger variety of ethnic groups may be a factor in sedition and rebellion. Is this a concern in the modern world?

_____
_____
_____
_____
_____
_____
_____

5. Does Aristotle seem to suggest that democracies are more stable than oligarchies? Why, or why not?

_____
_____
_____
_____
_____
_____
_____

**Group Exercise:** Relate Aristotle's article on revolution to Bamfo's article on current African problems. Should a professional political scientist have been able to predict these fairly accurately?

**Individual Project:** Locate and identify a contemporary newspaper article which reports on an existing struggle between democratic and oligarchic factions somewhere in the modern world.

# FACTORS IN POLICY-MAKING: HUMAN POPULATION AND TECHNOLOGY

## Lee M. Allen

### INTRODUCTION

Nothing interests people so much as the question: Should public policy be changed? When the answer is yes, some people will be happy to find out that their taxes are reduced, or that they have been granted new freedoms that they didn't have before. On the other hand, other people may find that their taxes are going up, that their property is confiscated, or their rights and privileges curtailed. This is the basis for the old saying that no one is safe when the legislature is in session and is making new laws and policies to control and regulate society. It is important to realize that we are living in a complex modern world in which our policies, beliefs and techniques are being continuously challenged. And if we do not know how to influence the policy-making process, then other people who do know how will pursue their own agendas, sometimes at our expense.

A concern over the causes and techniques of policy change is not new in political science. At least as far back as the *Politics* of Aristotle, people have focused on understanding the most fundamental policy changes, those which involve national survival and political revolution. Aristotle viewed constitutions as embodiments of conceptions of justice; people have different views of what justice is, and want different constitutions, or different public policies. Aristotle's writing style certainly seems a bit old-fashioned today, but as we read about his thoughts on the causes of revolution and the means of preserving political order, much of his argument seems very familiar to us. Sometimes dissidents change the constitution to convert democracy into elitism, or vice-versa. Everywhere inequality is a cause of revolution, and always a desire for equality (or privilege) will rise in rebellion.

For ancient authors, there were three main causes of political change: (1) psychological motives; (2) particular goals or desires; and (3) reaction to some triggering event, such as famine or war. Some people want change for personal reasons such as ego, power or revenge. Another cause of unrest and rebellion is conflict between different races or ethnic groups, especially if they lack a common patriotism. And goals, such as the desire for wealth, monetary gain, land or status and honor, may also underlie political activism for policy change. Fear of famine during the Great Global Depression led directly to WW II and indirectly in the United States to the New Deal and later social welfare programs. Minor issues, the Watergate and the Whitewater scandals, bribery, corruption, or even mere negligence, may be an occasion for voting out an entire government, let alone simply policy change.

But today there are many other factors which were not foreseen by the ancient writers, but which are resulting in great changes in public policy, not only in America but around the globe. These include new discoveries in human population growth, science and technology, environmental pollution. Even the pace of change itself is a problem, as individuals and institutions alike seem to be unable to cope effectively with the tidal wave of new things, new ideas, and demands for new public policies.

### HUMAN POPULATION GROWTH

What does the future hold for human beings on Earth? Will there be enough of us to both maintain our civilization and America's position among the nations of the planet? How does population cause policy change? Scientists have been working on techniques of trend analysis, to determine what are the major probable paths of change. One of the earliest trend analysts was Malthus, who back in the Eighteenth Century pre-

*A Clock is Ticking*

dicted that our human over-population would lead to over-utilization of the land, to be followed by famine and war. Although great advances in botany and agriculture warded off the early realization of his prediction, current events do correspond to his vision. To a certain extent, this gloomy forecast is supported by the beliefs of several religious groups, for whom the Divine answer is clear: catastrophe and doom for the planet and civilization, followed by only a spiritual rebirth. Unfortunately, modern techniques of trend analysis often depict a similar negative expectation. One thing is certain: that the global human population is rising dramatically.

Because of this population growth, many Americans can soon expect a drastic change in their quality of life, due to an impending revolution in environmental policy. Some of the factors leading to this change include an increasing population in a limited space, clashes of economic interests, and the retention of outmoded and self-destructive means of earning a living. Aggravating the situation are traditional public policies and political perspectives that forestall coordinated solutions to problems. What are some of these old traditional environmental policies that damage our lives and waste our natural resources?

Population growth is often depicted as the single most important factor in policy making. If it is too rapid, resources fail and war and famine results. If it is too slow, a manpower shortage may occur, and neighboring countries may attempt conquest and even enslavement. But much other research shows that this may be an exaggeration In fact, under-population, for example, seems to have been a small factor in the underdevelopment of some third-world nations; much more important was their remoteness from and lack of control over modern industrial production systems.

We live in a world in which countries such as China have been legislating a one-child limit for couples. Social movements such as Zero Population Growth advocate two or fewer children per couple. In our own society, with high rates of divorce and remarriage, even the calculation of the proper parents/children ratio is very confusing. However, one thing is clear: generally, having fewer children will be more environmentally (and socially) benign than having a very large number of children. Because you will have fewer economies of scale in childrearing, each additional child you have will eventually demand more greater economic production and social withdrawals (though whether this is a linear or non-linear function of demands is unclear). Moreover, if you have fewer children, slots will open up in the opportunity structure for more lower income children to receive more education and better employment.

If a proper balance is to be maintained between population growth and the environment, new strategies for individual living may be needed, both in family life and in consumer life. If you are concerned about population growth, instead of having more children, you can become a "big brother" or "big sister" to other people's children. Or you can become a grandparent and be more involved in the lives of your children's children. According to some scholars, if you do choose to have a child, you should also be checked out physically for your capacity to produce a healthy child, and if there are any doubts, an amniocentesis can be performed. For consumers, the strategies about consumer durables focus on choosing wisely and sharing whenever possible. Choices you may make about how to raise your child will also have environmental implications. You can attempt to create a private world for your child, in which case he or she will have higher environmental impacts during childhood and even higher consumption expectations during adulthood.

There are many reasons why our human populations tend towards increase even when there are food shortages, famine and war. Among these are the personal reasons, especially the desire for posterity. Additionally, other family members may bring pressure to bear on you to have children, based on a frustrated desire for children or for social and economic pattern maintenance. Businesses also have two vested interests in population expansion: their own desire for expanding markets and the desire for a large cheap labor supply. Churches have some similar motivations. Aside from their theological theories about the purpose of life, they are also concerned with "markets" and with the desire to maintain growth and ward off competition. Nations, of course, feel the need for all of these things: large populations mean large labor pools, expanding economic markets, and manpower for national defense. The result: a global outlook for high continued population growth. If we look at the World Wide Web, at the following address, anyone can track the continuing growing size of the human population. http://www.census.gov/cgi-bin/ipc/popclockw.

That figure, over five and a half billion people, is not only hard to imagine but is itself the focus of heated political debate. The official United census report lists only about 5,805,956,089 people in the world. The very existence of 80 million people is in doubt. The people who make up such lists will often skew the statistical numbers to achieve their policy objectives. But one thing is clear: there is a real growing number of people on the planet.

*When this article was written, on 12-02-96, at 9:16 in the evening, the entire world's human population, according to one webpage counter, was 5,861,742,641.*

## TECHNOLOGICAL CHANGE

Thousands of years ago the ancient Greeks made important contributions to many sciences—most notably astronomy, optics, acoustics, and mathematics. Greek technology also progressed through innovations in agriculture, building construction, mining, refining of metals, and military equipment. And yet few of these new and basic innovations drew to any significant degree on Greek science. Moreover, the Greeks' technological achievements were far less impressive than their scientific achievements, thus indicating the lack of any real necessary connection between the two. This lopsided pattern of development continued with the Romans, but in reverse.

Roman contributions to science were relatively minor, while Roman engineering (mainly in such things as the construction of great aqueducts) reached a high level of development. In any event, Roman technology had very little to do with science. Despite the views of some critics, the European Middle Ages were a time of slow but significant technological advances. For example, improved agricultural practices like crop rotation were introduced, along with new sources of power such as windmills, and then an effective horse collar allowing the effective use of a plow horse for the first time was also invented in that era.

Many of the major difficulties experienced by the centrally planned economies in achieving technological advances are the result of a basic tension between their system of economic management and the requirements of technological innovation. The centrally planned economies often rest on the assumption that most economic activities can be reduced to predictable routines. But in reality the course of most technological innovation is uncertain, and is notoriously difficult for us to predict. And the bureaucratic procedures that work tolerably well for the administration of routine productive tasks will usually fail when they are applied to basic technological innovation. A planning agency can set goals and quotas for the production of established goods, and various ministries can even oversee the actual operation of the individual enterprises through routine bureaucratic administration, but these procedures work much less well when innovation is the goal. Innovation is an activity full of risk and unpredictability, and it cannot easily be accommodated to the pre-programmed structures and activities.

To make matters worse, centrally planned economies attempt to motivate workers and managers through allocation of rewards that create disincentives for technological innovation. For example, a factory manager typically receives bonuses for the fulfillment and even the over-fulfillment of quotas for established products, as given by the central plan. Thus, the production of an innovative product is not rewarded, for it has not been stipulated by the plan.

Furthermore, technological innovation cannot always be traced to economic motives or even to the desire to address practical problems. To be sure, we tend to think of technology as the result of efforts to solve problems of this sort; after all, technology is often defined as the product of knowledge that is used in order to get something done. The very word "technology" conjures up images of useful devices. In fact, even the most practical of inventions may really owe its origin to a spirit that seems more closely connected to play than to "productive" work. When Willis Whitney served as the first official director of the research laboratory of the General Electric Company, he often asked his scientists and technicians there if they were "having fun." For Whitney, "fun" was working on problems that had stumped everyone. Pursuing these problems was nothing less than the most exciting thing that a person could do.

Robert Goddard, the inventor of the liquid-fueled rocket, later recalled that he really became interested in the topic while as a boy sitting in a tree, imagining how wonderful it would be to make some device which could ascend to Mars, and how it would look if sent up from the meadow below his feet. At the time he did not see the fruits of his labors: orbiting satellites providing global communication links, weather prediction, remote sensing of natural resources, and the deployment of new weapons. Young Goddard was energized by the dream of space travel; practical consequences were at best actually just a secondary concern. Even in a predominantly market-oriented society such as the United States, not all technologies have been generated and shaped by market forces.

This dreaming tendency is not confined to the new aerospace industry. There is a mounting concern about the financial costs incurred by the search for absolute physical health sought by idealistic modern medical technologies. While some medical advances have undoubtedly lowered the costs of medical care, many others have had the opposite result, without changing the ultimate reality of mortality. When faced with a choice between controlling medical expenses or saving lives and alleviating pain through the use of new and sophisticated technologies, it is difficult for any individual or society to exert any cost consciousness.

The case of space, military and medical technologies brings us back to the topic of factors in policy-making: the interplay of technology, population growth, and the political, economic and social context of decision-making. The economic considerations, important as they are, are certainly not the sole basis of decisions regarding the initiation, development, selection, and implementation of public policy.

Ironically, the very success of the modern technological lifestyle has created new global problems. Over-population, soil exhaustion, modern haphazard job security, job cut-backs, and land being over-developed, over-eroded, and coated with chemical toxins are evidence of technology gone awry. And although some industries have largely been able to develop strategies of environmental coexistence within modern technologies like the industrial and petrochemical industries, others have not. The seafood industry usually views all regulation to protect species of fish and shrimp as a basic nuisance, and sometimes as a positive evil that simply seems to adversely affect their own livelihood. They do not realize that without protection, there will be no shrimp to harvest at all.

Alexis de Tocqueville, an early observer of American culture, once indicated that our system of local responsibility for problem-solving, within our system of territorial democracy, is inferior to centralized planning only when the central powers are enlightened and the local authorities are ignorant. He also asserted that however enlightened or skillful any central power is, it cannot of itself simply embrace all of the details of the life of an entire nation. The Madisonian system of checks and balances, so effective at eliminating centralized tyranny, has some dysfunctional consequences: it leads to the creation of small independent groups of people largely isolated from majority pressure, even progressive pressure. These factional groups seem to be a modern-day equivalent of primitive tribal hunter-gatherer bands, who were suspicious of strangers and heedless of the harmful effects on others of their exploitative practices.

## Conclusion

Perhaps the greatest single factor in policy-making is the actual desire of the policy maker. What do we really want, peaceful and beautiful utopia, or a job-maximizing human beehive, or some combination of both? The social sciences, political scientists, and the policy analysts can help to enact sane and forethoughtful population and environmental policies by clarifying our desires.

In the future, management must use techniques of sustained yield husbandry, and attitudes of stewardship, not ownership, of natural resources. This should be encouraged by government leadership if necessary. But failures along these lines are already all too evident. Already, large and increasing areas of our coastal bays have been practically killed, ruined by toxins, and declared too polluted to allow fishing. Mammoths, sloths, passenger pigeons, all have gone the way of the dodo, wiped out by human recklessness. Now the fish in the seas in the Grand Banks are declared to be going too.

We have to choose between a short-term market place with an exploitation orientation or move to an integrated long-range environmental resource utilization as the model for our attempts to prepare for the future. Both perspectives are understandable, but we can only follow one. The short-term model is based on human fears and traditions of survival that were once helpful to the human race, but are now becoming counterproductive in our new global economic situation.

Scientists, intellectuals and policy analysts must tend to, and alter, our myths. There is no general consensus about strategies for coping with these problems; but there is consensus that competition between economic and social interests, long touted as a positive virtue, is aggravating the decline in the quality of life for earth's inhabitants. The policy sciences can help in this endeavor by sensitizing the human population to the positive values of conservation and husbandry of our precious biotic resources. If these changes in attitudes occur, then future generations will be able to stand on mother Earth in the twenty-first century and enjoy the fruit of their labors and trace the future in the light of bright stars as they gleam in a clear night sky.

# ALLEN

NAME: _____

SECTION: _____

DATE: _____

1. Explain how the apparently simple factor of human population growth can cause great changes in official government policies.

   _____
   _____
   _____
   _____
   _____
   _____
   _____
   _____

2. If you were in a position to influence policy in China or India today, would you try to change the pace of population growth? If so, why or why not?

   _____
   _____
   _____
   _____
   _____
   _____
   _____
   _____

3. Compare and contrast Allen's discussion on the weaknesses of centrally-planned economies with Bamfo's discussion of African economic difficulties. Is there fundamental agreement?

   _____
   _____
   _____
   _____
   _____
   _____

4. Regarding technological innovation, compare and contrast Allen's discussion on human dreaming and aspirational desire with the article describing a competitiveness model by Walters and Blake. Is there any fundamental disagreement?

___

5. Compare and contrast Allen's discussion of mythology with Saeger's discussion of post-revolutionary judicial philosophy. Should governments promote new ideas for cultural change?

___

**Group Exercise:** Discuss some of the possible consequences of space travel on the global population. Who would benefit, who might be disadvantaged, and over what time-frame of analysis?

**Individual Project:** Gain access to the world wide web and locate information on the size of the human population. Do you think it can continue to increase without political consequences? What consequences?

# POLICY HERE, POLICY THERE, POLICY EVERYWHERE

## Gary Misch

*The politician creates his little laws
And sits attentive to his own applause.*
CATO THE CENSOR (234–149 B.C.E.)

This essay briefly examines the use of symbolic words and phrases in the development of the omnipresent public policy. It defines the general meaning of public policy and cites examples of how symbolic words were used in the development of certain domestic and foreign policies. The essay suggests that symbolic terms used in political jargon may function as a type of user-shorthand that can be used to either depict political reality, or conceal reality.

## PUBLIC POLICY DEFINED

What is public policy? How is public policy developed in a very complex democratic society such as in the United States? The preceding articles in this book have provided the reader with a myriad of perspectives on the factional nature and behavior of government organizations. In general terms, public policy refers to a course of action that a government body intends and attempts to pursue overall on a particular subject or issue. Public policies are generally formed as a result of negotiations between or among powerful decision-makers. In certain instances, however, public policy may result from the decision of one executive decision maker acting in his/her legal capacity usually with consultation, but without concurrence by any other government authority. Executives such as the president, any cabinet secretary, agency administrator, governor, mayor, and other senior officials who are empowered by law to make certain policy decisions, do so routinely. The president, state governors and other officials have been trapped occasionally by the media into proclaiming new public policy during a news conference without prior discussion, analysis, or planning. This happens much to the dismay of their executive staffs who may attempt to shade, modify, or clarify what was really meant by the executive.

Public policy decisions may occur at all levels of government, i.e. federal, state, county, regional, city, etc. Government policies may be referred to as: laws, ordinances, statutes, rules, injunctions, codes, mandates, enacted bills, legislation, agency regulations, presidential executive orders, national security directives, et al. Political theorists have argued whether public policy is dictated by social events, inferring that it is only reactionary, or can public policy be proactive and effective in favorably influencing social events?

Aristotle's notion that "man is a political animal" (scheming) is as true today as it was 2300 years ago. Notable world leaders such as Mahatma Gandhi once described policy as a "temporary creed liable to be changed, but while it holds good it has got to be pursued with apostolic zeal." President Abraham Lincoln half-heartedly stated that "my policy is to have no policy." On the other hand, President Nixon reflecting on the art of policy-making in the age of the electronic media, noted ". . . what makes good television, makes bad politics." The interaction of the personalities of key decision-makers influences the tone of public policy. Personal attributes such as: intensity, charisma, physical appearance, reputation, actual or perceived power, motivation, powers of persuasion, factual knowledge, ability to make realistic assessments, and courage to act, will affect the outcome of any negotiations.

Political pundits in the media seem to enjoy comparing the policies of each political administration with its avowed principles of governance and pointing out the differences. This is quite acceptable, even entertaining, from the public's perspective because it actually assists the voters in the election process.

## POLICY DEVELOPMENT IS MORE ART THAN SCIENCE

The development of public policy is far more art than it is science. This should not be a great revelation to most persons in America, even those who possess only a rudimentary understanding of the U.S. political system of bargaining games in its decision process. It maybe be argued that "politics" is a term which defines the way that a democratic society decides what to do (policy), while "administration" is the way by which the government is going to do it (implementation). The results of the interaction between and among powerful political decision-makers, disparate advocacy groups within the government's executive branch itself, the general public, national media, foreign and domestic specia-interest groups, appear to shape most national policies.

The common denominator in the decision calculus is typically the *visible* amount of public dollars to be spent. If the taxpayers are fortunate, some consideration to tangible public benefits will be given by government decision-makers. The definition of a "public benefit," also known as a "public good," may be a matter of interpretation among politicians, government agency officials, and taxpayers. For example, most Americans would probably not agree that $19 billion per annum in foreign aid, a substantial portion of this aid in direct cash transfers to foreign governments, constitutes much of a "public good" to them. On the other hand, most Americans would probably agree that public expenditures for national defense, crime fighting, public education, housing, medical research, social security, public parks, and mass transportation seem more descriptive of a "public good." The concept of "cui bono" meaning "for whom is it good" is not always readily apparent in public policy. Public policy may not always directly benefit the general public.

## SYMBOLISM

A symbolic term essentially refers to any expression or sign commonly used to recall, typify, or represent an idea, thing or process. Persons having any interest in public policy formation should be aware of the symbolic words and phrases which attempt to portray, or perhaps conceal, what may be occurring.

Republican administrations under Richard Nixon, Ronald Reagan and George Bush appeared to have linked, or interchanged, the word "strategy" with "policy" at the national level on more than one occasion. This symbolism suggests that it could be more palatable in public relations terms for an administration to change its "strategy." A mere change in strategy infers a more fluid, tactical approach to problem-solving. This is more desirable to an administration than to frequently alter its "policy" or its "plan" which may appear to be more entrenched. The avoidance of the opposition's criticism to "waffle" on a policy, meaning to change or reverse a stated position, is a significant political consideration. An administration elected into office does not wish to appear weak, or lack vision and resolve in solving public problems. Politically inspired phrases such as: *stand firm, basically sound position, hold the course, opponent's flawed policy, political demagoguery, policy victory*, underscore the win/lose nature of U.S. politics in supporting a party's policies.

The definition of a successful policy, sometimes called a "winning policy" should be one that achieves its legitimate public goal within its approximate budget and timetable. There is a serious danger to the public when the symbolic winning policy is solely defined by public officials using the warrior mentality of winners and losers. The Republican party wins and the Democratic party loses or vice versa. The tendency of political parties to reject *not-invented-here* proposals suggests that a policy may not be evaluated solely on its potential public benefit. The political author is paramount! It is important politically that the sponsoring organization receive public credit for a successful policy. If the policy fails, the finger-pointing begins in an attempt to ensure that some person, political party, government agency, takes the responsibility and public criticism. Passage or amendment of a law, adoption of a government agency's regulation, inclusion of some special provision within an agency's administrative discretion, an improved organizational structure or procedure, a proposed change of po-

sition, are opportunities for new successes or failures in developing public polices.

Symbolic phrases or words such as: *policy reform, technical correction, technical rider, required amendment, promulgation, revised rule-making, modernization, restructuring, re-inventing, right-sizing, down-sizing, restoration, reconciliation, omnibus bill, harmonization, revenue enhancement, revenue neutral, user pay,* et al., characterize for the public's consumption what is meant to occur in public policy formation. Terms such as Roosevelt's "New Deal" in the 1930s, or Johnson's "Great Society" in the 1960s signaled a entire shift in national social policies. These terms were generally understood, if not entirely accepted, by the public. The national media will develop their own definitions of the latest terms which may not always agree with the views of their political authors. If the policy does not have a catchy working title, the media will fill that void.

Embarrassing political events and personalities are particularly rich material for inventive symbolism by the national media. Recent examples include: *Watergate, Irangate, Travelgate, Filegate, Welfare Queen, Tricky-Dicky (Nixon), Slick Willie (Clinton), Dole Man (Robert Dole), trust-gap,* and so it goes. The real meanings of symbolic terms may still be more political shorthand to insiders and pundits, than they are explanatory to the average person.

## SYMBOLISM IN DOMESTIC POLICY DEVELOPMENT

Recent examples of the importance of symbolic and pivotal words were the *National Energy Strategy* produced by the U.S. Department of Energy in 1992, and the *National Transportation Policy . . . Strategies for Action* (NTP) developed by the U.S. Department of Transportation (DOT) in 1990. Both were advertized as substantial policy initiatives by the Bush administration. Unfortunately, neither of these policy statements did particularly well in Congress, although they were developed with some rigor and public participation by their respective agencies. The statement on energy strategies was criticized by Democrats as not being sufficiently bold to meet the future energy requirements of the United States. The NTP fared somewhat better because it served as an agenda-setter for major transportation construction projects by the Bush administration.

The NTP promoted the passage of the Intermodal Surface Transportation and Efficiency Act of 1991 (ISTEA), also known as by its shorthand title of the "Highway Bill." This legislation was the most significant transportation legislation enacted since the Eisenhower administration built the U.S. Interstate System in the 1950s. The bill provided for the dispersion of an estimated $155 billion over five years from the U.S. Highway Trust Fund to all states for a variety of transportation-related projects. This included new construction, improvements to existing facilities, and demonstration projects. The term "demonstration project" was given some latitude in its interpretation.

Critics of the Highway Bill used the traditional symbolic nomenclature of "pork barrel" politics, while supporters preferred terms as a "comprehensive legislation," or "omnibus legislation." The final language of the bill, nearly 1000 pages, was developed by a Senate/House Conference Committee. The full text of the bill was not available until one hour before the final vote on 27 November 1991; however, conference aides developed a two-page outline which served as a guide to the Congress. In the House of Representatives, the congressional "debate" on $155 billion in expenditures took place between the hours of 4:00 AM and 6:00 AM on 27 November 1991. The Highway Bill passed overwhelmingly with 372 members voting for it and only 47 opposed.

Labor employment forecasts indicated that approximately 600,000 new jobs in construction and related fields would be produced as a result. President Bush seized the public relations initiative only briefly by hailing it as "the most important transportation bill" when he signed the bill on 18 December 1991. The significance of the legislation as a "jobs bill" was largely overlooked by the media and public because of the events of the Persian Gulf war. Unfortunately for the Bush team, the political initiative as a symbolic "jobs bill" was lost.

## Symbolism in Foreign Policy Development

Politically symbolic words and phrases used in developing government policies and actions are not limited to the domestic arena. They may also be used to denote a type of government scheme at work such as: *forward presence, global reach, strategy of deterrence, accommodation of diverse interests,* and *shuttle diplomacy.* A somewhat infamous and much overused symbolic word in the American political lexicon during the past thirty years was "detente." This is an adopted word of French origin, but it had nothing to do with the French as it is commonly used in American politics. At its core was the concept of limited disengagement between the superpowers of the former Soviet Union and the United States.

The concept of detente was pioneered by Leonid Brezhnev, general secretary of the Communist Party of the Soviet Union to promote peaceful co-existence with the United States. It was Brezhnev's desire to separate Soviet-U.S. relations from the events of the Vietnam War in 1968. This was not altruistic on the part of the Soviets since their strategy of disengagement was very self-serving. The Soviets envisioned that this era of peaceful co-existence could occur with the U.S. while the Soviet Union was attempting to increase and modernize its strategic military capability, pursue its "wars of national liberation," and neutralize its internal dissent.

Another significant goal of the Soviet version of detente was to improve its economy, particularly in consumer goods and agriculture. The policy of detente was a very ambitious policy initiative which had the potential of accruing long-term benefits for the Soviet Union. The Soviet policy of detente required the accommodation of the United States to negotiate how tensions might be eased.

This political initiative was embraced by President Nixon and his Assistant for National Security Affairs, Dr. Henry Kissinger. Kissinger's name became associated with the word "detente" when he served as head of the National Security Council (1969–73) and eventually as Secretary of State (1973–77). During his public career, Kissinger was very instrumental in shaping U.S. foreign policy. A positive U.S. response to the Brezhnev initiative was somewhat surprising since the principal goal of the Soviets, i.e. to promote class revolution and make the world communist, had not changed. During 1969, Nixon and Kissinger were seeking ways to ease tensions with the Soviets and most importantly at the time, to find a way to remove American forces from the Vietnam War. In short, they saw detente as a potential strategy to achieve limited U.S. goals. Nixon and Kissinger used the word to symbolically characterize the reason and the process of negotiation to end the cold war.

The reality of this vision was not shared by many average Americans and conservative members of the Republican party, namely Ronald Reagan, who remained suspicious and often critical of detente throughout his political career. In January of 1981, President Reagan commenting on the dangers of detente as the grand illusion. Reagan summed up the conservative views by stating ". . . so far, detente's been a one-way street that the Soviet Union has used to pursue it own aims."

President Nixon and General Secretary Brezhnev were able to negotiate some reductions in ballistic missiles (ICBMs) during the Strategic Arms Limitation Talks (SALT). The word "SALT" was the symbolic acronym of the treaty which was ratified by the U.S. Senate in 1972. The SALT negotiations produced some limited benefits on both sides, but the arms race continued. Although the SALT treaty expired in 1977, it continued to be observed as SALT II (second round) discussions were underway. President Carter and Brezhnev signed the second agreement, however the U.S. Senate would not ratify it. The entire detente process was discredited by the public, Congress, and many conservative Americans with the Soviet invasion of Afghanistan in 1979.

## DIFFERING INTERPRETATIONS OF A SYMBOL

A secondary goal of the Soviet's notion of detente, apart from the military, was to improve its economy through increased international trade principally in consumer goods and U.S wheat.

To accomplish this not only required a major shift in foreign policy for both countries, but also the development of some pragmatic methods of implementation. Since the Soviets did not have large sums of acceptable currencies to effect payment, they requested and received several concessions from the United States in creating a government-to-government trade agreement. This agreement ultimately required: special purchasing and payment arrangements based on international trading practices; direct loans; loan guarantees; and greatly improved access to U.S. ports by Soviet ships and aircraft. The Soviets realized that significant improvements in their own internal transportation and distribution structures would be essential. Some opponents of the agreement argued that the United States did not receive equivalent trade and transportation concessions from the Soviets to warrant the government-to-government trade deal.

The Soviets were seeking ways in which they could earn hard currencies in the international market. They chose maritime shipping and air transportation as two convenient methods which did not require the expenditure of large sums of money to enter the marketplace. They had the required technical abilities, but not the level of requisite commercial skills at the time.

An earlier U.S. wheat sale agreement with the Soviets under the Kennedy Administration in the 1960s had not been executed despite both governments reaching an accord on the general arrangements. President Kennedy gained political support for this change in foreign policy with the American Federation of Labor-Congress of Industrial Organizations (AFL-CIO). The AFL-CIO is a major coalition of labor unions which included both shore-based and sea-going maritime unions. The AFL-CIO was a strong supporter of President Kennedy and contributor to the Democratic party. As a condition of sale, the president specified that wheat shipments were to be made in *available* U.S. flag ships. American flag bulk cargo ships operating internationally are more expensive to use than their foreign flag counter-parts. These ships are employed only to carry cargoes which are owned, donated, or financed by the U.S. government. Large shipments of government-subsidized wheat to the Soviet Union on U.S. flag ships meant new sea-going union jobs and profits for American ship owners.

The wheat was to be supplied by grain companies in the United States, several of them foreign owned, who operated a core fleet of foreign flag ships. These grain companies immediately began to press the federal government for shipping waivers to relieve them of the obligation to use U.S. flag ships despite their availability. There was a great deal of sympathy by the U.S. State Department to grant shipping waivers to the US/USSR sales agreement which angered the maritime unions. The maritime unions believed that the U.S. government was not going to adhere to its maritime labor commitments as contained in the US/USSR wheat sales agreement. As a result, the International Longshoremen Union, an important component of the AFL-CIO at the time, refused to load *any* grain ships going to the Soviet Union and the sale did not materialize.

This situation exemplified the power of a major union to frustrate and alter U.S. foreign policy. Other than the U.S. exporters who lost the sale of the subsidized wheat to the Soviets, the actions of the U.S. longshoremen were praised by other unions and many Americans who distrusted detente.

Apparently, Dr. Kissinger and his State Department colleagues did not learn from recent history and the situation was nearly repeated a decade later in 1972. Under Kissinger's original agreement with the Soviets, no U.S. flag shipping provision was included. The President of the International Longshoremen Union, Teddy Gleason, ridiculed "Kissinger's detente" and the US/USSR wheat sale as against American interests. Gleason informed the federal government that no grain would move from a U.S. port to the Soviet Union unless there was a "deal" for U.S. seaman. This situation infuriated Kissinger, the State Department, and the Soviets. Gleason was clearly acting in the overall interests of the AFL-CIO since his union would be employed regardless of the flag of registry on the vessel to be loaded.

As a result of the longshoremen's ardent political stance, President Nixon approved further negotiations with the Soviets regarding the use of U.S. flag ships. On 14 October 1972, U.S. Secretary of Commerce Peter Peterson, and Minister of the Merchant Marine Timofey Guzhenko for the Soviet Union, signed an unprecedented government-to-government bi-lateral maritime agreement. In addition to opening several ports on both sides to the vessels of each nation, it called for U.S. and Soviet ships to carrying equal and substantial shares of cargo between the two nations. Substantial was defined as one-third of the total amount of yearly cargo. The balance would be for other flag vessels should they wish to compete. The ultimate result was that the U.S. taxpayers paid a substantial amount to subsidize the international wheat sale price, and the difference between the U.S. flag shipping rates to the Soviet Union and the world scale price of a similar service. Despite all the political rhetoric, American ships carried far less than the one-third portion as negotiated under the maritime agreement.

In addition to defending the U.S. goals of detente, the Nixon administration used the symbolic phrase of "American jobs" as a justification for the wheat and shipping subsidies. Perhaps the question of "cui bono" for whom is it good? . . . needed to be answered and conveyed to the public earlier in the decision process.

## OBSERVATIONS

Symbolic terms in the development and implementation of public policy at all levels of government is here to stay. The political history of the United States is rich with colorful examples of how certain symbolic words characterizing public policies may inspire Americans to take action, or garner their ridicule and distrust.

Persons who are interested in the development of public policies need to go beyond the symbolic shorthand used to describe them. Public policies must ultimately be evaluated in terms of their real outcomes, not rhetoric. For example, when is "reform" really a change in policy, procedure or structure? Is "reform" another way to carry on the same status quo under a different rubric, or is it really beneficial innovation?

This essay began with a little known quotation from a political figure of the Roman Republic, Cato the Censor. It simply suggests that politicians charged with making public policy seek the acclaim of the populous who are affected by these public policies. Because of this behavior, politicians may seek to express these policies in symbolic terms which are perceived to be agreeable, or at least tolerable, to the general public. In his time, Marcus Porcius Cato, was considered by many of his peers to be a Roman traditionalist who favored virtue and honesty. Cato served with distinction as military strategist, public administrator, politician, and scholar. Are these not desirable experiences for the political leaders of today?

# MISCH

NAME: _____
SECTION: _____
DATE: _____

1. What purposes does the term "symbolic" serve in Misch's article? What basic policy purposes do such devices promote?

   _____
   _____
   _____
   _____
   _____
   _____
   _____
   _____

2. Relate Machiavelli's article on the reputation of the prince to Misch's discussion of symbolism. Should rulers try to manipulate public opinion?

   _____
   _____
   _____
   _____
   _____
   _____
   _____
   _____

3. Compare and contrast American and Soviet goals in pursuing detente. In hindsight, was detente a good foreign policy? Defend your answer.

   _____
   _____
   _____
   _____
   _____
   _____

4. Compare and contrast Cato's quotation on Roman politicians to John Locke's discussion of the purposes of government. Should the ruler try to please the public with laws and policies?

5. Although symbolic sophistication may be a necessary skill, is rhetoric the true measure for the evaluation of policy? And if not, what is the true measure?

**Group Exercise:** Discuss the phrase: "Man is a political animal" and recast it in modern language to capture as many nuances as possible.

**Individual Project:** Locate and describe an article describing some symbolic political terminology that acts as a justification for special interest group subsidization.

# Comparative Public Policy: Environmental Policy in the United States and Germany

## Michael J. Baun

The comparative study of public policy yields many benefits. Using the comparative approach, we learn how the governments of different countries respond to similar policy problems, such as those presented by the economy, social welfare, and environmental degradation. Among other things, the knowledge gained from such comparison may prove valuable for improving the effectiveness of our own national policies. By focusing on the explanation of policy similarities and differences, the comparative approach also helps us understand the distinctive features of our own political system and those of other countries. Finally, as with the comparative study of politics in general, the comparative study of public policy provides us with a means of generating and testing specific hypotheses and theories about politics. This essay compares environmental policy in the United States and Germany. Although protection of the environment is a relatively new policy area, emerging only in the last two-three decades, it has become an important focus of government activity in all advanced industrial democracies. Increasingly in recent years, the environment has become an important policy issue at the global level as well. The United States and Germany are similar in that both are prosperous countries with relatively advanced environmental policies; both countries, it is generally agreed, have been environmental policy leaders. Nonetheless, there are also notable differences between the United States and Germany in this policy area. Through a comparative examination, we can better understand and explain these similarities and differences. The specific case of environmental policy also helps us understand broader differences in the political systems of the United States and Germany.

The next two sections of this chapter briefly examine, in respective fashion, the development of environmental policy in the United States and Germany since the 1960s. The third and final section draws some general comparative conclusions. Among the key factors affecting environmental policy development in the United States and Germany, it is argued, are national differences in political institutions and political culture.

## Environmental Policy in the United States

Environmental protection became an important issue in the United States in the 1960s. In this decade there was a dramatic upsurge of popular interest in the environment, fueled in part by the appearance of a number of influential books which alerted the public to environmental problems, such as Rachel Carson's *Silent Spring* in 1962 which warned about the dangers of the pesticide DDT. Also playing a role was a series of high-profile environmental accidents, including the 1969 oil platform explosion off the coast of Santa Barbara. A symbolic high-point for the new environmental movement was the first nation-wide "Earth Day" in April 1970. Responding to growing public concern about the environment, the federal government enacted several important new laws in the 1960s, including the Clean Air Act (1963), the Water Quality Act (1965), and the Endangered Species Conservation Act (1966).

Although not himself an environmentalist, Republican president Richard Nixon (1968–74) succumbed to political pressures and, in 1969, signed into law the National Environmental Policy Act.

The NEPA created the Council on Environmental Quality, a White House advisory body, and required all federal agencies to complete environmental impact statements on any government activity. In signing the Act, Nixon proclaimed the next ten years to be "the environmental decade." The following year Nixon created, by executive order, the Environmental Protection Agency (EPA), which would be the main instrument for implementing environmental policies and monitoring compliance with environmental regulations.

The early 1970s were a period of environmental policy activism. Among the new laws enacted at this time was the 1970 Clean Air Act, which set national air-quality standards that had to be met by certain deadlines and required that automobile producers limit pollution from engine emissions. Other important laws included the Water Pollution Control Act, the Marine Mammal Protection Act, and the Federal Environmental Pesticide Control Act, all enacted in 1972.

The oil shock of 1973–74 and subsequent recession brought to an end this burst of policy activism. During the Ford administration (1974–76), government attention focused mainly on restoring economic growth and combatting inflation. Economic hard times also increased the influence of groups opposed to environmental protection, including organized labor, farmers, and big business. By the late-1970s, a substantial backlash against the environmental movement had developed which championed economic interests and the market over environmental goals. This new environmental opposition, much of it centered on ranching, logging, and mining interests in western states, would play a particularly important role during the Reagan and Bush administrations.

Environmental policy enjoyed a brief resurgence of importance during the Carter presidency (1976–80). One area of action was the issue of toxic waste. In the wake of media coverage of the problems at Love Canal in New York, the Carter administration secured approval in 1980 of the so-called "Superfund," a special budget to pay for the cleanup of hazardous waste sites. Another Carter success was the Alaska Lands Bill (1980), which protected vast areas of wilderness in Alaska from economic development. Carter's efforts to ensure national energy independence also gave a temporary boost to energy conservation programs and the search for alternative energy sources.

The twelve-year period of the Reagan (1980–88) and Bush (1988–92) administrations, however, was a great setback for the environmental movement. With a primary commitment to deregulation and budget-cutting, the Reagan administration set out to virtually disembowel the federal government's environmental policy apparatus. Most symbolic of this intention was the appointment of noted anti-environmentalists to the key positions of Secretary of the Interior (James Watt) and EPA Administrator (Anne Gorsuch Burford). Both were eventually forced to resign in 1983; Watt because of his embarrassing outspokenness and Burford due to scandal and mismanagement. Their replacement by more respected professionals stopped the erosion of environmental progress in the remaining years of the Reagan presidency, but could not obscure the fundamental preference of this administration for the interests of business and industry over those of the environment.

The environmental policy situation improved only marginally under George Bush, despite his promise in the 1988 campaign to be "the environmental president." Bush got off on the right foot by appointing William Reilly, former head of the U.S. branch of the World Wildlife Federation, as EPA Administrator. Reilly's efforts were often undermined, however, by more conservative members of the White House staff, as well as by Vice President Quayle's Council on Economic Competitiveness, which assisted businesses in getting around EPA anti-pollution regulations. Bush administration actions also diluted federal policies aimed at protecting wetlands and endangered species, and opened federal lands to increased logging and mining. To its credit, the Bush administration did secure amendment of the Clean Air Act in 1990, which had been held up by Congressional gridlock since 1977.

Environmentalists hoped for much better days with the 1992 election of Democrat Bill Clinton. The Clinton administration was hobbled, however, by Republican control of Congress after 1994. Claiming they were elected with the mandate to pursue a "conservative revolution," Republicans in Congress sought to finish what the Reagan and Bush administrations had begun, by aggressively dismantling and rolling back a generation of environmental regulations. In the face of this attack the Clinton administration tried to hold ground, eventually reaping a windfall of public support for its efforts. Confronted by opinion polls showing that a great majority of Americans favored environmental protection even if it threatens jobs, many Republicans retreated from overt hostility to the environment and instead sought a middle ground. As the Clinton administration's second term began in late 1996, there was reason to hope for renewed environmental policy progress on the basis of bipartisan consensus.

# ENVIRONMENTAL POLICY IN GERMANY

In the Federal Republic of Germany, environmental issues first gained political importance in 1961, when the left-leaning Social Democratic Party (SPD) made reduced air pollution in industrial areas ("Blue skies over the Ruhr") an element of its electoral platform. It wasn't until the early 1970s, however, that environmental protection became a key focus of government policy. It was also about this time, somewhat later than in the United States, that a popular environmental movement began to emerge in Germany. At first this movement took the form mainly of localized citizen action groups, organized in ad hoc fashion to protest pollution from specific industrial plants or projects. By the mid-1970s, opposition to nuclear power became a dominant issue, and provided the catalyst for development of a truly nation-wide environmental movement.

Responding to growing environmental concerns among the German public, but also to developments in the United States and internationally, the Social Democrat-Free Democrat (FDP) coalition government of Chancellor Willy Brandt (1969–74) initiated a series of environmental policy initiatives. Key legislation included the 1970 "Emergency Program for the Environment," and 1972 laws on waste disposal and recycling and automobile and factory emissions. In 1974 the Federal Environment Agency was established, a body similar in purpose and design to the American EPA.

As in the United States and other advanced industrial countries, the economic effects of the 1973–74 oil crisis (in Germany economic stagnation and rising unemployment) led to a reduced priority for environmental goals. Instead, the SPD-FDP government of Chancellor Helmut Schmidt (1974–82) gave more attention to economics. The recession also allowed the unions and business interests, often in cooperation with each other, to more effectively mobilize opposition to environmentalist demands. An additional factor limiting the potential for environmental reform under the Schmidt government was the influence of the business-oriented FDP within the coalition. Although the FDP was only a small party, its governmental role was crucial since the SPD lacked a majority in parliament and therefore could not govern alone.

Despite its bias in favor of economic interests, the Schmidt government did produce some new environmental laws, including the "Waste Water Tax Law" (1976), the "Federal Nature Conservation Act" (1976), and the Chemicals Law (1980), although the latter was Germany's implementation of a European Community (EC) directive. Nevertheless, environmentalists complained that these laws were too weak, and that the government was not fully implementing existing environmental legislation.

Surprisingly, the switch to a more conservative, Christian Democrat-FDP coalition, government in 1982 did not produce a rollback of environmental policy similar to what was being attempted in the United States at this time under Reagan. Instead, the government of Chancellor Helmut Kohl (1982–present) has pursued a fairly progressive environmental policy course. One reason for this is the political success of the environmentalist Green Party. Established in 1980, the Greens first gained representation in the federal parliament in 1983. While the Greens have never held more than a small number of seats in parliament, their presence has helped keep environmental issues in the political spotlight, thereby exercising considerable influence over government policy and the positions of other parties. Also important has been the impact on public opinion of major environmental disasters, such as the May 1986 nuclear accident in Chernobyl (Ukraine), and later that year, the Rhine river chemical spill at Basel (Switzerland). In the 1980s, the emotional issue of Germany's "dying forests" also generated increased public support for environmental protection.

Under the Kohl government, much existing environmental legislation has been strengthened or updated, including laws pertaining to air and water quality and waste disposal and recycling. Germany has also taken a leadership role on environmental policy issues within the EC (since 1993 the European Union, E.U.) and at the global level. In April 1995, for instance, Germany hosted a major international conference on global warming in Berlin. In 1986, following Chernobyl, the Kohl government created a new cabinet-level Ministry for Environmental Protection. In 1994, revisions to Germany's constitution included the elevation of environmental protection to the status of an official state goal.

Two factors have greatly affected German environmental policy in the 1990s. The first of these is unification with East Germany in 1990, which simultaneously focused attention on the need for environmental cleanup in the east and generated new economic problems to overcome. The second is European integration. Especially since ratification of the Maastricht Treaty on European Union in 1993, German environmental policies are increasingly affected by the E.U. "Europeanization" tends to work in favor of German companies, since E.U. policies are often not as strict as German ones, and common E.U. environmental standards lessen competitive disadvantages for German companies which stem from German environmental laws. Unless Germany exerts its influence to push for tougher E.U. environmental regulations, however, the Europeanization of environmental policy could also lead to a reduction of environmental standards in Germany. For many environmentalists the fear is precisely this: that the German government will use the E.U. as a means for evading formidable domestic political barriers to a rollback of environmental regulations.

## COMPARING ENVIRONMENTAL POLICY IN THE UNITED STATES AND GERMANY

When it comes to environmental policy, the United States and Germany are similar in many ways. Both countries are advanced industrial democracies and demonstrate the strong link which exists between economic prosperity, the political salience of environmental issues, and high levels of environmental protection. In countries, although environmental movements took somewhat different shapes and followed different patterns of development, governments initiated environmental policies largely in response to growing popular pressures and concern about the environment.

In Germany and the United States as well, the progress of environmental policy was slowed or interrupted by the economic problems which followed the first oil shock in the mid-1970s, thus demonstrating the rule that in economic hard times, economic priorities tend to reassert themselves over environmental ones. In both cases, recessionary conditions enabled anti-environmental interests to more effectively mobilize their strength. In both countries the effectiveness of such groups was also enhanced by their privileged access to political leadership. In Germany, the Social Democratic Chancellor Schmidt was sympathetic to the needs of the trade unions and industry. In the United States, western ranchers, miners, and energy concerns had the ears of Presidents Reagan and Bush.

Both the United States and Germany also demonstrate, therefore, the important role of political leadership in environmental policy, although this can work in a positive as well as negative direction. In the United States, President Nixon went against his personal inclinations and initiated a wave of environmental legislation in the early 1970s. As an astute politician, Nixon was responding to rising popular concern about the environment and seeking to capitalize on this issue by playing an activist policy role. At about the same time in Germany, the reformist Chancellor Brandt was also launching a series of new environmental policy initiatives. In Germany since 1982 a much more conservative chancellor, Helmut Kohl, has favored continued environmental progress, for reasons which will be discussed below. In general terms, in both countries the course of environmental policy developments has been greatly influenced by the views and actions of executive leadership.

Despite these similarities, however, environmental policy in the United States and Germany also exhibits some important differences. Perhaps the most notable of these is the different trajectories of environmental policy in the two countries since the early 1980s. In the United States, trumpeting the values of economic growth and the market, the Republican Reagan and Bush administrations mounted a strong conservative counterattack against existing environmental regulations and policies. In Germany, by contrast, a conservative political turn after 1982 did not result in a similar attempted rollback. Instead, Germany became one of the most environmentally progressive countries in the world, at least as far as its government policies are concerned. Why the difference?

A major part of the answer to this question involves differences in national political institutions. In Germany, the combination of a fairly rigidified and closed (to new popular influences) party system and a modified proportional representation electoral system contributed to the emergence and success of the environmentalist Green Party. Frustrated by the inadequate response of the major political parties, especially the Social Democrats after 1974, environmental activists formed their own party and were able to gain seats in federal and state parliaments, aided by the rule that only five percent of the vote is required for parliamentary representation. The presence of the Greens in parliament (and in some state governments) since the early 1980s has been a key factor forcing the government and other political parties to address environmental issues.

Even the conservative Kohl government has not been able to ignore the strong environmental vote in Germany.

In the United States, by contrast, more open and flexible parties, especially the Democrats, rapidly absorbed environmental issues into their platforms. In addition, the majoritarian, "first-past-the-post" electoral system in the United States severely discriminates against small or third parties, making it almost impossible for an environmentalist party to establish itself. While a Green Party does exist in the United States, it has enjoyed only limited success at the local level. The absence of a politically significant Green party makes it easier for government and the larger parties to ignore environmental issues, or assign them a lesser priority in their attempts to aggregate a variety of different issues and interests.

Another institutional factor which differentiates environmental policymaking in the United States and Germany is the latter's membership in the E.U. Through the E.U., Germany has been able to reduce the negative competitive consequences of its domestic environmental policies by "Europeanizing" them; that is, by pushing for higher common environmental standards for the entire E.U. The United States, however, feels more directly the competitive consequences of its environmental policies since it is not part of such an integrative political community. This is even more the case with implementation of the North American Free Trade Agreement (NAFTA) in 1995, which exposes the United States to the competition of low-cost Mexican producers without supranational political structures that can impose common environmental standards. In the absence of such structures, the pressure to maintain competitiveness through a reduction of environmental regulations (and wages and social protection) is magnified.

In addition to institutional factors, there are political cultural reasons for the different course of environmental policy in the United States and Germany since the early 1980s. Scholars who have studied these two countries in a comparative fashion have long noted the difference between the more collectivist and "statist" political culture of Germany and the more individualist, anti-government political culture of the United States. The latter type of political culture favored an anti-environmental backlash in the United States in the 1980s, as part of a broader rejection of increased government regulation. In Germany, however, such anti-government feelings are not the norm, and the state is generally viewed as a useful and necessary social actor. Also, German conservatism is much more positively disposed towards government than its more libertarian American variant. Unlike its Republican counterpart in the United States, therefore, the Kohl government in Germany did not view a strong environmental policy role for the state to be in conflict with its conservative ideological beliefs.

## Conclusion

As this essay has attempted to demonstrate through a comparative examination of environmental policy in the United States and Germany, the comparative study of public policy is a useful way to illuminate policy similarities and differences between countries. Particularly in seeking to explain differences, we can identify factors which make countries unique and explain divergent national responses to similar problems and issues.

In the end, there are a number of factors which affect the development of public policy, including the nature and level of public demand for government action on a particular issue, the strategies and effectiveness of interest groups, and the economic and international political context of policymaking. Also important are the structure of political institutions, the role and effectiveness of executive leadership, and political culture. Through the comparative study of public policy, we can determine which factors are most influential in different countries, at different times, and in different policy areas. The comparative approach, therefore, helps us understand the unique features of different national political systems, while contributing to our broader theoretical knowledge of politics.

# BAUN

NAME: _____

SECTION: _____

DATE: _____

1. Describe how one group may benefit by studying another group's public policies. Do Aristotle and Machiavelli use this method? How?

2. Are there any common causal factors leading to the development of environmentally protective policies in Germany and the United States? If so, what are they and why would two countries have different reactions to them?

3. What are some of the trade-offs between technological development, economic competitiveness, and environmental protection? Compare Baun's article with the Allen article and the Walters and Blake article. Is there basic agreement among these authors?

4. Is there any relationship between the nature of a political party system, the governmental structure of a country, and its ability to support necessary policy innovation? If so, what are some of these relationships?

_____
_____
_____
_____
_____
_____
_____

5. If there is any common causality behind parallel development of environmental policies in America and Europe, do you think it will lead to more or less policy regulation in the future? Why?

_____
_____
_____
_____
_____
_____
_____

**Group Exercise:** Discuss the desirability of environmental policies. Then suggest ways in which you could change the political system of either Germany or the U.S.A. to effect your goals.

**Individual Project:** Locate and identify a professional journal article on environmental threats. Do these exist, and if so might they have significant political impact? What kind of impact?

*Chapter Nine*

# CONCLUSION

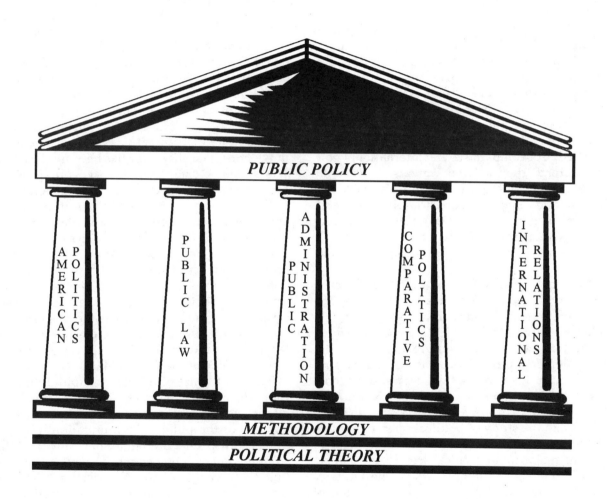

271

# Conclusion

It is important that students taking an introductory course in political science obtain some general sense of the nature of specialization within the academic discipline. Often students have no idea of the range of the field of study or of the variety of topics which political scientists explore. A course which is structured around the main subfields of political science specialization can provide students with the kind of understandings which they often develop in comparable introductory courses in sociology, economics, and psychology. For many reasons, introductory political science courses have focused on broad themes such as legislative power or the role of public opinion instead of on the various branches of the discipline. While students gain broad knowledge of comparative and international politics thereby, they are not conversant with the valuable contribution which political science as a field of study makes to American life in general. In particular, they often leave the introductory course with no sense of where the study of public administration or public and constitutional law fits in.

With these concerns in mind, *Political Science: An Overview of the Fields* has taken shape. The book offers readings in each of eight major subfields of study within political science. Moreover, the editors have put the subfields into an order that is depicted through the features of a classical building. In this way the field comes to life, conveys a sense of having undergone construction over time, and offers a sense of direction and purpose in the study of political science. As such the book can successfully introduce the field to persons majoring in political science and can accurately convey a picture both of the kinds of studies done and of the practical applications of the discipline to students seeking only a little exposure to the study of politics.

The picture of the classical building has meaning that extends beyond the individual features therein contained. Political theory and methodology constitute the foundation of the field of study. Students will become sensitive to the ways in which political philosophy animates the study of all key questions in political science. Hypotheses that guide the exploration of the other subfields are anchored in this foundation that stretches from ancient times to the late twentieth century.

The pillars cluster into two categories. The first cluster entails areas of study germane to the American setting. Articles on the field of American politics itself deal with both national and regional patterns. The writings on public law endeavor to demonstrate how the lifeblood of political relationships flows through the application of constitutional theory. The public administration pillar reminds us of the enormous growth of government since the 1930s and of how the management of public organizations in government and in the not-for-profit sector has become so critical. The second cluster includes two pillars which possess many points in common. In general, they pull Americans out the cocoon of self-absorption and demand attention to the outside world. The writings in the comparative politics chapter look at timely and important questions such as development, democratization, and representation in both developed countries and third-world settings. Essays in the international relations chapter center on critical issues such as the role of morality in world politics, the increasing impact of technology, and finally the implications for the foreign policy of the United States.

The last feature of the classical building is the roof which bears the label "public policy." Like all roofs it only maintains its position through the support of the pillars and foundation. Effective policies in specific human arenas flow naturally from theoretical perspectives as well as from detailed knowledge of the American and international settings. Like other roofs the policy subfield can also offer protection for all that is contained within the building. In this sense, policies offer protection, security, and safety nets from the randomness that potentially can harm any individual person. Through policy protection, persons are liberated for complete and successful lives that largely take place outside the political arena.

# BIBLIOGRAPHY

Advisory Commission on Intergovernmental Relations, (ACIR). (1984). *Regulatory Federalism, Policy, Process, Impact and Reform.* Wash. D.C.: The Advisory Commission of Intergovernmental Relations.

Allen, Lee M. (1988). Changing the Cultural Myth. In S. J. Curley (Ed.) *Living on the edge: Collected Essays on Coastal Texas.* College Station: Texas A&M University Press.

Allison, G., & Treverton, G. S. (Eds.). (1992). *Rethinking America's Security: Beyond Cold War to New World Order.* New York: W. W. Norton & Company.

Amacher, R. et al, *The Economic Approach to Public Policy.* Cornell University Press.

Amnesty International Report

Ancker, P. (1992). *IMAs Choose Quality: Citizen Airman.* Vol XLIV.

Appleby, P. (1950). *Morality and Administration in Democratic Government.* Baton Rouge: University of Louisiana Press.

Aristotle. (1905). *Politics* (Trans. Benjamin Jowett). Oxford: Clarendon Press.

Armstrong, B. (1975). *Texas Coastal Management Program: The*

Coastal Economy. Austin, Tx: General Land Office.

Babbie, Earl. (1992). The Practice of Social Research. 6th Edition. Belmont, CA: Wadsworth Publishing Co.

Barber, E. (1979). The Politics of Aristotle. New York: Oxford University Press.

Baum, Lawrence, (1989). The Supreme Court. Washington, D.C.: Congressional Quarterly.

Beer, Samuel H. (1981). "The Future of the States in the Federal System." In Peter Woll, ed. American Government: Readings and Cases. Boston: Little, Brown.

Behn, R. D. (1985). Policy Analysts, Clients, and Social Scientists. *Journal of Policy Analysis and Management, 4.*

Bork, Robert H. (1986). *Judicial Review and Democracy.* In

Encyclopedia of the American Constitution. Eds. Leonard W.

Levy, Kenneth L. Karst, and Dennis J. Mahoney. New York: Macmillian Publishing Company, pp. 1061–1064.

Bork, Robert H. (1996). *Slouching Towards Gommorah, Modern Liberalism and American Decline.* New York: Harper Collins Publishers Inc.

Bosner, C. (1992). *Total Quality Education?* Public Administration Review. Vol. 52, N. September/October. pp. 504–511.

Cable, Sherry, & Cable, Charles. (1995). *Environmental Problems: Grassroots Solutions.* NY: St. Martins Press.

Calvin, J. (1981). Institutes of the Christian Religion. In M. Curtis (Ed.) *The Great Political Theories.* New York: Avon, 249–262.

Campbell, A., Converse, P. E., Miller, W. E., & Stokes, D. E. (1976). *The American Voter.* Chicago: The University of Chicago Press.

Cannon, L. (1991). *President Reagan ... The Role of a Lifetime.* New York: Touchstone.

Caplan, N. (1976). Factors Associated With Knowledge Use among Federal Executives. *Policy Studies Journal, 4.*

Carson, R. (1962). *Silent Spring.* Boston: Houghton-Mifflin Co.

Carstsirs A. M. (1980). *A Short History of Electoral Systems.* Allen & Unwin. London.

Champney, Leonard. (1995). *Introduction to Quantitative Political Science.* New York: Harper Collins.

Chandler, R., and Plano J. (1982). *The Public Administration Dictionary.* John Wiley and Sons: New York.

Coffey, Peter. (1995). *The Future of Europe.* Brookfield, VT: Edward Elgar.

Comfort, N. (1995). *Brewer's Politics (rev. ed.).* Great Britian: Mackays of Chatham Ltd.

Corbin, L. (1993). *Reengineering: The Next Management Revolution.* Government Executive. Vol. 25. N. 9. September. pp. 26–33.

Cowan, L. (1986). Myth in the Modern World. In R. F. O'Connor (Ed.) *Texas Myths.* College Station: Texas A & M University Press.

Crowell, A. (1992). *Spirit of Change: Charleston Forges Ahead in Quality Revolution.* Citizen Airman. Vol XLIV. N. 1. February. pp. 3–5.

Curtis, M. (1981). *The Great Political Theories* (Vol. 1). New York: Avon.

Dahl, R. A., & Linblom, C. E. (1953). *Politics Economics, and Welfare.*

Dahl, R. A., (1958). Critique of the Ruling Elite Model. *American Political Science Review, 52.*

Deming, W. (1982). *Out of the Crisis.* Massachusetts Institute of Technology: Cambridge, Mass.

Deming, W. (1994). *The Government Learns About Quality in Japan: Transcript Recounts Deming's Presentation at 1980 GAO Roundtable.* Quality Progress. Vol 27, N. 3. March, pp. 39–46.

Doughty, R. (1986). From Wilderness to Garden: Conquering the Texas Landscape. In R. F. O'Connor (Ed.) *Texas Myths.* College Station: Texas A & M University Press.

Diamond, J. (1987, August). Soft Sciences Are Often Harder Than Hard Sciences. *Discover,* 34–39.

Dolbeare, K. (1974). The Impacts of Public Policy. In N. Cotter (Ed.) *The Policy Science Annual.* New York: Bobbs-Merrill.

Dye, T. R., & Zeigler, L. H. (1970). The Irony of Democracy. Belmont, CA.: Wadsworth.

Dunham, P. (1991). *Electoral behavior in the United States.* Englewood Cliffs, NJ: Prentice-Hall.

Easton, D. (1960). *The Political System.* New York: Alfred A. Knopf.

Easton, D. (1957). An Approach to the Analysis of Political Systems. *World Politics, 9.*

Easton, D. 1965. *A Framework for Political Analysis.* Englewood Cliffs, N.J.: Prentice-Hall.

Easton, D. (1965). *A System Analysis of Political Life.* New York: Wiley.

Edwards-Wilborn, L. (1992). *Reaching for Quality.* Citizen Airman. Vol XLIV. N. 1. February, p. 2.

Encyclopedia Britannica, Inc. (1992). *The New Encyclopedia* Britannica (15th ed.) (vol. 2). Chicago: Author.

Erikson, Robert S., Norman Luttbeg, and Kent L. Tedin. (1988). American Public Opinion: Its Origins, Content and Impact. 3rd Edition. New York: Wiley.

Etizoni, A. (1967). Mixed-scanning: A "third" Approach to Decision-making. Public Administration Review, 27.

Etizoni, A. (1968). *The Active Society: A Theory of Societal and Political Process.* New York: Free Press.

Eulau, H. (1963). *The Behavioral Persuasion in Politics.* New York: Random House.

Fagan, B. M. (1886). *People of the Earth: An Introduction to World Prehistory.* Boston: Little, Brown.

Fehrenbach, T.R. (1968). *Lone Star: A History of Texas and the Texans.* New York: Macmillian Publishing.

Fehrenbach, T.R. (1986). Texas Mythology: Now and Forever. In R. F. O'Connor (Ed.) *Texas Myths.* College Station: Texas A & M University Press.

Fisher, Louis. (1995). *American Constitutional Law.* New York: McGraw-Hill, 2nd ed.

Fraatz, J. M. B. (1982). Policy Analysts as Advocates. *Journal of Policy Analysis and Management, 1.*

Fry, B. & Mark, T. (1978). Some notes on the domain of public policy studies. *Policy Studies Journal, 6.*

Gallagher, M., Laver, M., & Mair, P. (1992). *Representative Government in Western Europe.* New York: McGraw-Hill.

Garson, D. G. (1973). Research on policy alternatives for America during the 1930s. *Political Inquiry, 1.*

Garson, D. G. (1978). *Group Theories of Politics.* Sage Publications.

Gant, M. M., & Luttbeg, N. R. (1991). *American Electoral Behavior: 1952–1988.* Itasca, IL: F. E. Peacock.

George, Stephen. (1991). *Politics and Policy in the European Community,* 2nd ed., London: Oxford University Press.

Gladden, E. N. (1972). *A History of Public Administration* (Vol. 1). London: Cass.

Glenny, Misha. (1992). *The Fall of Yugoslavia.* New York: Penguin.

Goetzmann, W. H. (1986). Keep the White Lights Shining. In R. F. O'Connor (Ed.) *Texas Myths.* College Station: Texas A & M University Press.

Gough, Ian. (1979). *The Political Economy of the Welfare State.* London: Macmillan Press, Ltd.

Gow, James. (1991). Deconstructing Yugoslavia, Survival 33, no.4 July/August, pp. 299–311.

Grodzins, Morton. (1961). *Centralizing and Decentralization in the American Federal System.* In Robert A. Goldwin, ed. *A Nation of States.* Chicago: Rand McNally: 1–3.

Grofman B. & Lijphart A. (eds) (1986) *Electoral Laws and Their Political Consequences.* Agathon Press: New York.

Grossman, Joel B. (1965). *Lawyers and Judges: The ABA and the Politics of Judicial Selection.* New York: John Wiley.

Grossman, Joel B., & Wells, R. S. (1988). *Constitutional Law and Judicial Policy-Making.* New York: Longman.

Grotius, Hugo. (1901). *The Rights of War and Peace* (Trans. A. C. Campbell). New York: M. W. Dunne.

Habermas, Jurgen. (1975). *Legitimation Crisis.* Boston: Beacon Press.

Hacker, Barton C. (1981). *Robert H. Goddard and the Origins of Space Flight* in Technology in America : A History of Individuals and Ideas by Carroll W. Pursell, Jr. ed. Cambridge, Mass: The MIT Press.

Hall, Kermit L.,ed. (1992). *The Oxford Companion to the Supreme Court of the United States.* New York and Oxford: Oxford University Press.

Hamilton, Alexander; Madison, James; Jay, and John. (1961). *The Federalist Papers.* New York: Mentors Books.

Harmon, M. J. (1964). *Plato Thought: From Plato to the Present.* New York: McGraw-Hill.

Harrigan, S. (1988, Oct.). Worked to Death. *Texas Monthly.*

Hastedt, Glenn P. (1997). *American Foreign Policy: Past, Present, Future.* Upper Saddle River, New Jersey: Prentice-Hall.

Heine, I.M. (1980). *The U.S. Maritime Industry . . . In the National Interest.* Washington, DC: National Maritime Council.

Hitler, A. (1963). Mein Kampf. In J. Somerville & R. E. Santoni (Eds.) *Social and Political Philosophy.* New York: Doubleday-Anchor, 441–462.

Hoff, J. (1994). *Nixon Reconsidered.* New York: Basic Books.

Horowitz, I., & Katz, J. (1975). *Social Science and Public Policy in the United States.* New York: Praeter.

House, P. W., & Shull, R. D. (1988). *Rush to Policy.* New Brunswick, N.J.: Transaction.

Hobbes, T. (1987). *Leviathan* (C. B. MacPherson, Ed.). New York: Penguin Classics. (Original work published 1651).

Jamieson, K.H. (1984). *Packaging the Presidency.* New York: Oxford University Press.

Janda, K., Berry, J. M., & Goldman, J. (1994). *The Challenge of Democracy: Government in America* (Brief, 2nd ed.). Boston: Houghton-Mifflin.

Jenkins-Smith, H. C. (1982). Professional roles for policy analysts: A critical assessment. *Journal of Policy Analysis and Management,* 88.

Jennings, M.Kent and Richard G. Niemi. (1968). The Transmission of Political Values from Parent to Child. American Political Science Review 62: 169–184.

Jensen, R. (1969). History and Political Science. In S. M. Lipset,(Ed.), *Politics and the Social Sciences.* New York: Oxford, 1–28.

Johnson, Loch. (1991). *America as a World Power: Foreign Policy in a Constitutional Framework.* St. Louis: McGraw-Hill, Inc.

Jordan, A. A., Taylor, W. J., Jr., & Korb, L. J. (1993).*American National Security: Policy and Process* (4th ed.). Baltimore: Johns Hopkins University Press.

Kaplan, M. (1957). *Systems and Process in International Politics.* New York: John Wiley & Sons.

Kaplan, Robert. (1993). *Balkans Ghosts,* New York: St. Martin's Press.

Kaufman, L. (1993). *The U.S. Forest Service: Decentralizing Authority.* Government Executive. Vol. 25. N. 3. March. pp. 23–24.

Kegley, C. W., Jr., & Wittkopf, E. R. (Eds). (1988). *The Global Agenda: Issues and Perspectives* (2nd ed.). New York: Random House.

Kunreuther, R. (1993). *Manner-of-performance Standards Bring Performance Appraisal into Line with TQM."* Government Executive. Vol. 25. N. 7. July. pp. 43–44.

Ladd, E. C. (1993). The American Polity: *The People and Their Government* (5th ed.). New York: W. W. Norton.

Langton, Kenneth P. and David A. Karns. (1969). "The Relative Influence of the Family, Peer Group, and School in the Development of Political Efficacy." Western Political Quarterly 22: 813–826.

Levine, H. (Ed.). (1983). *World Politics Debated: A Reader in Contemporary Issues.* New York: McGraw-Hill.

Lijphart A. (1994). *Electoral Systems and Party Systems.*

New York. Oxford University Press.

Lipset, S. M. (1993). The Significance of the 1992 Election. *PS: Political Science and Politics,* 26, 7–16.

Lasswell, H. D. (1941). *Democracy Through Public Opinion.*

Lasswell, H. D. (1956). *The Decision Process.* College Park, Md.: Bureau of Governmental Research, University of Maryland.

Lasswell, H. D. and Lerner, Daniel. (1951). *The Policy Sciences.* Palo Alto, Ca.: Stanford University Press.

Lasswell, H. D. (1963). *The Future of Political Science.* Atherton Press.

Lasswell, H. D. (1971). *A Preview of Policy Politics.* Elsevier.

Latham, E. (1965). *The Group Basis of Politics.* New York: Octagon Books.

Lemann, N. (1986). Power and Wealth. In R. F. O'Connor (Ed.) *Texas Myths.* College Station: Texas A & M University Press.

Lemonick, M. D. (1994, Ap.). Too Few Fish in the Sea. *Time*

Lerner, A. and Wanant, J. (1992). *Public Administration: a Realistic Reinterpretation of Contemporary Management.* Prentice-Hall: Englewood Cliffs, NJ.

Lewis, C. (1977). *The Treasures of Galveston Bay.* Waco: Texian Press.

Lieber, Robert J. (1997). *Eagle Adrift: American Foreign Policy at the End of the Century.* New York: Longman.

Linblom, C. (1959). The Science of "Muddling Through." *Public Administration Review, 19.*

Linblom, C., & Braybrooke, D. (1963). *The Strategy of Decision.* New York: Free Press.

Linblom, C. (1964). *The Intelligence of Democracy.* New York: Macmillan.

Linblom, C. (1968). *The Policy-making Process.* Englewood Cliffs, N.J.: Prentice-Hall.

Linblom, C. E. (1980). *The Policy-making Process* (2nd ed.). Englewood Cliffs, N.J.: Prentice-Hall.

Linden, E. (1994, March). Tiger, Tiger, Fading fast. *Time,143.*

Lippman, W. (1955). *Essays in the Public Philosophy.* Boston: Little, Brown.

Locke, John. (1823). *The Works of John Locke*, Vol. 5. London: Thomas Tegg.

Lodge, Juliet, ed. (1993). *The European Community and the Challenge of the Future*, 2nd ed., New York, NY: St. Martin's Press.

Loomis, L. R. (1943). *Aristotle on Man in the Universe.* Roslyn, N. Y.: Classics Club.

Lowi, T. (1967). The public philosophy: Interest group liberalism. *The American Political Science Review, 61.*

Locke, J. (1960). *Two Treatises of Government* (P. Laslett, Ed.). New York: Cambridge University Press. (Original work published in 1689).

Luther. (1981). Secular authority: To what extent it should be obeyed, 1523, and An open letter concerning the hard book against the peasants. In M. Curtis (Ed.) *The Great Political Theories.* New York: Avon, 238–249.

Lynch, T. (1990). *Public Budgeting in America.* 3d ed. Prentice-Hall: Englewood Cliffs, NJ.

Machiavelli, N. (1908) *The Prince.* (Trans. W. K. Marriott). New York: E. P. Dutton & Co.

Machiavelli, N. (1952). *The Prince.* trans. Christian Gauss. New York: Mentor.

Mackie T. T., & Rose. R. (1991). *The International Almanac of Electoral History.* London. Macmillan, 3rd ed.

MacRae, D. Jr. (1977). The social function of social science. *Policy Studies Review Annual.*

Madison, James. (1901). Federalist 10 and Federalist 51. In *The Federalist: A Commentary on the Constitution of the United States: Being a Collection of Essays Written by Alexander Hamilton, James Madison, and John Jay.* (Intro. E. Gaylord). Washington, D.C.: M. W. Dunne.

Marks, J. (1994, January 10). Remembrance of Things Past. *U. S. News & World Report*, pp. 28–35.

March, J., & Simon, H. (1958). *Organizations.* New York: Wiley.

March, J. (1955). An Introduction to the Theory of Measurement Influence. *The American Political Science Review, 49.*

Mason, Alpheus T., and Stephson, Donald G., Jr. (1993). *American Constitutional Law.* Englewood Cliffs, N.J.: Prentice-Hall, 10th ed.

Meadows, Donelia H., Meadows, Dennis L., Randers, Jorgen, Behrens III, William W. (1972). *The Limits to Growth: A Report for the CLUB OF ROME'S Project on the Predicament of Mankind.* New York, NY: Universe Books.

Meier, Kenneth J. and Jeffrey L. Brudney. (1993). *Applied Statistics for Public Administration.* 3rd Edition. Belmont, CA: Wadsworth Publishing Company.

Meltsner, A. J. (1976). *Policy Analysts in the Bureaucracy.* Berkeley: University of California Press.

Merriam, C. (1945). *Systematic Politics.* University of Chicago Press.

Mizaur, D. (1992). *Quality: Moving with Glacial Speed.* Government Executive. October. p. 69.

Moravcsik, Andrew. (1993). *Negotiating the Single European Act: National Interests and Conventional Statecraft in the European Community.* International Organization 45, no. 1: 19–56.

Morison, Elting E. (1977). *From Know-How to Nowhere: The Development of American Technology.* New York: New American Library.

Murphy, W. F. (1964). *Elements of Judicial Strategy.* Chicago: University of Chicago Press.

Nagel, S. (1969). *The Legal Process from a Behavioral Perspective.* Homewood, Il.: Dorsey Press.

Nelson, M. (1979). What's Wrong with Political Science. In C. Peters & N. Lemann, (Eds.), *Inside the System* (4th ed.). New York: Holt, Rinehart & Winston, 267–275.

Newcomb, W. H. Jr. (1986). Harmony with Nature, People, and the Supernatural. In R. F. O'Connor (Ed.) *Texas Myths.* College Station: Texas A & M University Press.

Nice, David C. (1987). *Federalism: The Politics of Intergovernmental Relations.* New York: St. Martin's Press.

Nie, N. H., Verba, S., & Petrocik, J. R. (1976). *The Changing American Voter.* Cambridge, MA: Harvard University Press.

O'Conner, James. (1973). *The Fiscal Crisis of the State.* Ny: St. Martin's Press.

Osborne, D. (1992). "Why Total Quality Management is only Half a Loaf." Governing. August. pp. 65.

Peltason, J. W. (1955). *Federal Courts in the Political Process*. Garden City, N.J.: Doubleday Short Studies in Political Science.

Peltason, J. W. (1961). *Fifty-Eight Lonely Men*. Urbana, Il.: University of Illinois Press.

Peterson, M. D. (Ed.) (1977). *The Portable Thomas Jefferson*. New York: Penguin Books.

Plato. (1914). Meno. In *Plato: With an English Translation* (Trans. Harold North Fowler). New York: G. P. Putnam's Sons.

Pohlman, H.L. (1995). *Constitutional Debate in Action: Governmental Powers*. New York: Harper Collins College Publishers.

Polishook, I. H. (1967). *Roger Williams, John Cotton and Religious Freedom*. Englewood Cliffs, N.J.: Prentice-Hall.

Popenoe, David. (1996). "A World Without Fathers." The Wilson Quarterly 20:12–29.

Portis, E. B. (1994). *Reconstructing the Classics: Political Theory from Plato to Marx*. Chatham, N.J.: Chatham House.

Prague, J. D. (1968). *Voting Patterns of the United States Supreme Court: Cases in Federalism 1889–1959*. New York: Bobbs-Merrill Company.

Pye, L. (1966). *The Concept of Political Development*. Boston: Little Brown.

Quade, E. (1977). Analysis for public decisions. *Policy Studies Review Annual*.

Rae. D. W. (1984). *The Political Consequences of Electoral Laws*. New Haven. Yale University Press.

Rago, W. (1994). *Adapting Total Quality Management (TQM) to Government: Another Point of View*. Public Administration Review. Vol. 54, N. 1. January/February. pp. 61–64.

Ranney, A. (Ed.). (1963). *Essays on the Behavioral Study of Politics*. Urbana, Il.: University of Illinois Press.

Reagan, R. (1990). *An American Life . . . Ronald Reagan . . . The Autobiography*. New York: Simon & Schuster.

Reeve A. and Ware A. (1992). *Electoral Systems: A Comparative and Theoretical Introduction*. Routledge, New York.

Reeves, Mavis Mann. (1990). *The States as Polities: Reformed, Reinvigorated, Resourceful*. The Annals of the American Academy of Political and Social Science 509 (May): 83–93.

Rodick, Burleigh Cushing. (1953). *American Constitutional Custom: A Forgotten Factor in the Founding*. New York: Philosophical Library.

Rohde, D. W., & Spaeth, H. J. (1976). *Supreme Court Decisionmaking*. San Francisco: W.H. Freeman & Company.

Rose, Richard. (1996). *What is Europe?* New York, NY: Harper-Collins.

Rosenbloom, D. (1993). *Public Administration: Understanding Management, Politics, and Law in the Public Sector*. Third edition. New York: McGraw-Hill, Inc.

Rosenbloom, D., Goldman, D., and Ingraham, P. (1994). *Contemporary Public Administration*. New York: McGraw-Hill, Inc.

Rosholt, R. L. (1966). *An Administrative History of NASA*. Washington: National Aeronautics and Space Administration.

Ross, R. S. (1993). *American National Government: Institutions, Policy, and Participation* (3rd ed.). Guilford, CT: Dushkin.

Rourke, J. T. (1989). *International Politics on the World Stage* (2nd ed.). Sluice Dock, Guilford, Connecticut: Dushkin.

Russel R. B. and Muther J.E. (1958). *A History of the United Nations Charter*. Washington, D.C.: Congressional Quarterly Press.

Rutland, Robert A., ed. (1994). *James Madison and the American Nation, 1751–1836: An Encyclopedia*. New York: Simon and Schuster.

Sabatier, D. & Mazmanian, P. (1980). The Implementation of Public Policy: A Framework of Analysis. *Policy Studies Journal*.

Sabine, G. H. (1961). A History of Political Theory (3rd ed.). New York: Holt, Rinehart, & Winston.

Sandholtz, Wayne and John Zysman. 1992:Recasting the European Bargain. World Politics 42, (Oct. 1989): 95–128.

Sarkesian, S. C. (1989). *U.S. National Security: Policymakers, Processes, and Politics*. Boulder: Lynne Rienner Publishers.

Scammon, R. M., & McGillivray, A. V. (1991). *America Votes 19*. Washington: Congressional Quarterly.

Schloming, G. C. (1991). *Power and Principle in International Affairs*. Washington, D. C.: Harcourt Brace Jovanovich.

Schnaiberg, Allan, & Watts, Nicholas, & Zimmerman, Klaus, eds. (1986). *Distributional Conflicts in Environmental-Resource Policy*. Aldershot, England: Gower Pub. Com.

Schnaiberg, Allan, & Watts, Nicholas, & Zimmerman, Klaus, eds. (1994). *Environment and Society: The Enduring Conflict*. Allan, NY: St. Martin's Press.

Schubert, G. A. (1960). *Constitutional Politics*. New York: Holt, Rinehart & Winston.

Schubert, G. A. (1965). *Judicial Policy-making*. Chicago: Foresman.

Schwartz, Bernard. (1993). *A History of the Supreme Court*. New York and Oxford: Oxford University Press.

Schwartz, Bernard. (1992). *The Great Rights of Mankind—a History of the American Bill of Rights*. Madison, Wisconsin: Madison House Publishers, Inc.

Scott, R. & Shore, A. (1979). *Why Sociology Does Not Apply: A Study of the Use of Sociology in Public Policy*. Elsevier.

Seidelman, R. (1985) *Disenchanted Realists*. Albany: State University of New York Press.

Seneca. (1981). Stoic Philosophy. In M. Curtis (Ed.), *The Great Political Theories* (Vol.1). New York: Avon, 106–113.

Sensenbrenner, J. (1991). *Quality comes to city hall*. Public Administration\the Annual Editions Series. Political Science Department, Southwest Texas State University. The Dushkin Publishing Group, Inc., Sluice Dock, Cn: pp. 123–128. Reprinted from the Harvard Business Review. March/April.

Shon, Louis B. (1965). *Cases on the United Nations Law*. Brooklyn: State University.

Shoop, T. (1993). *Headlong into Quality*. Government Executive. Vol. 25. N. 3. March. pp. 19–21.

Shoop, T. (1993). *IRS Leading the Way*. Government Executive. Vol. 25. N. 3. March. pp. 22–24.

Simon, H. (1952). Comments on the Theory of Organizations. *The American Political Science Review*, 46.

Simon, H. (1957). *Models of Man: Social and Rational*. New York: Wiley.

Singer, Max, and Aaron Waldovsky. *The Real World Order: Zones of Peace, Zones of Turmoil*. Chatman, N.J.: Chatman House Publisher, Inc.

Snow, D. M. (1987). *National Security: Enduring Problems of Defense Policy*. New York: St. Martin's Press.

Snow, D. M., and Brown, E. (1997). *Beyond the Water's Edge: An Introduction to U.S. Foreign Policy*. New York: St. Martin's Press.

Sómit, A., & Tanenhaus, J. (1967). *The Development of American Political Science*. Boston: Allyn & Bacon.

Spaeth, H. J. (1965). *An Introduction to Supreme Court Decision-making*. San Francisco: Chandler Publishing Company.

Spaeth, H. J. (1979). *Supreme Court Policy-making: Explanation and Prediction*. San Francisco: W.H. Freeman and Company.

Starling, G. (1982). *Managing the Public Sector*. Homewood, Il.: Dorsey Press.

*Statement of Argentina*. In United Nations Doc. A/37/PV.51 (Nov. 2, 1982).

Steiner, J. (1991). *European Democracies* (2nd ed.). New York: Longman.

Stone, Christopher. (1975). *Where the Laws Ends*. NY: Harper Torchbooks.

Swiss, J. (1992). *Adapting Total Quality Management*. Public Administration Review. Vol. 52, N. 4. July/August. pp. 356–362.

Swiss, J. (1991). *Public Management Systems*. Prentice-Hall: Englewood Cliffs, NJ.

Taagepera A., & Shugart, M.S. (1989). *Seats and Votes: The Effects and Determinants of Electoral Systems*. Yale University Press.

Talbott, Strobe. (1996). *Democracy and the National Interest*. Foreign Affairs, 75. November/December. pp. 47–63.

Taylor, F. (1987). *The Principles of Scientific Management*. In J. Shafritz & J. Ott (EDS). Classics of Organization Theory. 2nd ed. Chicago: Dorsey. pp. 66–81.

Theodorson, George A., and Theodorson, Achilles C. (1969). *A Modern Dictionary of Sociology*. New York: Harper & Row.

Tocqueville, A. *Democracy in America* (Vol. 1). New York: Mentor Books.

Tong, R. 1986. *Ethics in Public Policy*. Englewood Cliffs, N.J.: Prentice-Hall.

Toufexis, A. (1988, Au.). Our Filthy Seas. *Time*.

Townsend, P., and Gebhardt, J. (1986). *Commit to Quality*. New York: John Wiley and Sons.

Tribe, L. (1972). Policy Science: Analysis or Ideology? *Philosophy and Public Affairs*, 2.

Truman, D. (1951). *The Governmental Process*. New York: Knopf.

Truman, D. (1968). The Social Sciences and Public Policy. *Science*.

United Nations General Assembly Resolution (GA Res) 95 (I).

United Nations Security Council Resolution (SC Res.) 660, August 2, 1990, in 29 *International Legal Material*, 1325 (1990).

U.S. Department of Energy (1991). *National Energy Strategy . . . Powerful Ideas for America*. (Stock No. 061-00-00754-7). Washington DC: U.S. Government Printing Office.

U.S. Department of Transportation. (1993). *Carrying Forward National Transportation Policy*. Washington, DC.

U.S. Department of Transportation, Federal Highway Administration (1993). *Intermodal Surface Transportation Efficiency Act . . . FHWA Stewardship 1992 Putting ISTEA Into*

*Motion* (Pub. No. FHWA-PL-93-013, HPP-20/2-93[10M]E). Washington, DC.

Waldo, D. (1952). Development of a Theory of Democratic Administration. *The American Political Science Review*,46.

Walters, J. (1992). "The Cult of Total Quality." Governing. May. pp. 38–42.

Wengert, N. (1955). *Natural Resources and the Political Struggle*. New York: Doubleday.

Whitehurst, C.H. Jr. (1983). *The U.S. Merchant Marine . . . In Search of an Enduring Maritime Policy*. Annapolis, MD: United States Naval Institute.

Whiteman, Marjorie M. (1963–1973). *Digest of International Law*. Washington D.C.: U.S. Government Printing Office, Vol. 2.

Wildavsky, A. (1962). *Dixon-Yates: A Study in Power*.

Wildavsky, A. (1979). *The Politics of the Budgetary Process*. Boston: Little, Brown.

Wildavsky, A. (1979). *Speaking Truth to power: The Art and Craft of Policy Analysis*. Boston: Little, Brown.

Williams, P., Goldstein, D. M., & Shafritz, J. M. (Eds). (1994). *Classic Readings of International Relations*. Belmont, Ca.: Wadsworth.

Wilson, L. and Durant, R. (1994). Evaluating TQM: the Case for a Theory Driven Approach. Public Administration Review. Vol. 54, N. 2. March/April. pp. 137–145.

Wood, David M., and Yesilada, Birol A. (1996). *The Emerging European Union*. New York, NY: Longman Publishers USA.

Wright, Quincy. (1962). *The Goa Incident*. 56 American Journal of International Law (AJIL), pp. 617.

Ulmer, S. S. (Ed.). (1961). *Introductory Readings in Political Behavior*. Chicago: Rand-McNally.

Viguerie, R. A. (1981). *The New Right: We're Ready to Lead*. Falls Church, Va.: The Viguerie Company.

Volti, Rudi. (1995). *Society and Technological Change*. New York: St. Martin's Press. 3rd Ed.

Von Damm, H. (1976). *Sincerely, Ronald Reagan*. Falls Church, Va.: Green Hill.

Von Glahn, Gerhard. (1992). *Law Among Nations: An Introduction to Public International Law*. New York: Macmillan Publishing Company.

Wasby, S. L. (1970). *The Impact of the United States Supreme Court: Some Perspectives*. Homewood, Il.: Dorsey Press.

Wolfe, Alan. (1977). *The Limits of Legitimacy: Political Contradictions of Contemporary Capitalism*. NY: Free Press.

Yates, D. Jr. (1985). *The Politics of Management*. San Francisco: Jossey-Bass.

# INDEX

## A

Abortion, 80
Act of Settlement, 75
*Adair v. United States*, 127
Adam's Fall, and knowledge of good and evil, 20
Administration, public, 145–174
AFL-CIO, 260
Africa, 193–200
    history of economy, 194
    history of politics, 194
    implementation of economic development, 194–195
    regime change, 196
African Americans, and income, 91–92
Air Force Combat Command (ACC), 171
Alaska Lands Bill, 264
Albania, 26
Aldinger, Robert T., 167–174
Allen, Lee M., 55–62, 247–254
American Bar Association, 59
*American Electoral Behavior* (Luttbeg and Gant), 88
American Political Science Association, vii, 32, 34
American politics, 65–104
*American Voter* (Campbell), 87
*Analyzing the Causes of Revolution* (Aristotle), 240–246
Anti-Federalists, 79
Anti-Semitism, 24
*Antigone* (Sophocles), 76
Aquinas, St. Thomas, hierarchy of laws, 19
Argyle, Nolan J., 19–28, 30–38
Aristotle, 4–8, 31–32, 178–182, 240–246
    *Analyzing the Causes of Revolution*, 240–243
    Athens, 242
    and causation, 31
    citizen as member of community, 5, 179
    consitutions, types of, 178–180
    crafts, of inferiors, 6
    distinction between master and slave, 6
    elements of states, 179
    force and fraud, revolution by, 242
    king, vs. statesman, 4
    and man as political animal, 255
    and oligarchy, 178, 240–242
    and political theory, vii
    *Politics*, 178–180, 247
    revolution, threat of, 240–243
    ruler, virtue of, 5, 242–243
    state, as community, 4
    tyranny, 5–6
    "Varieties of the Main Types of Constitutions," 178–182
    voice, gift to man, 4
Article I, Section 6 (of U.S. Constitution), 79
Article III, 80
Article VI, 138
Articles of Confederation, 137
Aspin, Les, 232
Atom bombs, 154
Australia, House of Representatives, 203

## B

Balkans, 26
Bamfo, Napoleon, 193–200
Baun, Michael J., 263–270
Behavioralism, and political methods, 34–35
Behavioralists, 114
Bible, 22, 211
Bickel, and deference to legislative process, 132
Bill of Rights, 81, 162
Blackmun, Justice, 114
Blake, David H., 223–228
"Blessing of liberty," 159
Block grants, 99–100
Bolingbroke, 75–76
Bonaparte, Napoleon, 78
Bork, Robert, 141
Bosnia, 26
Brandeis, Justice, 78–79
Brandt, Willi, 266
Brennan, William, 114–116
Brezhnev, and SALT, 259
British political parties, 88
*Buckley v. Valeo*, 78
Burger, Warren, 141
Bush, George, 87
    Bush administration, 257
    and environmental issues, 264
    and foreign policy, 232
    and language, 256
    and New Federalism, 100

## C

Calvin, and theocracy, 20–21
Calvinist model, 22–23
Cardozo, Benjamin, 130
Carson, Rachel, 263
Carter, Jimmy, 91–92
    and environmental policy, 264
    as Southerner, 93
Catholic, and voters, 92
Cato, 255, 260
Causation, and Aristotle, 31
Chamberlain, Houston Stewart, 24–25
Champney, 48
Chernobyl, 265
Chirac, Jacques, 188
Christian right, 22
Christianity, and Reagan, 22
Christopher, Warren, 232
Church, as unifying force, 23
Citizen, nature of good, 5–6
*Civil Rights Cases*, 140
Civil War, and advent of Industrial Age, 140
Clean Air Act, 263, 264
Clinton, Bill, 87–88
    and Bork, 142
    and Democratic party, 92
    and enlargement of world economy, 230
    and environmentalists, 264
    and fiscal policy, 100
    and New Federalism, 100
    second election, 91
    as Southerner, 93
    and Whitewater, 90
CNN, and Gulf War coverage, xii
Coalition government, 205
Code of Justinian, 113
Coke, Justice, 76
Cold War, 229–233
*Commentaries* (Story), 78
Commerce Clause, 118
Commission of the European Communities, 187
Committee of Regions, of European Union, 187
Common-law rules, and English feudalism, 126
Communist party, 88
Community, citizen as member of, 5
Compact Theory, 19–23
    and nature of state, 19–23
Comparative politics, 177–208
"Concerning the Secretaries of the Prince" (Machiavelli), 146–147
*Congress and Its Members* (Davidson and Oleszek), 89
Congressional hearings, and public adlministration, 153
Conservation, and population growth, 251
Constitution (U.S.), preamble, 20
Constitution, interpretation of, 113–122
    judicial decision making, 117–119
    Meese-Brennan debate, 114–116
    objectivism, 113–114
    subject/object dichotomy, 113
    subjectivism, 114, 116–117
Constitutional setting, 75–86
    elements of constitutionalism, 75–77
    implied powers, 81–83
    separation of powers, 77–81
Constitutionalism, elements of, 75–77
    Friedrich, 77
    modern views, 77
    Sutherland, 77
Continental Congress, 79
Contingency view, 35–36
Contingency, and law, 123–136
    classical legal consciousness, 125–127
    modern reconstruction, 129–133
    pre-classical consciousness, 123–125
    realist challenge, 127–129
Cooperative federalism, 98
*Coppage v. Kansas*, 126–127
Cotton, 22
Council of the European Union, 186
Creative federalism, 99–100
Croatia, 26

## D

Dayton Agreement, 232
DDT, 263
De Gaulle, Charles, 184
De Gobineau, Count Arthur, 24–25
Declaration of Independence, and Locke, 76
Deductive reasoning, ix
Defense Department, cutback proposals, 232
Deming's fourteen points of TQM, 169–170
Democracy
    and Aristotle, 178, 240
    forms of, 180
Democratic reform, in Africa, 193
Democrats, and party identification, 50, 87
Department of Energy, 257
Developed nations, technology in, 223–228
*Dictionary of legal terms*, 57
Dole, Bob, 87, 88, 97
Dole, Elizabeth, 87
Domestic fields, 63–174
Domestic policy development, 257–258
*Downward Spiral* (Sandbrook and Baker), 195
Dr. Bonham's Case of 1610, 76
Dual federalism, 97–98

Due process of law, 75, 162
Dynasty, defined, 180

# E

Earth Day, 263
Eastern Europe, 25–26
Economic and Social Committee, of European Union, 187
Eisenhower administration, 257
Elections, 201–208
   and British working-class, 204
   defined, 201
   electoral systems, 201–203
   presidential, 92
   proportional representation, 203
   types of, 90–93
Electoral systems, 201–203
Ellerbee, Sarah, 137–144
Elza, Jane, 55–62
Empiricism, as challenge to normativism, 32
Endangered Species Conservation Act, 263
Engels, 25
*Engle v. Vitale*, 23
Environment, and Germany, 265–267
Environmental policy, U.S., 263–264
Environmental Protection Agency (EPA), 264
Equal protection, 162
ESPRIT (European technology project), 226
Europe, fascism in, 128
European Atomic Energy Community (EURATOM), 184
European Central Banks, 188
European Community (EC), 265
European Council, subgroups of, 186–187
European Court of Justice, 187
European Economic Community (EEC), 183
   and technology, 225
European Federalist Movement, 184
European high-technology projects, 226
European Parliament, 187
European Union, 183–192
   European Council, 186–187
   and environment, 265–266
   institutions of, 185–186
   member state interests, 188–189
   origins, 183–185
   prospect of united Europe, 189
   and U.N. Charter, 217
European unity, 188–189
Executive power, distrust of, 78

# F

Fair Labor Standards Act, 117, 118
Falwell, Jerry, 22
Family, and organization, 152
Family, and survey research, 47–54
Family politicization, 47–48
Fascism, in Europe, 128
*Federalist* No. 10, ix, 66–69
   causes of faction, 67
   republic vs. democracy, 68–69
*Federalist* No. 51, 69–72, 79
   federal principle, 72
   guarding against oppression by rulers, 71
   and national defense, 70
   predominance of legislative authority, 70
   republican cause, 72
   separation of powers, 69–70
   and single government, 71
*Federalist* No. 78, x, 106–112, 141
   appointing judges, 106
   Constitution as fundamental law, 107
   Constitution against legislative encroachments, 108
Federal Environmental Pesticide Control Act, 264
Federal principle, 72
Federal Quality Insititute, 169
Federalism, 97–104
   creative federalism, 99–100
   doctrine of cooperative federalism, 98
   doctrine of dual federalism, 97–98
   doctrine of national supremacy, 97
   fiscal federalism, 98–99
   future of, 100–102
   New Federalism, 100
Federalist party, 138
Federalists, vs. Jeffersonians, 139
Fields, domestic, 63–174
Fields, integrative, 237–270
Fields, global, 175–236
*Finding the Law* (Cohen), 57
Fiscal federalism, 98–99
Fisher, Louis, 75–86
Flatterers, and Machiavelli, 146
Food. *See* Human population
Force de Frappe, 223
Ford, Gerald, 91
   and New Federalism, 100
Foreign policy, American, 229–236
   domestic pressures, 231–232
   objectives after WWII, 230–231
   policy themes, 232–233
Foreign policy development, and symbolism, 258–259

Formal organization, defined, 151
Foundations of political science, 1–62
Fourteenth Amendment, 162
France, and European Union, 188–189
Freedom of Information Act, 57
Friedrich, Carl, 77
Fundamentalists, 22
*Fundamentals of Legal Research* (Jacobstein), 57

# G

Gallup poll, 49
*Garcia v. San Antonio Metropolitan Transit Authority*, 100, 114, 118
Gay rights, 88
Gender gap, and voting, 93
General Administration Office (GAO), 170
General Electric, purchase of RCA, 226
Georgia Laws, 58
Germany
    and environment, 265–267
    and environmental policy, 263–270
    and European Union, 188
    legislature, and representation, 203
    and Social Democrat-Free Democrat coalition, 265
*Gibbons v. Ogden*, 115
Glen, Carol, 183–192
Global fields, 175–236
Good man, Seneca's definition of, 20
Gore, Al, 87, 88
    and ACC, 171
Government agencies, organization of, 154
Government efficiency, 167–174
Governors, 101
Great Depression, 25, 80, 140, 247
Green Party, 266–267
Grotius, Hugo, 210–214
Guarding against oppression by rulers, 71

# H

Habeas Corpus Act, 75
Habeas corpus, writ of, 83
Hamilton, Alexander, 82
    and *Federalist* No. 78, x, 106–112, 141
    writing as Pacificus, 82
*Hammer v. Dagenhart*, 140
Heidegger, Martin, 25
High definition television (HDTV), 225
Hindenburg, 25
Hitler, Adolph, viii, 25, 48
Hobbes, Thomas, 21–23
Hooker, 123

Hoover, Herbert, 98
Human population, 247–254
    growth, 247–249
    technological change and, 249–250
Hungary, 26
Huntington, Samuel P., 81

# I

IBM computers, 223
Imperialism, German, 24
Implied powers, 81–83
Independents, and survey, 50
Industrial Age, and judicial review, 140
*Inquiry into the Lawfulness of War* (Grotius), 210–214
Intermodal Surface Transportation and Efficiency Act (ISTEA), 257
Internal Revenue Service, 98
    and TQM, 171
International Criminal Code, 216
International relations, 209–236. *See also* Foreign policy
Interstate system, 257
Iraq-Kuwait Conflict. *See* Persian Gulf War

# J

Japan, and technology, 224–226
Jason, Aristotle's view of, 5–6
Jay, John, 79
Jefferson, Thomas, 82
    and Declaration of Independence, viii
    and Lockean Compact, 22–23
    and Marbury, 138
Jeffersonians, vs. Federalists, 139
Jesus (quoted in Bible), 22
Jews, and income, 92
Johnson, Lyndon, 77
    and Great Society, 257
    as Southerner, 93
Judicial decision making, 117–119
Judicial review, 137–144
    in democratic society, 141–142
    Great Depression, 140
    history of, 137–138
    Industrial Age, 140
    *Marbury v. Madison*, 138–139
    in modern world, 140–141
    New Deal, 140
    Taney court, 139
*Jus gentium*, defined, 75
Juvenile crime rate, 48

## K

Karen Quinlan case, 130
Kemp, Jack, 87
Kennedy, John F., 90
King, Larry, 88
King, vs. statesman, 4
Kissinger, Henry, 258–260
Knox, Henry, 79
Kohl, Helmut, 188, 265, 267
*Korematsu* case, 132
Kurland, Philip B., 81

## L

LaPlant, James, 47–54
Latinos, and income, 92
*Legal Research and Citation* (Teply), 57
Legal thought, manistream, 123–136
Lincoln, Abraham, and public policy, 255
Livy, 211
Locke, John, 13–18
    American adaptations of, 22–23
    and civil society, 14
    and Declaration of Independence, 76
    ends of political society, 15
    and freedom, 14
    and laws of nature, 13
    "A Letter Concerning Toleration," 23
    and men's violence, 14
    and Plato, 21–22
    and political theory, viii
    and property, 13–18
    and punishment of offenders, 14–15
    state of nature, 13–15
    and supremacy of legislative power, 76
Lockean Compact, and Jefferson, 22–23
Love Canal, 264
Luther, Martin, and nationalism, 24

## M

Maastricht Treaty, 185
Machiavelli, Niccolo, 9–12
    and Compact Theory, 23–24
    as first modern political scientist, 32
    flatterers, 146–147
    and political theory, vii
    *The Prince*, 9–12
    "Secretaries of the Prince," 146–150
Madison, James, ix, 66–74, 82
    and *Federalist* No. 10, 66–69
    and *Federalist* No. 51, 69–72, 79
    and Hamilton, 82
    as Helvidius, 82
    and Marbury, 137–139
Magna Carta, 75
Management By Objectives (MBO), and public administration, 168–169
Mansfield, Lord, 124, 130
*Marbury v. Madison*, 137–139
Marine Mammal Protection Act, 264
Marshall, John, 81, 82, 97, 115, 138, 139
Marx, 25
Marxism, 133
Marxism-Leninism, in Africa, 195
Master and slave relationship, 6
*McPherson v. Buick Motors Company*, 130
Meese, Edwin, 114–116
Meese-Brennan debate, 114–116
Member state interests, in European unity, 188–189
    France, 188–189
    Germany, 188
    United Kingdom, 189
Mensch, Elizabeth, 123–136
Methodology of political science, viii-ix, 29–62
    formative period, 34
    history of, 32–34
    timeline, 33
    transition years, 34
Ministry of Trade and Industry (MITI) of Japan, 225
Misch, Gary, 255–262
Mitterand, Francois, 188
Modes of analysis in political science, 30–38
Montesquieu, 113
Morris, Dick, 90
MTV, 88

## N

National defense, 70
National Environmental Policy Act (NEPA), 263
*National League of Cities v. Usery*, 117–118
National Security Council, 258
National Socialist German Workers' Party, 25
National supremacy, doctrine of, 97
*National Transportation Policy*, 257
Nationalism, 23–24
    and Eastern Europe, 25–26
    and Machiavelli, 23–24
    and Nietzsche, 24–26
NATO, 26, 231–232
Nature of state, and Compact Theory, 19–23
Neagle (*in re Neagle*), 82
New Deal, 91, 98, 131, 140, 257
New Federalism, 100
*New York Journal and Weekly Register*, 138

Nietzsche, 24–26
Nixon, Richard, 77, 81, 141
   and language, 256
   and National Environmental Policy Act, 263
   and New Federalism, 100
   and public policy, 255
   and SALT, 259
   and Soviets, 258–260
   *United States v. Nixon*, 141
Nobel prizes, 223
Nordic culture, 24
Normativism, 32

# O

Objectivism, and Constitution, 113–114
Oligarchies, and Aristotle, 178, 240–242
Organization, of family, 152
Organization, formal, 151–152
Ottoman Empire, 26

# P

Parliamentary-Cabinet systems, 202
Partisanship, 87–89
Pearl Harbor, 153
Perot, Ross, 88
Persian Gulf War, 216, 229, 258
Peterson, James W., 229–236
Petition of Right, 75
Plato, 19–28
   allegory of the cave, 19
   American adaptations of, 22–23
   and Calvin, 20–21
   and Hobbes, 21
   on learning and remembering, 39–46
   and Locke, 21–22
   In@Index2 = *Meno*, ix, 39–43
   nature of state, 19–20
   and Seneca, 20
   *Statesman*, 113
   and subject-object dichotomy, 113
   and teaching of virtue, 31–32
Political appointees, and TQM, 169
Political efficacy, defined, 49
Political parties, and demographics, 50
Political socialization, and the family, 47–54
Political theory, defined, vii
*Politics* (Aristotle), 247
Politics, comparative, 177–208
Popenoe, David, 48
Population
   defined, 49
   world, 248
   and worldwide web count, 249
Portis, Edward Bryan, 19
Post-Cold War period, 229–233
Postbehavioralism, 35
Predominance of legislative authority, 70
Presidential veto, 80
*Prince, The* (Machiavelli), 9–12
   avoiding being despised and hated, 9–10
   vs. conspirator, 10
   and external powers, 10
   keeping faith, 9
   and nobles, 10
   reputation of, 9–12
*Principles of the Administrative Law of the United States* (Goodnow), 162
Privacy Act, 57
Private administration, vs. public, 153
Procedural due process, 162
Public administration, 145–174
   defined, 151–158
   efficiency as goal, 154
   formal organization, 151–152
   "good practice," 154–155
   governmental vs. non-governmental, 153
   growth of, 154
   legal approach to, 162–163
   managerial approaches to, 159–166
   nature of, 151
   performance in, 167–174
   political approach to, 161–162
   public vs. private, 153–154
   universality of, 152–153
Public administration, performance in, 167–174
   Management By Objectives, 168–169
   public vs. private goods, 167–168
   total quality management, 169–172
   traditional measurement, 167
Public law, 105–144
Public policy, 239–270
   defined, 255–256
   and environment, 263–270
   and language, 255–262
   and symbolism, 256–257
   and two-party system, 256
Public vs. private goods, public administration, 167–168
Publius (Hamilton), 109
Publius (Madison), 69, 72
Pufong, Marc G., 215–222
Punnett, Malcolm, 201–208
Puritan Compact, 22
Puritans, England of, 22

# Q

Quayle, Dan, 264

# R

Race, and Eastern Europe, 25–26
Race, theory of, 24–25
RACE (European technology project), 226
Reagan, Ronald, 100
   and Christianity, 22
   and detente, 258
   and environmental issues, 264
   and New Federalism, 100
Refuse, and federal employees, 159
Representation, proportional, 203
Republicans
   and party identification, 87
   Republican cause, 72
   and survey, 50
   and voting, 92
Research, legal, 55–62
   and abortion, 56
   *Roe v. Wade*, 55–56
   and Supreme Court, 56
Revolution
   accomplished by force or fraud, 242
   American, 123, 137
   and Aristotle, 240–246
   fear as cause of, 241
*Roe v. Wade*, 22, 23, 55–56, 130
Roman Empire, and universal brotherhood, 23
Romania, 26
Roosevelt, F.D., 80–81, 98, 140, 257
   and New Deal, 257
Roosevelt, Theodore, 83
Rosenbloom, David H., 159–166

# S

Saeger, Richard T., 97–104
Sample, defined, 49
Schmidt, Helmut, 265–266
Scientific method, elements of, 47
Semiconductor Manufacturing Technology Initiative, 225
Seneca, and Plato, 20
Separation of powers, 69–70, 77–81
Serbia, 26
*Shephard's Citations*, 59
Shepardizing, defined, 59
Sherman Anti-Trust Act, 140
*Silent Spring* (Carson), 263
Simon, Herbert A., 151–158
Single government, concept of, 71
Single Transferable Vote (STV) system, 204
Single-party government, 205
Sixteenth Amendment, 97
*Slaughterhouse Cases*, 140
Slovenia, 26
Smithburg, Donald W., 151–158
Social Democrat-Free Democrat coalition (Germany), 265
Socialist party, 88
Socialization, and family, 47–54
Socrates, 113
   dialogue with Meno, 39–43
   Socratic method of reasoning, 31
   and the soul, 39–43
Soil exhaustion, and over-population, 250
Sophocles, 76
South Africa, and foreign policy, 232
Southerner, as voter, 93
Soviet Union, 229–230
Spoilsmen, defined, 159
Spurious relationship, defined, 51
*Stages of Economic Growth* (Rostow), 194
START agreements, with Russia, 232
State, as natural, 4–5
State, nature of, 19–23
*Statesman* (Plato), 113
Statesman, vs. king, 4
Story, Justice, 78
Structural adjustment, and Africa, 196
*Study of Public Administration* (White), 160
Sub-Saharan region, 194
Subject/object dichotomy, of Constitution, 113
Subjectivism, and Constitution, 114, 116–117
Substantive rights, 162
"Sunset" provisions, of administration, 161
"Sunshine" provisions, of administration, 161
Supremacy Clause, 118, 138
*Supreme Court Reporter*, 57–58
Supreme Court, 59
   and implied powers, 81
Survey research, on family, 47–54
Sutherland, Arthur, 77
Syllogism, defined, 31
Symbolism
   differing interpretations of, 259–260
   in domestic policy development, 257
   in foreign policy development, 258–259
   and national media, 257
   in public policy, 256–257

# T

Taft, William Howard, 83
Taney, Roger, 97, 139

Technology
 in developed states, 223–228
 and economic motives, 249
 and GNP, 226
 and human population, 247–254
Television, and politics, 255–256
Tenth Amendment, 81, 97, 117–118
Theocracy, Calvinist, 20–21
Theory, political, 3–28
 link with practical politics, 19–28
 Plato's, 19
 of political socialization, 47–48
Thompson, Victor A., 151–158
Total Quality Management (TQM), 169–172
 Deming's fourteen points, 169–170
 difficulties in public sector, 169–170
 downside, 170–171
 emergence, 169
 future of, 171–172
 and Japanese manufacturers, 169
 as organizational culture, 169
 in public administration, 169–172
 as shift in focus, 169
 upside, 171
Trade balance, U.S. high tech, 224
Traditional measurement, public administration, 167
Treaty on European Union (TEU), 185
Twenty-sixth Amendment, 90

## U

United Kingdom, and European Union, 189
U.N. Charter and post-World War II obligation, 215–216
UNDP, 194
United States Bank, 81
U.S. Department of Energy, 257
U.S. Department of Transportation, 257
U.S. Highway Trust Fund, 258
U.S. Interstate system, 257
U.S.-Japanese technological partnerships, 224
*U.S. Reports*, 57
*U.S. Term Limits v. Thornton*, 101
*United States v. Butler*, 114
*United States v. Darby*, 117
*United States v. Nixon*, 141
*United States v. Willow River Power Company*, 130

## V

Variable, dependent vs. independent, 48

"Varieties of the Main Types of Constitutions" (Aristotle), 178–182
Veto power, and governors, 101
Vietnam War, 88, 229, 232
Viguerie, Richard, 22
Virtue, as knowledge, 31
"Volk," and theory of race, 24–25
Voter turnout, 89–90
Voting behavior, 87–96
 age factor, 90
 partisanship, 87–89
 turnout, 89–90
 types of elections, 90–93

## W

*Wabash, St. Louis & Pacific Railway v. Illinois*, 140
Wagner, Richard, and Chamberlain, 24
Wall Street, crash of 1929, 140
Walters, Robert S., 223–228
War, Bible on, 211
War, and Grotius, 210–214
Warren, Earl, 140–141
Washington, George, 79, 138
Water Pollution Control Act, 264
Water Quality Act, 263
Whitewater, 90
Willis, Clyde, 113–122
Wilson, Woodrow, 80, 98, 160
Winder, David W., 87–96
Working-class, British, 204
World Bank, and Africa, 194–197
*World Development Report*, 193
World War II, 88, 132
 and European Union, 183–185
 foreign policy after, 230–231
 and Great Depression, 247
 state of obligation after, 215–222
World War II, state of obligation after, 215–222
 European Union and, 217
 International Criminal Code, 216
 and Iraq-Kuwait Conflict, 216
 UN Charter and, 215–216
 Yugoslavia Conflict, 217–218

## Y

Yugoslavia, 26, 217–218

## Z

Zero Population Growth, 248